Praise for *War on the*

"Kevin Slack's *War on the American Republic* is outstanding. It blends strong moral seriousness with impressive scholarly analysis. Slack both explains and responds to the relentless attack on the manly, Christian republicanism of the older America by successive waves of liberalism, each one more radical than the last. This book is the best available panoptic view of the transformations in America's moral-political orientation over the course of its history."

—Thomas G. West, professor at Hillsdale College, author of *The Political Theory of the American Founding*

"This is a thoughtful and interesting book, to be read by scholars and students alike, that corrects the record of generations of popularized and fake concepts describing how America got to its rotten state, where things may go from here, and how to correct our trajectory. This learned book should be read by people on both left and right."

—Arthur Milikh, executive director of the Claremont Institute's Center for the American Way of Life

"Finally, a comprehensive treatment of the American left. A thoughtful, immensely well-researched, and spirited intellectual history of American decline."

—David Azerrad, assistant professor at Van Andel Graduate School of Government in Washington, D.C.

"This is a powerful book, exhaustive without being exhausting. Kevin Slack offers a bold new history of American society and politics, ranging from the founding all the way to our current despotic kleptocracy and beyond. If you want clarity about what lies ahead, understanding the past is essential, and there is no better place to start than this book."

—Charles Haywood, editor of *The Worthy House*

War

on the

American Republic

How Liberalism Became Despotism

Kevin Slack

New York • London

First American edition published in 2023 by Encounter Books,
an activity of Encounter for Culture and Education, Inc.,
a nonprofit, tax-exempt corporation.
Encounter Books website address: www.encounterbooks.com

Manufactured in the United States and printed on
acid-free paper. The paper used in this publication meets
the minimum requirements of ANSI/NISO Z39.48-1992
(R 1997) (*Permanence of Paper*).

First paperback edition published in 2024
Paperback edition ISBN: 978-1-64177-417-8

THE LIBRARY OF CONGRESS CATALOGING-IN-PUBLICATION
DATA IS AVAILABLE:
Cataloging information for this title can be found at the Library of Congress
under the following ISBN 978-1-64177-417-8 and LCCN 2024023849.

This will be the practice of the king who will reign over you: He will take your sons, and appoint them for himself, for his [armies].... And he will appoint captains over thousands, and captains over fifties; and will set the people to plough his ground, and to reap his harvest, and to make his weapons of war.... And he will take your daughters to be his sweetmeats, and to be cooks, and to be bakers. And he will take the best of your fields...and give them to his courtiers and servants. And he will tax your possessions, and your lands, to give to his officers and administrators. And he will take your young men and women, even the best and brightest, and put them to his work. He will take a tenth of your belongings, and you shall be his slaves. And you shall cry out in that day because of your king that you chose over you; and the Lord will not hear you.

—I Samuel 8:11–17

State is the name of the coldest of all cold monsters. Coldly it tells lies too; and this lie crawls out of its mouth: "I, the state, am the people." That is a lie! It was creators who created peoples and hung a faith and a love over them: thus they served life.

—Friedrich Nietzsche

And he causeth all, both small and great, rich and poor, free and bond, to receive a mark in their right hand or in their foreheads, that no man might buy or sell, save he that had the mark or the name of the beast or the number of his name.

—Revelation 13:16–17

Hence as all History informs us, there has been in every State and Kingdom a constant kind of Warfare between the Governing and the Governed: the one striving to obtain more for its Support, and the other to pay less. And this has alone occasion'd great Convulsions, actual civil Wars, ending either in dethroning of the Princes or enslaving of the People. Generally indeed the Ruling Power carries its Point, and we see the Revenues of Princes constantly increasing, and we see that they are never satisfied, but always in want of more. The more the People are discontented with the Oppression of Taxes; the greater Need the Prince has of Money to distribute among his Partisans and pay the Troops that are to suppress all Resistance, and enable him to plunder at Pleasure. There is scarce a King in a hundred who would not, if he could, follow the Example of Pharoah, get first all the Peoples Money, then all their Lands, and then make them and their Children Servants forever. It will be said, that we don't propose to establish Kings. I know it. But there is a natural Inclination in Mankind to Kingly Government. It sometimes relieves them from Aristocratic Domination. They had rather have one Tyrant than 500. It gives more of the Appearance of Equality among Citizens; and that they like. I am apprehensive, therefore, perhaps too apprehensive, that the Government of these States, may in future times, end in a Monarchy. But this Catastrophe I think may be long delay'd, if in our propos'd System we do not sow the Seeds of Contention, Faction and Tumult by making our Posts of Honor Places of Profit.

—BENJAMIN FRANKLIN,
CONSTITUTIONAL CONVENTION, JUNE 2, 1787

The right of suffrage is certainly one of the fundamental articles of republican Government....In several of the States a freehold was now the qualification. Viewing the subject in its merits alone, the freeholders of the Country would be the safest depositories of Republican liberty. In future times a great majority of the people will not only be without landed, but any other sort of, property. These will either combine under the influence of their common situation; in which case, the rights of property & the public liberty, will not be secure in their hands: or which is more probable, they will become the tools of opulence & ambition, in which case there will be equal danger on another side. The example of England had been misconceived. A very small proportion of the Representatives are there chosen by freeholders. The greatest part are chosen by the Cities & boroughs, in many of which the qualification of suffrage is as low as it is in any one of the U.S. and it was in the boroughs & Cities rather than the Counties, that bribery most prevailed, & the influence of the Crown on elections was most dangerously exerted.

—JAMES MADISON,
CONSTITUTIONAL CONVENTION, AUGUST 7, 1787

I dedicate this book to the young citizens of this country, especially my students, who are disgusted by our rotting plutocracy and fortified by the moral confidence to shame those so clearly repugnant to life and liberty. They have seen that all the kleptocracy can promise them is subjection in an isolated and degrading servitude and praise by a ludicrous priesthood that deifies profit, degeneracy, and self-hatred.
I dedicate this book to the New Right.

CONTENTS

FOREWORD

War on the American Republic was mostly finished by fall 2020, with updates and final edits in spring 2022. Supply chain delays postponed its release until spring 2023. It was foremost written as a historical companion to the study of American political theory, and amidst the crises of 2020 it was meant to be a chronicle of politics under the COVID-19 regime—one of the defining moments of our time—in the awareness that much would be forgotten.

For students of American political thought, this book supplements original works by Woodrow Wilson, John Dewey, Herbert Marcuse, and John Rawls that are often assigned in the field. Moreover, it intends to provide a new kind of history, dividing the American regime into various eras and connecting each to changes in institutions and mores. Thus, it had to immerse the reader in details. Recounting the changing views of human nature that informed each era, it places the great thinkers in engagement with each other.

The book is also a critical history for a New Right. It begins with critiques of conservative groups. In fairness, some of these groups, like the Heritage Foundation, have since changed their messaging for the better. The book's controversial statements were meant to be a litmus test for its readers. The year 2020 was a gut check: it exposed one's instincts. The passing years have vindicated those who opposed governmental propaganda and policies on COVID-19 and identity politics. The New Right was born of Western youth who watched their rulers consume their inheritance. They challenged the intellectuals who, when their liberties were at risk, complied with and rationalized every mandate, soiling everything they touched.

The book concludes with the United States at a turning point, the end of the neoliberal regime: not because it is without power but because that power is losing its legitimacy. While it continues to attack Christianity and what it calls white supremacy, young males increasingly no longer believe in or have loyalty to the regime. Despite the myth that scientific geniuses fill its ranks, government bureaucracy and the wealthy zip codes around Washington, D.C., and New York City are filled with incompetent, corrupt, degenerate *midwits*.

As it loses legitimacy, the globalist American Empire must apply greater force to control the populace. FBI agents demand private information from banks and stores and visit the homes of those who voice dissident opinions. Google supplies them the names, addresses, phone numbers, and user activity of those who view certain content. They spy on Catholic Latin Masses.

The first great enemy of the ruling class (indeed, the title of the book) is the American Republic, whose citizens it seeks to degrade and replace. The river of 2 million illegal aliens that crossed the border under Joe Biden in 2021 has become a flood of almost 10 million, driving up crime and rent, grocery store and home prices. In 2023, the average US home cost $495,000. Biden's horde of foreign invaders—more than the population in thirty-eight individual states—join another 22 million already in the country. The ruling class secures their presence. It campaigns to legalize mail-in ballots with no proof of citizenship, creates sanctuary cities, refuses to enforce employer sanctions or to prosecute aliens for crimes against citizens, encourages these aliens to serve in the military to swell flagging recruitment numbers, and provides them entitlements: free shelter, education, and medical care. This immigration policy against popular consent proves Our Democracy™ is a farce. Biden's illegal aliens alone will count for thirteen congressional districts in the next census.

The ruling class also wages war against human biology. The cosmopolitan regime poisons, sterilizes, and disposes of human life. One must pay more for unprocessed food without poison in it. The youth are awash in a sea of endocrine-disrupting chemicals; testosterone levels among men have decreased 25 percent since 2000. One-fifth of teenagers today identify as LGBTQIA+. This massive grooming campaign has sealed the fate of an entire generation of young women, 50 percent of whom will be single and childless by 2030. Everyday throughout the land, in bureaucracies and in corporate HR departments, palace intrigue plays itself out among catamites, eunuchs, and harems, the bulk of whose positions contribute little to the national welfare.

Optimism for a New Right

Still, the book is optimistic, and for good reason. It does not appear that Western youth will quietly accept the yoke of servitude and technological management, or that the spark of their spirit will be quenched in unquestioning submission. They are indignant at their plight, and they have the moral high ground. What is important is their ethos, not numbers.

But this is more than a youth movement. Since the book's publication, the American people have shifted to the right. Biden's disastrous open border policy has given Donald Trump a lead in the 2024 presidential race. The majority of Americans reject the DEI priesthood. Black Lives Matter is now a joke after its leaders used two-thirds of the $90 million they raised as a slush fund, with no improvement for black lives. Americans have pushed back against the cultural elites' sexual mutilation of children and inclusion of biological men in women's sports. Governor Ron DeSantis has started a reclamation of education for the people of Florida. Trump's campaign proposes new ways to drain the swamp. DEI really is a clown car. As grifters and affirmative action hires manage the economy, basic road maintenance decays; Boeing doors blow off; airline pilots, doctors, and educators become second-rate.

The American people now question imperial wars. The US thwarted an early peace settlement between Ukraine and Russia in

April 2022, sacrificing the flower of Ukrainian youth. Cosmopolitan whites, fed by US state propaganda that Ukraine was winning, flew Ukrainian flags long enough to support the $134.3 billion boondoggle by US defense contractors. US sanctions punished American citizens with inflation and pushed Russia out of the dollar. The Rainbow Coalition further fragments over Middle Eastern policy. Despite receiving up to 50 percent of its campaign funds from Jewish Americans, the Democratic Party has increased the flow of immigrants from Muslim countries; they angrily protest the bombings in Gaza. Their more radical adherents chant "Death to America!" in Dearborn, Michigan.

There has been improvement in American trade policy. Even cosmopolitans see that China threatens to create a global monopoly on semiconductors. Politicians concede that Americans must build their own production facilities. China was an agricultural backwater that American elites built up into an existential threat from their own greed and delusion that it would become a liberal democracy.

The real test will be whether the Republicans will enforce employer sanctions, pass a stricter immigration law, and follow through on mass deportations. Greg Abbott's bussing of illegal immigrants to northern sanctuary cities was largely a stunt, but it made cities like New York and Chicago acknowledge that their political party abetted the chaos at the Texas border. The answer to these questions is a matter of conservatives' political will. Time will tell.

On the Old New Right and a Red Caesar

This book did not have the space to treat each school of the 1960s fusion of libertarianism, neoconservatism, and traditionalism. Each taught some useful truths in response to liberal failures: liberal regulation was a problem; the Soviet Union was a tyranny; America must be more than an abstract idea. Where each erred was in abandoning the true star and compass, which is our republican *polis*: global trade, outsourcing, and open borders weakened our country and hollowed out our middle class; interventionist foreign policy hurt Americans and only benefitted special interests; traditionalism unmoored from the lifeblood of a people often produced silly performances. The 1980s conservative intellectuals took dogmatic but false positions on what became the crucial issues of our time: trade, immigration, and war.

The book's single use of the phrase "Red Caesar" amusingly sucked it into the Left's hysteria. I stated my own views in both an article, "What We Talk about When We Talk about 'Red Caesar'," and in an interview, "The *Guardian* Falsely Accuses Conservative Academics of Being Pro-Dictator." The question of a caesar, as the book shows in its opening quotations, was at the forefront of our Founders' minds. When citizen virtue is gone, according to Franklin, Madison, and Adams, republics devolve into a clash of oligarchic and caesarist titans—the great devourers of humanity—both sides adopting a pseudo-aristocratic ethos, each with trained praetorian guards and private armies. With the decline of Roman virtue, Julius Caesar challenged Marcus Tullius Cicero's attempt to revive the republic. Caesar believed that Rome could not go back: a different regime was necessary.

The great irony is that the people who fret over a caesar's arrival are the very ones preparing his way. Caesar was not an outsider like Trump but a general who emerged from an oligarchy of consolidating imperial forces. A modern caesar needs centralized law enforcement and a centralized economy: an intelligence state, militarized police, and monopoly capitalism. In our time, a blue caesar is more probable. During an economic or political crisis, he would claim to save "democracy" from enemies like "semi-fascism" or "whiteness" by usurping power or fixing elections. He might imprison political challengers, destroy constitutional protections, pack the Supreme Court, use intelligence agencies to "monitor and censor" Americans online, spy on religious groups, infiltrate and entrap right-wing groups, attack homeschooling as anti-democratic, force so-called "diversity, equity, and inclusion" trainings, and preserve open borders to buy votes.

This book was written with, and still keeps, Cicero's republican hope—at the local, state, and national levels. But it also recognizes that the founding of this country was a sacred compact—with obedience dependent upon the securing of natural rights. During the pandemic the American people displayed the spirit to challenge unjust edicts. If the people did not possess an inheritance of republican virtue, the elites would have no need to import a new populace. Niccolò Machiavelli's great critique of the feudal aristocrats was that, distrusting their own people, they resorted to securing themselves in fortresses. But the greatest fortress, the founders of the modern nation-state knew, was the people themselves.

"What is to be done?" is the fundamental *political* question. Yet the book also begins in derision of professors in the field of political *philosophy* who appeared to live a noble way of life, but were exposed in 2020 to be at best imperial grifters, or worse, abject middle-aged men terrified of a sickness: in sum, Aristotle's definition of cowardice. They had abandoned the deepest questions of nature and the good life, and how they intersect with politics. This book's references to religion and philosophy intended to tie them to a history of our regime and, more importantly, to our own experience. While political action is not the only end of thought, much of what passed for political philosophy was useless for living. Suffice it to say that to preserve political philosophy, it must first be rescued from those who have turned it into a portrait of their own life-denying existences.

INTRODUCTION

Americans look around at their country and no longer recognize what they see. The very category of citizenship is denied. Millions of illegal immigrants stream across an unprotected border and are escorted into the interior of the country, where they receive government welfare. Americans have learned that all their rights as citizens can be removed, not by elected representatives but by unelected bureaucrats claiming emergency powers. Under the authority of *health*, which used to mean human flourishing, Americans were told they must reduce their lives to bare preservation. They watched their demoralized neighbors become habituated to wearing face masks and line up for endless experimental vaccines. Journalists who disagreed were censored. The assistant secretary of *health* and the nation's first *female* admiral, report state media, is a *man* who, declaring himself a woman, had his own penis removed. Little girls in California schools are told to question their genders and then, without the consent of their parents, are injected with irreversible, sterilizing puberty-blockers and courses of testosterone. Mainstream media outlets like *USA Today* run stories to destigmatize pedophilia. When polled, surprising numbers of Democrats approved of fines (55 percent), home confinement (59 percent), and prison (48 percent) for those who resisted or publicly challenged mandates for masks and COVID vaccinations. Twenty-nine percent approved of removing their children. Under the authority of *anti-racism*, Americans see their leaders promote vicious anti-white racial hatred, justifying a new Jim Crow for whites. For an entire year Americans watched Black Lives Matter and Antifa rioters burn great American cities, desecrate ancient churches, tear down historical monuments, break all laws, and injure law enforcement, only to be told that the riots were peaceful and the rioters had a right to destroy others' property and livelihoods. The government creates record levels of inflation and disrupts supply chains, and Americans are told to embrace the new lower standard of living.

In sum, the ideas that most Americans had tolerated as absurd and relegated to academia—transgenderism, anti-white racism, censorship, cronyism—are now endorsed and carried out at the highest levels of political power. What formerly were the ideals of a radical Left are now the policies of an entire cosmopolitan class that includes much of the entrenched bureaucracy, the military, the media, and government-sponsored corporations. It seems there is little that can be done. While 70 percent of Democratic activists—those who lead the party—express shame of their own country, the sentiment extends to Republicans. Leading conservative intellectuals attack the country's founding traditions and principles as a failure to the point of rejecting republican principles altogether. Among other conservatives, there is a general uncertainty as to what republican principles even are. As a professor of politics at Hillsdale College, perhaps the most politically conservative college in the country, I am often asked by my students and visiting friends of the college: "How did we get here?"; "What intellectual and cultural changes took place to bring us to this point?"; "What recourse do we have?" This book is my answer. It is written for them. While I am not a political insider, nor do I aspire to be a pundit, this book is also written in the spirit of the times. It is filled with both facts and controversy. It intends to be iconoclastic, especially for its conservative audience in a world where the old conservative gods are dead. Those gods, this book hopes to show, were newer in their construction, and they are experiencing a timely demise. And despite this book's dour implications, I hope the reader will share in some of its optimism. History is for the living, and there is a rising generation of young conservatives who, in the face of the ruling class's incompetence, corruption, and degeneracy, is finding much worthy to conserve for all Americans.

Republicanism

Students will someday be required to memorize a few facts about the American empire: the original republic's foundations, its rise to become the wealthiest and most powerful regime the world had ever seen, and its fall. The key to American success was not simply natural resources, nor capitalism, but a republican political order, a way of life or character expressed in public and private institutions. The American regime, like every *political* community, presupposed a common mind, agreement as to the just and the unjust, the advantageous and the disadvantageous. Barring this rule by virtue, hedged by institutions, there is only rule by pleasure and pain. Every community must claim itself exceptional if only to preserve itself. Alexander Hamilton succinctly defines American exceptionalism in *Federalist 1*: "It seems to have been reserved to the people of this country, by their conduct and example, to decide the important question, whether societies of men are really capable or not of establishing good government from reflection and choice, or whether they are forever destined to depend for their political constitutions on accident and force." Hamilton and James Madison both agreed that the success of the American regime would "decide forever the fate of republican government." But Benjamin Franklin also reminded those present at the Constitutional Convention that "there is a natural Inclination in Mankind to Kingly Government," to live under the rule of force: "It sometimes relieves them from Aristocratic Domination. They had rather have one Tyrant than 500."

To be clear, this book is a defense of an older way of viewing the American regime. And it aspires to be a bit more, a brief genealogy of our political order in order to know what it is by knowing how it came to be. As a brief history, it describes broad changes in American political ideas about the regime's ends, the resulting changes in political institutions, and its decline from a republic to a despotic kleptocracy. Providing succinct descriptions of these movements—of progressivism, liberalism, and radicalism—is this book's contribution. As a brief political and social history, I have written it with my undergraduate and graduate students of political theory as well as the many friends of Hillsdale College in mind. This justifies its treatment of institutional and academic details that historical surveys normally omit.

The history of political ideas and peoples is not one of slow gradation of change. Rather it is a series of conflicts resulting in inversions of mores. Scholars often revel in indecision and ambiguities of pluralist traditions and hide behind the appearance of detached intellectualism. They may challenge the terms *progressivism*, *liberalism*, and *radicalism* by pointing to exceptions. Progressive Era philosophy, for example, included rich philosophical disagreements among John Dewey, William James, and Josiah Royce and heated political disagreements among Theodore Roosevelt, William Howard Taft, and Woodrow Wilson. And there are certainly continuities between these movements—progressives who supported the New Deal or liberals who embraced sexual revolution. Still, few would disagree that a fundamental shift occurred in the Progressive Era; a new regime emerged that shaped American minds and hearts. The words *progressive*, *liberal*, and *radical*, as we commonly use them, presuppose some political order, and these orders are best understood when compared and contrasted to one another. To understand *neoliberalism*, for example, one must compare it to what it sought to replace: midcentury *liberalism*. In this account, I omitted much information, including several chapters on the nineteenth century. But much I have attempted to include. The book's excursions into Progressive Era health mandates, Liberal Era torture of prisoners of war, and 1960s radicals' programs of racial awareness training are, I think, necessary in describing each of these distinct movements.

The second purpose of this book is to offer conservatives a more informed treatment of American liberalism. The word is often used confusingly to refer to *both* the early nineteenth-century regime of limited government that protected individual rights and the mid-twentieth-century regime that expanded government and subverted those older rights. This confusion allows scholars to attack a vaguely defined *liberalism*, into which they lump every thinker from John Locke to John Rawls. Many intellectuals present grand five-hundred- or even two-thousand-year narratives, placing all so-called liberalisms on a continuum. In most of them, modernity is the enemy, set against classical and medieval regimes (as if Christianity had not undone the ancient order and "turned the world upside down"). Such narratives are romantically seductive. Well-paid cosmopolitan peddlers of ingratitude teach privileged students to loathe the American people and to wax nostalgic for unrealistic visions of ancient and medieval communities. They teach bookish college students to think of themselves as aristocrats staving off the tide of vulgarians. And they promise redemption on earth: we are entering a post-liberal era, they prophesy, with cursory speculation on contemporary politics or the proper role of church and state. Scholars educated in Platonic dialogues, though generally uninterested in and ignorant of American history, make specious connections in American philosophy and law. They use Alexis de Tocqueville, for example, as an authoritative shortcut to save themselves the time of learning about the actual material: the American people.

Such abstract political narratives prove false. Theorists who argue that *liberalism* destroyed marriage and the family often ignore changes in marriage law, such as the move from *contract* to *status* or the creation of family courts. In morals, they ignore the actual morality during most of the American republic's history so that, appealing to their young listeners, they may contrast liberal "selfishness" to the altruism of magical earthly kingdoms. They discuss *liberalism* as divorced from Christianity yet know little of the American republic's support for religious organizations. Until the 1960s Catholic Mass would have been uncomfortably orthodox to the crunchiest of today's traditionalists. Scholars accuse liberal philosophers of corroding Christian faith yet remain silent about the theologians who welcomed an alternative authority, as if theology were the dim-witted stepbrother of philosophy. In sum, political theorists still employ the word *liberalism* in the context of the worn-out scholarly republicanism-liberalism debate that few today take seriously. Because individual freedom was inseparable from republican duties in the early American regime, I will hereafter refer to classical liberalism as *republicanism*.

This book hopes to provide a historically grounded record of American republicanism. Its central thesis is that progressivism, liberalism, and radicalism break from each other in distinct ways. I first set my thesis against the teaching that there are three waves of modernity, with the final wave of relativism culminating in nihilism. Leo Strauss, for example, exhorted the youth to return to the study of nature in ancient political philosophy to stem the West's moral decline. But each American movement, rather than rejecting human nature, appealed to it as an authority. Indeed, the teaching of nature adopted by many of Strauss's students—that of the philosophic soul removed from spiritedness—has contributed more to the West's decline than anything from the pages of Locke. What Strauss called nihilism is simply the revelatory authority of today's pseudoscience and part of what the ancients called the cycle of regimes. I also set my thesis against the discontinuity thesis, which treats pluralism as the key to American politics. Pluralist studies help us question the myths that are used to unify or divide a people. But they fail to appreciate *politics* as an architectonic art—at some point, young men fight to defend a common way of life. When scholars refuse to defend a certain way of life, they abet the liberals attacking the right while forever yielding ground for their inability to demarcate what is sacred. Lest we adopt the inane view that all wars are misunderstandings, we must hold some things—ideas, land, language, culture, religion—as worth defending. The pluralists' solution of reviving *institutions for conflict resolution* is inadequate, not just because those institutions no longer exist in any meaningful sense but because their only justification is a principled view of citizenship, which makes the pluralist squeamish in his aversion to absolutes. Moreover, if republicanism means the habits informed by a framework of natural law that underpinned the republican nation state, it not only still resides in the hearts of many Americans, it remains the only alternative to prescriptions for a return to an ancient politics or some vague and undefined future global order.

The final purpose of the book is to reflect on the future of conservatism. The old idols of conservatism—neoconservatism, constitutional originalism, libertarianism, performance traditionalism—are dead. The reader need only look to the political positions taken by intellectuals who have peddled the above theories about *liberalism* and who failed to conserve anything. For years decent Americans gave money to think tanks, centers on "democracy"—cartons of eggheads speaking at lavish black-tie dinners on saving the family with "new natural law" or property rights—without a single victory. Today the American Enterprise Institute embraces the trans revolution. The Heritage Foundation adopts the Left's position on big tech, immigration, and systemic racism. The Acton Institute presents the outsourcing of American manufactures and the demoralization of its populace as a brief hiccup toward global progress. Catholic integralists teach open borders and accuse those who disagree with them of racism. Political theorists who long criticized liberal democracy's concern with bare preservation (as opposed to philosophic courage and friendship) are the first to teach online classes, veil their faces in terror of sickness, and dilute their Great Books programs with subpar thinkers when the identity politics priesthood demands. The president of the Association for Core Texts and Courses confesses, "I suffer from [white privilege] too." Worst of all, Christian ministers were the first to accede to state orders to shutter their doors, wear masks, and preach the Black Lives Matter dogma. Establishment conservatism is exposed as a half-witted ideology for a kleptocracy that funds its teaching positions, master's programs, scholarships, and think tanks. We must reassess what conservatives failed to conserve, Americanism, to define what the American people must conserve if they wish to survive.

Method

By Americanism I mean, in a word, republicanism. The American people were a *people* who shared a common way of life and made their land into a home. The political, legal, economic, and social institutions expressed that fact. The nation state that developed in the sixteenth century offers a mean between the failed city-state and the empire. It was a *patrias*, a fatherland that depended on certain religious and moral teachings. The American founders never meant to supplant virtue with institutions; republican freedom, they said, depended on citizen virtue. John Adams said, "We have no government armed with power capable of contending with human passions unbridled by morality and religion.... Our Constitution was made only for a moral and religious people. It is wholly inadequate to the government of any other." Or in the words of Franklin: "Only a virtuous people are capable of freedom." The decline of faith and freedom would bring the return of empire and tyranny.

My approach is simple. I provide a genealogy of the movement from American republicanism to kleptocratic despotism. Each of the book's seven chapters describes a major era in American politics and each political order's view of the good life. The first chapter briefly illustrates the republican order and its responses to the crises of the nineteenth century: that of federalism, resulting in the institutional compromises of the early republic; that of immigration, resulting in limits on who could join the body politic; that of slavery, resulting in the Civil War. At the end of the nineteenth century, the Americans still handled the new political challenges—urban machine corruption, the rise of the trusts, and cheap immigrant labor—in the older way, but a new class of social scientists championed different solutions that subverted the older republicanism.

The Progressive Movement (1880–1920) grew from a spiritual crisis, and it constituted a fundamental break with the old order. Christian faith and republican citizenship gave way to the new authority of science and the ethical ideal, administrative rule by a scientific aristocracy. *Science* here meant absolutism or philosophical idealism, the culmination of a teleological historical process that could undergird empirical methods. Progressives leaned toward a simple Darwinism in psychology and presumed that they could direct mental and moral evolution to altruistic ends by altering the social environment. Individuals would achieve their highest end in willing the collective good. Under the new science of economics, cooperation could replace the competitive motives of capitalism. Threatened by big business above and the religious, racial, and ethnic groups beneath, the white Anglo-Saxon Protestant middle class created institutions to control both the trusts and the surge of southeastern European laborers. They argued, on the one hand, for more democratic procedures by which to circumvent the old constitutional structures, and, on the other hand, the rule of an elite class by which to secure their influence in an unelected bureaucracy. Politically, progressives aimed to undermine the separation of powers and forwarded a theory of the administrative state in which Congress would delegate lawmaking powers to impartial experts who could resolve the complex questions of commerce and monopoly. Moreover, they claimed, by the authority of science, the right to rule over decisions of health or life itself and began to absorb the free institutions of civil society, such as church and family. In foreign policy, progressives applied their view of a colonial, racial struggle between world historic peoples to internationalism and adventurism, which purported to uplift uncivilized peoples. For the first time, a sizable number of Americans, believing that democracy was locked in a global struggle against autocracy, aspired to empire. The apex and nadir of progressivism was the First World War, in which the WASP pieties came under severe criticism.

The *liberals* (1933–1969), composed of a rising urban constituency, rejected the progressives' philosophical idealism. Science no longer meant absolute truth but a pragmatic attitude and an instrument of inquiry; nature meant the scientific attitude as set against supernatural explanations. Liberals in psychology viewed mind not in terms of an ethical ideal but as competing enduring instincts that could be adjusted in therapy and counseling. Rejecting the progressives' ideal of apolitical, impartial administrators, the liberals argued for regulation of business and the profit motive in state capitalism: government and industry would together plan the economy. Where progressives promoted the ideal of a scientific aristocracy to decipher the will of the sovereign people, liberal *democracy* discarded the pretense of popular government for expert management of the people. Rejecting progressive nationalism, the liberals celebrated pluralism, religious toleration, and racial "colorblindness." In an American struggle of the orders, religious and ethnic elites partnered to create a managerial state that abandoned the rule of law for a regulatory morass. This bureaucratic elite would use the older associations of economic class, religion, sex, and race for social planning. Administrative boards would balance the interests of labor and management. Religious traditions were used to promote a new ecumenical "Judeo-Christianity" against Soviet atheism. Counselors would adjust family members to greater harmony and sexual permissivity. And ethnic identities could be recast as economic groups. In this "affluent society," the liberals believed that all problems of wealth creation had been solved, and they created a new regulatory regime to both plan the economy and provide new entitlements for the growing population. In foreign policy, liberals dreamed of a "world state" (in reality American-led internationalism) and went to war over global control against fascists and communists. In the postwar order, they created international economic institutions to manage and adjust foreign peoples. Liberalism met its own crisis in the 1960s as the radicals challenged both its claims to authority and the effects of state planning and foreign interventions.

In the 1960s, a generation of *radicals* revolted against liberal hypocrisy on race, class, and gender and the meaninglessness, even absurdity, of the authority of science as an instrumental method. In philosophy, existentialists and critical theorists challenged liberal pragmatism, which, rather than acting as a neutral tool, was a method of adjustment that impeded consideration of the highest human ends. Even worse, it was an instrument for corporate control. The new progressive psychology rejected the liberals' teaching that repression was necessary for civilization. Appealing to human nature in its teaching of human potential, it taught a new ethic of authenticity and autonomy. A new value-laden science could be used to achieve "health" and "well-being," the mores of the cosmopolitan elite. The teaching of authenticity dovetailed with the Christian charismatic movement, the new Black Liberation Theology, and deep ecology. In sociology, the radicals challenged the liberal "power elite" under state capitalism, in which privileged industrial capitalists had profited from population management. Politically, they crafted an identity politics for a new proletariat, in which white radicals would side with oppressed race and gender groups in a revolt against the white middle class. Students of the New Left coopted the older liberal institutions, ensconcing themselves in bureaucracy and universities to implement race and gender politics. In economics, they promoted democratic socialism. Liberal state capitalism, they argued, exploits minorities and women and colonizes Third World peoples. In foreign policy, the radicals espoused globalism to overturn the nation state that, they argued, could no longer solve world problems. They were willing to sacrifice the American middle class for the good of a future world order. But 1960s identity politics was only the Leftist component of a broader class divide between the elites and the old industrial middle class.

In the *neoliberal* consensus (1977–2009), a class of center-right and center-left elites in the new "knowledge economy" formed an oligarchy. Rejecting the concept of liberal democratic *citizens* for that of *consumers*, it adopted social libertarianism and free-market principles in trade and deregulation as well as financial centralization. After America went off the gold standard in 1971, the Right and Left in the neoliberal consensus disagreed about who should receive the fiat money first. Compassionate conservatives claimed to side with low-wage workers in the growing service-sector economy against the industrial middle class. Innovators would create the wealth that would trickle down to consumers as well as help them in charity. The New Democrats, breaking with big fiscal policy, balanced their support of financial centralization with bureaucratic centralization to help the disadvantaged first. A privileged class of bureaucrats promised to aid the Democratic base, single women and minorities, with preferential treatment in their competition for jobs with white males. The middle class lost its traditional economic, social, and moral supports. The family began its long decline under sexual liberation, feminism, and economic insecurity. Poor blacks became a permanent underclass. Turning its back on industrial unions, big business and the civil rights lobby colluded to flood the country with immigrants, who provided votes for Democrats and cheap labor for Republicans. The neoliberal system fortified the entitlement state by outsourcing American manufactures, deficit financing, and building an empire to secure the dollar as the world's reserve currency. Neoliberals used international institutions to loan money to developing nations for the purposes of political and economic control. They fomented regime change around the world. The collapse of the USSR changed little. Globalization, i.e. outsourcing and immigration, proliferated under Bill Clinton and George W. Bush, who started an unending War on Terror. The failed wars in the Middle East and the 2008 housing market crash marked the crisis of neoliberalism. Barack Obama continued Bush's domestic and foreign policies, but neoliberalism had lost all credibility.

No political order can last without religious legitimacy. The Leftist elite, consisting of the 1960s radicals in the universities, administrative agencies, and education, had become an order of *identity politics* priests who served as the conscience of the neoliberal elite. By teaching the identities of race and gender, they controlled those groups' political allegiance and used their influence in bureaucracy to benefit their constituencies. While neoliberals pushed quantification in the economic and social sciences, the purveyors of identity politics in the liberal arts completed their systems of critical race theory, gender studies, queer theory, and trans identity. The identity politics priesthood had worked with neoliberals for increased immigration and affirmative action, but in many ways it had remained neoliberalism's greatest critic. Its ultimate vision was to provide moral authority for a truly global order. It regularly prognosticated demographic, environmental, and racial apocalypses. Meanwhile, it directed hatred toward the old white Christian middle class and the American nation as the sources of all the world's problems. But the neoliberal gods were now dead. In the so-called Great Awokening of Obama's second term, the neoliberal oligarchs, choosing between the economic nationalism of the populist Right and the identity politics of the Left, sided with identity politics against the American people. Donald Trump represented a rallying cry of the old middle class, not just in the United States but all over the West. Fearing a populist uprising, the oligarchs supported Democrat Joe Biden and then used his victory to turn the full force of the state against political dissenters.

The final chapter, "Despotism," provides a description of the American kleptocracy. Claiming the authority of science and identity politics, an increasingly incompetent, corrupt, and degenerate ruling class seeks to use despotic measures to manage and subdue the populace. It has used the COVID-19 pandemic, BLM riots, and the supposed insurrection at the Capitol to justify its deployment of state agencies to destroy the remnants of republicanism, to reduce once-citizens-now-consumers to abject servility. Government-sponsored corporate monopolies align with the identity politics priesthood in the universities and bureaucracy to control subjects through animalistic pleasure and pain. In the name of science, not as a method of inquiry but an authoritative institution, the kleptocracy uses new modes of control, and it divides the people by tribal identities of race and gender. With the rise of this ruling class, the United States stands on the brink of a return to an ancient politics, the one our founders knew all too well: between a decadent elite living in gated communities and a degraded vulgar mob of dependents. This class of cosmopolitans, using the intrusive powers of the state, manages imperial decline. Viewing the world as its playground, it travels to exotic places, samples various cultures, and experiences new pleasures of sexuality, food, and drink. It erects the bars of its human zoo and even feeds the animals. The decline of the American people has accompanied the decline of the institutions that secured their freedom. But this push to kleptocracy was predicted by the American founders, who themselves revolted against a world empire. And there is hope for those who choose liberty over tyranny. A New Right, sick of the ruling class's treachery, has only begun to rise up to fight for the American way of life and to conserve the American people.

I

REPUBLICAN CITIZENSHIP

The American Revolution was born out of a hundred-year dispute. In the British Empire, all were born subjects owing allegiance to the crown, not citizens with inherent rights. Privileges and status were accorded through various hierarchical and overlapping identities based on tradition, statute, and common law. But common law rights did not extend to settlers outside the realm of England. As subordinate polities of conquest or discovery, the colonies were ruled by royal prerogative. The settlers had no inherent claim to English law or representative institutions but enjoyed them at the "will and pleasure" of the crown, which could override colonial legislatures, erect courts without juries, make governors' instructions legally binding, and even revoke the charters altogether. Far from the administrative eyes of an England racked by civil war, the New England colonists had continued in self-government. Annoyed by their defiance of the Lords of Trade, in 1686 Charles II collapsed the eight colonies into a single dominion, ruled by a military governor. But John Wise, minster at Ipswich and a powerful wrestler (and Ben Franklin's boyhood hero), refused to assist the order to tax the colonists without their consent. Arrested and tried, he appealed to Magna Carta and English law, but a judge retorted, "[Do] not think the laws of England follow [you] to the ends of the earth... Mr. Wise, you have no more privileges left you, than not to be sold as slaves."[1] The colonial charters that Charles had repealed were restored after the 1688 Glorious Revolution but absent some of the older privileges. And now Parliament added its own claim to sovereignty over the colonies. The Board of Trade moved to repeal the New England charters four more times before 1724.

Unable to ground their claims in English law, the settlers drew on other sources of authority in defense of their rights. In 1717 Wise published a treatise grounding the English freedoms to representation in legislatures and juries on the "Law of Nature." In 1721 Massachusetts agent Jeremiah Dummer argued that the settlers' claims to the soil originated not in the crown but *in their own labor* and the risks they had undertaken to purchase and improve the land. Minister Solomon Stoddard repeated the claim in 1722. One of the popular arguments for natural rights that circulated in the colonies was *Cato's Letters*, which compared the liberties of the ancient Roman Republic to imperial Rome, when a decadent, wealthy elite managed a vulgar mob. It was written in response to the 1720 collapse of the South Sea Company, a government-created monopoly (with King George as its governor). In the speculative bubble, stock prices rose tenfold before plummeting and ruining investors. It was just one reminder of the mother country's possible tyranny in an era where popular parties fought royal governors throughout the colonies. The American settlers, contesting British jurisdiction, selectively converted the liberties of Englishmen under common law into a universal theory of rights. Drawing on the natural law tradition, they argued for a natural right to emigrate and then establish both property rights and political authority in the New World. In this contractual view of colonization, the empire was not a unitary state but equal sovereign dominions united in allegiance to a common monarch conditional on his securing their rights. By the time of the 1765 Stamp Act crisis, appeals to natural right had become a fixture of colonial politics and were irreconcilable with the British imperial order.

A natural law consensus underlay the American states' bills of rights. It grounded sovereignty in the people, who conferred political legitimacy by consent, challenging imperial claims to right based on tradition or force. The very word *right* logically presupposed a mutual recognition of justice that informed the law and thus a voluntary contract; without consent, rule was founded on mastery and force, a state of war. These natural rights included the individual rights to life, liberty, acquisition and possession of property, conscience, and speech. Locating sovereignty in the people meant that it must be returned periodically in elections; it could not be permanently deposited in bodies made unaccountable to the people. And it required limited government because the people only ceded certain alienable rights to protect the inalienable. If a government were to fail to secure these rights, it forfeited its legitimacy to demand obedience by the governed. Absolving the ties of government, a people returned to a state of nature.

The state of nature was no mere abstraction. It referred to any time humans interacted outside of properly functioning government without standing, promulgated laws, an impartial judge, or a common executioner. It was not synonymous with war or license but supposed a standard of natural law accessible to reason. Absent government, only God (nature's lawgiver) or his human agents were left to enforce natural law and secure their rights, thus the patriot "Appeal to Heaven." Samuel Adams told the Congress that men are God's "humble instruments and means in the great Providential dispensation."[2] In political society, the state of nature reemerged when there was no magistrate around, in moments of conscience where one must enforce the laws of nature himself. It was the state of the Indian tribes and on the contentious frontier, where civil law was often unknown or unenforced. And it was the state of nations in foreign affairs, where there was neither international law nor a common sovereign to enforce it. While the state of nature was better than tyranny, one's rights were insecure. Thus, individuals consented to form a political society and choose a government that would erect civil laws to protect their natural rights. Social compacts actually occurred. In 1747 the factions in Pennsylvania, facing broken government, united to create an extralegal militia "in Defence of...Liberty and Property."[3] Denouncing British tyranny, Virginian Patrick Henry declared in 1774, "We are in a State of Nature."[4] The colonists, overthrowing British rule, declared independence and announced their break with Britain and their return to a natural state of equal status with other peoples of the earth. Franklin said they were "without any laws or government."[5] Massachusetts's 1780 Constitution stated, "The body politic is formed by a voluntary association of individuals; it is a social compact by which the whole people covenants with each citizen and each citizen with the whole people that all shall be governed by certain laws for the common good." It was a revolution in claims to sovereignty.

Social contract theory introduced a revolutionary notion of citizenship based on choice. In 1789 David Ramsay affirmed that "the principle of government" had been "radically changed by the revolution"; the "political character of the people was also changed from subjects to citizens."[6] The new state compacts were not between a sovereign government and subjects to be ruled but among the sovereign people themselves. Americans denied the unequal status of subjects and feudal relations of perpetual allegiance, and they claimed a new republican relation between free and equal citizens. The claim to equality was prior to liberty: unlike those who claimed a right to rule by their natural superiority, equals could only be ruled by consent. Not all were equal and entitled to political rights. Children and the mentally ill, those not having attained reason, had no right to rule, and criminals who had demonstrated a moral inequality had forfeited it. Nor did equality mean citizens' unequal capacity in "their virtues, their dispositions, or their acquirements"; James Wilson observed, "it is fit for the great purposes of society that there should be, great inequality among men" in their talents and occupations.[7] Natural equality was rather a moral principle. All were equal in their natural rights and duties, which informed the two principles of justice: one has a right to the fruits of his labor and to the honor of his merits. The end of government was the equal protection of property for both the strong and the weak. Property in its fullest sense meant the exercise of one's faculties, by which one accrued an unequal share of wealth or honor. Republican government was thus defended as the means to a natural aristocracy, or rule by the best, rather than rule based on birth, wealth, or education.

Republican citizenship unified individuals under natural law into one community that excluded outsiders, upheld a way of life, and legally shared in common privileges, immunities, and duties. A citizen swore loyalty and obedience to the law, to pay his taxes, and to risk his life to defend the rights of all. One had a natural right to emigrate but only according to law so that he could not shirk his pledged duties. And while all had the right to form their own associations, only those in the compact could determine whom to admit, for whatever reason whatsoever, and demand assent to certain ideals. While patriot leaders supported nonimportation agreements and resistance to taxation without consent, the morally indignant Sons of Liberty enforced them. They smashed windows, trashed businesses, tarred and feathered customs officials, and burned ships. During the war, unity was forged through oath-taking and revolutionary committees and at the barrel of a gun. Loyalty to the community was demanded in test acts with oaths and pledged support for the cause. Thousands were made to swear oaths, post bail, or surrender for punishment before committees of safety and special courts. Those indicted for treason who refused to take oaths were "ordered to depart," their property confiscated, or they were fined and taxed, their civil rights revoked.[8] In 1777 the Maryland legislature required all preachers to swear an oath of political allegiance. Pennsylvania patriots overthrew the Quaker-dominated Assembly and overturned citizenship based on landholding for that of militia service, or bearing arms in defense of the country. In Massachusetts, committees of public safety and county conventions seized power from the governor and county court system. Religious dissenters and inhabitants of rural counties and the backcountry challenged centers of power in the law, church, and military, and they demanded a broadened franchise on a republican basis as a condition of revolution. In 1783 the Maryland Assembly required all solicitors and attorneys be "well affected to the present government of this State, and the principles of liberty and independence, as established by the late revolution."[9]

Under the new conception of citizenship, only republican forms of government were legitimate. A sovereign people could only be represented by an elected legislature, which, by the logic of compact, must rule by standing and promulgate laws for the general good and not for a particular interest or class. The government's primary task was to protect citizens' lives, liberty, and property from criminals and invaders, requiring a criminal law and public defense. A law, by definition, must be universal (applied to all) and necessary (enforced equally), else it is fiat rule, which marks a return to a state of nature. The legislature could neither tax property without consent, reducing citizens to slaves, nor seize private property for the public good without just compensation. Nor could a legislature delegate lawmaking authority to another body. Otherwise the people would lose sovereignty and suffer rule under officers unaccountable by election. To secure natural rights from government, the American state constitutions experimented with the separation of powers, instituting legislative checks and new balances for the three branches of government. The state bills of rights were partial lists of these freedoms. Americanizing the common law, they included legal provisions to shape future jurisprudence; barred practices such as ex post facto laws, monopolies, hereditary privileges, and titles of nobility; and clarified procedures of due process, trial by jury, and the right to confront one's accusers.

Achieving a Republican Form

While Americans agreed on republican principles, they disagreed over their implementation. The modification of republican forms of government to best protect rights began with the recognized need for union in 1775 and was only resolved with the Twelfth Amendment in 1804. Under the Articles of Confederation, the states ceded their claims to Western territory. The introduction of new territories in the 1787 Northwest Ordinance reproduced the "articles of compact between the original States and the people." The great feat of the new constitution, as stated in *Federalist* 9 and 39, was securing citizens' "civil liberty" with a new "republican form." At the constitutional convention, the concern over consolidated government animated the small states, which feared tyranny by the populous states. The bicameral legislature and the Electoral College gave disproportionate representation to smaller states as a condition of union. The Constitution established a process for statehood whereby new states with differing interests could enter the union if submitting a republican government "in conformity to the principles of the compact" as adjudged by Congress.[10]

Federalists, fearing the spirit of party and faction, believed that a strong military and economy depended on a more centralized government and enlightened national character. *Federalist* 2 had proclaimed that Providence had established "one united people...descended from the same ancestors, speaking the same language, professing the same religion, attached to the same principles of government, very similar in their manners and customs, and who, by their joint counsels, arms, and efforts, fighting side by side throughout a long and bloody war, have nobly established general liberty and independence." Those "once scattered all over Europe," wrote J. Hector St. John de Crevecoeur, were "melted" in the "great American asylum," whose climate, government, religion, and employment created a "new race of men."[11] As treasury secretary, Hamilton planned federal investment in agriculture, trade, transportation, and manufacturing.

The national bank established credit with foreign investors and limited state governments' expenditures by assuming their debts. In *Chisholm v. Georgia*, the Supreme Court ruled that former Loyalists could sue states for property, and by 1793 federal courts had struck down numerous laws that prevented foreign creditors from collecting prewar debts. But a broad consensus emerged among *both* Federalists and Republicans for the Eleventh Amendment (1795), which secured state sovereign immunity and denied federal courts the power to arbitrate suits against states. The union would be a *compound* and not *consolidated* government.

The question of national character extended to the naturalization of immigrants, whose corrupt habits could threaten rights. The 1794–95 Congress condemned the "facility by which, under existing alien law, aliens may acquire citizenship," and Republicans agreed to extend residency law to five years and to keep out both propertyless Irish and French radicals and aristocrats seeking asylum.[12] But following the 1797 XYZ Affair and Quasi-War with France, the Federalists challenged the old residency law along with seditious speech: if French intrigue, aided by universal principles of the "rights of man" removed from faith and nation threatened national allegiance, then American nationality (common religion, manners, habits, customs, language, and political principles) must defeat it. One Federalist explained, "It is not the establishment of an abstract theoretical point of Government for which we are to contend, but for the real and substantial enjoyment of our liberty and existence as a nation."[13] America must not be an "asylum to all nations" but must prevent the "hordes of *foreigners* immigrating to America" who "corrupt the public morals" and "prevent the establishment of a national character" through "assimilation." Federalists created a new Department of the Navy, levied new federal taxes, and authorized the president to borrow money to raise armies for war. The Naturalization, Alien, and Sedition Acts instituted a fourteen-year residency requirement, a national "registry" and surveillance of all resident aliens, the deportation of "alien enemies," and a prohibition of "false, scandalous, and malicious" writings against the government—the expulsion of dangerous foreign ideas.

Republicans saw Federalist nationalism as a threat to liberty and as the machinations of the Eastern commercial and merchant classes. They agreed with the deportation of aliens "dangerous to the peace and safety of the United States,"[14] but they suspected that the Federalists preferred rich immigrants over useful laborers. The Federalists would crush dissent while creating an army and navy to fight an unnecessary war, expand the government with placeholders, and subdue the states. By contrast, the Republicans promoted a union of contracting peoples, of independent farmers in local associations and state citizenship—relations more formative and preservative of a national character. Threatening civil war, nullification, and secession, Republicans protested in the Kentucky and Virginia Resolutions and won the Pennsylvania governorship. Journals published anti-tax protests from the backcountry along with protests against a standing army, national debt, and land laws that benefitted speculators. The petitioners claimed that their natural rights (free assembly, speech, and press) were under assault by the Alien and Sedition Acts and were best protected by republican governments in the states. The federal government had unlawfully assumed undelegated powers, like punishing libels. In the Republican victory of 1800, when President Jefferson said, "We are all republicans: we are all federalists," he assented to the need for union but not national consolidation. America would be the land of states' rights and local governance without centralized authority. The Judiciary Act and Alien Acts were repealed, and the Sedition Act expired in 1801. The Louisiana Purchase created an agricultural empire of small farmers. It led to an expanded electorate, in which states defined and defended the rights and duties of citizenship.

Americans associated republican citizenship with the self-sufficiency of independent farmers rather than the groveling of servants or serfs. At the Constitutional Convention, John Dickinson recommended "vesting the right of suffrage in the freeholders of the Country," who possessed a stake in society and independent wills.[15] They were "the best guardians of liberty; And the restriction of the right to them as a necessary defence [against] the dangerous influence of those multitudes without property & without principle with which our Country like all others, will in time abound." Defining "freehold" was a dilemma. The concern was that the propertyless masses would either unite under a demagogue to redistribute property or, worse, sell their votes to oligarchs who would form a "rank aristocracy." Yet in the revolution, as in the War of 1812, men who bore arms for their country successfully claimed the right to vote in the elections that determined when they would sacrifice their lives. Tying suffrage to a landed class had proven disastrous to freedom, yet small land ownership could secure greater independence. Oliver Ellsworth asked, "Ought not every man who pays a tax, to vote for the representative who is to levy & dispose of his money? Shall the wealthy merchants & manufacturers, who will bear a full share of the public burdens be not allowed a voice in the imposition of them—taxation & representation ought to go together." As state populations grew, the increasing number of disenfranchised propertyless citizens pushed for suffrage. In one estimate, the right to vote expanded from 65 percent of adult male citizens in colonial days to 85–90 percent in the 1790s.

The Twelfth Amendment, which placed presidential and vice-presidential candidates on "distinct ballots," completed the republican revolution by institutionalizing political parties, which channeled local interests and stabilized politics. James Madison had defended parties as a security to republican government in the "party press" essays of 1791–92. One function of the party was to draw voters to the polls. In an era of small agriculture and limited government, voting was a small part of citizenship, and turnout was low in national elections (10 percent in 1820, 27 percent in 1824). But the party popularized various interests, coordinated them, and channeled them into the political process. Under the Second Party System, average citizens participated in choosing policies on the tariff, internal improvements, and expansion. Voter turnout from 1840–96 was consistently 75–85 percent in presidential elections.

A Federalist and Republican consensus on the role of the federal government was achieved after the crises of the War of 1812. States had continued to trade openly with the enemy, supplying grain to British forces in Europe. Some refused to mobilize their militias or threatened to withhold taxes and troops. The New York militia refused to cross into Canada, halting the invasion. The governor of Massachusetts suggested a private peace with Britain followed by hints of secession at the Hartford convention. John Adams asked, "Are We One Nation Or 18?" The chaos culminated in 1814 with the burning of Washington, D.C. Republicans, ever suspicious of consolidation, accepted the need for a strong military for defense and expansion and even a national bank, but they rejected alien and sedition acts. In 1817, Adams wrote that Madison's administration had "acquired more glory. And established more Union, than all his three Predecessors...put together." James Monroe's presidency, the Era of Good Feelings, reflected that common sentiment. The declining Federalists left their legacy in the judiciary by standardizing American law.

Republicanism informed economic policy. Even in an agricultural nation, there was broad support for Hamilton's argument to protect infant industries. Laborers as well as farmers, he argued, displayed republican virtue. The Society for Political Inquiries, established in 1787 to discuss matters of republican governance and whose founding members included Franklin, Wilson, Benjamin Rush, Robert Morris, Tench Coxe, and Thomas Paine supported protection of domestic industries and sin taxes to promote republican virtues. The nation's first tariff in 1789 levied 7.5–10 percent "for the discharge of the debts of the United States, and the protection of manufacturers." In 1799 Madison warned that importing cheap British manufactures threatened American freedoms. British free trade was really moved by a "spirit, and system of monopoly" that kept the US dependent on British commerce by strangling US manufactures in their birth.[16] Exhortations to independence from foreign manufactures increased during the 1809 Embargo and War of 1812. The Pennsylvania governor asked the legislature to "devise means to encourage domestic manufactures; not only because they eminently contribute to national independence, and add to our national resources, and individual wealth; but also, because they... preserve and perpetuate our republican institutions."[17] In 1823, American political economist Daniel Raymond, critiquing Adam Smith's laissez faire philosophy, systematized the argument that infant industries should be protected until they had achieved proper scale. "The true system embraces agriculture and commerce, and considers them both as essential to national wealth."[18] Smith had incorrectly presumed that one naturally prefers employment that is advantageous to society. The idea, wrote Raymond, "that national and individual interests are never opposed... if adopted in practice, would destroy all government, and tear up the very foundations of society." The individual's right to property was only secure insofar as republican government could protect it. "But for the social compact no man could have an exclusive right to any spot of this earth." Still, the tariff would exacerbate regional interests as the North industrialized, coming to a head in the 1828 Tariff of Abominations.

The Family and Moral Virtue

A free republic must be founded in choice, but it must be maintained by tradition. Every political order reproduces a certain character, or type of soul, to preserve itself, a *constitution* in the truest sense of the word. Republicanism refers not simply to political institutions but to the type of citizen that demands them and whose habits sustain them. Political rule, different from the rule over slaves, requires an education in the noble and ignoble, honorable and shameful. "It is the manners and spirit of a people which preserve a republic in vigor," wrote Jefferson, and "a degeneracy in these is a canker which soon eats to the heart of its laws and constitution."[19] Citizen virtue, said Madison in *Federalist 51*, was the "the *primary* control on the government" to secure republican freedoms. Samuel Dana wrote that the American people's "character has been formed and fixed by such institutions"; tethered by affection to family, church, private associations, and local government, their participation in "numerous republics... enjoying powers for their own welfare... mutually supporting and supported" unified their love of freedom with the rule of law.[20] According to Zephaniah Swift, "These popular privileges have a powerful effect upon the personal character. Every inhabitant of a town, in virtue of his corporate rights, feels that he is of considerable consequence among his fellow citizens. He does not feel himself degraded to the low rank of a slave, who has nothing to do, but to obey; but from the share which he has in the government, he is conscious of the dignity of a freeman, and has a personal pride and interest, in the support of a government in which he is entitled to so much consideration and respect."[21] This Don't Tread on Me attitude was unfathomable to those bred for dependency. When the founders wrote that a vicious people must be ruled despotically, they did not just mean that a corrupt people required rule by force. Rather servile people *want* to be ruled, like the lower animals, by pleasure and pain.

The republican family foremost provided the care and instruction to produce citizens of good character who would practice the virtues necessary for a well-ordered society. Marriage, besides being part of natural law, wrote John Witherspoon, holds "a place of the first importance in the social compact. It is the radical relation from which all others take their rise."[22] Considering the "peculiar" sexual function of man, Wilson included marriage among the "natural rights of individuals" under natural law.[23] The parties must be single (barring polygamy), consensual (barring underaged and arranged marriages), and not incestuous.[24] *Natural* did not mean spontaneous, but ethical, or with a view to the comprehensive human good. Given the permanent differences between the sexes (John Gros and Francis Wayland argued that the "relative duties of man...flow from the constitution of the sexes") as well as their mutual needs, marriage was the best arrangement for human thriving and for uniting the happiness of individuals with the common good.[25] Swift wrote, "The connection between husband and wife...when founded on a mutual attachment and the ardor of youthful passions, is productive of the purest joys and tenderest transports that gladden the heart."[26]

Because marriage was not spontaneous, it had to be secured by civil law. Leading jurists recognized marriage as a contract. Theophilus Parsons, chief justice of the Massachusetts Supreme Court, wrote, "Marriage is, unquestionably, a civil contract, founded in the social nature of man, and intended to regulate, chasten and refine the intercourse between the sexes; and to multiply, preserve and improve the species."[27] Marriage institutions were public because they were essential for the procreation, education, provision, and establishment of children. Marriage was then both private and public, a contract *and* a "civil institution" with its own special rules, with each state legislature negotiating its terms. "The fundamental part of the contract," wrote Witherspoon, is lifelong "fidelity and chastity."[28] Like debts contracted in business, marriage was an oath to pay future obligations. Contracts, which aligned the interests of the parties with the aims of society, protected marriage from the whims of passion. Law obliged husbands to "maintenance," or to support their wives and children; women were obligated to intimacy, or living under the same roof. Marriages also affected property. Joseph Story wrote, "A man has just as good a right to his wife, as to the property acquired under a marriage contract. He has a legal right to her society and her fortune; and to divest such right, without his default, and against his will, would be as flagrant a violation of the principles of justice, as the confiscation of his own estate."[29] Marriage was viewed as the best means to support women and protect children, both physically and from the stigma of illegitimacy.

While today the word *contract* implies vulgar economic exchange, to the Americans it meant *freedom* to enter into the duties of partnership and to take on mutual obligations. Wilson compared the Christian republican family to servile feudal relations in ancient societies, where inequality bred polygamy and the extremes of "female servitude" and "licentiousness."[30] "Polygamy," said Justice James Kent, "may be regarded as exclusively the feature of Asiatic manners, and of half-civilized life, and to be incompatible with civilization, refinement, and domestic felicity."[31] Americans associated empire with adultery, concubinage, and sex slavery, and barbarism with polygamy. But republican marriage, Witherspoon argued, was by nature. Men were raised to equal status with other men. Women were elevated to equality, dignity, and security from harems and de facto polygamy. One popular American encyclopedia informed its readers that the "greatest evils" resulted from "unrestrained promiscuous intercourse": it would "destroy the health, and prevent the propagation of the species," subvert "the tender and benevolent charities, either between the individuals themselves, or towards their offspring," and "promote endless contentions among mankind."[32] Living together outside of marriage and sexual promiscuity undermined the "restraint of marriage institutions." The first annihilates the advantages and duties of marriage; the second discourages marriage and defeats its purpose. Sexual promiscuity erodes a culture because it weakens shame, leads to a lewd and coarsened society, and forms habits of libertinism that "incapacitate and indispose the mind for all intellectual, moral, and religious pleasures." It also violates republican equality. In adultery or promiscuity, Judge Jacob Rush told a grand jury, one is tempted to apply a different standard for himself or his friends. But the "true criterion" for any action is "the result to society if every *other person* did the same thing."[33] A violation of the marital oath "tends directly to destroy the peace of families, and to tear up the very foundation of society." Adultery and "*universal* and *unrestrained* intercourse...between the sexes" bring a "universal depravity of morals...as must utterly destroy society."

Courts of law upheld the oaths of marriage and supplemented the right to marry with religious forms, such as a ceremony with authorized persons to officiate and witnesses.[34] Society, wrote Witherspoon, has a right to know when and with whom marriage is contracted "in order to prevent causeless separations [no-fault divorce], to ascertain the legitimacy of the offspring, and determine the right of succession [inheritance]."[35] Civil law established mutual responsibilities of spouses, parents, and children. Criminal law both forbade conduct injurious to the formation and stability of families and instituted punishments for violations, such as adultery, sodomy, fornication, prostitution, bastardy, and abortion, the "destroying and murdering of bastard children."[36] Some states prohibited remarriage to discourage separations. Some brides went to the altar pregnant because the laws encouraged marriages, upon punishment of fines, in such cases.[37] In *Fenton v. Reed* (1809), cited throughout the 1800s, the New York Supreme Court legally recognized cohabitation as a formless, or "common law," marriage contract that had the same rights and obligations.[38] This method ensured, in an era of limited government (and resources), that a majority of citizens were assigned legal status, hence rights and duties, within the institution of the household.

State involvement was necessary to procure a divorce. The South Carolina Court of Chancery noted, "The remarkable facility of contracting matrimony in this State, is strongly contrasted with the impracticability of dissolving the contract."[39] Under civil law, one party dissolving a contract without mutual consent was by definition antithetical to the concept of contract. Moreover, because marriage was also a contract with the public, both parties could not agree to exit. Story wrote, "Marriage is not treated as a mere contract between the parties, subject, as to its continuance, dissolution, and effects, to their mere pleasure and intentions. But it is treated as a civil institution.... Upon it the sound morals, the domestic affections, and the delicate relations of and duties of parents and children, essentially depend."[40] The general rule for divorce was that the misbehaving party was forced to pay. Divorce was grounded in fault, or breach of contract, requiring that one spouse plead that the other had committed adultery, abandonment or desertion, insanity, bigamy, cruelty, abuse, or impotence. The other spouse could plead, in a variety of defenses, that the other was also culpable. A judge could find that the respondent had not committed the alleged act or that both spouses were at fault. Either was sufficient to defeat an action for divorce, and the parties remained married. New York only allowed divorce in cases of the crime of adultery. Alabama's 1819 constitution required the consent of a court of chancery and a two-thirds vote of both houses of the legislature.

Women were an essential part of the citizenry, and they vaunted their role in securing republican liberty as wives and mothers. "Mothers," said one 1794 textbook arguing for female education, planted the "seeds of virtue and knowledge" that schools and colleges only cultivated.[41] Lydia Child's *Mother's Book* was dedicated "to American mothers, on whose intelligence and discretion the safety and prosperity of our republic so much depend."[42] Child's *The American Frugal Housewife* (in its twelfth edition by 1833) praised the virtues of "industry, economy, and integrity" that enabled women to fulfill their duty in the domestic sphere by "management of a small household."[43] Mothers tended to the "health and morals" of children, whose development was "uncertain" when left at home or "with domestics." Wayland described these separate spheres: "It is the duty... of the husband to provide for the wants of the family; and of the wife, to assume the charge of the affairs of the household. His sphere of duty is *without*; her sphere of duty is *within*."[44] Socially, women created hierarchies in voluntary and charitable associations. Female chastity and modesty were a means of controlling others' behavior. In the Petticoat Affair, Floride Calhoun led D.C.'s ladies in snubbing the adulterous Peggy Eaton—it was they who would be the gatekeepers of polite society. American women showed their moral superiority by removing themselves from men's clubs and politics, with their vulgarity and drunkenness. Touting their superiority to aristocratic women (who were either fragile, naïve, or lewd), they displayed unbearable pride to their European visitors. Female citizens held some political rights under state law, such as the right to sue in court but not to serve on juries. And deemed to have no political "will," their property was placed under that of their husbands. The two could conflict. For example, in 1805 a woman's legal obligation to remove with her loyalist husband to Canada was ruled a renunciation of American citizenship, though her son was allowed to inherit her property.[45] In equity courts single women received the legal right to sue, contract in business, sell property, and be attorneys in fact but not in law, but this included no more than 10–15 percent of the female population. Wincing at women's legal status as one person with their husband under common law (ignored in equity courts), in the 1820s states began to grant married women property rights under civil law.[46] Women voted in several states, but this was the exception. When female suffrage was removed in New Jersey in 1807, there was no outcry.

The greatest safeguard against tyranny, wrote Madison in *Federalist 57*, was republican virtue: "above all, the vigilant and manly spirit which actuates the people of America, a spirit which nourishes freedom, and in return is nourished by it." American governments mandated moral instruction. To the classical virtues of temperance, resolution (fortitude), justice, and prudence, they added the industry and frugality necessary for a free citizenry in a commercial republic. The virtues were taught at home, school, and church as good for their own sake or noble, such as courage to stand up for one's rights and to defend one's community. In the words of Harvard's Levi Frisbie, "It is the common sense of men, that the best actions are those which proceed from a regard to virtue itself."[47] The laws educated virtues as useful by arranging the citizen's confrontation with necessity: industry and frugality in the face of old age and sickness; resolution in the face of failure and death; social cooperation in the "little republics" of local government.[48] Under good laws, wrote Franklin, the virtuous were rewarded with profit and honor and the idle and profligate allowed to fail: "Some of those who grow rich, will be prudent, live within Bounds, & preserve what they have gained for their Posterity. Others fond of showing their Wealth, will be extravagant and ruin themselves."[49] America was made stable, prosperous, and happy by a large "middling element" that prized self-sufficiency and freed it from the mechanisms of tyrants, such as debt and fear. A middle class does not see itself in conflict with the rich because it aspires upon its merits to become wealthy just as the poor hope to enter the middle class. It despises aristocratic nepotism and patronage. Similarly, the middle class despises the idle poor for their sloth and dependence. Local magistrates sent vagrants and beggars to poorhouses to earn the fruits of their labor.

Because governmental administration constantly threatens tyranny, an education in "literature and the sciences," in "wisdom and knowledge, as well as virtue," was necessary for citizens to understand when their rights were being violated.[50] Henry St. George Tucker wrote of education in the right principles: "Man only requires to understand his rights to estimate them properly: the ignorance of the people is the footstool of despotism."[51] Free institutions were overturned by the "usurpations or contrivances" of those in "administration," but "Science counteracts this mechanical monopoly of knowledge." "An enlightened people, who have once attained the blessings of a free government, can never be enslaved until they abandon virtue and relinquish science." Students should be rooted in history, and they should learn to distinguish and value their own nation. The American orthodoxy, combining natural law philosophy, Scottish common sense moral psychology, republicanism, and Protestant Christianity, dominated American colleges in textbooks such as John Gros's *Natural Principles of Rectitude...Comprehending the Law of Nature* (1795) and Francis Wayland's *The Elements of Moral Science* (1835). Leading scientists Joseph Henry, Benjamin Peirce, Benjamin Silliman, and Louis Agassiz defended it. Religious questions about life and death were part of every education; every college president before 1860 was an ordained minister.

Civil Society and Private Associations

The preservation of the family and morality required government support for religious associations (chronicled by Thomas G. West) while respecting the natural right to free conscience.[52] As the foundation for the social compact itself was an oath, Jacob Rush lectured a grand jury in 1796, a free people required belief in a monotheistic God who would punish oath-breakers. National and state governments made public professions of faith. Legislatures paid chaplains to open their sessions in prayer, and the Supreme Court convened with invocations for divine aid. While Congress could make no establishment of religion, the New England states established Protestant churches. States incorporated Bible reading and prayer in public schools, and they instituted blasphemy laws and blue laws requiring Sunday closings (Sunday mailings caused fierce disagreement). Most importantly, religious associations, unlike other corporations, were given tax-exempt status. Congregationalist and Presbyterian churches saw themselves as schools for republican government. In 1789 American Presbyterians removed the passage in the Westminster Confession requiring the magistrate to punish blasphemy and heresy, replacing it with "as nursing fathers, it is the duty of civil magistrates to protect the church of our common Lord, without giving preference to any denomination of Christians above the rest."[53]

The revolution did much to forge a Catholic and Protestant agreement on a moral natural law, which included the right to private judgment or conscience. General Washington canceled the Guy Fawkes Day "childish Custom of burning the Effigy of the pope": "We ought to consider as Brethren [Catholics] embarked in the same Cause...the defence of the general liberty of America."[54] In 1773 John Carroll, who would become the first American Catholic archbishop, waged a pamphlet war against Tory Daniel Dulany in making the case for Catholic Whiggism. Carroll celebrated Catholics who shed their blood to secure their natural rights, and he appealed to social contract theory: "Americans associated into one great national union, under the express condition of not being shackled by religious tests; and under a firm persuasion that they were to retain, when associated, every natural right, not expressly surrendered."[55] He could thus harmonize "civil toleration" with intolerance over theological matters.[56] Still, Protestants like John Jay were suspicious of granting civil rights to Catholics who might appeal to the authority of the Church to deny them religious liberty. Only six states allowed Catholics all rights of citizenship, such as holding office.

Churches were but one type of association or social contract in the political order. Samuel Dana's 1802 *A Specimen of Republican Institutions* showed republican habits as the common element, from families and private associations to district, town, county, and state governments, all the way to federal union. Each was voluntary and regulated by law. New York passed a general incorporation law for religious societies in 1784, colleges and academies in 1787, municipalities in 1788, libraries in 1792, and medical societies in 1806. A jurisprudence developed around the formation and limits of these contracts. In resolving disputes, courts looked to the constitutions and bylaws of associations and churches. Incorporation became common in business. In New England, 171 charters had been granted before 1799; from 1800–75, there were 11,357 business corporations, 8,119 created by special acts and the rest by general acts. In 1805, a Massachusetts law enumerated the "general powers and duties" of turnpike corporations, followed by a law for manufacturing companies in 1809. Business corporations were not seen as simply good. Each charter required a special act of the state legislature, and each petition for incorporation was weighed according to whether it would "promote the interest of the public."[57] With war looming in 1811, New York passed the first limited liability law (limiting capital stock to $100,000) to encourage incorporation and "convince foreign nations that [the US was] not dependent on them for manufactures."[58]

The constitution recognized the states' reserved powers as well as the "police powers" of the people to pass reasonable laws in the regulation of public health, safety, and morals. This included quarantines to stop the spread of deadly diseases, surveyors inspecting the integrity of privately owned bridges, and testing the flammability of illuminable oil.[59] State regulation secured equal access to transportation and markets, defined property rights, and enforced contracts. "Three principles" writes Joseph Postell, defined the republican model: "Regulation would be defined as much as possible by legislatures, where the elected representatives of the people would make policy decisions. It would also follow the rule of law by involving the courts of law and would be local and accountable through decentralization." Administrators could not hide in anonymity; they were subject to suits by citizens and arbitrated by the courts. Zealous officers operating beyond the law became subjected to notoriety and dismissal.

Health meant *both* the right of citizens to make decisions for their own care and happiness and the state's obligation to protect the rights of others from injury. While every state government regulated verifiable threats to public health, the underlying legislative principle was that of liberty; individuals with freedom of conscience were presumed capable of making decisions about their own diet and well-being, for which they sought books and dictionaries to inform themselves. Personal injuries were settled in civil courts under tort law with a jury determining fault. Infectious persons could be sued under the common law offense of public nuisance or for "negligently imparting a disease" such as smallpox and scarlet fever.[60] In the face of deadly diseases and pestilences (smallpox, yellow fever, and cholera), state governments passed sanitation and quarantine laws to regulate what experts argued were the sources, noxious odors from putrid water and interpersonal transmission by ship. With the outbreak of yellow fever in Philadelphia in 1793, which infected eleven thousand and killed five thousand, or one-tenth of the population, Pennsylvania revived its Act to Prevent Infectious Diseases and, along with New York, passed health and quarantine laws that established health commissioners and boards of health. The boards reported their findings to the legislature on disease and sanitation and executed health bylaws ordered by mayors to fill low lots and clean streets, yards, cellars, and public places of stagnant putrid water. In Massachusetts, if an official had reason to believe noxious odors were emitting from a business or private dwelling, he must obtain the aid of a justice of peace, who would fill out a warrant for inspection and justify the interference of a constable. To stop the spread of disease, public health officials in New York hailed every incoming vessel and queried as to its crew whether there was pestilence and whence it came with power to collect reports, search the ship, assess the health risk, and impose a quarantine. Governors and mayors were empowered to quarantine ships and cut off commercial trade with other cities and states by stopping ferries and incoming vessels. Physicians and boardinghouse owners were required to report the names of sick travelers or patients to the health inspector or board. While contagious residents of the city were confined to their homes, others were taken to hospitals like New York's Marine Hospital or Philadelphia's Lazaretto.

Following Benjamin Waterhouse's introduction of cowpox vaccination to protect against smallpox in 1800, governments worked with private associations to encourage vaccination. In 1810 Massachusetts passed a law ordering that every town, district, and plantation where no board of health existed choose three or more persons to *supervise* the inoculation of the inhabitants with cowpox along with the earlier restrictions for those exposed to smallpox.[61] It was no mandate. In the town of Milton, which Governor Gore called an exemplar, "The Superintendents are invited to call upon every family, and use their best exertions, to persuade all that are exposed to the small pox, to attend."[62] Legislatures incorporated institutions, such as the Massachusetts Medical Society (1781), and private institutes sprung up to vaccinate as many as possible at no expense.[63] However, Massachusetts repealed its earlier vaccination laws in 1837. A report of the Medical Society before the Joint Committee on the Judiciary complained that the laws passed in 1792 and 1797 were "useless, vexatious and burdensome, that personal rights were interfered with, individuals and the public subjected to unnecessary expense, deprived of the comforts of home by removal to public hospitals and that physicians were now compelled to report these cases to the proper authorities and thus subject their patients to the provisions of severe and as they believed unnecessary laws."[64] The surge of Irish immigrants reintroduced the question of whether the state could compel its citizens to be vaccinated as a matter of public health. In 1855 Massachusetts passed the first compulsory smallpox vaccination, requiring managers and superintendents of incorporated manufacturing companies, almshouses, state schools, lunatic hospitals, prisons, and all state-supported institutions to vaccinate all workers, inmates, and entrants. It also required town authorities to vaccinate their inhabitants. Without a physician's note, a parent could be fined five dollars if his child had not been vaccinated before the age of two. But there was no efficient enforcement machinery in place. New York had instituted a "free system of public vaccination," and the city inspector in 1861 suggested vaccines for immigrants and vaccine certificates to attend public school, but wide noncompliance made him conclude that it was "unreasonable to attempt their enforcement."[65] Rather, "an appeal to the good sense of our citizens will be almost sure to be answered by their general cooperation." Still, they waited "until the disease has actually exhibited itself with virulence."

States also passed laws that required a license to practice surgery and medicine. Again they relied on private associations and medical societies to inform the legislature on public health and on pharmacopoeia societies to classify various compounds and their medicinal effects. The Massachusetts Medical Society published a pharmacopoeia in 1808. The oldest standards-developing organization in the United States is the US Pharmacopeial Convention, which published standards for 219 drugs in 1820. The informed patient could then choose a doctor or purchase a cure for himself. While twenty states and the District of Columbia had medical licensing laws "to practice physic or surgery" before 1850, most were repealed, beginning with Illinois's in 1826. The laws were, writes Ronald Hamowy, "short-lived and poorly enforced": "Five states attached no penalty to practicing without a license and six more provided that, at worst, unlicensed practitioners could not sue for recovery of fees."[66] In only four states, practicing without a license could result in imprisonment. One of those states, New York, incorporated societies that would vote on issues of malpractice and then deliver their findings to the district attorney, who would serve charges and handle the prosecution.

The republican mind aided the demise of licensing laws. Americans trusted their own experience and rejected social elites' authoritative claims. Orthodox medicine, described by Dr. John Beck in 1829, applied treatments of "bleeding, vomiting, blistering, purging" and massive doses of mercury, antimony, and other mineral poisons as purgatives and emetics.[67] "If the illness continued, there was *repetendi*, and finally, *murderandi*; nature was never to be consulted or allowed to have any concern in the affair." This "heroic therapy," based on a theory of balancing four humors, killed many patients, including President Zachary Taylor, "Old Rough and Ready," whose doctors managed to do by bleeding and emetics what the Mexican Army and Texas heat could not. The public challenged the ineffective cures of established medical practice, which in turn fueled alternative medical schools and easier access to degrees. Two sects with competing educations arose to challenge the orthodox "regular" medicine. Samuel Thomson, a New Hampshire farmer, founded eclectic medicine in 1813, which prescribed botanical (as opposed to metallic) remedies, steam baths, and rest (Benjamin Waterhouse, mentioned above, was an avid Thomsonian).

Samuel Hahnemann, a German doctor, criticized regular medicine and founded homeopathy in 1796 on the healing powers of the organism itself—the recuperative powers of nature. Introduced to America in 1825, its two premises were that the appropriate drug for a disease would be that which induced similar symptoms in a healthy person and applying minute doses in its administration (regular medicine equated larger doses with greater efficacy). Eclectic and homeopathic remedies of fresh air, sunshine, rest, proper diet, and personal hygiene made sense to average citizens and provided an alternative to regular therapy. In 1830 New York law explicitly prohibited the use of its provisions to "debar any person from using or applying for the benefit of any sick person any roots, barks, or herbs."[68] While the percentage of homeopaths and eclectics remained small, by 1860 the US had a larger number of doctors per capita than any country in the world. Regular physicians organized the American Medical Association in 1847. Its ethical code barred association with competing sects.

The Citizenry

Republicanism requires clarity about who is a citizen and who else may be admitted. The consensus was that the American citizenry should be European, Protestant, and industrious. Most Americans, 3.14 out of 3.93 million, were white, and whites were 60 percent English, 85 percent British, and 99 percent Protestant. Indians were not deemed to be part of the original people. By the 1820s, Americans viewed Indian assimilation as a romantic dream. In the tribal way of life, rivals kidnapped women and children and ritualistically tortured their captures. Men shunned agriculture as degrading women's work for hunting and warfare, and there was no virtue of female chastity protecting patrilineal bloodlines. In tribal matrilineal societies, boys were raised by uncles and grandfathers. The tribes were not sovereign but existed as "dependent nations" whose relation resembled "that of a ward to his guardian."[69] The policy of Indian Removal in the 1830s revolved around a central question: whether a sovereign people may determine its citizenry and thus who may live within its borders. Indian tribes could not claim sovereignty while living within sovereign states with police powers over their internal territories.[70]

In 1790, 757,000 Africans, mostly slaves, lived under the new government. During the Revolution, 10,000–20,000 blacks had fled from their masters, while 5,000 had sided with the Patriots. States, proclaiming the natural rights philosophy, freed 10,000 blacks, some immediately and some on Pennsylvania's gradual abolition plan. The number of free blacks grew from less than 3,000 to 30,000 in Virginia between 1782 and 1810 and became a large portion of all blacks in Maryland and Delaware. In the debates over the 1780 Massachusetts constitution, some advocated citizenship rights to free blacks, who received the privileges and immunities of citizenship under the Articles of Confederation. Antislavery societies expanded and assaulted slavery in the press. In congressional debates, slavery was cast as a necessary evil, detestable, against republican principles. The Northwest Territory banned slavery but guaranteed the return of fugitive slaves. Slavery, Madison recalled, constituted "the real difference of interests" at the Constitutional Convention.[71] The question was how to secure the "principles of the Revolution" with a political union yet get the South to make compromises over slavery. None of the southern delegates promoted slavery as a positive good; some readily lamented the contradiction between principle and practice. As to slavery in the South, in 1790 Congress admitted there was little it could do but levy a duty on the importation of slaves or offer to purchase and resettle them. But ideals soon faced the harsh southern reality. After the 1791 Haitian revolution, where black revolutionaries carried an impaled white baby as their standard, representatives ceased discussing the issue.

But the Revolution had created the *problem* of free blacks, now present in large numbers. Free blacks voted in the ratification of the Constitution, but it was not clear whether they were citizens. Nor was black citizenship simply about belief in African equality. While most whites did not hold to African equality, many of those who did denied the possibility of civic harmony. Mutual animosity born of "prejudices" between whites and blacks, Madison and Jefferson argued, were "permanent and insuperable," creating divisions of race that would "produce convulsions which will probably never end but in the extermination of either one or the other race."[72] Virginia congressman and law professor Henry St. George Tucker forwarded a gradual abolition scheme, but he did not favor civil equality. Blacks had a right to be free of slavery and to emigrate, but they did not have a right to become citizens. Nor did Americans have to admit them. Men have, "when they enter into a state of society, a right to admit, or exclude any description of persons, as they think proper."[73] Prejudices, he wrote, were a fact; right or wrong, they ought to be respected and were no worse than those who "depreciate the...national character" out of misguided charity or a destructive integrationist ambition. His position was, he wrote, a "middle course, between the tyrannical and iniquitous policy" of slavery and "turn[ing] loose a numerous, starving, and enraged banditti, upon the innocent descendants of their former oppressors." It was inconceivable that blacks, who represented a disproportionate number of the prison population, would be capable of citizenship. In this conflict between the natural rights to liberty and self-preservation, the latter had required the unjust institution of slavery. The only true solution was self-emigration or colonization.

In the republican system, each state determined the terms of citizenship. Legally, free blacks were neither aliens nor naturalized citizens with permanent rights. They had the legal status of denizens, or inhabitants granted some legal rights and privileges subject to change or repeal.[74] In Maine, free blacks possessed almost all the rights of white citizens without citizenship. But in no state did they have complete civil and political equality that included rights such as marriage. Most states and territories passed anti-miscegenation laws: Massachusetts (and Maine) and Rhode Island did so in 1786 and 1798, respectively. Blacks formed their own communities and an African American identity in religious and private associations. In 1789, free blacks could vote in ten states, but after mass manumissions, their voting rights were restricted and their civil rights curtailed.[75] In interpreting the status of blacks under state constitutions, jurists opined and courts ruled that they may have been free but were not "freemen" or citizens with voting rights.[76] "Negroes," concluded Justice Kent, "are natural-born subjects, but not citizens."[77] Northern states secured the natural rights of blacks while discouraging their immigration and presence. In the 1780s New Jersey and Connecticut barred the importation of slaves as a threat to "white labour." Local municipalities, such as Boston, barred blacks from public schools. In 1833 Connecticut banned the creation of private schools for black nonresidents to discourage the growth of the black population, which contributed "thereby to the injury of the people."[78] The 1802 Ohio Constitutional Convention *both* banned slavery and denied voting rights to black males while granting blacks some civil rights; to discourage black immigration, Ohio only permitted them upon proof of freedom and the payment of prohibitive bonds (as high as $1,000). The Ohio bill of rights banned not only slavery but black immigration and any form of indentures that might be used to circumvent the ban. Indiana, Illinois, and Michigan banned *both* slavery and black immigration, the latter by barring their employment, voiding all contracts—even marriage contracts—made with them, and even appropriating money for their emigration. The Indiana Supreme Court concluded, "The policy of the state is...clearly...to exclude any further ingress of negroes, and to remove those already among us as speedily as possible."[79] By 1850 blacks constituted less than 2 percent of the northern population and less than 1 percent in territories. In the South, legislatures curtailed the privileges of free blacks as a threat to the planter class. Facing slave revolts and war with Britain, Virginia, Maryland, Delaware, and Kentucky banned their entry and removed their civil and legal rights. Factually, blacks could not become US citizens because the

Eleventh Amendment prohibited them from suing states for national privileges and immunities.

At the federal level, the 1790 Naturalization Act barred blacks from citizenship while extending citizenship to "any Alien" that was "a free white person" of "good character" who had resided "under the jurisdiction of the United States" for two years and had been a yearlong resident "in any one of the States." The 1792 Militia Act prohibited blacks from joining American militias, a key criterion of citizenry in the Revolution. In 1798, during the Quasi-War with France, the Department of War ordered that "No Negro, Mulatto or Indian" could enlist in the Marine Corps, and the Department of the Navy barred "Negroes or Mulattoes" from serving aboard naval vessels and all revenue cutters.[80] Negroes, like foreigners, were prohibited from captaining American merchant ships. US Attorney General William Wirt stated in 1821 that "it seems very manifest that no person is included in the description of citizen of the United States who has not the full rights of a citizen in the State of his residence."[81] Thus, "Free colored persons in Virginia are not citizens of the United States."

The solution for those who despised slavery but doubted the possibility of civic harmony was to stop the spread of slavery and promote black colonization. The 1820 Missouri Compromise limited the spread of slavery to the Arkansas Territory. Supporters of the American Colonization Society, including Jefferson, Madison, Monroe, Clay, and Lincoln, wanted to purchase land in Africa for black resettlement. The society's first president was Supreme Court Justice Bushrod Washington (George's nephew). Feasibility was an issue: the 1830 census reported two million slaves and 319,000 free colored people. Still, Liberia was founded in 1822 as a colony for freed slaves, with its capital named after Monroe. Exercising their own right to exclusive republican government, black settlers from America barred native Africans from citizenship.

Naturalization was restricted to whites, but it was no matter of open borders. Americans debated which Europeans were fit for citizenship and how many they should accept. The first consensus was that citizenship should be encouraged by suffrage laws as well as restricted for reasons of national unity and security. While Congress held power over naturalization, states had long prevented vagrant or pauper immigrants and restricted their movement. They controlled which aliens, who did not possess the rights of citizenship, could buy land and engage in business. States determined alien residents' rights to vote, own real estate, and hold political office. At least twenty-two states and territories, seeking to attract European settlers, gave white resident aliens the right to vote after either a period of residency or stating their intent to naturalize. Congress reenacted the 1787 Northwest Ordinances to give voting rights to aliens with fifty-acre freeholds after two years. The Northwest Ordinance suffrage law was a model for the Orleans, Michigan, and Mississippi Territories as well as the congressional enactment for state constitutional conventions in Ohio, Indiana, Michigan, and Illinois.[82] Ohio gave voting rights to white male residents without property qualifications and full citizenship after a one-year residency and payment of the requisite taxes. Illinois allowed resident aliens to vote but let citizens alone hold office. But importantly, states changed their laws after the War of 1812, which stirred nationalistic sentiment and affirmed the importance of loyalty. The six newly created states prohibited alien suffrage, and six others that had permitted it revoked it.[83]

As the nation grew in population, laws requiring voter registration prior to elections followed concerns about voter eligibility and fraud. Twelve states denied paupers the right to vote from 1792 to 1876, and eleven states barred felons from voting from 1776 to 1821 and twenty-four by 1858. "The need for residency rules," writes Alexander Keyssar, "was widely agreed upon," though states differed on lengths of time: "the average requirement tended to be one year in the state and three or six months in an individual township or county."[84] In southern locales, voting was oral and public (thus the push for written ballots to eliminate intimidation). From 1800 to 1830 numerous states changed their constitutions to distinguish "citizens" from "inhabitants," with almost all new states from 1800 to 1840 granting the right to vote *only* to citizens: aliens were almost universally barred from the polls. This required lists of eligible or "enrolled" voters and proof of citizenship. Massachusetts passed a voter registration law in 1801. In 1807 New Jersey only admitted "enrolled" "free, white, male citizen" voters to the polls, cross-checked with tax rolls, and imposed stiff penalties for fraud.[85] South Carolina required voter registration for citizens in Columbia in 1819, and in 1821 New York required that voters present "proper proofs" of eligibility. The same year Massachusetts required the mayor and aldermen in Boston to compose a list of all eligible voters. By mistake, Samuel Foster, local inspector of elections, excluded taxpaying resident Joseph Capen in 1831. In *Capen v. Foster*, the Supreme Court of Massachusetts upheld the law. In the words of Chief Justice Shaw, "The constitution, by carefully prescribing the qualifications of voters, necessarily requires that an examination of the claims of persons to vote, on the ground of possessing these qualifications, must at some time be had by those who are to decide on them. The time and labor necessary to complete these investigations must increase in proportion to the increased number of voters; and indeed in a still greater ratio in populous commercial and manufacturing towns, in which the inhabitants are frequently changing, and where of necessity many of the qualified voters are strangers to the selectmen." Voter registration laws accelerated in the 1830s with the rise of transient Irish immigrants. Whigs accused Democratic areas of allowing illegals to vote. In 1836 Pennsylvania required the assessors in Philadelphia to compose a list of qualified voters. Connecticut passed a voter registry system in 1839; New York passed one for New York City in 1840. Other states implemented literacy tests and "waiting periods" to vote in the 1850s.

Another debate ensued over whether immigrant laborers undermined republican independence. The ideal of free labor conflicted with both slavery and cheap immigrant labor. Honest, productive work, with the possibility of social mobility, provided the basis for citizen independence and virtue, whereas permanent wage-labor and dependence upon an employer was akin to slavery. The citizenship question followed the Irish Potato Famine and the 1830–60 immigrations. Unlike the Germans who migrated to the frontier, Irish immigrants crowded into tenements in large cities, providing cheap labor, breaking strikes, driving down wages, and consistently voting Democratic. Deadly riots ensued over whether states would fund Catholic schools or require Catholic students to read from the Protestant Bible. Crime and welfare costs soared. Cincinnati's crime rate tripled between 1846 and 1853; poor relief in Boston rose threefold. And immigration accelerated between 1850 and 1855 to five times that of the previous decade. In response, six more states revoked alien suffrage.[86] To protect native jobs, states required business licenses and excluded foreigners from civil rights and holding offices. Tavern license restrictions in Chicago erupted into the 1855 Lager Riots. State laws excluded foreign paupers and criminals. Massachusetts and New York developed extensive systems to restrict destitute foreigners and deport them back to Europe. Massachusetts law restricted legal residency to US citizens; any denizen seeking relief at a public almshouse was subject to deportation to "any other state, or to any place beyond [the] sea, where he belongs."[87] Officials raided almshouses and asylums. Steamship companies had to pay a $1,000 bond for each feeble-minded, aged, or infirm person, conditional on whether such person became a public charge within ten years. Another law restricted legal settlement to US citizens after a period of residency; all others remained non-naturalized aliens. Massachusetts imposed a $2 head tax for the support of foreign paupers. While the US Supreme Court found this and a similar New York act unconstitutional in 1849, the Massachusetts law had already been amended and would be several more times.

Where Congress had regulated immigrants as early as 1819, the lack of federal action reflected political and regional divisions. Anti-immigrant and trade union interests in the North and South conflicted with business and Western interests. Western states like Nebraska and Oregon passed land laws to encourage white citizens, immigrants, and investment. Democrats in the North wanted immigrants for the party machinery, while those in the South defended slave labor and opposed the new immigrants, who as a rule opposed slavery in the territories. The Know Nothings won 40 percent of the vote in most Southern states, and Alabama, Mississippi, and Maryland prohibited aliens from purchasing land. Stephen Douglas, both pro-immigrant and pro-slavery, held the party together with the "great principle" of popular sovereignty: let both sides vote on slavery in the newly created states as the nation expanded westward. He elided the difference between slavery and denizenship. But the Whigs and Know Nothings, which supported tariffs, clashed over immigration and slavery and faced a dilemma in building a national party. Northern industry and financiers favored cheap labor for internal improvements, while the Native American Party lobbied to stop immigration from Catholic countries, repeal the naturalization law, and increase the residency requirement to twenty-one years. It won numerous state legislatures and offices throughout the country in the 1854–55 elections.

The 1856 Illinois Republican platform cleared a middle path by both encouraging white immigration and opposing unpopular immigrant demands, such as Catholics' proposals for changes in public education. Lincoln believed the solution lay in channeling white immigrants into growing industries that would both destroy the slave power and solve the labor shortage in industry, mining, and agriculture. Enabled by Lincoln's native genius and his relative obscurity, the motley Republican Party platform wedded agrarian and industrial interests in protective tariffs, internal improvements (a transcontinental railroad), and the Homestead Act, which offered citizens and white aliens up to 160 acres of land. In his debates with Douglas, Lincoln adopted the Jeffersonian republican mantle, now openly rejected in the South, and courted Know Nothings by tarring the Democrats as the party of slavocracy, where a lordly landed class ruled poor whites. The issue was slavery, not "negro citizenship," which Lincoln opposed.[88] He called slavery an evil but insisted that he was not arguing for "social and political equality" for blacks (the right to vote, serve on juries, and hold office). He wanted to preserve the union by impeding the spread of slavery and encouraging small farmers and free labor. Accused by Douglas of plotting miscegenation, he replied, "I protest against that counterfeit logic which concludes that, because I do not want a black woman for a *slave* I must necessarily want her for a *wife*."[89] But neither did denying blacks the political rights of citizenship conflict with the undergirding principle of natural right. In that second sense, "in her natural right to eat the bread she earns with her own hands...she is my equal, and the equal of all others."

The problem of the status of free blacks became a crisis in 1861 as confiscated, impoverished black slaves fled their Confederate masters into the Union. Lincoln recurred to self-deportation and colonization in his second annual message to Congress, in which he affirmed, "I strongly favor colonization." The 1862 Emancipation Act emancipated slaves in D.C. and appropriated $100,000 for their voluntary emigration to "the Republics of Hayti or Liberia, or such other country." Prominent blacks supported the proposal; hundreds signed up for the first voyage to Chiriquí, Panama. Congress appropriated another $500,000, attracting numerous colonization schemes. That year Lincoln invited a five-member black delegation to the Executive Mansion, where he blamed blacks for the war because they would not leave. Both races had suffered, he said, but even were slavery destroyed, unequal "physical differences" would remain, with blacks "cut off from many of the advantages" that whites enjoy.[90] "You and we are different races," he concluded, and it was "better for us both...to be separated." Yet Lincoln's final views were not fixed. The Emancipation Proclamation and recruitment of blacks into the armed forces cleared the way for his final endorsement of admitting blacks to expanded *state* civil rights. In his last public address, addressing Louisiana's new state constitution that barred blacks from voting, he preferred that the right to vote be "conferred on the very intelligent [blacks], and on those who serve our cause as soldiers."[91] He had in mind political rights based on military service—dependable Republican votes in the South—with a threshold of education such as that exemplified in Frederick Douglass. Still, Lincoln focused primarily on restoring "those states to their proper practical relation with the Union," not on black citizenship.

Seven hundred and fifty thousand Americans died to settle the questions of slavery, voluntary secession, and the place of the states in a federal system, crystalized in the Thirteenth Amendment prohibiting slavery. The South was a conquered people, carved up into military governorships, with Republicans divided on terms of readmission. The returning Southern states wanted the old position of enslaved black labor. In the 1865–66 Black Codes, they used the Thirteenth Amendment, which allowed for "involuntary servitude" in criminal cases, to re-enslave the freedmen. But following their 1866 victory, the Radical Republicans passed the Civil Rights Act, which guaranteed blacks the right to make contracts, give evidence in court, own property, and enjoy "full and equal benefit of all laws…as is enjoyed by white citizens." Recognizing the alternatives of continued de facto servitude and the equal rights of citizenship, they passed the Fourteenth and Fifteenth Amendments over President Andrew Johnson's veto and without Southern assent. The first, which was passed under constitutionally dubious means, granted citizenship to all blacks born in the US (and not under a foreign sovereignty) and required "limited absolute equality" in certain basic civil rights, allowing for "reasonable" racial classifications. The same Congress, for example, required segregation in D.C. public schools. The second, disallowing "race, color or previous condition of servitude" as criteria for denying suffrage, ensured Republican victories. With the enfranchisement of black males and the extensive use of loyalty oaths to disenfranchise some whites, blacks used their new citizenship to elect six hundred blacks to southern legislatures; twenty-two blacks served in Congress between 1870 and 1901.

In 1870 Congress extended naturalization law to blacks. Citizenship on the new white and black basis introduced a tension between separation and "uplift." The first meant securing the freedmen equal protection under the law while allowing states to determine full civil rights. Prominent Republicans like William Seward, Charles Sumner, Salmon P. Chase, Rufus Dawes, and George Boutwell supported *both* black legal equality *and* race segregation. The Force Bill, for example, attempted to crush the Ku Klux Klan. In the second, reformers sought to show that both the freedmen and Indians could, by a process of education, behave as whites, whereupon they would receive full political rights.[92] While the Freedmen's Bureau provided food, health care, and education on a color-blind basis, northern missionaries descended to the South to uplift the freedmen, often by means of race preference. Fearing both northern white paternalism and southern white reprisal, Booker T. Washington stressed the economic basis of black independence, and Frederick Douglass stressed political equality and the right to be left alone.

By 1872, Americans increasingly opposed Union occupation and federal central control, and they favored amnesty and a return to republicanism. Wealthy southern whites threatened by populist uprisings helped suppress Klan violence. The Supreme Court struck a compromise between republican self-government and federal management by limiting the Fourteenth and Fifteenth Amendments. In the Slaughter-House Cases (1873), it applied privileges and immunities only to prohibition of state action. In the Civil Rights Cases (1883), it overturned the Civil Rights Act of 1875, which mandated "equal enjoyment of the accommodations, advantages, facilities, and privileges of inns, public conveyances on land or water, theaters, and other places of public amusement" for "citizens of every race and color." This, said the Court, was an unconstitutional regulation of "private rights." Civil rights did not include "the social rights of men and races in the community" but only "those fundamental rights which appertain to the essence of citizenship," such as the right to travel, "equality of access on public conveyances," and the right to contract in business.[93] Nor must state legislatures guarantee every citizen the right to vote but could restrict voting rights based on sex, literacy, and property. *Plessy v. Ferguson* (1896) reflected the consensus; requiring equal accommodations, it hinged on the citizen's equal right to travel and engage in commerce, which could not be denied by private carriers. But it also sanctioned southern and de facto northern segregation. Equal protection meant that citizens could sue in federal court to secure their essential privileges while the states determined most civil rights. In varying state legislation, for example, eleven states repealed their anti-miscegenation laws before 1887, while thirty states (sixteen in the South) kept them.

The above restrictions on citizenship and the republican ideal were tied to an inward looking, noninterventionist foreign policy, removed from entangling alliances with European powers or Latin American republics. It made no sense to expand to include those incapable of citizenship. The Constitution had planned for the creation of new states, each with a republican character, and this included vigilance against both chaos on US borders and European powers aspiring to colonize North America. Manifest Destiny was not a policy of ruling conquered peoples without their consent but in expanding US territory. There was a legitimate question as to where exactly in the Pacific the US should stake its claim, but it did not expand to incorporate or rule over new subjects. Despite Commodore Matthew Perry's own aspirations, it did not seize the Ryukyu Islands in 1853. After purchasing Alaska for $7.5 million, Congress passed a resolution that there would be no more acquisitions until it had paid off its Civil War debt. The Senate rejected Grant's bid for Santo Domingo, and it did not oppose French interventions in Panama. Congress signed a reciprocity treaty with Hawaii instead of seizing it in 1875. In 1885 Cleveland affirmed that the nation should "not favor a policy of acquisition." By 1890, it was clear that the US must expand to secure North America from foreign fleets, thus the attraction of Samoa, Hawaii, Cuba, and Puerto Rico. But following the 1893 Hawaiian coup, Cleveland ordered an investigation and withdrew the treaty from the Senate. Secretary of State Gresham said the US could not "annex a people against their consent." Private churches would send missionaries to save the souls but not the politics of foreign lands.

Postwar Challenges

Republicanism required ruling and being ruled while addressing the most egregious examples of corruption. In the golden age of political parties, the machine, led by the party boss, carved up cities into districts, wards, and precincts. Ambitious vote hustlers climbed their way up the party by delivering votes. The winning party distributed the spoils—government jobs and contracts—to supporters. At conventions, state delegates met to haggle over interests and select candidates to carry out their compromises. The parties handed out their own ballots in order to know whom to reward when the voter left the booth. Thousands of federal post office jobs went to loyal supporters and changed hands in defeat. In the 1880s one could find an ad in a D.C. newspaper: "Wanted—a government clerkship at a salary of not less than $1,000 per annum. Will give one hundred dollars to anyone securing me such a position." Outside of pensions for veterans and their widows, political parties and charitable organizations distributed welfare. Churches were power brokers that provided food for parishioners and refuge for freedmen and new immigrants. The party gave financial help, legal advice, coal to families in winter, and turkeys at Christmas. Functionaries showed up with gifts at weddings and baptisms and condolences at funerals. The justice of the era was called *honest graft*. The party benefitted its supporters and also fulfilled its public duties: competent policies meant improvements and reelection. Boss Tweed hired top experts to build much of New York City.

Dishonest graft benefitted the party at the expense of the public. Tweed also stole $81 million from New York by charging it to the city's credit. Receipts for the county courthouse included $3 million for "stationery." When corruption became too rife, citizens elected good government reformers ("goo-goos") to clean out the bureaucracy and start anew. At the national level, corruption attended the wartime growth in federal bureaucracy and government contracts, and Republicans were divided over the open patronage of the spoils system.

After a deranged office seeker assassinated President James Garfield, the 1883 Pendleton Act reinstituted President Ulysses Grant's three-member Civil Service Commission, which, like similar state commissions, oversaw exams for appointments and conducted investigations into public mismanagement and removals for partisan reasons. Democrat Grover Cleveland attracted the Mugwump (Republican Reformers) vote in 1884 by supporting civil service reform, a proposal to regulate promotions based upon merit instead of patronage and free the president from the deluge of office-seekers. The commissions were an independent investigatory arm of legislatures that reported on testing results, competitive bids, sanitary conditions, and graft. Journalists aided the commissions by publicizing corruption. In response to the charge that the new civil service would constitute a "permanent office-holding community" where a "privileged class controls all the offices," the Civil Service Commission affirmed in 1888 that there were probationary periods and never "permanent appointment[s]."[94]

The second challenge to republicanism was the rise of large corporations, whose business decisions subverted the economic independence and political autonomy of small communities. Businesses increased their demands for protective tariffs from 1865 to 1900, and the 1890 McKinley Tariff scheduled rates up to 50 percent. The business lobby killed trade reciprocity with Canada in 1865 and Mexico in 1883, and it opposed the annexation of Hawaii, which would undercut US sugar interests, in 1893. "Free trade" Democratic "Bourbons" did not challenge protection but Republican *overprotection*, tariffs that secured profits for industries that already outproduced foreign competitors. Manufacturers had long formed short-lived, unstable pools to limit domestic production and prevent price wars. But government subsidies, foreign investment, and now investment banks (like J. P. Morgan) provided vast capital for industry. Andrew Carnegie's US Steel gained a monopoly by controlling every phase of the steel-making process, consolidating iron ore mines, shipping, short line rails, and smelting furnaces. John D. Rockefeller's Standard Oil monopolized refineries, thereby controlling the oil industry. These integrated, efficiently organized industries with large economies of scale and capital requirements challenged the assumption that free markets would always undercut inefficient monopolies. Rockefeller and Carnegie slashed steel and oil prices. The consolidation of the rail lines brought lower passenger and shipment rates while curbing rate wars and preventing upstarts from speculating in rail line takeovers.

In 1879 Rockefeller made a secret agreement with the stockholders of Standard Oil, called a trust, to place control of the decisions of thirty separate companies in dozens of states to three trustees. Trusts soon emerged in whiskey, cottonseed oil, and sugar. These consolidations of wealth and power jolted the view of America as the land of equality. Single businessmen had private armies of Pinkerton guards and more wealth than the national treasury. It was the first tension between efficiency and size, where the very meaning of *competition* was ambiguous, and between economic production and political classes. Corporations formed "natural monopolies" in markets or resources that threatened republican self-sufficiency and divided the American identity between that of consumer and citizen. As interests intensified, the first view of citizens as consumers, often guided by abstract theories (both laissez faire and socialist) made politics and republicanism secondary. Large corporations preferred cheap, docile laborers. William Seward had long questioned the "preference for native American citizens over foreigners."[95] It was "un-American," he said, to distinguish between "native-born

Americans" and immigrants; all Americans were aliens. America had needed foreign cheap labor for five thousand miles of canals and sixteen thousand miles of railroad. Moreover, "The ingress of the foreign population into this country" was "a fixed and unchangeable fact." Those fleeing poverty and oppression in Ireland, Germany, and China would come, obeying inexorable "laws of supply and demand."

The republican consensus was that government should break apart the trusts. Ohio representative John Sherman called the trust "a kingly prerogative, inconsistent with our form of government, and [it] should be subject to the strong resistance of the State and national authorities." All but a few states had banned corporate consolidations, trusts, and pools under common law. Some had inserted anti-monopoly provisions into their constitutions, prohibiting combinations in restraint of trade. New York prohibited corporate consolidations in manufacturing until 1867 and even then confined it to single industries. In the 1880s numerous states criminalized trusts. Focusing on railroad trusts, by 1887 fourteen states had created commissions to inspect railroad safety and to investigate rate and service discrimination. More commissions were created for gas and electric utilities. These were advisory commissions that provided information for legislators with the power of publicity; a poor report would lead railroads to stabilize prices and reform practices. They could present information to the attorney general for prosecution in the courts. In 1890 Congress overwhelmingly passed the Sherman Antitrust Act, which prohibited every contract, scheme, deal, or conspiracy for the "restraint of trade."

The challenge of the trusts from above paralleled the plight of the farmers and laborers below. Farmers had built homesteads by borrowing greenbacks that funded the war. Frustrated by fluctuating rail rates and costly storage fees, they watched their incomes depreciate from the deflationary policy of retiring greenbacks in a return to the gold standard. Populist movements pushed bimetallism, or monetizing silver, to inflate the currency and ease mortgage payments. The Patrons of Husbandry (the Grange) organized eight hundred thousand Midwestern farmers in the 1870s, supporting any candidate who promised to restrain the railroads. In Illinois, Iowa, and Wisconsin, grangers united with small businessmen to elect legislative majorities that would set maximum railroad rates for storage and shipment. In *Munn v. Illinois* (1876), the railroads argued that Illinois had both unconstitutionally regulated interstate commerce and deprived them of property without due process. The Court sided with the grangers: the public, where affected by private property, had the right to regulate its use "for the common good."[96] But after the appointment of five new justices, the Court reversed its position in 1886, declaring that railroads, as interstate commerce, could only be regulated by Congress.[97] Congress subsequently passed the Interstate Commerce Act in 1887, prohibiting pools, rebates, and rate discrimination; rates must be published, "reasonable and just." It created a bipartisan five-member federal advisory commission based on state models. The Interstate Commerce Commission only had the power to investigate violations, compel witnesses to testify over a "specific breach of law," collect the relevant information from railroads, and petition a case to a federal circuit court. Even after Congress legislated ICC assessment of damages, Chairman Thomas Cooley preferred that juries make those decisions: "The less coercive power we have, the greater...will be our moral influence."

Protecting the separation of powers, the Supreme Court ruled that a federal commission was a "mere board of inquiry" and "not a judicial body"; it had neither the right to investigate the activities of a private business nor to compel it to open its records.[98] The federal government, as creditor, could sue in court like any private creditor. The Constitution required that all action under judicial power stem from a suit made "*by a party who asserts his rights in the form prescribed by law. It then becomes a case.*"[99] Only this legal form provided a forum "for forensic litigation and judicial decision." Justice Sawyer opined, "A general, roving, offensive, inquisitorial, compulsory investigation, conducted by a commission without any allegations, upon no fixed principles, and governed by no rules of law, or of evidence, and no restrictions except its own will, or caprice, is unknown to our constitution and laws; and such an inquisition would be destructive of the rights of the citizen, and an intolerable tyranny." The ICC could not fix maximum rates nor even determine whether a rate was reasonable: the latter was a judicial matter requiring due process not obtained in administrative procedure.

Given the rise of industry and giant impersonal factories employing thousands, the common law notions of personal and lasting employer-employee relations became unworkable. The solution was a new legal principle of at-will contracts, created in 1877 and cited by the courts thereafter. At-will contracts had no fixed duration, and either party could terminate them.[100] Thus the "right of the employee to quit the service of the employer, for whatever reason," said the Court, "is the same as the right of the employer, for whatever reason, to dispense with the services of such employee."[101] Individual laborers suffered debilitating wage cuts and gruesome dismembering workplace accidents. In one grisly incident, "In plain sight of a hundred fellow-workmen, Martin Stoffel was cut into small pieces at the Philadelphia Caramel Works.... He was dragged into the machinery and his head severed.... A second later both legs were cut off. Then one arm after the other fell into the lesser wheels below, both being cut into many parts. Before the machinery could be stopped, Stoffel had been literally chopped to pieces." Workers needed private associations to strengthen their hand. Laborers' efforts to organize gained national attention in their violent pitched battles with federal troops during the Great Railroad Strike of 1877. The Knights of Labor, enlisting seven hundred thousand, won a decisive victory against Jay Gould's Wabash Railroad in 1885. Father Michael McGivney founded the Knights of Columbus to provide insurance for laborers in 1882. Samuel Gompers created the American Federation of Labor for skilled workmen in 1886. From 1877 to 1914, hundreds of Americans died in battles between management and labor. In response to lockouts and strikes, press and citizens called for labor bureaus and arbitration boards, such as that in New York created in 1886, which reported to the legislature. The board could not force intervention but made overtures to resolve labor disputes. Management and labor agreed to submit their grievances to the board for arbitration. The board reported that "without the law, and clothed with only the prestige of having been created by the State for purposes of arbitration, [it] ha[d] accomplished much."[102] Labor posed its own abstract countervailing theories to republicanism. Edward Bellamy and Lawrence Gronlund made arguments for communal property. But the success of the American Federation of Labor (AFL) hinged, Gompers knew, on "bread and butter" issues, not a socialist agenda. He attacked anti-nationalist unions and steered clear of government sponsorship, which he argued would subject the union to government and then business control.

The key to strengthening union power was slowing cheap foreign labor. From 1880 to 1921, the US population doubled from 50 to 106 million. Immigrants crowded into unsanitary cities to work in factories. MIT president Francis Walker argued that immigrant labor both degraded the American worker and discouraged families from having children. Rather than importing immigrants to do jobs that natives would not, it created classes divided by labor; the Irish now refused to work Italians' jobs. Both political parties voted to accept Irish and German immigrants and exclude Asian immigrant laborers for reasons of expense and assimilation. The Irish had not only become so numerous that such arguments were impolitic, they had unionized in opposition to cheap labor. The AFL and the Knights of Labor saw the threat of "Asiatic Coolieism" to unionization. In the words of Dennis Kearney's Workingman's Party, "To an American, death is preferable to life on a par with the Chinaman.... Treason is better than to labor beside a Chinese slave."[103] Theodore Roosevelt warned that "Chinese immigration" threatened to reintroduce a "slave-holding oligarchy."[104] Spending more to house Chinese prisoners than it received in Chinese immigrant taxes, California required a license to mine and altered its constitution to limit land ownership to aliens of the "white race or of African descent."[105] After the Supreme Court ruled state alien restrictions unconstitutional in 1875, Congress passed the Page Act, which prohibited "undesirable" Asian workers and banned Asian women suspected of being concubines or prostitutes (the majority were). It excluded convicts and prostitutes and provided for their deportation. Justice Stephen Field questioned whether Chinese laborers with despotic habits, "residing apart by themselves, and adhering to the customs and usages of their own country," could assimilate, and he likened their immigration to a peacetime invasion.[106] A nation that could not "exclude aliens" would be "subject to the control of another power." The 1882 Exclusion Act added "idiots, lunatics, and persons likely to become public charges"; that of 1885 added foreign contract laborers; that of 1891 added "paupers, persons suffering from loathsome or dangerous contagious diseases, and persons assisted by others to come." It was not simply a matter of race. The Supreme Court upheld the confiscation of Mormon lands if the Church did not abandon the barbaric practice of polygamy, which it did in 1878.[107] Following President William McKinley's assassination, Congress barred anarchists as a threat to republican government in 1903.

Laborers were not the only workers to organize. Facing overcrowding, professional associations sought to drive up their members' wages and status. The AMA had long complained that there were too many doctors. The profession "ceased to occupy the elevated position it once did; no wonder that the merest pittance in the way of remuneration is scantily doled out." In Chicago the number of medical schools peaked at fifteen in 1900; from 1870 to 1916 the number of law schools grew from one to nine (and law students from 59 to 2,327). To increase wages, the AMA lobbied governments to pass medical licensing laws, reduce the number of institutions of learning, and require a longer period of study. It appealed to the improvement of industry standards and used sensationalistic journalism to warn of diploma mills and the dangers of malpractice. From 1868 to 1880, twenty states and territories passed laws requiring that doctors obtain medical degrees or pass license exams to practice medicine. But most laws simply required that physicians present a diploma or evidence of training and file their name and business with a county clerk. A few states established boards of medical examiners to evaluate credentials, but they could not accredit medical schools or write the licensing exams. Moreover, the laws grandfathered or exempted practicing physicians from the requirements. By 1890 an equilibrium had been reached as the AMA, in lobbying for state laws, was forced to cooperate with unorthodox medical associations, who weakened most state boards' demands for compulsory examination standards, which proved an effective method of reducing doctors and driving up wages. By 1887, seventeen states had established medical examination boards, though only six made examinations mandatory. By 1890 twenty-eight states had passed registration laws for doctors, most requiring evidence of a medical degree, without delegating legislative powers to a state board of examiners. But the laws passed before 1884 did little to prevent itinerant doctors. They were seldom enforced and tended to be easily evaded. Citizens, it was presumed, needed little protection from Indian medicine men selling magic elixirs. The republican resolution for medical malpractice was criminal and civil suits, a seldom used tort that rose dramatically after 1850.

The fourth challenge was that of sanitation and health, where the concerns that rose during the war increased even as the commissions erected to control them were dismantled. From 1830 to 1860, New York City's population, fed by immigration, had exploded from 185,000 to over one million, creating problems in burials, street cleaning, maintenance of city markets and piers, unhealthy tenements, sewage, drainage, slaughterhouses, livery stables, and garbage and offal removal. Deaths among immigrant children under the age of five outnumbered all those between five and sixty. In 1861 Daniel Delavan, inspector for the Sanitary Bureau, turned to both sound regulation and private associations: "The power of remedy does not rest in...the departments over which I...preside, but is to be found in the erection of hospitals for the sick children of the destitute, where they can be removed from...these abodes of death."[108] When the city passed a penal law requiring all ministers and physicians to furnish their departments with "regular and exact returns of marriages, births, and deaths," the effort failed. Roman Catholic divines "peremptorily [refused] to comply with the provisions of the law, for reasons" that "compliance with the statute would involve a violation of that confidence" necessary to the "confidential relation with parties joining in marriage.... The constitutionality of the law was equally denied, and opposition threatened to its enforcement." A "large majority of the medical faculty" refused "on the grounds of its interference with their personal interests and convenience." New Yorkers did not think private information was the city's business, and Delavan agreed. He defended the law as important in "ascertaining and determining rights of property dependent both on births and deaths" and resolving matters of "titles to estates." He added that it was unnecessary "for the further efficiency of this department that it should become the nursery of students of medicine—a plan suggested by a limited class of physicians in this city." The Citizens Association of New York, organized in 1863 for the "voluntary work of municipal reform and public improvement," had its own Council of Hygiene and Public Health "for Sanitary Inquiry and Advice" to report on sanitation problems in the city.[109] Members took pride in their "*voluntary effort*" and expertise, highlighting both their civic republicanism—concern for the "welfare of the community, and benefitting all classes in the city"—and their techniques of the new science. James Ware's dumbbell tenement was not the creation of a city employee but the winner of an 1879 design contest in the magazine *Plumbing and Sanitation Engineer*.

The final challenge to republicanism was securing the police powers of the state while protecting the citizen's substantive due process rights to life, liberty, and property. The Supreme Court had noted in

1878: "It is confessedly difficult to mark the precise boundaries" of police powers.[110] The federal courts settled on key criteria. It required that a legislature's object be permissible, that its means have a substantial relation to the end, and that it not infringe upon fundamental rights. Nor could a law be arbitrary, unreasonable, or oppressive. In matters of property, the courts turned to scientific evidence to determine whether the state had regulated on a rational basis.[111] Striking a republican balance, the Court mostly deferred to state police powers, only interfering in cases where states had violated "social justice," property rights, interstate commerce, or the Contract Clause.[112] While upholding states' granting of discretionary powers to boards of health over details of implementation, state courts recognized two limits. In the case of compulsory vaccinations, there could be no delegation of lawmaking power. "The state board of health," ruled the Wisconsin Supreme Court, "is a purely administrative body, and has no legislative power, and none can constitutionally be delegated to it."[113] Moreover, the boards' decisions must be reasonable or even limited to periods of public health emergencies.[114]

The challenges facing Americans at the end of the century need not have concluded in an abandonment of republican principles. But several factors foreshadowed change. The rise of progressive social science effectively undercut the American republican orthodoxy and produced a legacy of new ideas. It constituted, said its leading thinkers, a complete rejection of the older principles and so became the dividing line between the American republic and its descent into empire. Its foremost advocates were Anglo-Protestant crusaders, who saw in the new ideals a chance to redeem the world. Second, the tide of economic immigrants with no understanding of republican government created ethnic divisions, political instability, and anxiety among a shrinking Anglo majority. Finally, economic inequality led to a constitutional revolution as the majority sought to control the trusts above and the immigrants below. The Supreme Court best captured the dilemma in 1898; the railroads, it said, were entitled to "the fair value of the property being used for the convenience of the public."[115] How the nation would decide "fair value" and regulate private property would spark an anti-republican revolution called progressivism.

PROGRESSIVISM

The progressive political revolt against the old republicanism originated in a spiritual crisis. Progressivism was birthed in strict Protestantism, which emphasized a conversion experience (often to the point of breakdown) and vocation. Christian reformers channeled this religious energy into social reform. Since the 1840s, The American Home Missionary Society had warned that Catholic immigrants and disorderly Western settlements threatened Americanism. But those reformers experienced a crisis of faith. Under the withering assault by biblical textual criticism, Darwinian evolution, and German idealism, educated Americans increasingly rejected the Christian and republican orthodoxy. Abandoning the ministry and mission field, they underwent a secular conversion in new vocations in settlement houses, journalism, education, and social work. They recast Christian faith anew in social science, the religion of Social Gospel, and the administrative state. They abandoned republican citizenship for the "ethical ideal," or "democracy," which referred to a spiritual identity detached from the old institutions. It meant the creation of an insulated elite, drawn from the middle class, that would convert the trusts above and the immigrants and laborers below. To carry out this task, it claimed the right by the authority of science to regulate civil society (business and the family) outside the rule of law.

The Collapse of Faith

In 1882 Yale President Noah Porter described the "collapse of faith." After the attacks by "modern science and the deeper insights of modern philosophy," there was the "prevailing conviction that faith is not only failing, but that it is doomed to a slow but certain dissolution."[1] Christian faith had long been challenged by German scholarship on the "historical Jesus" and "higher criticism," which by textual analysis disputed the authorship of the Bible and subverted it as a chronicle of miracles that proved the divinity of Jesus. The theory of evolution gave additional force to atheism and agnosticism. If theological concepts of God expressed philosophical notions of form and teleology, then evolutionary theory challenged the very possibility of mind and absolute truth; it, said Porter, "not only destroys faith but strangles science."[2] After Charles Darwin's insights, what humans had perceived as mind, the agent of order, now appeared the result of a mindless process of random mutations preserved in violent struggle—nature, "red in tooth and claw." Young philosopher John Dewey had been raised a Christian—his mother often pressed him if he were "right with Jesus"—but the attack on philosophic certainty disturbed him more. He searched out authors like John Fiske, whose cosmic theology was one of many evolutionary cosmologies in the late nineteenth century that attempted to rein in the chaotic implications of evolutionary theory. Darwin, Fiske said, was actually "the best of religious teachers" because he "unfolds the way in which God works."[3] The new systems hearkened to the dense German schools of Kantian idealism and Hegelian historicism, to which we are here by necessity forced to turn.

Immanuel Kant's idealism had long been used to show the inadequacies of scientific materialism (where external causes determine thoughts) and skepticism by referring to an ideal realm of mind. Rather than a passive sponge of brute sensory data, mind actively conditioned and categorized experience according to certain, knowable laws. G. W. F. Hegel's historicism, applying Aristotle's concepts of potentiality and actuality, argued that Kant's categories of understanding had developed within time. What seemed like chaos and blind passion could be demonstrated to have meaning; there had been an unconscious movement toward consciousness of freedom. Thus the providential Christian God could be salvaged as a historically vital way of viewing the world. What men call God was this spirit of freedom stirring itself in material nature. A study of history revealed a dialectical logic, in starts and stops, progressions and regressions, in the development of human freedom, both *in-itself* and *for-itself*. *In-itself* meant that one becomes conscious of himself as free, a secularized teaching of Christian free will called "autonomy"—one obeys a law that he himself has given. Opposed to the ancient view of fate, Western man had become conscious of his capacity for choice and thus could be held accountable for his good or evil intentions. *For-itself* meant that one only becomes certain that he is free by his actions in the world, in the mutual recognition of other free individuals, and in the choices made possible in political institutions: the family, civil society, and law. Thus the foundation for a new progressive politics: the state organized the ethical substance of individuals and society into a "system of right," "the realm of actualized freedom."[4] Humans' spontaneous inclinations were perfected (a "second nature") in a teleological historical process, beginning with Asia (Africa, Hegel said, had played no part in world history) and ending in 1830s Prussia.[5] The new science of bureaucracy constituted the highest development of right because it transcended mere civil society or the protection of private property. The administrative state would train impartial experts—scientific knights of a new order—to regulate the economic interests of a large populace and channel the more sublime inclinations to religion and art. It actualized the highest freedom in the divine activity of reason in philosophy, or "absolute mind."[6] Instead of drinking hemlock, the philosopher received an endowed chair at a research university, where he would provide the logical underpinning for the new empirical sciences.

In his trenchant 1882 critique, American philosopher William James claimed to only understand Hegel's system after he got high on nitrous oxide. It was "a mouse-trap.... Safety lies in not entering."[7] Still, German idealism provided a balm for the anxieties of a young generation. It became one of "the most potent influences" in Britain and America. The dialectical science promised certainty, a means to absolute truth. The "completed Method of Philosophy" and "fulfilling of the ideal" wrote Dewey, was found "chiefly in Hegel and his 'Logic.'"[8] But it was "no mere intellectual formula"; "Hegel's synthesis of subject and object, matter and spirit, the divine and the human...operated as an immense release, a liberation."[9] It dissolved walls between the individual and society, the private and public, and reconnected religious sentiment to secular life in the state. Hegel showed "how a free natural life is possible; how a man can live as a whole."[10] British neo-Kantians and neo-Hegelians such as F. H. Bradley and T. H. Green inspired a new generation during the surge in American higher education. Twenty-five new scientific graduate programs were founded in the 1860s, and they sought status by hiring German-trained faculty. Some ten thousand American students studied in Germany, a world leader in culture. Dewey latched onto William Torrey Harris, America's leading Hegelian and founder of its first philosophical periodical in 1867. In 1876, Columbia hired German-trained John Burgess, who started the first graduate program (and journal) in political science. In 1886 Johns Hopkins University was founded on the German research model; with the "needs of graduate work in mind," President Daniel Coit Gilman hired German-trained historian Herbert B. Adams and economist Richard T. Ely. The Hopkins program produced leading political scientists Westel W. Willoughby and Woodrow Wilson, one of Dewey's classmates. Wilson became convinced that American politics, rife with corrupt city machines and a confused national government, must borrow the "impartial science" of politics from "doctors in Europe" employing "only foreign tongues."[11]

Historicism provided a sense of purpose. Theologians downplayed scientific problems in theology by reconfiguring Christianity into an active faith, an ever-evolving, missionizing political religion of Social Gospel. It was the response of a pious people (church attendance was 75 percent in 1900) that resonated with evangelicals who lacked theological backing and mainline Protestants who saw in Christianity allegories for scientific truth. Moreover, Social Gospel preached a vision of perfect justice, heaven on earth, and a moral teaching of self-sacrifice and uplift. Baptist theologian Walter Rauschenbusch said, "All history becomes the unfolding of the purpose of the immanent God who is working in the race toward the commonwealth of spiritual liberty and righteousness."[12] Christian love, he said, "is supreme freedom," thus "Christianizing the social order" requires "a state in which even moral compulsion ceases because goodness has become spontaneous." "It is the mission of Christianity," Ely wrote, "to bring to pass [in 'this world'] a kingdom of righteousness and to rescue from the evil one and redeem all our social relations."[13] Someday, he prophesied, the people will realize the "advantages conferred upon society by the men who speak the truth" and see that the humble altruistic scientists "who stand between the fighting social factions, and receive merciless blows from both sides, are their saviors, are the 'missing coupling' to unite the various discordant elements of society."[14] One Progressive Era novel described the passionate love affair between two reformers, Philip and Gloria: "Gloria proselyting the rich by showing them their selfishness, and turning them to a larger purpose in life, and Philip leading the forces of those who had consecrated themselves to the uplifting of the unfortunate. It did not take Philip long to discern that in the last analysis it would be necessary for himself and co-workers to reach the results aimed at through politics."[15] In their world historic role, the Americans would either bring the world to its highest development of freedom or allow its relapse into barbarism.

Josiah Strong's bestselling *Our Country* (1885) warned that Americans needed a new sense of purpose to overcome the "perils which threaten our future."[16] Thus "the world is to be Christianized and civilized." Uplift became the new piety for an urbane middle class, which could rule justly by means of the new social sciences.

Victorian Americans were ascetic. Too embarrassed to use words like *breast, thigh,* and *leg,* they said *white* and *dark* meat. Discussing bodily functions, in an era without air conditioning and with stuffy dress, was taboo in mixed company. Distinguishing oneself from laborers required stolid aloofness to profuse sweating, ubiquitous horse manure on shoes and in dress seams, and the sexual deed itself, which seems to have been little discussed among middle-class women. A man did not frequent saloons, the dens of Irish corruption. He wore a hat, not a cap, and never left the house or answered the door in shirtsleeves (without a jacket). Women had guests wait in the parlor while they made themselves presentable. The afternoon brought a culture of calling cards, left by visitors on special tables in the parlor. Middle class families did have fun; they strived to be urbane in music, entertainment, and education. But they showed a balanced concern with the growing consumerism, the purchases of their proudly displayed parlor-room clutter. Roosevelt celebrated "the strenuous life" of physical fitness, men "anxious to work...with all their might and strength, and ready and able to fight at need, and anxious to be fathers of families."[17] Virtuous young men and women, wrote leading psychologist Grenville Stanley Hall, "glory in occasions when they can display the beauty of their forms without reserve."[18] The healthy young man "should have fought, whipped and been whipped, used language offensive to the prude and to the prim precisian, [and] been in some scrapes." The YMCA built a gymnasium and swimming pool in every major city during the 1870s and 1880s to educate the "spirit, mind, and body" of single young men. At one of them James Naismith, studying the human frame, invented basketball as the first a priori scientific sport for health and morals. It was a winter sport for young men when not playing baseball or the incredibly violent football, whose deaths were defended by its ascetic virtues: "If the world can sacrifice lives for commercial gain," said William Harper, president of the University of Chicago, "it can more easily afford to make similar sacrifices on the altar of vigorous and unsullied manhood."[19]

Such a moralistic people revolted at the idea of an economy held hostage to imprudent or immoral speculators; of increasing economic inequality; of industrial tycoons as lords over faceless workers; of unsanitary, dangerous living and working conditions; of democracy, light of freedom to the world, mired in petty calculations by party hacks; of cities rotting with prostitution, venereal disease, and anarchist immigrants. In *How the Other Half Lives*, Jacob Riis used the new flash photography to expose the unsanitary and violent conditions of city life. But the salvation of the cities also made possible the birth of a true nation. Like missionaries, reformers Jane Addams and Ellen Starr went to live among the urban and working poor. Bessie and Marie van Vorst worked alongside factory women, publishing exposés in *Everybody's*. Uplift aimed at social unity. Socialism, said Roosevelt, was "the most mischievous" theory because it taught that "progress is to be secured by the strife of classes."[20] These problems, progressives believed, stemmed from the failure of political institutions, shaped under the older individualistic view, to evolve to keep up with changing conditions.

Progressives, couching their political ideas in evolutionary jargon, had an unbridled faith in the authority of science and its promise to alter human conditions. The new politics focused on biological evolution, both in intellect and morals, within a social and racial organism. Humans, rather than born equal and free, are born into a social mind (the unconscious history of their race), and they must be educated to become individuals. "The end of Christianity is twofold," explained Washington Gladden, "a perfect man in a perfect society."[21] *The state is the people*, the embodiment of the individual and collective will, an ethos, and not a superimposed political structure based upon abstract ideas.[22] "Democracy," said Herbert Croly, "must stand or fall on a platform of human perfectibility."[23] The "ethical ideal which animates the new political economy," wrote Ely, means "the most perfect development of all human faculties in each individual, which can be attained."[24] This was no leveling down to mass man. It "means any thing rather than equality. It means the richest diversity." Geniuses only thrive in the right environment.[25] Ely distinguished between the "naturally gifted," the lower classes, and "Negroes"; intellectuals require four times more possessions (books, travel, and salary) than the lower classes, while blacks may best develop as "servants for superior families."[26] Progress depended on a racially inherited ability of foresight. Individuals in advanced civilizations had also evolved a stronger sense of the collective and thus had a greater sense of duty, the precondition for freedoms in the state.[27] Because a change in environment could alter the biology and motives of human beings, sociologists studied social forces—family, education, culture, and economy—with a view to "social control."[28] Lester Ward, first president of the American Sociological Association, taught the evolution of human nature toward collectivism and cooperation and away from individualistic competition. Ward's "sociocracy" was "a government by society" based on "the true principles of social science" that would be guided by the "brilliant achievements of the elite of mankind."[29] By controlling the environment, humans could guide the process of evolution instead of being chaotically tossed about by it.

The first form of uplift was racial and celebrated Anglo-Saxon political achievement. Strong argued, "This race…is destined to dispossess many weaker ones, assimilate others, and mold of the remainder until…it has Anglo-Saxonized mankind."[30] The new historicist view was not that of separate peoples with equal station in the world but that of a competition between races for world hegemony, "warfare of the cradle."[31] Anglo law and German freedom had birthed the unique American people, which would be destroyed by ignoring its racial roots and admitting other races, particularly Slavic immigrants. From 1900 to 1915, more than fifteen million immigrants entered the country, more than during the previous forty years. Sociologist Edward Ross, followed by leading statistician Richmond Mao-Smith, warned of "race suicide" in 1891. "Race suicide," said Roosevelt, was "infinitely more important than any other question."[32] Finding themselves awash in immigrants seeking only economic security or patronage, Christian missionaries were torn between saving immigrant souls and needing to control and moralize them. After describing the different habits of races, which evolved over long periods, Ross concluded, "Since the higher culture should be kept pure as well as the higher blood, that race is stronger which, down to the cultivator or the artisan, has a strong sense of its superiority. When peoples and races meet there is a silent struggle to determine which shall do the assimilating. The issue of this grapple turns not wholly on the relative excellence of their civilizations, but partly on the degree of faith each has in itself and its ideals."[33] Hall noted that this "enmity against the lower races...has exterminated" some of them "and is *reducing* so many lower human ethnic stocks to make way for favored races."[34] Congress used racial classifications as a way to both segregate and educate and thus morally uplift blacks in the 1890s. As Negroes were at an inferior stage of development but displayed a "capacity" for civilization, wrote feminist Charlotte Perkins Gilman, "compulsory labor" might accelerate their intellectual and moral development.[35]

The second form of uplift was moral. "Sin," preached Roosevelt, "evolves along with society."[36] Original sin meant the old social system that pitted individuals against one another in economic competition, shaping them into acquisitive, selfish creatures without cooperative virtues. Its solution was a conversion to a new selfless consciousness, where "the conditions of life for the first time" would be "placed upon unselfishness."[37] All in the social organism, being complicit in its evils, have a duty to uplift their fellow man. The state must care for the soul in ways formerly reserved to churches. In his 1888 bestseller *Looking Backward*, Edward Bellamy's Mr. Barton explains how by the year 2000, America had become a Christian socialist utopia: "My friends, if you would see men again the beasts of prey they seemed in the nineteenth century, all you have to do is to restore the old social and industrial system, which taught them to view their natural prey in their fellow-men, and find their gain in the loss of others."[38] Evolution progressed with the victory of "the instincts and processes of race-preservation" over "self-interest."[39] Progressives believed they could accelerate this process by altering the social conditions that created conflict and belligerence within the race, which perverted natural development and threatened extinction. The "highest form [of virtue] is loyalty to the largest common interest," while egoism is an evil descent in the natural hierarchy of social creatures.[40] Conflict between the individual and society, wrote Ely, is no longer necessary. "Self-development for the sake of others is the aim of social ethics. Self and others... are thus united in one purpose."[41]

For progressives like Dewey, education did more than promote democracy—it *was* democracy. Democratic education aimed to mold American individualists into a common mind to advance the social organism. Not satisfied with kindergartens (a German import), Gilman argued for the creation of "baby gardens," where babies could evolve a collective consciousness, a sense of "we" instead of "I."[42] As social consciousness develops, so does the growth and sophistication of the human brain as a product of both superior stock and social environment. Hall theorized that the human mind grows in recapitulation of evolutionary stages, and he pioneered the study of "adolescence." The youth's "esthetic sensibilities are presentiments of a superior stage of the race that will develop out of the present human type," "the superanthropoid that man is to become."[43] A new science of education would solve the problems of immigrant assimilation, child labor, and individualistic education within the home. From 1900 to 1910, public school enrollment increased from 12.5 to 16 million, and the number of school days from 86.3 to 113. Warning of the "American peril" of international industrial competition, educators initiated industrial and vocational training ("differentiation"), first in high schools, then in elementary schools, to track students for industrial labor. William Wirt's "Gary Plan" provided industrial education to fourth graders. Educators added personal and social hygiene to tailor the individual to the social organism. Girls learned home economics, including cooking and sewing. "School," said Hall, "has become the method of colonization and completes the work of conquest by armies." To reject mandatory education was heresy, but the real challenge was how to tell whether the increase in the number of schools paralleled an evolution in mind measured by the new authority of science.

The New Conception of Health and the Family

The ethical ideal, under the mantle of scientific authority over *health*, inverted the older republican view of individual rights by extending the power of the state to the activities of bare life. Experts claimed that by vocation and training they were value-free and public spirited and thus had the right to rule. Referring to sanitary and medical practice laws, Dr. H. C. Markham argued in 1888 that physicians "are alone competent to measure the evils against which this legislation is aimed" because of their "self-sacrificing exercise of charity...toward the individual sufficient to include the public."[44] Health included happiness and human flourishing. Dr. Samuel Dixon, Pennsylvania commissioner of health, said in a 1905 address to the AMA, "On state medicine depends the happiness of our people and the success of our nation.... The nation which is vigorous in its individual citizens will be strong as a whole."[45] Rome was not destroyed by invaders but by "the physicial degeneracy of a race enfeebled by luxury and the diseases which luxury entails.... It is health that nerves the arm that wields the hammer and the sword, that gives keenness to the eye that sights the gun and that penetrates the mysteries of the microscope."

Medical scientists promised both to relieve suffering from the diseases that plagued cities and soldiers in the late war and to preserve the nation against the immigrant infection. "We hope," said Dixon, "to perpetuate a vigorous race of American parentage," contrasted with "the constantly swelling tide of immigration which, attracted by the success of our efforts, is now sweeping in, actuated by no higher motive than the accumulation of weath, bearing...the ignorance, the vices, the follies and the pernicious political heresies of the lowest and most dangerous stratum of European society." But it was not just immigrants. Progressives did not think *American citizens themselves* should control their health decisions. "The great majority of mankind arc neither wise enough voluntarily to submit themselves to the requirements of sanitary law for the sake of preserving their own health and those of their loved ones, or righteous enough to be willing to exercise self-denial and repress cravings of avarice to save others from sickness, suffering and death." Physicians, declared Dr. Ephraim Cutter in 1897, should rule as lawmakers: "The effect of physicians in their own department being ruled over by lay people is embarrassing, harassing, if not paralyzing."[46] Education alone was insufficient; state medicine required the force of law. Morals and good citizenship meant obedience to science and possession of "sufficient self-control, both individually and collectively, to be willing to submit to the enforcement of the legal [health] enactments."[47]

As science grew in authority, the fragmented medical sects could agree to restrict avenues to power by pursuing national regulation. In 1889 the AMA proposed a draft law, passed in several states, requiring a liberal education in order to obtain a license to *study* medicine. In 1892 the *Journal of the American Medical Association* reported, "Within the last very few years" and even "the last very few months—there has been a rustling...indicative of a change of thought, an evolution of sentiment amounting to a tacit demand.... The several State legislatures are...enacting laws having for their purpose an elevation of the standard of educational requirements for the privilege and right to practice medicine."[48] By 1916, forty-five out of forty-eight states had empowered their medical boards to refuse to recognize medical degrees from substandard colleges. States had enacted over four hundred laws to harmonize them with the state medical societies and the AMA.

In the late 1890s states (Iowa did so in 1897) began to delegate legislative powers to boards of health. The year 1905 was a landmark one in state legislation. Pennsylvania's statute creating a new health department was "the most comprehensive and effective legislation for the protection of public health ever enacted."[49] Dixon was named commissioner of its board of health and given a seat in the governor's cabinet. It was, he said, a new administrative form whose efficacy was "due to concentration of authority, coupled with absolute power of initiative" that unified previously separated powers. The advisory board's principal duty was to prepare health regulations, while the commissioner's executive power was expanded to enforce regulations, appoint officers, and "issue warrants" to law officers "to apprehend and to arrest such persons as disobey the quarantine orders or regulations of the department." The commissioner was also delegated authority to inspect and issue permits for all future projects involving public waters. In 1906 the state hired 1,200 officers to register all births and deaths and work with doctors across the state to report communicable diseases. The commissioner appointed sixty-six county medical inspectors to order the enforcement of health regulations as well as supervise seven hundred more officers in rural districts. It was crucial in rural areas that all be made "directly responsible to the Department of Health and dependent upon it for their remuneration.... The state badge carries a weight of authority not conveyed by that of a township constable, and the officer does not hesitate to perform his duties because of the fear of incurring the animosity of his neighbors and so losing his place." The AMA pushed for a federal Department of Health, with a secretary of health to both advise the president and provide authoritative statements to Congress "to see to it that no member voted wrongly" in securing "the biologic developments of man." Dr. Cutter had called for the federal Congress to delegate lawmaking authority to a "department of public health in the cabinet."[50]

The new authority of health meant reconfiguring the older conception of liberty. "It is idle," said Dixon, "to prate of the enforcement of
sanitary laws as an infringment of personal liberty.... The individual
who insists on what he is pleased to call his own rights in defiance of
law and the detriment of the common weal is 'an undesirable citizen
of the republic.'"[51] *JAMA* suggested prior restraint and censorship to
silence criticisms of the Public Health Service in a 1905 yellow fever
epidemic: "If it is treason in time of war for a man to betray his country's military plans, it certainly should be made treason for a man or
a publication in time of deadly peril from disease to foment by false
allegations public lack of confidence in the government's plan of rescue,
and in the integrity and ability of the men who risk their lives to save
the community from unnecessary deaths.... Stringent penalties [are
needed] for their crime against the nation, against humanity."[52] Health
also meant expanding the intrusions of medical science. "The family,"
said Dr. Cutter, "is the unit of the nation. If one is sick and feeble the
other is so.... None are better able to tell how to have heathy families
than physicians. If states need such laws, physicians should make
them."[53] These laws, said Dixon, must reach into "all the relations of
human life," including registration of births, deaths, and marriages;
notification and tracking of transmissible diseases; the "control of
epidemics by domiciliary quarantine" and use of "prophylactics and
disinfectants"; "the construction, heating and ventilation of our homes
and public buildings"; protecting water supplies and restoring purity
to polluted streams and lakes; the "occupations and industries of the
people"; protecting food and drugs from adulteration and impurity;
"the education of physicians, dentists and vetinarians."[54]

The courts' interpretation of substantive due process rights and
the limits to state police powers followed their deference to expertise.
Hearing 560 cases challenging state regulatory laws from 1887 to
1911, the Supreme Court only struck down three for violating "social
justice" and thirty-four for violating property rights, interstate commerce, or the Contract Clause.[55] In 1903 state supreme courts began

to uphold the delegation of lawmaking powers to boards of health, and in *Jacobson v. Massachusetts* (1905), the Supreme Court upheld a Massachusetts state law that gave authority to municipal boards to require vaccination. Henning Jacobson had refused, claiming that he and his son had experienced "great and extreme suffering" from earlier vaccinations. He produced evidence that questioned the vaccine's efficacy and protested his denial of due process right to a trial. But the Court, citing "common belief...maintained by high medical authority," ruled that constitutional liberties were not "absolute" in cases "necessary for the public health": "It is within the police power of a State to enact a compulsory vaccination law, and it is for the legislature, and not for the courts, to determine in the first instance whether vaccination is or is not the best mode."[56] In response, the Anti-Vaccination League was founded in 1908 to pressure legislatures to oppose compulsory vaccinations, which, it argued, exposed individuals to involuntary risks. In 1922, the Court ruled that a state could "delegate to a municipality authority to determine under what conditions health regulations shall become operative"; public school authorities could require vaccinations for admission.[57]

During the 1918 influenza pandemic, local communities applied police powers to close theaters, opera houses, saloons, and schools. *Variety* reported, "Entire Country Near Closed."[58] Closings were local and brief as citizens themselves decided when to reopen. At the Progressive Public Health Association meeting in Chicago, scientists professed helplessness and ignorance of key facts as to the cause of the disease. There was a consensus that it was located in the respiratory tract and spread by "droplets diffused by sneezing and coughing" and that those who contracted it were immune. But they disagreed over what to do. The two methods were "individual care and prophylaxis" and "community health control."[59] As to the first method, there was no consensus on masks, which were a barrier between mouth and hand but "could not prevent the spread of the droplets and [were] totally inadequate for that purpose." In numerous cases "physicians and nurses were infected in spite of their wearing masks," and deaths rates had increased in San Francisco where masks were used but not in Los Angeles where they were not. Dr. Frederick Hoffman "remarked that statistics were never so much abused as by the doctors and health officers in the epidemic and that most of the statistics were worthless." Several doctors argued for the importance of illusion: masks had no demonstrated prevention but stopped the spread of fear. Dr. Robertson, health commissioner of Chicago, said, "It is our duty to keep the people from fear. Worry kills more people than the epidemic. For my part, let them wear a rabbit's foot on a watch-chain if they want." Vaccinations showed more promise in one study of four thousand employees. Still others concluded, "The greatest value of vaccine therapy was in fact that it reduced *fluphobia*, as it has been clearly demonstrated that worry and fear had to be controlled." The second method was control by social action, and doctors again reported a dearth of evidence. Local ordinances had come too late, and not all physicians reported. With thousands of untreated cases, it was impossible to know how many had been infected. Doctors regarded "prevention of overcrowding" as the most important measure to stop the spread, but many health officials questioned its efficacy. There was little uniformity in shutdown measures, even within communities, where some businesses and schools were closed while others deemed essential remained open. Dr. Copeland pointed out the absurdity of closing schools for eight hundred thousand New York children while sending them home to crowded tenements.

Faced with this inefficacy, Dr. Price concluded that "the greatest method of prevention and control of the influenza epidemic is in public health education in its *broadest* sense." He called for a "revolution," a political order governed by a different conception of *health*.[60] The US must "establish new [federal and state] agencies for public health conservation." Impartial experts would provide "proper medical attention, both preventative and curative." The American Public Health Association was not just "the greatest life-saving crew in the civilized world" but a veritable aristocracy, the "dukes, marquises and barons of public health." Dr. Hastings said that democracy meant extending the concept of health to include all of one's life activities. Dr. Hoffman's plan presupposed "the physical and medical examination of all children and young persons from infancy to majority." "[Raising] the level of national health," said Dr. Lecky, "is one of the surest ways of raising national happiness." It included rectifying wealth inequality and malnourishment—low wages lead to poor health and disease, while higher minimum wages and compulsory state social insurance improve diet, housing, clothing, and medical care. To achieve public health, said Hastings, "we require centralized authority...the appointment of a generalissimo." What was needed was "nationalizing of public health activities of the country by giving greater scope and power to the Public Health Service and broadening its functions to embrace a nation-wide authority over disease prevention, rural hygiene, and milk and food control." Thus, said Dr. Frankel, "We must become a propagandist body, working every day to carry the doctrine of prevention into every city and town. We must improve the status of local and county health officials. Health work must be dignified. It must be wrested from the hands of the politicians. The office must have permanency and continuity." The power of health officers must extend beyond "police power" to all areas of "social improvement." One recommended slogan was "Register Hogs—Why not Babies?"

The scientific authority over bare life extended to human procreation. Progressive feminists, uniting middle-class women's issues with medical wellness, crusaded for laws to protect women and children from unsanitary conditions, high infant mortality rates, and poor nutrition and to promote hygiene and baby care. In the new Bureau of Child Welfare in 1912, Julia Lathrop began recording birth statistics. In 1921 Lathrop, Florence Kelley, Dr. S. Josephine Baker, and other health activists lobbied for the Sheppard-Towner Act, a joint federal-state matching funds program that paid for prenatal and nutritional care in 3,000 clinics, 180,000 infant care seminars, and three million home visits by traveling nurses. The bill required professional licensing for birth attendants, including physicians. While midwives continued to practice in rural and minority communities, the bill destroyed the profession for highly skilled yet uncredentialed women.

Addressing the conflict between the individual and society in sexual mores, progressives argued that sex should improve both individuals and society's racial stock. They united love and racial duty in teachings of chastity, the family, and motherhood. Chastity had evolved as a "comparatively modern virtue" that led to "the highest personal happiness" in "romantic love."[61] Science confirmed the superiority of monogamous marriage; sexual perversion (promiscuity, homosexuality, masturbation) caused venereal and mental disease. Humans had developed an *instinct* to monogamy, which proved superior for procreation and social support by channeling individual sexual desire and ensuring the continuance and civilization of the race. For progressive feminists, work outside the home would free women from economic parasitism and make marriage a true union of equals. This contradicted their view that there was, in the words of Ellen Key, "a higher plane, the equilibrium between self-sacrifice and self-assertion, which finds its most perfect realization in motherhood."[62] Looking askance at romantic portrayals of social work, Roosevelt reminded women to "recognize that the greatest thing for any woman is to be a good wife and mother" who chooses to bear children with an eye to social improvement.[63] Social work and the "desire to be 'independent'—that is, to live one's life purely according to one's desires" were no "substitutes for the fundamental virtues, for the practice of the strong, racial qualities without which there can be no strong races—the qualities of courage and resolution in both men and women. . . . The man or woman who deliberately avoids marriage, and has a heart so cold as to know no passion and a brain so shallow and selfish as to dislike having children, is in effect a criminal against the race, and should be an object of contemptuous abhorrence by all wealthy people."

While the "science of human breeding" could aid in the "evolution of man as a rational animal" and consciously fulfill his nature, it was a double-edged sword.[64] One trouble with philanthropy and science, recounted Ely, was that they kept "men alive who would otherwise perish," bringing a decline in physical vigor and increasing the "parasitical classes."[65] Hiram Stanley called for both negative and positive measures. Negatively, experts would offer guidance on imprisonment, contraception, celibacy, sterilization, and medical certification to procreate; positively, they would encourage the most fit to marry and breed. Dixon proposed eugenics as a form of good "husbandry": "In order to build up a race fitted to cope with these dangerous masses [of immigrants]," the gardener "attacks [human weeds] with the cultivator, the mattock and the hoe."[66] Most progressive economists, including Ely and Simon Patten, endorsed laws restricting marriage and procreation. Margaret Sanger promoted birth control and eugenics to improve the race and to prevent "feebleminded offspring."[67] Beginning in 1907, most states passed eugenics laws, resulting in some sixty-five thousand forced sterilizations, twenty thousand in California alone. State eugenics boards enforced sterilization of inferiors; reformer Marie Stopes argued for its extension to racial groups. In *Buck v. Bell* (1927), Justice Oliver Wendell Holmes cited *Jacobson v. Massachusetts* to include procreation in state police power: "The principle that sustains compulsory vaccination is broad enough to cover cutting the Fallopian tubes.... Three generations of imbeciles are enough."

Progressives inverted the older view of sex by promoting governmental control over private sexual acts that did not impact the family and by creating an administrative apparatus to manage families outside the rule of law. Prostitution, outlawed in most states by 1900, had only been enforced against streetwalkers. Most cities tolerated whorehouses with or without payoffs to police, and some cities imposed fines on them to fund education.[68] But newspapers began to publish lurid stories of "white slavery," sex trafficking in farm girls. Middle-class women crusaded against prostitution, which courted poverty and disease as well as undermined marriage. Gilman wrote that the "one unmixed evil in human life" in all ages is "'the social evil' consisting of promiscuous and temporary sex relations."[69] The prostitute, a product of capitalist alienation, sells her right to natural selection for subsistence, a return to barbarism.[70] Disease and feeble offspring are evolutionary byproducts of morbid sexual relations, with oversexed males and females attracted to one another at unnatural levels. Females disempower themselves when they flaunt their sexuality rather than their intellect and spirit and suppress their caring and nurturing natures to fulfill abnormal sexual desires. By 1910 most states passed stricter laws and began to enforce them. "Vice commissions" operated in twenty-one major cities. The 1911 Mann Act prohibited interstate sex trafficking and defined "prostitution" not by sale but as "indiscriminate" sexual intercourse. It was first used to prosecute black heavyweight boxing champion Jack Johnson, who preferred white prostitutes. To avoid jail, he married one, Lucille Cameron.

Sex education, where experts taught sex hygiene, was a progressive innovation to replace stodgy Christian teachings of original sin that hid or fearfully repressed sexual truths. "Greater knowledge," said Annie Riley Hale, advocate to Congress, was "the supreme demand of the day": "I should like to suggest that that we start with frankness— a little wholesome truth-telling.... A good beginning would be for woman to speak the truth about sex; to say that she has failed to lift man to a higher sexual life, because she has failed to dominate and spiritualize her own sexual emotions."[71] The first Purity Congress was held in 1895; Jane Addams, Charles Eliot, G. S. Hall, and Roosevelt sponsored the "purity movement," which anticipated the social and mental hygiene movements, the first mainstream efforts to discuss sex frankly with middle-class girls. In 1905 Dr. Prince Morrow, warning of the rash of venereal diseases, established the American Society of Sanitary and Moral Prophylaxis, which preached both sex education in schools and chastity to middle-class men. The Chicago Social Hygiene Society, organized in 1906, became instrumental in the battle to introduce sex education, formerly reserved to family and church, into the public school system in 1913. It was essential, said Dewey acolyte Ella Flagg Young, to safeguard the morals of Chicago's youth. By this she meant not swarthy Italian immigrants but Anglos tempted to dance halls and brothels.

In 1880 divorce rates, driven by war, frontier dislocations, and immigration, had increased to one in twenty-one marriages and by 1900 to one in twelve. Progressives saw a crisis. In his definitive study, George Howard traced marriage's "disintegration" to the view of marriage as a contract.[72] Leading jurist Roscoe Pound blamed the founders' "theories of natural rights and of a social contract," which had led to "ultra-individualism in legal thought."[73] Citing the "idea of evolution" that proved the interrelatedness of an adapting organism, he rejected the older "separation of powers and checks and balances."[74] Abstract individual rights could not ground law because it was an instrument of "social justice" informed by "economic and sociological thought."[75] Progressives sought to protect marriage and the family by elevating it from the base realm of necessity (common law marriages, procreation, and finance) to spiritual unions. They expanded the Supreme Court's 1887 romantic redefinition of marriage. The Court had refused to strike down a no-fault divorce in the Oregon Territory as a violation of the Contract Clause on the grounds that marriage was a *status*, not a *contract*.[76] The rise of large cities, said Pound, required it; decentralized government could work for a homogenous, pioneer, religious people jealous of its freedoms but not for cities plagued by immoral immigrants who were racially incapable of legal freedoms intended for Anglos. The family was no longer to be viewed as a contract or a private entity within domains of kin, neighborhood, and church, but as part of a web of social institutions with evolving standards directed by a growing body of experts. Domestic relations were "more of an administrative character" requiring "adequate administrative facilities

and a staff of social investigators, and even…a psychological laboratory."[77] "Less than a generation ago," noted Pound, "we were echoing
the outcry of our fathers against governmental paternalism. To-day,
not only have we swung over to this condition in large measure, as
our increasing apparatus of commissions and boards and inspectors
testifies…but we are beginning to call for what has been styled governmental maternalism."[78]

Legally, the first solution to the dissolution of family life among
poor white ethnics in crowded cities was criminalization of male
offenses that had formerly been treated as violations of private contract. From 1890 to 1915, every state enacted laws that criminalized a
husband's desertion and nonsupport of his wife and children. Punishments included imprisonment and hard labor. Criminalization was
a means to the second solution: the creation of family courts that
channeled the new criminals into courts of equity, which removed
domestic matters from adjudication under due process to greatly
enlarge the scope of administration by social scientists. The first
domestic relations courts were city courts of limited jurisdiction in
Buffalo, New York City, Boston, and Kansas City. The celebrated
Chicago court, created in 1911 (the work of progressive female lobbying), was given broad jurisdiction to hear cases of nonsupport,
illegitimacy, child abduction, and statutory rape. Family courts would
not rule on "mere contract" under due process protections. Rather
the judge issued orders based on maxims of equity, considering the
social good in light of "sociological jurisprudence." Failure to obey
constituted contempt of court, which gave the judge almost unlimited
authority. "The powers of the star chamber," said Pound, "were a
trifle in comparison with those of our juvenile courts and courts of
domestic relations."[79] The court, wrote journalist Ida Tarbell, would
mend private conscience "by furnishing two great needs of men and
women in trouble—a confessional and a hand of authority."[80] The
moral basis was that of redemption; the court refocused from punishment to "sound preventative work," especially in divorce. Trained

experts would resolve marital disputes case by case by applying the latest statistical information from social science. The key to saving marriages was to move beyond a concept of fault, tied to the law, and toward Christian forgiveness, which transcended base contractual negotiations. It would be a secular confessional, wrote Tarbell. For the program to work, "an offender must be broken down, made to admit his wrongdoing. The judges become extremely skillful in finding the way to a man's heart, his conscience, or his pride. If ever children were played for all their great worth in the marriage relation it is in this court. Nine times out of ten, Judge Goodnow declares, you can arouse a man to remorse or to effort by his child." Tarbell shares a story of a "big, ugly, red-haired driver who had been brought in for nonsupport and who stood before the bar unmoved by the story of his wife and the reproaches of the judge." But when ordered to hold his cooing baby, "the surly brute broke down in a moment and, every trace of bravado gone, burst out: 'For god's sake, Judge, let me go back to my babies, I swear I'll do the square thing!'"

The family courts expanded their services and jurisdictions. Judge Harry Fisher praised the benefits of an investigative social service department: "Our court has become much more a great social agency than a court."[81] Pound agreed that family courts were a "cross between an imperial ministry of justice and a legal aid society." "But that is what a municipal court must be in a large city."[82] To control working-class men, states introduced probation—from six states in 1900 to every state by 1920—increasing supervision, under the constant threat of jail time, with the goal of rehabilitation. In 1915, thirty-three states passed or extended probation laws, and by 1920 every state permitted juvenile probation. "By the early 1920s, almost half the state prison population was serving indeterminate sentences, and more than half the prisoners released were on parole."[83] In 1917 the National Probation Association proposed that every family court "should have exclusive jurisdiction of the following cases: Non-support, desertion, all children's cases, including contributory delinquency; adoption and guardianship; bastardy; divorce, and alimony."[84] It would be funded for staff, including probation officers, "special investigating officers," and "psychopathic-psychological laboratories for proper diagnosis." It should have "power to make mental and physical examinations." Above all, it was not to be bound by domestic relations law, and all proceedings should be secret. Judge Charles Hoffman, of the Cincinnati Court of Domestic Relations, looked to "the great departments of psychology and sociology of our colleges" to provide "proper education and treatment."[85] In 50 percent of divorce cases, he estimated, experts could reveal the underlying "pathological and social conditions of parents that have existed from their childhood." Probationary forces were needed to investigate "the alleged grounds for divorce, and the home conditions and environment of the children of the parties involved... and for supervising the homes and children after the decree is granted." Investigative officers for the St. Louis Court collected a comprehensive list of information to make a statistical and psychological assessment of the divorce that may be used to reconcile the couple. Judge Edward Waite pushed for family courts in Minnesota and to give them jurisdiction over desertion, nonsupport, illegitimacy ("adjusting the mother, and making collections from the father"), juvenile matters, adoption, divorce, alimony, and the "enforcement of... payments" in support cases.[86] Women, far more than men, quickly utilized the social services and arbitration of the new courts, which subordinated the male status in the household before authoritative family experts. In the Chicago court in 1914, the female was defendant in only 61 of 2,796 cases. Waite observed, "The social workers, a keen and tireless group, are to be reckoned with; and the newly enfranchised woman is not likely to be long delayed in pursuing her ideals for the betterment of family life." A growing bureaucracy replaced household governance in the management of family affairs. And lawmakers noticed that a large stream of revenue could be drawn from non-supportive husbands.

The New Political Science

In his 1902 summary of the field, Charles Merriam concluded that political science had rejected the founders' obsolete political theories and replaced them with new "systematic and scientific" German methods.[87] "All political scientists" scorned both the state of nature and social compact theory as historically false; states originate by force and fraud, not consent. "Natural law and natural rights" had been "discredited and repudiated" and thus had been "with unanimity discarded." No one any longer held to "inherent and inalienable rights of a political or quasi-political character which are independent of the state." The old idea of liberty was dangerous and ahistorical. Rather, the "state is the source of individual liberty." Liberty describes a "sphere of action" or "a domain in which the individual is referred to his own will"; it is the "reward of the races or individuals properly qualified for its possession." Given differing capacities for liberty, some races have the broader goal of civilizing mankind. If incapable of evolution, then "barbaric races...may be swept away." If the state is composed of several nationalities, it should not give liberty equally to all. As the older limited function of the state—protection of life, liberty, and property—supplied a mere negative liberty, it must be supplemented with (or supplanted by) a new positive conception of liberty. The government must broaden its scope to provide for each individual's physical and mental cultivation. Rights, said Dewey, must be effective and not merely formal. He redefined the right to life to include old-age pensions and adequate working conditions. The right to mental freedom included education "in thought and sympathy."[88] The new conception of spheres of personal freedom required a balance of interests between individual and community, and "fear of centralization" of federal power, argued Frank Goodnow, "is no longer reasonable."[89] Thus there were no limits to the state in principle; its end, said Theodore Woolsey, was to cultivate man's "spiritual nature."[90]

The Progressives rejected the older view of republican citizenship, folkways tied to legal procedures of self-government, for the ethical ideal, or membership in the social organism. It meant unifying a fragmented American society, North and South, city and country. It also meant the triumph of a moral majority seeking to secure its power from below and above. From below, it faced both the question of the citizenship of the freed slaves and the deluge of Southern and Eastern European immigrants preyed upon by political machines rife with voter coercion and employee intimidation. Anglo-Americans must recognize the "vast differences in political capacity between the races, and that it is the white man's mission, his duty and his right, to hold the reins of political power in his own hands for the civilization of the world and the welfare of mankind."[91] At home and abroad, uplift was a process of education necessary for the privileges of citizenship. Anglos would accelerate the moral development of the lower races and guide them, if possible, to equality, and thus liberties. Against the trusts above, an insulated elite, a "rule of the few," purified by a scientific education and sensitive to the public welfare, must teach business to put the social good before profit.[92] Thus there should be two levels of citizens: first the experts who, knowing the good of the social organism, are empowered to rule outside of or contrary to law, and a second, lower tier of citizens with fewer privileges and immunities.

A new constitutional structure must replace the old separation of powers and checks and balances, which, Wilson said, now only secured a "ruling class" of plutocrats.[93] He contrasted the founders' older Newtonian view with the new Darwinian view. Life requires intelligence and quick cooperation: "No living thing could have its organs offset against each other as checks, and live." Frank Goodnow, another founder of scientific administration, agreed that the separation of powers was "unworkable as a legal principle."[94] A new "living" constitutionalism was needed to reinterpret the document for a changing social organism. The old constitutional questions had been historically solved in favor of democracy and majority rule, but now, as society became more complex, the need arose for a "science of administration" that could act with efficacy and speed in response to changing purposes. The new separation of powers would be between *politics* and *administration*. Congress embodies the people's will and deliberates over "constitutional questions," then delegates lawmaking authority to scientifically trained administrators who formulate and implement policies.[95] Administrative questions were of a "semiscientific, quasi-judicial" character combined with legislative and executive powers.[96] The older view had separated the reason and will of the people into different branches precisely because of the possibility of faction. But now the study of administration could transcend mere ethical prescriptions and become a true science, uniting reason and will in a professional bureaucracy. Civil servants would receive a moral preparation, a training in the universal (and not particular) interest, that cultivates selfless efficiency and integrity. As reason was now unified with will, tyranny became impossible, and so America could dispense with limited government in principle. Administrators would be not passive instruments but agents and would receive "large powers" and "unhampered discretion" to enforce their choices.[97] "The nation cannot be corrupted," said Wilson, "and we have ceased to fear a Caesar."[98]

Administration, said Wilson, was more like business than politics, with the goal of efficiency. He argued that taxation, punishment, and defense were matters of expertise that bureaucrats, not elected representatives, should decide; each area could become as efficient as the US Post Office. To control transportation and the railroads, the government "must make itself master of masterful corporations," requiring a national commissioner of railroads and administrative oversight.[99] Wilson reasoned that administration could only become transparent and accountable if it had vast unitary powers. "Public opinion," he added, would "play the part of *authoritative critic*." Bureaucracy itself would determine the public's role, "shutting it out" when it makes decisions. Moreover, bureaucrats must educate the public or teach the "people what sort of administration to desire and demand." For this education, political scientists would teach new "principles" of government to future politicians while training civil servants to be "sensitive to public opinion." Bureaucrats would be "statesmen...removed from the common political life of the people," with loyalty only to the people and the ability to best implement their laws. The greatest obstacle to the new political theory was the old American republicanism that remained suspicious of bureaucracy. Public opinion lagged; it was disunited, slow to organize, inefficient, and full of compromise. The solution, argued Wilson, was good rhetoric that makes the public willing to listen to the right things and desire change. Progressives repackaged the new principles in the old language to rouse opposition to a new economic tyranny.

There was no single progressive economic philosophy, but ideas like Henry George's single tax became veritable religious crusades. The key to American prosperity, argued George, had been hard work and initiative, but vast tracts of land had become means to speculation, which suppressed production and caused depressions. The solution was to make natural resources public property. This would include municipal utilities like street lighting, water, and railways. A single tax on land would change incentives by encouraging those who did not use their land to sell or develop it. George endorsed both free trade and a universal basic income funded by the new land rents. Ely, founder of the American Economic Association, began to systematize these policies in a science of Christian sociology in the 1890s. Dismissing a natural right to private property and business for social regulation of "quasi-public industries," he pushed for public ownership of utilities, transportation, and communication, "compulsory arbitration or public regulation of wages," profit sharing, and new inheritance laws.[100] Business must subordinate profit to the collective good. With state regulation, experts would resolve each case on its own merits in workplace safety, workers' insurance, health, and foreign trade.

The key economic issue was the trusts. The Court's odd interpretation of the Sherman Antitrust Act, which distinguished manufacturing from commerce while overturning pools, had led to a "consolidation craze"; from 1897 to 1904, 4,227 firms merged into 257 combinations.[101] There were three competing strategies to deal with corporate consolidation. Louis Brandeis's "regulation of competition," which focused on the "curse of bigness," would reduce protective tariffs while passing stronger antitrust legislation to smash all trusts.[102] The alternative, he said, was between "regulated competition or regulated monopoly."[103] Expert commissions would promulgate and promote scientific management, transparency, and business efficiency while allowing producers to *fix prices* to retailers, even if at greater cost to shortsighted consumers. The cutthroat prices under monopoly suppressed competition by "exterminating the small independent retailer" and barring market access.[104] Charles Van Hise rejected Brandeis's alternatives of competition or monopoly. Considering the obsolescence of small business and the economic advantages of concentration such as efficiency that lowers consumer prices, he argued for delegating rulemaking power to administrative commissions, which would pass broad regulations for large industries (with none allocated more than 40–50 percent market share) and be subjected to congressional oversight.[105] Finally, in Roscoe Pound's judicial model, Van Hise's administrative decisions and fact-finding would be subjected to oversight by an appellate specialty court, which would, on a case-by-case basis, slowly create precedent for an industrial common law in specialized bodies of legal doctrine. His view of a "living constitution by judicial interpretation" corrected the older mechanistic and individualistic view of law by adding a new "sociological jurisprudence" that focused on social justice, adjusting relations of men to each other and society.[106] Judges, he said, are "a progressive and enlightened caste whose conceptions are in advance of the public and whose leadership is bringing popular thought to a higher level."[107]

Progressivism began with reformist city mayors who took aim at nineteenth-century graft. Hazen S. Pingree, a shoe manufacturer, was elected mayor of Detroit in 1890. His "Potato Patch Plan" provided vacant city lots for residents to garden after the '93 panic. Pingree sold his prize horse to buy farming tools and seed. He championed municipal ownership and operation of public utilities, including streetcars, electricity, and gas. The city, he argued, could charge less and operate more efficiently than private corporations because it received lower interest rates for loans. The public, he said, should receive free water utilities at the expense of the rich and "railroad companies and other institutions" that were not paying their fair share.[108] Public ownership, he argued, would tend to prioritize the working conditions of laborers and reduce user charges instead of making higher profits. The danger of a public "spoils system" was real, but social moral pressure would mitigate it, and it was less dangerous than the "demoralizing influence of great wealth under private management."[109]

The city commissioner plan and city manager system embodied the progressives' twin thrusts of democracy and efficiency. Staunton, Virginia, implemented these systems in 1908; they spread to more than four hundred middle-sized cities by 1915. Cities, said journalist William Allen White, had been run by illiterate legislators who formed into "combines" to support the "rights of vice" of a corrupt political class.[110] To fight corruption, reformers turned to the new "scientific study of government" and "municipal engineering" that separated government from administration.[111] Rejecting the old separation of powers, they would combine "the legislative of policy-determining function with...executive of policy-executing power."[112] Abolishing the office of mayor, voters elected a city council to hire and oversee a nonpolitical, professionally trained administrator to manage the city. The manager, a "city engineer," took control over the city's administrative and executive work, heard citizens' complaints, made budgets, purchased city supplies, advised and assisted the city council, and oversaw the various departments. By this logic, the system was democratic because the city council was elected, and it was not corrupt because little-paid elected officials would oversee the decisions carried out by an expert.

At the state level, William S. U'Ren's Oregon System embodied progressive *democracy* as a solution to corruption. Special interest money and patronage, he claimed, had corrupted the party nomination system and prevented good citizens from running for office. Political parties must no longer be private tools of business but rather heavily regulated government organs. In 1902 Oregon passed an initiative and referendum amendment with 92 percent of the vote to circumvent elected officials by direct vote of the people. It established a direct primary to prevent special interests from nominating candidates, provided for the recall of elected officials, limited campaign contributions to prevent the "corrupting use of money," prohibited campaigning on election day, and required candidates to furnish information to voters. By 1884, most states had introduced the secret, or Australian, ballot to prevent voter intimidation in presidential elections. To circumvent special interests in state legislatures, progressives promoted the popular election of senators. To further weaken the parties, states established nonpartisan offices, including judgeships. As governor of Michigan, Pingree proposed replacing the party delegate system, ballots, and conventions with open primaries with no test of party affiliation. He also proposed same-day voter registration and a single primary voting day to cut costs and prevent voter fraud.

The turn to *expertise* was epitomized in Wisconsin's "Fighting Bob" La Follette, whose progressive career began after a Republican senator offered him a bribe to fix the verdict of a trial. The problem, as he saw it, was railroad and lumber interests' domination of Wisconsin politics. He won the governorship in 1900. While adopting the ballot initiative and referendum, the "Wisconsin Idea" was about expertise: in a complex modern world, to counter business interests, legislators needed their own experts to help them assess both the value of railroad land for tax purposes and the sale of public land to private interests.

La Follette forged a mutually beneficial relationship between the state government and the distinguished economists at the University of Wisconsin. Van Hise, Ely, Selig Perlman, and John R. Commons endorsed progressive policies, and in return they received prestige and high salaries. The state would use boards of expert economists, who knew as much about economics and law as businessmen, to provide public services. Pingree similarly made the "principle effort" of his administration the creation of an expert Board of State Tax Commissioners that would fairly assess the value of railroad and corporate property, which would cause tax revenues to double. La Follette also backed regulatory laws for businesses that required close inspections of operations. In 1905 Wisconsin, following Iowa (1897), created the first "fully fledged...administrative commission," delegating to it rate-making and regulatory authority, first over the railroads, then over all public utilities in 1907.

Three Progressive Presidents

At the national level, competing presidents Roosevelt, Taft, and Wilson shaped the progressive agenda. *Progressivism* does not refer to trust-busting, nor to Roosevelt's threat to use the army to work the mines to end the 1902 coal strike. Nor does it refer to the leadership role embraced by Roosevelt and Wilson, their use of press conferences or novel appearances before Congress. Nor was it their use of boards and commissions to investigate industries, arbitrate disputes, or report to Congress on monopolistic practices. There was nothing revolutionary about the 1906 Pure Food and Drug Act, which prohibited the adulteration of foods and medicines by processors engaged in interstate commerce, required that companies accurately label ingredients, and created an executive agency to investigate and enforce the law. Manufacturers of "feel good" elixirs now had to list cocaine as an ingredient. It was similar with meat inspection. Upton Sinclair's stories of piles of rat poop in Chicago slaughterhouses horrified readers, but the 1906

Meat Inspection Act, prompted by the Neill-Reynolds report, only *updated* the 1891 meat inspection act (which amended the 1884 act) to require more thorough federal inspection of meatpacking plants involved in interstate commerce. Poultry inspection had to wait; Americans slaughtered their own chickens at home. It was similar with conservation. Roosevelt's power to set aside national monuments and tracts of land, granted by Congress in the 1906 Antiquities Act, only continued efforts by the General Land Office and the Forest Reserve Act of 1891, which authorized presidents to withhold forests in public domain from private ownership. Recognizing the threat of private exploitation, the goal was conserving national resources and wildlife for *public use* and enjoyment. It limited the amount of land a president could preserve to "the smallest area compatible with the proper care and management of the objects to be protected." Few quarrels sprang from the policy; the Court upheld Roosevelt's 1908 creation of Grand Canyon National Monument. In two years, he added 125 million acres to national forests, tripling their size, and reserved for future use sixty-eight million acres of coal deposits, five million acres of phosphate beds, several oil fields, and 2,565 sites for irrigation and hydro-electric dams.

Progressivism properly refers to the implementation of administrative rule that constituted a regime change. It is summarized in Roosevelt's assessment that business "combination and concentration should be... *supervised* and within reasonable limits *controlled*."[113] At the federal level, the Hepburn Act in 1906 launched the administrative state by expanding the ICC's jurisdiction to cover all railcar companies, pipelines, and vehicular transportation through an express delegation of rate-making power. After a hearing that found rates unreasonable or unjust, the ICC was empowered to fix "just and reasonable... routes and joint rates as the maximum to be charged" as well as set the division or apportionment of those rates and order compensation. Carriers were required to publish their rates and notify both the commission and the public thirty days in advance as well as submit data on contracts, agreements, arrangements, and accounts. The act was a compromise between progressives who argued for a broad model of judicial review of administrative orders and those who wanted review narrowed to questions of law (not fact). Before, suits were filed in a district court, and the ICC's orders were only preliminaries, subject to lengthy legal challenges. Now complainants could file suit in a federal district court, but "the findings and order of the Commission shall be prima facie evidence of the facts." The commission's expert judgment as to whether "transportation is just, fair, and reasonable" received court deference. Its cease and desist orders, with threat of fines and even imprisonment for violators, took effect within thirty days. The courts could set aside, annul, or suspend the commission's orders, but the law required five day's notice to the ICC before an injunction, allowing it broad discretion. If carriers failed to comply, the "Commission in its own name, may apply to the circuit court" for writs of injunction and mandamus to enforce the order.

In the 1907 Bankers' Panic, the stock market fell nearly 50 percent from its peak in 1906. It was the fourth panic in thirty-four years. It was only resolved after J. P. Morgan locked up the nation's financial elite in his library until they could agree on mergers and acquisitions to clean the worthless assets off bank books and provide liquidity to increase investor confidence. Partnering with Roosevelt to end the panic, Morgan received federal funds with assurance that his mergers would be free from antitrust suits. Morgan partner George Perkins became executive chairman of the Progressive Party in 1912. Roosevelt now condemned Sherman Antitrust as "profoundly immoral," seeking "to forbid honest men from doing what must be done under modern business conditions."[114] He attacked the judicial model as dependent on outmoded economics and even praised the German price-fixing cartel, a commission that could set quantities, maximum prices, and labor conditions. If managed, even an "absolute monopoly" was tolerable.[115] He argued for "a commission to supplement (or supersede) antitrust" and distinguish reasonable from unreasonable restraints against unfair competition.[116] Because combinations were inevitable, a commission should regulate "methods of competition": "improper rebates, discrimination, and unfair competition...which has *no necessary connection with combinations.*"[117] Roosevelt flirted with licensing and preapproval for interstate commerce.

Roosevelt had appointed William Howard Taft governor of the Philippines with a goal of educating the Filipinos to self-government. The Philippine Commission, the upper house of the bicameral legislature, combined legislative and executive functions, with the people represented in a lower house. Taft set up a civil service as well as one of the first surveillance states. Roosevelt next picked Taft as his presidential successor. Taft oversaw ninety antitrust suits in four years, twice that of Roosevelt. But Taft was a "conservative" in that he differed with Roosevelt in his judicial model. He wanted to implement progressive administration with a bureaucratic soul, seeking to use both legal precedent and the party as an instrument of organized, slow change. "The Court is a continuous body," he said, "and the law of its being is consistency in its judicial course. Presidents come and go, but the Court goes on forever."[118] Roosevelt's earlier radical opposition to business, he concluded, lacked "the most sensitive consideration of the methods by which...progress might be safely attained. Precedents and their influence which are essential in a judicial system, to secure uniformity in the application of the law, did not greatly appeal to him."[119] Taft agreed with delegation of lawmaking power, but he was concerned about the unification of "administrative, legislative, and judicial functions."[120] Thus he signed the 1910 Mann-Elkins Act, which extended the ICC's power to telephone and telegraph industries and cable lines, and he delegated it power to suspend rate advances when new rates, regulations, practices, or classifications were filed with the commission (or of its own motion). It also reasserted the ICC's right to regulate long- and short-haul rate disparities. But Taft, like Pound, argued for a judicial resolution of antitrust questions, a specialty court of equity that could develop a new common law for industrial relations.

As Sixth Circuit Court justice, Taft had constructed the "rule of reason" test, interpreting the Sherman Antitrust Act to bar only direct or unreasonable restraints of trade. By *reasonable* Taft did not mean mere judicial preference but statutory language that referred to "well understood meaning at common law—to wit, restraint of trade, monopoly combination, and conspiracy."[121] Thus courts were not "assuming legislative power" but applying a "well-measured and definite yardstick." In the Standard Oil and American Tobacco antitrust cases, judges tailored decisions to "stamp out the evil of monopoly...yet [left] the capital and plant ably organized, to reduce the cost of production, and to carry on legitimate business for the benefit of the public." The "chief civil remedy provided by the anti-trust law" was "the elastic and many sided remedies afforded by procedure in equity," which, unimpeded by juries, held the "power of punishment by summary contempt proceedings for violation of the provisions of the decree." Taft oversaw the creation of a specialty Commerce Court to hear appeals from ICC decisions with power of review over its "legislative function" of rate making. Its judges would be superior to Circuit Court justices in their expertise over the "great volume of conflicting evidence" and thus better exercise "effective, systematic, and scientific enforcement" of railroad law, chiefly in protecting the railroad's reasonable profits. Seeing the court as a threat, progressives abolished it in 1913.

To please progressives, Taft supported the Sixteenth Amendment (income tax), ratified in 1913. To please big business, he signed the Payne-Aldrich Tariff, which raised already high rates (45.6 percent) on more than two hundred items. And Taft had backed Speaker Joseph Cannon, whom progressives had overthrown in the "Cannon Revolt." Taft, said progressives, had allied with big business. The final straw was his termination of Gifford Pinchot, Roosevelt's favorite forester. Entering the 1912 election, Roosevelt outlined a broad program, the "New Nationalism," which included women's suffrage, a federal minimum wage for female workers, the abolition of child labor, a limitation on courts in labor disputes, and social insurance. But Roosevelt, popular with the voters, lacked support by party leaders. Losing to Taft at the Republican Convention, he attacked the organ of the political party itself. He launched his own Bull Moose Party, promising to greatly extend government control. He would expand the powers of the advisory Bureau of Corporations to regulate the trusts rather than dissolve them. With an elite staff of lawyers and economists, it would be an "interstate trade commission" delegated broad powers to regulate manufacturing, wholesaling, and retailing, with a last resort of direct price regulation.

New Jersey governor Woodrow Wilson, reputed scholar and reformer, entered the race as a progressive Democrat, blaming Roosevelt and Taft for the recent economic crises. Brandeis, Wilson's economic advisor from 1912 to 1916 (and later Supreme Court appointee), helped craft his platform, the "New Freedom." Opposing Payne-Aldrich, Wilson's promised a lower tariff, the intensified prosecution of trusts, and vague banking reform. With a split in the Republican Party, Wilson won with 42 percent of the popular vote. He quickly signed Underwood-Simmons, reducing tariffs by 15 percent. To make up for lost revenue, he called for corporate and modest personal income taxes. Next was the creation of a central bank, a "lender of last resort," that could provide liquidity (short-term loans) to financial institutions or markets to help calm financial panics. As an alternative to Carter Glass's plan for a decentralized system of private banks, Wilson successfully proposed a centralized board of directors with presidential appointment of a majority. The 1913 Federal Reserve Act established a private central bank with power to issue currency, loan money, and oversee twelve district banks. By raising and lowering interest rates, the Fed could control the number of notes in circulation. The *New Republic* called it one of the greatest administrative bodies in the world. Lengthy tenure would insulate it from politics and business, securing "supreme impartiality and disinterestedness."[122] It would also "intervene in industry in the interest of national coordination" and limit "over-speculation and . . . inflated business," a "great development towards an increasing governmental control over industry."

Progressive principles informed Wilson's policies. Herbert Croly noted in 1914 that Wilson often concealed his principles for political reasons.[123] As part of his trust-busting platform, Wilson adopted Roosevelt and Taft's model of delegation. To enforce the 1914 Clayton Antitrust Act, which fined corporations for stifling competition, Congress authorized the Federal Trade Commission to issue orders barring "unfair methods of competition in commerce." The five-member FTC, designed to be preventative rather than punitive, would demand annual reports from corporations and investigate business practices, prevent mislabeling, and frustrate price fixing. Wilson pushed for prosecutorial authority and broad judicial review of its determinations. As an overseeing agency during the war, it made 370 wartime cost-finding inquiries in 1917–18, and by 1920 it had issued 400 "cease and desist" orders. When Democratic majorities in the House and Senate shrank in 1914, Wilson courted Roosevelt's supporters by backing his New Nationalist legislation, such as the 1916 Federal Farm Loan Act, which provided low-interest credit to farmers, and the short-lived Keating-Owen Act, which prohibited child labor. Congress, in the Adamson Act, claimed the emergency of war to fix the terms for service and overtime pay for interstate railroad workers.

Wilson's view that "government and business must be associated closely" meant that private property should be viewed more like public streets. He used the example of a "tenement house" in Glasgow. Police officers were not confined to the street but monitored the halls, listening at the doors, for evidence of crime. In Wilson's mind, business firms were quasi-public thus less entitled to property rights. They must provide regulatory agencies data and be open to inspections for violations. The power of supervision stems from the power to collect information for prosecution. But the courts frustrated these attempts, both denying the ICC the power to compel witnesses and narrowly interpreting its right to collect information to matters under complaint.[124] Following the Court's narrow interpretation, Congress expanded the power of ICC information collecting in 1910, and it wrote compliance requirements of reporting into the FTC's organic statute. But when the FTC demanded broad information about legal violations from business, it was overturned by a unanimous Court. Justice Holmes wrote, "Anyone who respects the spirit as well as the letter of the Fourth Amendment" and embraces the "first principles of justice" never would "believe that Congress intended to authorize one of its subordinate agencies to sweep all our traditions into the fire…and to direct fishing expeditions into private papers on the possibility that they may disclose evidence of a crime."[125]

In foreign policy, all three progressive presidents rejected republican noninterventionism for the "uplift of humanity," a spiritual redemption of the world in the education of inferior peoples to democracy.[126] There were other arguments, such as the need to vent American energies and markets after the settling of the frontier and that America needed a modern two-ocean fleet with island bases and coaling stations to protect trade. But the most compelling one was that empire was not selfish: wars were justly waged on behalf of foreigners. The Cuba Libre movement called for American intervention to free Cubans from Spanish concentration camps. Congress's 1898 authorization to use force cited the "cause of humanity" and renounced intent to annex Cuba. But following the "splendid little war," the US was uncertain what to do with its acquisition of Spanish colonies. They could neither be returned to tyrannical Spain nor be independent, so the answer was to "uplift and civilize and Christianize them."[127] Senator Albert Beveridge defended annexing the Philippines, Puerto Rico, Guam, and Hawaii lest Americans "rot in our own selfishness." It would be a long commitment: Taft told McKinley that "our little brown brothers" would need "fifty or one hundred years" of close supervision "to develop anything resembling Anglo-Saxon political principles and skills."[128] Statehood did not accompany the mission of uplift. Rather "the consent of the government... is conditioned upon capacity for political action. If a population is not capable of democratic self-government, then they must be subjected to a process of political education, until such time as they can govern themselves."[129] In the dependencies of Guam, Puerto Rico, and the Philippines, Americans for the first time set to rule other peoples without their consent. In the Insular Cases, the Supreme Court created a new jurisprudence to do so: self-government no longer followed the American flag.

The US had employed Filipino nationalist Emilio Aguinaldo to overthrow the Spanish, but realizing American intentions, he led a second revolt. By 1902, 4,200 Marines and 250,000 Filipinos had been killed, with atrocities and massacres on both sides, at a cost of $160 million (of a $572 million budget). After inviting Aguinaldo to parley, the US seized him, forced him to surrender, and installed Taft as governor. Americans boasted to have acted against their own military and economic interests: they brought ports, roads, railroads, schools, hospitals, and civil rights. They enforced a rigid public health code and built an electrical and telecommunications grid for military intelligence. With infrastructure rose Taft's repressive multitiered security state, which included the Constabulary, a paramilitary police force with a secret service, to patrol the countryside, contain radical elements, and spy on popular gatherings. Pacification required an intensive police state, firearm confiscations, and prosecutions of 30 percent of Manila's populace for violations of colonial law. In this new imperialism, the US built a Panama Canal "for the benefit of the world" (said Taft),[130] liberated Cuba, and became, said Roosevelt's Corollary, an "international police power." Wilson proclaimed that it was dangerous, unfair, and disgraceful to pursue foreign policy based on material self-interest; rather the US would "teach the South American republics to elect good men."[131] He established military protectorates in Haiti and Nicaragua, sent Marines to Vera Cruz to punish Mexicans for not saluting the US flag, and supported Venustiano Carranza in the bloody Mexican civil wars. World War I offered a greater opportunity for righteousness.

Condemning old world militarism, Wilson assured Europeans that the interests of democracy could never conflict with those of humanity. He stayed out of the war to remain morally above it, courted disaster by allowing US ships to travel in war zones, and then joined at the end to exert moral authority for reshaping the postwar world. The US, he proclaimed, was not fighting for material interests, money and power, but to "vindicate the principles of peace and justice in the life of the world as against selfish and autocratic power."[132] Germany must be defeated as an enemy of mankind. Global peace required the "partnership of democratic nations." Abandoning the idea of separate autonomous nations, Wilson's internationalism posited the impossibility of the coexistence of "democracy" with "autocracy," which led him to believe that democracies must overthrow all undemocratic regimes. France and Britain used Wilson's promises for a moderate peace to deceive Germany into an armistice.

Progressivism peaked in World War I. The Eighteenth and Nineteenth Amendments (Prohibition and women's suffrage) were the work of WASPs in a period of moral fervor and national sacrifice. The first, directed against the taverns at the center of German and Irish city machines, condemned the use of grain for Hun beer instead of food for allied soldiers. Progressive women demanded the right to vote not because they were the same as men but because they were angelic beings that would purify politics and double the WASP vote threatened by anarchist immigrants from Italy. The Committee on Public Information saturated the public with war propaganda against German "Kultur." Seventy-five thousand "four-minute men" gave patriotic speeches during film intermissions. The 1918 Sedition Act prohibited "disloyal, profane, scurrilous, or abusive language about the form of government of the United States...or the flag of the United States, or the uniform of the Army or Navy." Progressives celebrated the new planned economy. Federal spending increased tenfold, and the number of bureaucrats doubled from 400,000 in 1916 to 950,000 in 1918. The 1917 Lever Bill gave the president control over fuel, food, fertilizer, and requisite machinery. The War Industries Board, headed by Wall Street financier Bernard Baruch, supervised all lower production boards. The United Railway Administration, headed by Wilson's son-in-law William McAdoo, planned the nation's railroads. While the shipping board could produce ships twice as fast as the Germans could sink them, the Aircraft Production Board, commissioned to construct 22,000 planes, only delivered 1,200.

Laying a Wreath on Uplift

Progressive leaders were divided over the war, and Americans tired of its intrusions. In 1917 La Follette condemned US entrance into the war over the "right of an American citizen to travel upon a foreign vessel loaded with munitions of war."[133] Roosevelt called him a "sinister enemy of democracy," its "worst enemy now alive."[134] But La Follette only echoed the earlier Anti-Imperialist League, whose leading statesmen opposed the Spanish-American War. Expansion, they had argued, was unprincipled, ignoble, inefficient, and self-destructive. Empire abroad meant empire at home, subverting freedom, centralizing government, exacerbating domestic divisions, and degrading culture. They denied that distant foreign powers posed any real threat and questioned supposedly altruistic American motives. US-owned sugar plantations displaced Puerto Rico's jíbaros, and Marines were deployed to protect the interests of American investors, who owned 40 percent of Mexico's assets. Smedley Butler, two-time recipient of the Congressional Medal of Honor, reflected: "I spent thirty-three years...in active military service, and during that period I spent most of my time being a high-class muscle man for Big Business....I was a racketeer, a gangster for capitalism. I helped make Honduras right for the American fruit companies in 1903. I helped purify Nicaragua for the International Banking House of Brown Brothers in 1902–1912. I helped make Mexico and especially Tampico safe for American oil interests in 1914. I brought light to the Dominican Republic for the

American sugar interests in 1916. I helped make Haiti and Cuba a decent place for the National City Bank boys to collect revenues in. I helped in the raping of half a dozen Central American republics for the benefit of Wall Street."[135] Most Americans came to believe that WWI had been fought for corporate interests. J. P. Morgan & Co. underwrote British and French war bonds; by mid-1915 it was purchasing $10 million per day in American goods for the British, including arms and wheat. By 1917 Americans had loaned the British $2.3 billion and Germany $27 million. After the war, Wilson was caught in between. Those who most fervently supported his idealism denounced his betrayal of world democracy and the Fourteen Points at Versailles, while most Americans had become weary of his moralistic reforms and economic planning. The income tax for the highest earners had risen progressively to 77 percent. Leading progressives Hiram Johnson, Henry Cabot Lodge, and William Borah opposed Article 10, the League of Nations, whose collective security obligation threatened the creation of an entangling alliance. But the spirit of empire remained. The US immediately forged alliances to control international arms buildups. It implemented the Dawes Plan in postwar Germany to secure profits from the massive loans brokered by J. P. Morgan for private investors.

In 1920 Americans voted for Warren G. Harding's "return to normalcy," meaning the business-friendly McKinley Era. Many progressive Republicans had wanted to reform business, not destroy it. By the "New Era," reformists had eased concerns over concentrations of wealth in industry. The top US companies appeared to share in a stable universal pattern with similar growth strategies, and reformers did not mind the profits from their investments. Progressivism was in part a victim of its own successes. Reformers had achieved much—on state election reforms, women's suffrage, Prohibition, and immigration—leaving them with little to do. The Emergency Quota Act of 1921, followed by the immigration Act of 1924, "scientifically" limited immigrants from each European country to 2 percent of their total number in the 1890 national census. It passed without a recorded vote in the House and 90–2–4 in the Senate. Progressives' views on immigration matched their discomfort with classism. They preferred nationalism and Anglo finance to urban radicals. Among workers the divide between farmers and labor weakened La Follette's Progressive Party candidacy in 1924; it had no state or municipal tickets. Failing to forge a coalition, the movement ceased to be relevant. Forty-seven former "supporters of…Roosevelt and the Progressive Party" publicly expressed their "resentment" at La Follette's use of the name: the Progressive movement, they said, had not been "radical. Its purpose was to improve American institutions, not to substitute others for them. It stood for political and social justice, not economic revolution. It believed in democracy, not socialism."[136]

Progressives had also succeeded in creating a new political model. While the number of bureaucrats was tiny and their scope small (in 1902 federal expenditures totaled $572 million, while local expenditures totaled $959 million), the idea of scientific management had sprouted among elites and the urban middle class. The Transportation Act (Esch-Cummins) of 1920, which returned railroads to private operation after the war, extended the ICC's powers to set minimum rates and created the Railway Labor Board (RLB) to make nonbinding proposals to settle railway disputes, but the latter failed. After the RLB ordered a wage reduction for workers in 1921, followed by support for a federal injunction of a strike in 1922, unions refused to use it for mediation. The 1920 Water Power Act created the Federal Power Commission to license and regulate hydroelectric power companies and their utility rates. Despite their delegated authority, the regulatory commissions hardly seemed a political threat. They depended on cultivating good relations with the three branches, each in turn seeking to wrest the bureaucracy under its control. The ICC and FTC nursed relations with Congress that a jealous judiciary threatened. The Supreme Court ruled that the FTC's power to determine "unfair" trade practices was too broad, an encroachment on its own power. Staffed with incompetent commissioners who had conflicting views of their mission, it limped throughout the 1920s; the federal courts eviscerated the Clayton Act. But despite these failures, precedent had been set. The FTC remained an independent "quasi-judicial" and "quasi-legislative" administrative body, which fourteen years later would be used as a tool for expansive New Deal legislation.

The war had resulted in a new cynicism—for the Americans, the "Lost Generation." Progressive idealistic appeals to transcendence of self-interest, presupposing an undependably high level of virtue, conflicted with reality. Bureaucracy introduced a different sort of spoils for an educated elite. Presidents extended civil service protections to cover their partisan appointments. From 1883 to 1900, the percentage of protected civil servants rose from 10 to 50 percent. The 1912 Lloyd-LaFollette Act gave federal workers due process and whistleblower protections before removal. Bureaucrats, like headless nails, once pounded in were impossible to extract. College professors and instructors claiming the right to shape public policy rose from seven thousand in 1900 to thirty-three thousand by 1920. In 1903 William James complained about the "Ph.D. Octopus" at Harvard, a "grotesque tendency" of "the Mandarin disease" to the antagonistic aims of "multiplying...the annual output of doctors" and "raising the standard of difficulty in passing." Other professionals formed cartels, such as the "medical trust," under the claim of impartial scientific authority. And courts deferred to state powers to require licenses to practice medicine, law, and education.

Bureaucrats could be dedicated public servants or corporate shills who formed alliances with the industries they were supposed to regulate. In 1892, incoming attorney general Richard Olney reported on the ICC to the Burlington Railroad: "The Commission...is, or can be made, of great use to the railroads. It satisfies the popular clamor for a government supervision of the railroads, at the same time that that supervision is almost entirely nominal.... The older such a commission gets to be, the more inclined it will be found to take the business and railroad view of things." In 1904 ICC Commissioner Charles Prouty had a different view: "If the [ICC] were worth buying, the railroads would try to buy it. They have bought pretty nearly everything in this country that is worth buying, and the only good reason they have not tried to purchase the Commission is that this body is valueless in its ability to correct railroad abuses." After securing more power for the ICC in the 1920 Esch-Cummins Act, Representative John Esch took a seat on the commission. Seven years later the Senate denied his reappointment after learning he had changed his vote to approve preferential rates for coal transportation in Pennsylvania. The Bureau of Chemistry's Harvey W. Wiley, crusader for the 1906 Pure Food and Drug Act, became so disgusted with industry's use of the act that he entitled his reflections *The History of a Crime Against the Food Law*. State workman's compensation and insurance boards deteriorated into slush funds and were bankrupt or replaced by the end of the century.

The greatest casualty was republican government and the rule of law. Wilson admitted that bureaucracy presented a danger of Prussian officialdom, but a science of administration, he promised, would be "Americanized" and would adapt European despotism's efficiency to American decentralized government without its tyranny. He presumed that the love of liberty was a constant in the American character independent of its shaping institutions; because of "democracy," he believed, it is "impossible to snatch power over a...people by [seizing] its central offices."[137] But if moral virtue depended upon the older institutions, which progressives detached from the people and placed in the hands of experts, then the progressives accelerated what they feared. Expert oversight makes people dependent, uncertain of themselves, less responsible. Women were told that cooking, motherhood, and housecleaning were sciences: "Selection and preparation of food should be in the hands of trained experts."[138] In the 1914 Smith-Lever Act, for the first time the federal and state governments jointly funded home economics programs. The price paid for a new scientific and academic priesthood was the loss of self-government that the progressives claimed to save. By 1915 it had become obvious to John Burgess, who warned: "It is high time, for us to call a halt in our present course in increasing the sphere of Government and decreasing that of Liberty, and inquire carefully whether what is happening is not the passing of the Republic, the passing of the Christian religion, and the return to Caesarism."[139]

Democracy was a casualty too. The attack on the nineteenth-century party structure had immediate effect. The secret ballot, which was introduced to end voter intimidation and bribery, subverted the democracy it claimed to support. Where the party ballot had appealed openly to solidarity and rewards, now uninformed voters had no help comprehending the information on a complicated ballot. In the South, the secret ballot operated as a de facto literacy test for blacks. Voters no longer had skin in the game; turnout plummeted from 75 to 85 percent to 50 to 60 percent. Direct primaries drew a minority of partisans less willing to compromise. In civil society, Social Gospel contributed to the demise of the churches. Dealing with the urban poor, Protestants like Gladden and Rauschenbusch, and Catholics like Father John Ryan (a Kantian idealist and promoter of Ely's "ethical ideal"), preached that government should take care of their constituents' bodies while they ministered to their souls. As we will see, it was the first of three deals with the devil: decentralized government had secured churches' power and authority over the soul by tying it to bodily needs. Reformers of soul or body, the spoilsmen noted, easily rationalized the privileges they received in accepting the proffered tentacles of power. Theologians agreed to welcome state intervention in exchange for recognition and offices to administer its treats.

Progressives initiated the turn to rule by emergency, or exception to the law, in decisions made by experts and not legislators—whether for reasons of war, economics, or health—in forced vaccinations and sterilizations. The Supreme Court upheld the Adamson Act, which, under the power to regulate commerce, used an "emergency" to set the terms of labor contracts to increase worker wages, raising costs to the railroad and thereby raising prices. In that 5–4 decision, Justice Day's dissent warned that it was the first time that Congress had "fix[ed] the rate of compensation…under coercive influence of a threatened public calamity."[140] But no emergency could justify removing citizens' Fifth Amendment rights, depriving them of property without due process. It "exceeds the bounds of proper regulation" and was an ominous departure from the protection of property.

By the 1920s, progressivism was dead as an intellectual movement. Its demise stemmed from a fatal contradiction that lay at its core. Progressives never reconciled their teleology in an absolute historical process with their scientific aspirations, which rejected a priori logic. The professional philosopher would seem to chronicle, perhaps at best articulate, the changing social organization, while scientists in narrowing, specialized fields slowly replaced the need for encyclopedic thinkers. Positivists and the new physiological scientists each transgressed the boundaries of the old philosophy, staking their turf. The new "liberals," rejecting progressive "absolutism," challenged the progressives' supposedly scientific foundations of authority. They rejected Social Gospel and German idealism for the new pragmatic philosophy that underpinned the idea of a *truly* "scientific" state, one not proceeding from a social organism but managing plural groups. Elites like Walter Lippmann and Lincoln Steffens, seeing how easily reformers and voters were coopted by corporations, lost faith in the very people they had set out to redeem.

In a 1926 article "Where Are the Pre-War Radicals?", *The Survey* gave an autopsy from older progressives who had agreed that the movement was over. Stuart Chase proposed the nation "lay a wreath on the Uplift Movement in America."[141] Roosevelt, Wilson, Tom Johnson, and La Follette were dead. On seeing what they had wrought, most of the old progressives, even Ely, were critical of the New Deal, and many were hostile to it.[142] In 1936 the *New York Times* printed a Letter of Bull Moosers endorsing Alf Landon for president against Franklin Delano

Roosevelt. The dream of a unified nation, embracing rural American morals, was shattered by an urban pluralism. The ethical ideal for a social organism gave way to a new conception of pluralism and the scientific management of competing ethnic and economic interests. The new movement was not progressive but liberal, and it spoke a language of ethnic diversity, class warfare, and internationalism.

3

LIBERALISM

Walter Lippmann, George Soule, and Herbert Croly, founders of the *New Republic,* first popularized the term *liberalism* in its contemporary meaning. "The word," wrote Lippmann in 1919, "was introduced into the jargon of American politics by that group who were Progressives in 1912 and Wilson Democrats from 1916 to 1918."[1] Progressivism, he argued, was not a united political movement but a hodgepodge of policies, primarily at the local and state levels. After their break from Roosevelt's progressive party and disillusionment with Wilson, the *New Republic* crowd (funded by J. P. Morgan) needed a new name. They borrowed *liberalism* from British politics, where the Liberal Party had, by the end of the nineteenth century, rejected limited government for the idea of the organic welfare state. But they wanted more than a name. They saw the need for a new philosophy requiring both an intellectual detachment from and a means to a new politics. Roosevelt had ended his friendship with Croly and Lippmann after the journal attacked his Mexican policy, and Wilson, in the minds of his idealist followers, had betrayed his promises at Versailles. The war had discredited progressive faith in absolutes like teleology and nation. It was time to grow up. Finding that progressive idealism could not solve existing problems, liberals seized upon John Dewey's instrumentalist strain of pragmatic philosophy, and it became the basis for a new political order of state capitalism and scientific planning.

Renascent Liberalism

Dewey, father of "renascent liberalism," had been a progressive.[2] But as professor of philosophy and psychology, he found that he could not demonstrate the validity of Hegel's metaphysics for science. Darwin, he concluded, had indeed destroyed the concept of essence that underpinned two thousand years of Western metaphysics.[3] Mind did not require an a priori logic to develop in time. What philosophers had called the forms had emerged from constant adaptation with, even a struggle against, the changing environment. Thus science and even mathematics were not the pursuits of absolute truth; scientists had built systems of geometry and physics upon certain axioms that did not grasp truth in reality but that had developed historically as useful tools for concrete ends. The same was true for ethics and morality. Moreover, the old philosophy collapsed under psychological questioning. Dewey confessed that his own attraction to philosophy had been a religious quest for certainty too easily satiated by a logic that united all facts into a grand system. Idealists who set out to find a presupposed order unsurprisingly always found one. But absolute questions, he concluded, demanded a revelatory knowledge that exceeded human intelligence, and they were answered in untestable systems removed from the very reality they sought to explain. They were also ineffectual. Philosophers, in their search for absolute Good, ignored the plurality of goods that science could achieve in this world. Dewey adopted a radical empiricism that philosophers had demoted as the realm of appearances. He sought to extend to every inquiry, especially mind and ethics, the experimental scientific attitude judged by its utility to the individual and collective good.

Dewey recast the old notion of an unchanging human nature as a function that channeled enduring instincts within a spectrum of possibilities. Intelligence was a human's greatest instrument for adapting, constructing ideas, and testing hypotheses as tools for action. It enabled humans to predict and shape outcomes and thereby adjust themselves and the world.[4] What the philosophers had called essences amounted to the sum of functions and values that arise and accrue from these inquiries.[5] Humans may ascertain the logical structures of inquiry in human language, but they should never confuse thinking with accessing eternal truths; the forms are never severed from experience, i.e., pragmatic questions with possible answers. Thus inquiry defined the good life. The scientific method was the highest *activity* of mind, the actuality of human potential as a problem-solving creature, while the philosophic quest for certainty was, underneath, a longing to rest or to stop thinking.[6] A scientific attitude opposed all "system making and programs of fixed ends" and "impotent...creeds and all-inclusive ideals."[7] Its "general adoption...in human affairs," predicted Dewey, "would mean nothing less than a revolutionary change in morals, religion, politics and industry." Lippmann called Dewey's ideas world historic.[8] Randolph Bourne hailed him as a "prophet": "After reading him, you can see nothing again in the old terms."[9]

Dewey did not naively think anyone could be a scientist who challenged authoritative hypotheses. To be politically effective, the "collective intelligence" of science must become an authoritative belief whose province would extend from the physical sciences to all society. Science could combine "authority and freedom" into an "intimate and organic union."[10] This did not affirm the old progressive faith in altruism and selfless reform but an authoritative new *method* that united individualistic aspiration and community testing. Individuals would (theoretically) be encouraged to independently challenge authoritative opinions with new hypotheses that require experimental confirmation (in replication) by the scientific community. Only scientific planning provided an alternative authority to the twin absolutisms of socialist faith in a future communist consciousness and capitalist faith in principles of laissez faire (leading to fascism). Because most could never understand complicated scientific mechanisms, the state would have to drape decisions with the sacred mantle of democracy, an alternative political order. It would be what Dewey called a "Common Faith."

Liberalism was America's first truly secular movement. The "conflict between science and religion" wrote Dewey, "was essentially a conflict of claims to exercise social authority."[11] The 1933 Humanist Manifesto, signed by Dewey, extolled the scientific method, denied supernaturalism, and exalted human nature, affirming that man was on his own in the universe. Sigmund Freud argued that the science of psychoanalysis had disproven religious and moral authority. Religious feelings were regressions to infancy, through either a return to a maternal oceanic feeling of oneness or a state of dependence upon a providential father. Philosophic systems, he noted, included the same rites as religious obsessive-compulsives, who scrupulously perform repetitions that bring a sense of certainty and promise to control external events. Moral compunction always betrayed a contradiction between a man's moral claims and his underlying sexual motives; virtue is never for its own sake.[12] Freud prophesied the "future of an illusion." With religious sentiment detached from its authority, a new priesthood of lay analysts would hear the people's confessions.[13] Citing Freud, Lippmann argued that Western civilization, now stripped of religious belief, must grow up from its infantile stage. The new social science was the offspring of Anglo utilitarianism, German profundity, and American revivalism. As a sect it preached a conversion to reason (rebirth in agnosticism) with examinations of consciousness to root out both guilt and moral sentiment (and its indignation) as primitive or superfluous forms of self-management. Denying absolute essences, liberals found purpose in social control, a crusade to convert the world to rationality.

Pragmatism dominated growing academic circles in the universities. Dewey's pupil John B. Watson purified instrumentalism to found behaviorist psychology "upon natural science."[14] Behaviorism rejected the older questions of meaning and consciousness via introspection:

"the problem of 'meaning' is a pure abstraction. It never arises in the scientific observation of behavior." Detaching themselves from religious and moral sentiment, scientists only studied objective, verifiable facts, not values: "Psychology is not concerned with goodness or badness of acts, or with their successfulness, as judged by occupational or moral standards. Because a man fails... to get his food... or to live in harmony with his wife, is no reason for rejecting him as a psychological subject. *We study him for his reaction possibilities and without prejudice.*" The study of "instincts" or unlearned emotional reactions (fear, rage, and love), which by proper conditioning were almost infinitely malleable, replaced the older study of habits and virtues. The liberal scientist forsook the progressive scientist's pursuit to know what was just or impartial for "the prediction and control of human action." The quest for certainty was replaced by certainty in efficacy, and the scientist's rule was justified by power: "Behaviorism's primary contention is that *if its facts were all at hand the behaviorist would be able to tell after watching an individual perform an act what the situation is that caused his action (prediction), whereas if organized society decreed that the individual or group should act in a definite, specific way the behaviorist could arrange the situation or stimulus which would bring about such action (control).*" Moral standards change with each historical epoch, but the psychologist would discover the "laws and principles which underlie man's behavior" and that he, "having chosen human behavior as his material, feels that he makes progress only as he can manipulate or control it."

Social scientists would control all human life "from even before birth until death."[15] Their probabilistic view of the world required data collection and quantitative analysis, which first began in the 1920s. A key liberal tenet was that culture did not matter. Humans were all the same; a knowledge of nature or their instincts could be used to direct subjects to humane ends. To uproot the older commonsense views, social scientists filled citizens with fear and doubt. "Until we know more about the control of behavior during the tender years of infancy," said Watson, "it seems almost a dangerous experiment to bring up a child." Most people, he warned, fail in "making satisfactory adjustments to society"; indeed, "Every human individual needs the data and laws of behaviorism for organizing his own daily life and conduct." While the older mental hygiene had focused on "right living" or a "mind that found itself," behaviorists claimed that only "systematic, long-sustained, genetic studies upon the human species begun in infancy and continued until past adolescence, will ever give us this experimental control over human conduct so badly needed both for general social control and growth and for individual happiness."[16] Watson promised the possibility of molding children into any profession. "Give me a dozen healthy infants, well-formed, and my own specified world to bring them up in, and I'll guarantee to take any one at random and train him to become any type of specialist I might select—doctor, lawyer, artist, merchant-chief and, yes, even beggar-man and thief, regardless of his talents, penchants, tendencies, abilities, vocations, and race of his ancestors."[17] Successful "experimental manipulation" required placing humans in laboratory-like settings where variables could be controlled, such as the experiment to condition nine-month-old "little Albert" to become terrified of white rats. After Watson left his wife for his graduate assistant, the new couple used behaviorism to educate their two sons, spurning motherly tenderness and seeking to strip them of the need for religious meaning in life (both later attempted suicide).

Where academic psychology promised to adjust individuals, psychoanalysis promised to cure maladjustments and shape character. Parents now obsessed over their child's fixations and toilet training. Supported by government funding and private insurance, psychoanalysis's influence peaked between the world wars, where American soldiers experienced debilitating levels of shell shock and combat fatigue (today called post-traumatic stress). Psychotherapists adopted Freud's teachings of repression, sublimation, and renunciation: stifling sexual mental energy; sublimating it to socially useful activities like art, reason, and science; and openly discussing sexual drives, gaining control over them. Repression is the basis for civilized pleasures because there always remains a core of actual neuroses, or self-denial. In a secular teaching of conscience, Freud argued that humans were by nature selfish and destructive: *"Homo homini lupus."*[18] "Our mind," he wrote, "is no peacefully self-contained unity. It is rather to be compared with a modern State in which a mob, eager for enjoyment and destruction, has to be held down forcibly by a prudent superior class."[19] The defense of repression was not that it constituted a "best" way of life; questions of "right" or "meaning" (no such things existed) were those of a sick mind and had no place in science. His view was tragic: civilized man would ever be discontent because the growth of his duties accompanied a growing repression and its concomitant anxiety.

Liberals preached an ethic of proper emotional adjustment for intelligent behavior. They discarded the progressives' faith in evolved altruistic morality for solving the problems of adjustment, "interactions between an individual and the social environment."[20] Social institutions, wrote Dewey, are not "means for obtaining something for individuals. They are means for creating individuals."[21] Liberal virtues included piety for science, toleration, skepticism of religious and moral certainties, openness to diversity, and confidence in technology. As educational techniques produced personality or character, a scientific education would adjust individuals' unique competing demands of pleasure, conscience, and society to realize their ends in a social purpose. Schools would teach democratic morality by stripping away the old American "cult of individual success" and adjusting students to one another in collective experiences.[22] Teachers would focus on total personal development, including sex, customs, and hygiene. The failure to integrate, Dewey thought, is the cause of mental disease; the solution was greater conformity or the "recovery of an integrated individual."[23]

Liberal political science, attempting to apply the scientific method to administrative rule, rejected the older progressive ideal of the social organism and its view of citizenship, participation, and administration as a "consummate juvenalism" that had led to world war.[24]

Rejecting "uplift," which presupposes that minorities need to be uplifted, liberals substituted the ideal of a "great community," an equal, diverse citizenry. As the belief in absolutes was a pathology, liberals championed routinization, bureaucratic rule by scientific method that dispensed with dangerous charismatic leaders. The new conception of right was solving immediate crises of maladjustment through "continuous inquiry." Democracy now meant balancing interests in a pluralist society (economic, racial, and religious) lest one interest rise to dominate the others. Political scientist William Bennett Munro called the older progressive democracy a "necrocracy," founded on dead principles, and lectured on the "myth of popular sovereignty": "Sooner or later, democracy and efficiency obtain a divorce for incompatibility of temper."[25] Lippmann argued that elites must use propaganda to "manufacture" popular consent: "As a result of psychological research, coupled with the modern means of communication, the practice of democracy has turned a corner. . . . It is no longer possible . . . to believe in the original dogma of democracy."[26] Even Dewey's democracy, often viewed as antithetical to Lippmann's, required no fixed constitutional procedures or institutions; the individual's legitimate sphere of social participation would be determined experimentally. Merriam now argued for replacing the study of political theory with quantitative political science. Experts using new methods in polling could gauge public opinion and identify the plural publics' interests before making administrative decisions for the collective good. Institutions are then democratic if they facilitate deliberation and thereby express and refine the public interest as well as clarify the tasks of the administrative specialist.

Pluralism

The liberals promised to use the scientific method to manage a pluralist society, directing its sexual and aggressive urges and solving race and class conflict with social science. They championed an ethnic and class identity politics unknown to older progressives. Liberalism was an American struggle of the orders that produced a new coalition of cosmopolitan Anglos, labor, and diverse ethnics, the inverse of the older rural Americanism. The urban reformers of the WASP elite and the Irish, Jewish, and Italian ethnics began to make turbulent concessions and intermarry to form an elite class with a new morality of sex, race, and class.

Among cultural elites, the rise of psychoanalysis in the 1920s undermined the progressive conception of reality and morality. Because the basis of human action is always egoistic, even sexual, the individual and society are locked in tension. Indeed, society itself caused neuroses; the mentally healthy and pathological lie on a continuum of neurotic individuals. Liberals touted their detachment from indignation, holding stiff Anglo reformist mores in contempt. Charlie Chaplin made a career mocking them. Among elites, moral certainties became an opportunity for parlor game speculations on infantile sexual fixations. At their core lie "man's narcissism," which, noted one psychiatrist, "comes to mean the whole of racial pride," the trivial claims to meaning as a member of a race or "national destiny."[27] Leading intellectuals affirmed that anxiety-ridden American culture was especially neurotic, even barbaric, compared to stress-free primitive life: sexual freedom before marriage, toleration of homosexuality, and flexible conjugal life. Chastity was a "disease," not a virtue. The egoistic flapper who separated sex from procreation replaced the drab progressive feminists who preached bearing children for the state: "Is it not high time," asked *Harper's*, "that we laid the ghost of the so-called feminist?"[28] H. L. Mencken, Sinclair Lewis, and Theodore Dreiser mocked "Puritanism" in prohibition and chastity. They derided both populist revivalism (the preaching of Billy Sunday *and* La Follette) and William Jennings Bryan's democratic defense of school boards' right to control class materials in the 1925 Scopes Trial. Small town life in Lewis's *Main Street* was close-minded, sexist, racist, jingoistic, and ultimately irredeemable. Jazz, the very word a euphemism for sex, replaced band music and Protestant hymns. Celebrating downward mobility, white New Yorkers danced to black music in segregated clubs. Radical artistic and literary circles in Chicago and New York's Greenwich Village circulated theories of innate bisexuality, infantile sexuality, incest, transsexualism, and sex changes. Where progressives swooned over romantic friendship and race progress, Mencken asked, "Are platonic relations possible between the sexes? ... Many a woman of the new order dismisses the problem with another question: Why without sex?"[29] Freudo-Marxist Wilhelm Reich proposed a "sexual revolution" against all moral repression. In the new "work democracy," an elite class of scientists would guide the population by managing their sexual desires.[30] D. H. Lawrence, priest of love, presented the sexual act as one of religious fulfillment and self-realization, the sacred encounter of two primordial ids.[31]

Freud winced at libertinism. He wanted a softer sexual revolution, where civilized people could talk about, not act out, their sexual fantasies. He advocated traditional sexual mores and attacked free love advocates. Social order required repression, but creating well-adjusted personalities and marital relations depended on healthy sexual expression, especially the long-neglected feminine sexuality. Average Americans were taught that they needed scientific counseling to achieve individual fulfillment and familial adjustment. Sex gratification within romantic marriage aided self-realization and diminished neuroses. Maturity meant recognition of *both* the pleasure and reality principle, adjusting sex and duty, the rational regulation of pleasure for its greater fulfillment. This would require sexual experts, not moral prudes, to educate young women about their physical needs. Marital counseling in the 1930s became sex confessionals, measuring genitalia and the frequency of intercourse and orgasms and discussing inhibitions and sexual frigidity. The point was to use the authority of science to relax the old asceticism. In their clinical reports, psychologists Dickinson and Beam, after chronicling "the isolated and depressed Jewish woman," the Roman Catholic woman who fears pregnancy, and the "wives of Protestant ministers" who "display moral reluctance toward the sensual," concluded: "The reproductive function is important not because of what it actually does or does not do within the organism, but because it is a determinant for conduct and thinking and for social control."[32] The successful patient, stripped of his older moral foundations, may even embrace a soft hedonism. Liberals analyzed deviant behaviors—pre-marital sex, cohabitation, and promiscuity—without any appearance of moral disapproval except for perhaps sexual jealousy. They challenged patriarchal sex roles. Most women (Dewey guessed 80 percent) would desire to stay home, but career women should receive equal treatment. The new feminists split between wealthy Republicans advocating legal equality in the workplace and Democrats seeking unequal treatment to protect female industrial workers.

In the Roaring Twenties, Anglo businessmen courted the "high society" and "conspicuous consumption" despised by men like Morgan and Rockefeller. They partnered with social science, which developed statistical methods from factory quality control, to manipulate consumers. Fired by Johns Hopkins for his sexual indiscretion, in 1920 Watson took a job with advertising agency J. Walter Thompson. Freud's nephew Edward Bernays, who had previously served on the Committee for Public Information, became a corporate consultant. He championed the marriage of social science and industry as "propaganda for peace" using psychoanalysis in advertising to channel erotic and aggressive impulses toward consumption instead of war. The new psychology could "engineer" consent: the public's "mind is made up for it by...those persons who understand the manipulation of public opinion," especially in the "acceptance of minority ideas."[33] Rejecting the behaviorist model, which focused on repeated advertising as conditioning and coupons as rewards, he looked to shape the unconscious motives of buyers for sex and status. After the American Tobacco Company hired Bernays to increase market share among women, he consulted psychoanalyst A. A. Brill to assess the female smoking taboo. He learned that cigarettes were phallic symbols of power, socially imposed to confine women to certain roles. To subvert the taboo, Bernays procured a list of debutantes from the editor of *Vogue* and pitched the idea that they could expand women's rights by publicly lighting up on Fifth Avenue during New York's annual Easter Parade. He then notified the press, which gave international coverage to the "Torches of Freedom Parade." Asking "Who is it that influences the eating habits of the public?", Bernays boosted bacon sales for Beechnut Packing by reporting surveys of doctors (those with status) who recommended eating a "hearty breakfast."

Racial conflict grew with diversity. Despite the immigration acts of 1921 and 1924 that reduced their numbers, the urban population swelled with a flood of Southern and Eastern Europeans into factories and universities. Courted by Anglo industrialists promising work and higher wages, blacks moved in great migrations to northern cities like Detroit and Chicago. They crowded into segregated neighborhoods bordering white ethnics, with whom they competed against for jobs and territory. While finding better wages, the black family dispersed and crime soared. While the white homicide rate remained constant from 1919 to 1927 at 5.3 per 100,000, black homicide increased from 30.5 to 43.8. Cities like Chicago exploded in race riots between white ethnics and blacks initiated by violent flare-ups of racial solidarity. The membership of Marcus Garvey's black nationalist United Negro Improvement Association exceeded that of the NAACP. In rural areas, the Ku Klux Klan, borrowing the idea of bed sheets from D. W. Griffith's 1915 film, *Birth of a Nation*, surged to four million members. After a black man was accused of rape in Tulsa, blacks organized for armed conflict, getting the best of whites in several armed exchanges before whites torched the black side of town, thirty-five square blocks. The ferment in the Democratic Party was best captured by Irish, urban, anti-prohibitionist Al Smith's campaign for the presidential nomination against McAdoo's rural prohibitionists in 1924. Smith's 1928 campaign, said one journalist, was defeated by "Prohibition,

Prejudice and Prosperity." Still, Republicans' former hold on cities was broken. Jews, who constituted a sizable minority in elite universities, law schools, and graduate schools, often saw themselves as outsiders seeking to overturn the old Anglo order. They made up a disproportionate share of radical socialists and anarchists. At the New School, Jewish students hotly debated Trotskyism and Stalinism. WASP progressives attacked Jews as purveyors of sexual perversion and economic revolution. Not until the 1930s, recalled Norman Podhoretz, could Jewish intellectuals say America was their own country, worth defending instead of subverting. Attacking the Anglo elite, Jewish lawyers led lawsuits for the ACLU and NAACP and dominated the organizations' national leadership.

Liberals rejected the progressives' view of race differentiation and introduced "race relations" courses in the universities. Israel Zangwill celebrated the "great Melting Pot...the harbour where a thousand mammoth feeders come from the ends of the world to pour in their human freight. Ah, what a stirring and a seething! Celt and Latin, Slav and Teuton, Greek and Syrian,—black and yellow...Jew and Gentile."[34] By the 1920s, leading anthropologists like Franz Boas, whose students included Ruth Benedict and Margaret Mead, argued for the "plasticity" of human types: the word *race* was almost meaningless.[35] Social scientists declared racism a mental pathology and promised that it could be cured and race consciousness transcended. The very idea of race difference, recalled sociologist Lewis Killian, was unscientific and laughable. Robert E. Park, a Dewey student and sociologist at Chicago, offered the idea of pluralist conflict resolution, a four-stage cycle of contact, competitive conflict, and accommodation culminating in assimilation. He developed the theory of marginality, or "marginal man," to describe individuals caught between two cultural groups. Marginal man was an adaptive character, "a personality type with characteristic forms of behavior"; his mind was where "conflicting cultures meet and fuse" and thus where the "process of civilization" may best be studied.[36] The vanguard of civilization was the "community of races" in the universities.[37] But assimilation disturbed minorities who would preserve their group identities. Horace Kallen, a Jew, and Alain Locke, a black homosexual, each formulated a theory of teaching race pride for Jews and blacks while promoting the "cultural pluralism" of American identity. Jewish groups, lobbying to *both* increase their own numbers *and* promote diversity, took the lead fighting the national origins quotas of the 1924 Immigration Act and worked for its repeal. To preserve a "separate national existence" for Jews free from anti-Semitism, Zionist Maurice Samuel argued for a secular US identity removed from religious, moral, and ethnic traditions.[38] "If America had any meaning," it was the founding of a "state [as] purely an ideal," and thus its duty was to secure "the most elementary human right, the right of asylum."

Class conflict increased as the urban population first outnumbered the rural in 1920. In the 1919 postwar recession, 3,600 labor strikes involved four million workers. Eugene Debs (arrested for sedition in 1918) and the International Workers of the World (IWW) promoted socialism. The IWW had 150,000 members at its peak in 1917 before it was crushed by the government. Debs had won 12 percent of the popular vote for president in 1912; he received one million votes while imprisoned in 1920. The Red Scare, warning of a bloody Bolshevik revolution, was marked by bombings (in April 1919, dynamite-filled packages were sent to thirty-six prominent politicians), thousands of arrests, and hundreds of deportations. Business in response tarred unionism as anti-American, and the courts upheld yellow-dog contracts that prohibited workers from joining unions. Court injunctions against labor strikes doubled, and labor unions declined during the prosperity of the 1920s. Gompers, who had attacked the IWW, died in 1924, and AFL membership decreased from four million in 1920 to less than three million in 1925.

By the 1929 stock market crash, liberal economic planning was not just a response to class conflict; it constituted one of three world systems (with communism and fascism) that competed for imperium in the West. Communists had preached international solidarity and party rule in the name of the workers. And urbane liberals sympathized with Bolshevism: they were armchair-general theorists allied with a simple, hardworking, hedonistic "proletariat" that longed to be engineered. Lapsed Anglo Protestants romanticized backward peoples, seeing them as fellow atheist underdogs in need of a sponsor. They had contempt for businessmen and found a sense of meaning in political revolution after the death of God. In the 1920s ships full of Americans traveled to the Soviet Union (85 percent of its visitors). While businessmen wanted to export goods and ideas, intellectuals like Rexford Tugwell had seen the future. They returned with glowing stories of economic planning and wrote dozens of books praising the Soviet model. Stuart Chase's *A New Deal* asked, "Why should Russians have all the fun remaking a world?" Communist sympathizers and spies infiltrated every level of the US government. Stalin, courting the liberals in order to destroy them, applied a strategy of international chaos, pitting Western liberal nations against Germany and Japan.

The liberals found a devil in Benito Mussolini and Adolf Hitler's national socialism, which also had its American supporters. Hitler, a German in liberal Austria-Hungary, opposed the empire's multicultural policy of balancing ethnicities. He accused it of favoring minorities like the Czechs, thereby working toward the "slow extermination of the German nationality."[39] His "greatest spiritual experience" came from reading about Prussian military glory—he "became a nationalist." The turn to "blood and soil" was a rebellion against cosmopolitanism, which used a class of intelligentsia to uproot all identities and reduce sacred traditions to base economic calculations. Social democracy, he wrote, was really bureaucratic rule, a slow rot, an unstable halfway house en route to communism, which itself was not what it seemed. Rather than a workers' movement, it was a cabal of Jewish international bankers who stirred class and race conflict (like Slavic pride) in order to weaken all other races and, by financial leverage, reduce them to "interest slavery." Hitler's solution was fascism: to lay aside guilt for German identity and unify conflicting classes in a love of nation. This required a single party to dominate all aspects of life, from youth bunds to working with the Jewish Agency to finance the emigration of sixty thousand German Jews to Palestine to euthanizing the unfit. Imagining a renewed era of European colonial rule, Hitler wanted to seize Russian land to provide an agrarian base for German industry, after which he would form a grand alliance with Britain's sea empire. At first Nazism appealed to only a few, those humiliated by Versailles and disgusted with the hedonism and weakness of Weimar, a regime floated by foreign loans in the US Dawes Plan. But it rose to power in the Great Depression as a reaction to communist proliferation. Middling artisans voted for a return to the prewar economy that balanced small and large business and agriculture and industry and tied unions to cultural, not merely economic, ends. Under a legal authorization to emergency power, the Nazis ruled by exception to the law, removing legal protections from all opponents. In his view of a global racial struggle, Hitler promised to use "the most extreme and brutal means" to destroy the "Jewish-Bolsheviks" endangering the nation. He created Dachau, a concentration camp, for dehumanized races, political prisoners, and ideological dissenters.

Many liberals, accusing American populists of fascism, idealized the communist struggle abroad as a projection of both their political aspirations and struggle with the older American traditions.[40] In 1935 Raymond Swing warned that Father Coughlin, Huey Long, and Francis Townsend were "forerunners of fascism." But the US was poor soil for both fascism and communism. Social strata and class did not divide American businessmen and financiers (embodied in Morgan and Rockefeller) as they did in Germany, where an old, militaristic aristocracy expressed an ethos of elitist contempt. Nor did American laborers possess peasants' reciprocal hatred. Hitler could court a landed class and industrialists, and Lenin could set degraded peasants against the decent, hardworking farmers he called capitalist "kulaks." But

US laborers shared common mores with businessmen and aspired to more than European peasant hedonism. Americans had also largely conserved a theory of representation that resisted the Bolshevik and Nazi destruction of opposition political parties. Liberals articulated their own view of economic planning in the New Deal.

Quantitative Liberalism and the New Deal

At the outset of the Great Depression, leading Republicans and Democrats embraced social engineering, and intellectuals argued that a planned economy could provide equal access to the material conditions for freedom. Franklin Delano Roosevelt's Commonwealth Club Address placed experimentalism at the center of his 1932 presidential campaign. In his reworking of the social contract, he declared that the people give power to the government, which in turn gives them rights. The statesman's task was to redefine these rights for each generation. Based upon "self-evident" "economic truths," he added new rights: "a useful and remunerative job," "recreation," "a decent home," and "adequate medical care."[41] The "new goals of human happiness and well-being" would be measured by efficacy or "how fully these and similar rights have been carried into practice." Adolf Berle, Rexford Tugwell, and Raymond Moley (FDR's "brain trust") promoted "a policy of cooperative business-government planning.... It was the duty of government to devise, with business, the means of social and individual adjustment to the facts of the industrial age."[42] Berle and Tugwell distinguished their own view from Theodore Roosevelt's and Woodrow Wilson's: government, instead of policing or breaking apart private industry, would become its senior partner.[43] Tugwell likened capitalist market speculation to philosophic speculative systems, and economic planning offered a scientific alternative. Economists, with the help of industrialists, would plan production and consumption for each industry with increasing data and accuracy; it would mean, literally, the death of private business. Berle argued that shareholding in the modern corporation required a new concept of property: corporate boards, whose decisions affected the business cycle, stewarded public wealth, not just shareholder profits.

Liberals initiated the new economic planning in FDR's Hundred Days. The 1933 Banking Act created the twelve-member Federal Open Market Committee to make the key decisions affecting the cost and availability of money and credit in the economy. The new economic science rejected long-range price stability for year-to-year monetary interventions by the central bank. While old progressives had feared inflation, the new currency managers saw that the gold standard (John Maynard Keynes called it a "barbarous relic") impeded government's market manipulation. To stop investors from fleeing to gold, FDR confiscated all gold reserves by executive order, then devalued the dollar by 40 percent. New "alphabet agencies" provided not just "relief" through government employment and home and farm loans but also "recovery"; they would grow the economy. The 1933 National Industrial Recovery Act, in which government partnered with industry, was the idea of General Electric president Gerard Swope. To end needless competition, it set industry codes (right down to strippers' tassels) and fixed prices and wages. The 1933 Agricultural Adjustment Act, a partnership between the largest growers and the USDA, instituted subsidies, price controls, and marketing orders to regulate production. Its goal was "parity" through wage controls so farmers would make the same wages as in 1909–14. To raise prices, the government ordered farmers to kill six million piglets and 220,000 pregnant cows and to plow under one-quarter of the cotton crop. While the Court struck down the NIRA and AAA as unconstitutional delegations of lawmaking authority, Congress quickly reinstituted their key elements in the National Labor Relations Act of 1935 and Soil Conservation Acts of 1935 and 1936. Now the government paid farmers to conserve the soil by growing nothing. At its most ambitious, government would, in the Tennessee Valley Authority, compete with private enterprise in production itself.

To collect their subsidies, farmers expelled three million tenant farmers from 1933 to 1935. It was another opportunity for social planning. Via the Resettlement Administration, Tugwell oversaw their removal to supervised rental farms as well as the relocation of city dwellers to low-cost neighborhoods. Financing long-term commitments in home ownership was the ideal form of social planning. Only 47.8 percent of Americans owned their own homes in 1930; mortgages were ten-year loans with 50 percent down payments. The 1933 Home Owners' Loan Corporation Act sold bonds to lenders to purchase and refinance more than one million non-farm home mortgages. To prevent foreclosure, it refinanced mortgages from shorter loans to fully amortized, twenty- to twenty-five-year loans on non-farm homes worth under $20,000. The 1934 National Housing Act created a Federal Housing Authority to insure mortgages and thereby secure low interest rates and longer terms. WASPs relocated to suburbs outside the city while funneling blacks and white ethnics into housing projects. The 1936 FHA Underwriting Manual included "deed restrictions" and zoning regulations to protect the new neighborhoods from "adverse influences," including "the infiltration of business and industrial uses, lower-class occupancy, and inharmonious racial groups."[44] In the management of pluralist groups, stability in home values, neighborhoods, and local schools required segregating those of "a far lower level of society or an incompatible racial element." The new deeds included twenty-year restrictions on building design and racial occupancy. Under a 1937 act, municipalities could build low-rent housing with federal loans and grants. The first such agency, the Newark Housing Authority, used federal money to create two Irish, one black, two Italian, and two Jewish projects. Government workers moved to planned suburbs like Greenbelt, Maryland (designed by Tugwell and Eleanor Roosevelt), where applicants were screened for race, religion, income, health, family size, cleanliness, and community spirit. Wives were not allowed to work.

To manage the economy, Congress delegated broad lawmaking powers to the ICC and FTC and created four more regulatory commissions to form the "Big Six": the Securities and Exchange Commission (SEC), Federal Communications Commission, Civil Aeronautics Board (CAB), and Federal Power Commission. The SEC, created in 1934, was delegated broad rulemaking authority to solve problems in security trading, including a lack of transparency, unregulated or over-the-counter exchanges, and the use of commercial funds for investment banking. James Landis, the obsessive son of missionary parents, law clerk to Brandeis, and professor at Harvard Law, was hired to create the administrative state. In the 1933 Securities Act, Landis included legal executive mechanisms to hinder securities fraud: disclosure requirements for new companies, subpoena powers making noncompliance a penal offense, cooling off periods for issuance of securities, and stop orders. The 1934 Securities Exchange Act regulated stock exchanges, first by granting power to the Fed to set margin requirements for trading (to prevent the kind of leverage that led to the stock market crash). It also barred certain sales practices under certain circumstances, to be decided by federal regulators, and required financial reports from all trading companies. The SEC, which was staffed by Landis himself, administered both acts. FDR named business-friendly Joseph Kennedy to the commission to tame Wall Street fury and restore investor confidence. The new SEC attracted top lawyers, an elite bureaucracy of seven hundred to register thousands of corporations in three dozen exchanges.

But Landis's views went beyond regulation. "In terms of political theory," he argued, "the administrative process springs from the inadequacy of a simple tripartite form of government."[45] Government needed a new administrative branch of government, "quasi-legislative, quasi-executive, quasi-judicial" in function.[46] He did not intend to punish businessmen but to create "cooperation" between government and industry and channel human incentives within institutions; scientific knowledge of investor psychology could benefit the public.

Industry must self-regulate and become "keen about the Act rather than opposed to it." He praised expertise, which "springs only from that continuity of interest, that ability and desire to devote fifty-two weeks a year, year after year, to a particular problem." Not only would experts replace elected officials, he foresaw a proliferation of regulatory agencies: "Efficiency in the process of governmental regulation is best served by the creation of more rather than less agencies." And Landis promoted not just regulation but rule by "advanced advice," or agency guidance, in formal and informal opinions, which the SEC began to issue by the thousands.

Government agencies proliferated. They treated more markets (such as broadcast frequencies or air routes) as scarce resources that must be regulated in the "public interest." Congress expanded ICC powers to regulate all trucking and water carriers. It delegated broad powers to the formerly weak FTC to prohibit "unfair and deceptive acts or practices." In 1938 it created the five-member Civil Aeronautics Authority, delegating it power to conduct investigations, issue and amend orders, and make "general or special rules, regulations, and procedure" as well as oversee an administrator with power to license air carriers and allocate aviation routes. The 1938 Federal Food, Drug, and Cosmetic Act delegated broad authority to the FDA to oversee the safety of food, drugs, medical devices, and cosmetics. All organic statutes included conflicting mandates to both impartially promote industry and protect consumers. The CAB, for example, must "encourage and foster the development of…air commerce" but also ensure "just and reasonable…rates, fares, and charges" by air carriers.

Illiberal speech did not go unregulated. Updating the regime created by the 1927 Radio Act under Calvin Coolidge, the 1934 Federal Communications Act delegated lawmaking and judicial powers to the FCC to allocate portions of the electromagnetic spectrum, not just requiring standards for licensing but holding hearings to determine which radio stations should receive priority according to the "public interest." Owners could not operate a broadcast service to benefit their own private business.[47] The FCC could deny licenses for broadcast material that failed to "sufficiently represent local interests" or that it found inimical to public health.[48] It denied or withdrew licenses where illiberal religious or labor groups sought to use stations to further their own views. Vulgarity and anti-Catholic broadcasts were barred along with astrological predictions and marital advice.[49] The FCC worked with the National Association of Broadcasters, which in 1939 established a fairness doctrine to ban Father Charles Coughlin (with some 30 million listeners) for his anti-Semitic remarks as well as controversial topics like birth control and labor disputes. In its 1940 Mayflower decision, the FCC banned on-air editorializing by station owners: "A truly free radio cannot be used to advocate the causes of the licensee."[50] The FCC's later Fairness Doctrine, under the "right of the public to be informed," required "well-rounded," adequate coverage of certain issues and equal representation.[51] Stations must "seek out, and encourage the broadcast of opposing views."[52] Meanwhile, the FCC silenced information, such as the Soviet massacre of twenty-two thousand Polish military officers at Katyn.

To legitimize the administrative state, liberals championed legal realism, the brainchild of Jerome Frank, and rejected Roscoe Pound's progressive sociological jurisprudence, which had maintained that law was rooted in popular sovereignty. Frank, after six months of psycho-analysis, had adopted a factual skepticism and legal pragmatism that jettisoned the concept of law as universal and necessary. Jurists had hitherto presented logical systems of rules that they believed would introduce certainty in decisions but in truth made decisions based on unconscious biases—racist, sexist, or classist—at the most elementary level of fact-finding. The solution was to reject the "belief in a body of infallible law" and to adopt a new attitude of doubt recognizing the law's inherent mutability.[53] Pound, he argued, had not given up the quest for certainty as demonstrated by Pound's exemption of property law from his evolutionary legal theory of human relations. Pound advocated for a slowly evolving common law, shaped case by case, instead of granting an almost unlimited rulemaking authority to agencies. Frank was appointed chairman of the SEC, later Second Circuit Court justice, and Pound, once a supporter, became a critic of the New Deal. The courts nodded to legal realism in various cases. A new type of administrative lawyer rose to the fore, specializing in compliance and undoing basic republican liberties with labyrinthine tests. Equal protection, which had been used to overturn segregationist municipal zoning laws and violation of contract, could also be used for preferential treatment for "discrete and insular minorities."[54] In "civil liberties," liberals crafted a hierarchy of rights in different levels of judicial "scrutiny" (strict, intermediate, and reasonable) to balance various rights. This legal gymnastics reflected the amalgamation of Anglo experimentalism with "Jewish legal tradition" to the end of locating sovereignty in an elite caste, who under a sacred mantel of *stare decisis* used "law" to manage individuals and associations by fiat regulation.[55] Judge David Bazelon, finding no legal ground for an opinion, would wink at his clerks and tell them to write a "*writ of rachmones*"—in Jewish law, "*compassion.*"[56]

In the so-called Second New Deal (1935–36), the Democratic Party brokered a coalition of the disadvantaged to redistribute wealth to the elderly, poor, laborers, and minorities. "Necessitous men are not free men," proclaimed FDR to support insurance for old age and sickness. The Social Security Act instituted a social insurance system for the elderly funded by a Federal Insurance Contributions tax based on a life expectancy of fifty-nine (forty workers to support each recipient). Politicians could not let that money sit for long. They soon added survivors (1939), followed by the disabled (1956). After working three years and paying $24.75 into the system, Ida Fuller received her first check of $22.54 in 1941. She lived until age one hundred and collected $22,888.92. The act's Aid to Dependent Children recast child nonsupport as a federal problem, culminating in a massive, intrusive welfare system in which the lives of welfare recipients became a primary concern of the government. Single mothers received support to continue their "natural" tasks of childcare and housekeeping. States distributed monies to welfare boards, which decided who received aid, how much, and under what terms. They implemented rules like "suitable home," "socially acceptable," and "man in the house" to disqualify women with suspect moral standards from aid. Caseworkers could stop by to investigate at any hour. They snooped through homes, looking for male razors and other evidence of sexual promiscuity. One woman complained, "All they was trying to find out was, did you have another man."[57] Welfare agencies kept extensive case records, including "evaluations of a welfare woman's housekeeping, her ability to budget her small income and pay her bills, and her 'moral standards.' Likewise, she is often scorned for activities that take her outside the home." In New Jersey, Old Age and Disability recipients were checked every three months, welfare women every month. Vague rumors spread that noncompliance meant an end to the checks or even removal of children.

Liberals had used the Depression to secure laborers' support. They called for government recognition of labor to compensate for past anti-union discrimination. The Davis-Bacon Act of 1931 mandated prevailing regional wages to privilege union contracts (over cheap black labor), and the 1932 Norris-LaGuardia Act prohibited both yellow-dog contracts and federal courts from issuing injunctions in labor disputes. The crucial 1935 Wagner Act, the work of Tugwell's student Leon Keyserling, delegated power to a National Labor Relations Board (NLRB) to arbitrate disputes and settle labor violations claims. Agents visited factory floors to see if workers wanted to unionize. To identify victims of labor discrimination, the NLRB conducted administrative hearings and fact-finding investigations with the power to order offending parties to "cease and desist from such unfair labor practice, and to take such *affirmative action*, including reinstatement of employees with or without back pay." Designed to avoid the slow, rigorous process of criminal law, the NLRB required a less stringent standard of "substantial evidence" for fact-finding. Its evidentiary standard of discrimination included the statistical assessment of percentages of union members fired, laid off, or refused. The NLRB then negotiated agreements with employers to avoid punitive sanctions. Its trial-like due process was subject to judicial review, and congressmen preferred indirect influence by committee oversight to the formalities of congressional hearings. In 1938 Congress further empowered the NLRB to administer the Fair Labor Standards Act, which instituted a forty-hour workweek, a national minimum wage, overtime pay, and "child labor" laws.

As blacks began to picket storeowners to hire them in their own neighborhoods, liberals were caught between two contradictory policies: color blindness and race preferences in quota hiring, the latter in principle the position of southern segregationists. Liberals in the NAACP who adopted the former found themselves set against black nationalists, who defended "fighting segregation with segregation— transmuting segregation into power that would bring an end to racial discrimination someday."[58] The National Urban League supported race quotas, while the NAACP proceeded cautiously since similar discrimination might emerge in white areas. The liberal solution, borrowed from labor law, was the contradictory "affirmative action," or preferring black applicants while rejecting racial quotas as a violation of racial equality. Following the sociological argument that a disadvantaged race should expect statistical representation, by 1940 New Deal agencies adopted a standard of race proportions in federal employment. The Public Works Administration implemented the nation's first policy of racial hiring quotas, based on proportionate representation of blacks using 1930 census records for various trades. Quotas were used in the TVA (11 percent black employees) and the US Housing Authority (for both employees and tenants). During the war, FDR's "Executive Order 8802: Prohibition of Discrimination in the Defense Industry (1941)" cited the need for national unity of American manpower "regardless of race, creed, color, or national origin." In response to A. Philip Randolph's threat to march on Washington,

FDR created the President's Committee on Fair Employment Practices (FEPC) to monitor defense contracts for discrimination. It sought to enforce nondiscrimination policy without racial quotas. It had neither power to issue subpoenas and cease and desist orders nor standing to sue in court, but it could threaten to cancel contracts.

Historian Paul Moreno has pointed out that government recognition of the unions constituted a labor cartel that discriminated by definition to exclude competitors and increase wages.[59] Thus it also came with a hitch. A closed-shop union, unlike other private associations, was subject to regulation. The Supreme Court decided that union representation for its members must be "fair," not based on "irrelevant differences" such as race.[60] A union must either give up its closed-shop status or admit black employees to full membership.[61] But neither did the courts require unions to hire black workers. The FEPC, calling race an "artificial criterion" distinct from "individual qualifications," continued its strong stand against quotas. Justice Frankfurter, agreeing with union leaders *and* civil rights groups, wrote for the Court that a "quota system," especially in a nation "made up of so many diverse groups," would encourage racial animus.[62] Still, he suggested that businesses might voluntarily implement their own quotas. After Congress ended the wartime FEPC, New York (followed by twenty-five more states) created its own State Commission Against Discrimination (SCAD). It applied a lower threshold for discrimination than criminal and civil courts, and it used "conference, conciliation, and persuasion." After a public hearing, it could issue orders to "cease and desist" and require "affirmative action," including "hiring, reinstatement or upgrading of employees, with or without back pay, or restoration to membership in any respondent labor organization." When businesses did not comply, it could seek judicial enforcement with its own findings of fact.

The state civil rights commissions borrowed the NLRB's evidentiary standard of discrimination, using disproportion in race as evidence of discrimination. The courts, however, applied a standard of "disparate treatment" rather than "disparate impact." The legal charge of discrimination required demonstrable instances of unequal treatment, focusing on particular facts of intent to discriminate, while the pattern-centered approach considered discrimination systemic, unintentional, and impersonal. Because the courts had rejected the concept of systemic racism, general statistics could not prove discrimination since they failed to consider the qualified minority applicant pool within an area. Thus the commissions combined evidence of an applicant's qualifications with sociological arguments about patterns of disproportionate employment. SCAD, which did not collect statistics, argued that this was actually its strength. Its real weapon was publicity, using moral suasion (not compulsion). This both relieved anxious employers and avoided the rigorous standards that protected individual rights in courtrooms. Still, civil rights groups were frustrated that FEPCs did not allow them the same role as labor unions in the NLRB: picking cases and crafting rules.

The Second New Deal reframed the liberal partnership with business by equating cartels with fascism. In 1935 Congress passed the Public Utility Holding Company Act, which gave the federal government power to regulate electric power companies. Waging war against private holding companies that controlled 80 percent of the nation's electricity, it required them to file with the SEC, which could initiate proceedings to separate its utility from nonutility interests. Holding companies sold off their subsidiary companies, which were reduced from 1,983 to 303 by 1948. Congress also passed the Revenue Act, introducing a "wealth tax" of 75 percent on the highest incomes (over $1 million). Reversing the trend of mergers in the 1920s as well as the 1933 cartelization of industry and agriculture, in March 1938 FDR appointed Thurman Arnold to head the DOJ's Antitrust Division, expand antitrust enforcement, and formulate a coherent policy. Arnold championed democracy, the "ideal of a society of competing business men and farmers," against Germany's centralized cartels and "socialistic legislation."[63] He increased the number of lawyers from

15 in 1933 to 583 by 1942. In five years, he initiated almost half of all the government's cases in its first fifty-three years. FDR successfully recommended congressional hearings on economic concentration, which produced forty-five volumes on the problem of monopolies.

Thus the Democratic Party secured its power and became the party of the "common man." It controlled the twelve largest cities in six straight presidential elections, where residents rejected the Republicans' message of letting alone. By 1941, there were 10.5 million unionized workers; 31.5 percent of all workers were union members in 1950. In 1936, blacks, who had voted 75 percent Republican in 1929, voted 75 percent Democratic. As Democrats increased public assistance, they fought to remove or reinterpret pauper laws. One-quarter of states still prohibited those unable to support themselves from voting.[64] This new administrative government required a new class of managers and a new kind of lawyer who specialized in regulations and compliance. The number of federal bureaucrats increased from six hundred thousand to one million. From 1929 to 1939, the federal government's share of nonmilitary government spending rose from 30 to 55 percent; local governments' share declined from 57 to 28 percent.

Economic planning extended to liberal foreign policy, where the US refinanced German war repayments (the Young Plan) and initiated a free trade agreement in 1934. Secretary of State Cordell Hull argued that protectionism had brought world war and that international free trade could bring peace. Yet from 1931 to 1937, the US actively protected its investments and trade in East Asia by building a massive navy (and triggering an arms race) to retain its regional hegemony and stifle Japanese advances.[65] The US and Stalin aided China in the 1937 Sino-Japanese War. As conflict over China and in Europe threatened a second global war, Congress placated public concerns by passing several neutrality acts. FDR and Hull resentfully complied while implementing sanctions on Japan and taking action to aid the Allies. Facing opposition from the eight-hundred-thousand-member America First Committee that wanted neutrality, FDR directed a series of maneuvers (cash and carry, destroyers for bases, and Lend-Lease) to "arm and support" the Allies and China with the "arsenal of democracy." It was a de facto declaration of war. FDR had run in 1940 on keeping the nation out of war, so the public was subjected to intense propaganda (much of it Soviet) to justify intervention.[66] Liberals even capitulated to Stalin's demands on federal appointments.[67] Bypassing the State Department, the Treasury Department under Henry Morgenthau Jr. and Harry Hopkins directed an aging FDR throughout the war. Liberals saw a "second opportunity to make the world safe for democracy."[68] The August 1941 Atlantic Charter, signed by FDR and Churchill, was a liberal manifesto for a new world order. It was a pact to avert future wars by free trade and disarming "nations which threaten, or may threaten, aggression outside of their frontiers." The Commission to Study the Organization of Peace rejected obsolete national sovereignty. For the postwar world, Hull designed a United Nations Organization. Private internationalists, led by Clark Eichelberger, formed the Citizens Council for the United Nations, which drew support from business organizations like the Rotary Club to change public opinion by sponsoring radio addresses that pushed for US entry into a future world organization. In May 1943, 74 percent of Americans favored an "international police force."

The Postwar Liberal International Order

Both parties accepted a liberal consensus to oppose the competing ideology of fascism by instituting an international order. Key Republican Arthur Vandenberg was named delegate to the San Francisco UN Charter, which passed the Senate in 1945, 89–2. Popular press celebrated what Albert Einstein called a "One World State." Sponsored by the group World Republic, he preached over the radio that given "weapons of war . . . the only hope for protection lies in the securing of peace in a supernational way. A world government must be created which is able to solve conflicts between nations by judicial decision.... A person or nation can only be considered peace loving if it is ready to cede its military force to the international authorities."[69] The US adopted "global meliorism," a program of rebuilding, reshaping, and bringing "democracy" to the postwar world and so created a new economic and military order.[70]

The 1944 Bretton Woods global financial system launched "embedded liberalism," a compromise between Allied nations that (in the name of global stability) secured their interventions in other states while preventing the industrial chaos fomented by free trade and an international division of labor in their own. Free trade was a tool to undermine other nations' sovereignty. Since Germany's economic self-sufficiency, argued Morgenthau, had brought the war, all nations must become dependent on Allied financing and materials, with the US first among equals or, in the words of Hull, "German economic capacity must be converted in such a manner that it would be so dependent on imports and exports that the country could not by its own devices reconvert to war production."[71] The Army's Decartelization Branch, tasked to break up German cartels, would "convince the German people that economic democracy is a necessary basis for political democracy."[72] The 1947 General Agreement on Tariffs and Trade (GATT) reduced tariffs and trade barriers. By 1950 the US held about 75 percent of the world's monetary stock, establishing the dollar as the world's reserve currency, freely convertible to gold. Claiming a need for international financial stability, the US pushed for global institutions to implement its creditor-oriented rules. Instead of reparations, it would finance balance of payment deficits through the International Monetary Fund and the World Bank, in which US diplomats alone could veto policies not in their national interest. Other countries had to follow the US's trade and investment rules to obtain gold or dollars for their currency backing. The US dominated capital movements and restricted foreign nationalization of natural resources, the public domain, local industry, and banking systems. Growing foreign economies sought exports, followed by liberalization of trade and money, thus the military component of the economic system. As gold poured into the US, the US weakened the dollar with large deficits in military spending, beginning with the 1950 Korean War. Becoming the leader of the free world, the US created a huge military establishment with permanent allies and obligations in Europe and Asia.

Liberals waged unbounded war. They rejected the older conception of autonomous states and thus abandoned the distinction between war against an enemy state's soldiers and its private citizens. Combatants all, they became *enemies of humanity*, justifying Allied bombing of civilian populations, the expulsion of twelve million German civilians from their homes on account of their race, the looting of private property and vital industries, and forced slave labor.[73] German POWs were given over to the French and British for years of forced labor in mines and factories. The Morgenthau Plan, signed by FDR and Churchill, would have stripped Germany bare of industry and turned it into a backward agricultural province that provided serf labor to the Allied powers; it was abandoned only after its details became public. Instead the US Army conducted FDR's plan to punish the German people.[74] To avoid compliance with Hague and Geneva Convention protections, Eisenhower created a new category, "Disarmed Enemy Forces," under which fifty thousand German POWs starved to death in American concentration camps.[75] War now included unconditional surrender followed by the right to alter a conquered people's rulers and customs, their very way of life. To destroy fascist ideology, Congress approved $3 billion to purge militarism in Germany and Japan and turn them into democracies. Said one US War Office film, "We cannot live next to a disease-ridden neighbor.... We must prevent...diseases of the mind, new brands of fascism." Germany was carved into occupation zones, colonies without rule of law. Japan's military was disbanded. Its new constitution, modeled on "New Deal liberalism," also "renounced war as a sovereign right" and pledged to pursue "international peace based on justice and order." Denazification did not work as promised.[76] In practice, it set up large bureaucracies to harass, punish, and starve *at least* two million German civilians (a nation "converted to a starvation prison") while publicly exonerating elites like Leni Riefenstahl and conscripting over seven hundred Nazi scientists for the next war against communism.[77]

While the Soviets wasted little time with farcical legal trials, liberals extended their fictitious idea of domestic *law* to "international law" to justify their management and execution of Axis prisoners. They contradictorily traced their moral authority to brute force. "We sit," said the American judges at Nuremberg, "as a Tribunal drawing its sole power and jurisdiction from the will and command of the four occupying powers."[78] Council No. 10 made crimes of "wars of aggression," "crimes against humanity," and "membership in...a criminal group," which was defined as "membership in a criminal group declared criminal by the International Military Tribunal." Any "accessory" to such crimes was guilty. This assigned collective war guilt to the German people, who were subject to any punishment the Allies should mete, including "deprivation of some or all civil rights," "forfeiture of property," and death. The goal was to level the German social class of capitalists and landowners, which is why industrialists at Flick, IG Farben, and Krupp were indicted.[79] Jettisoning Anglo legal tradition, American lawyers at Nuremberg prosecuted Germans for ex post facto crimes while excluding rules of evidence: defendants were withheld information, access to witnesses, and cross-examinations. Judges denied evidence considered not "relevant" while admitting hearsay and double hearsay against the accused.[80] Disapproving of Justice Robert Jackson's participation in the trials, Chief Justice Harlan Stone called them a "high-grade lynching party" under the "pretense" of "running a court and proceeding according to common law." It was "too sanctimonious a fraud."[81]

The 405,000 American deaths and 671,000 wounded, along with the horrors of World War II, brought a new sacred order. General Eisenhower used an air fleet to bring journalists, congressmen, and churchmen to see the camps. Nazism became synonymous with evil, its supporters inhuman, and the Holocaust a sacrifice that justified the liberal postwar order. The word *fascist* applied to all heretics who questioned liberalism: small businessmen who opposed government regulation, white ethnics who opposed integration, traditionalists who opposed permissive views on sex and the family. While resistance to the war dissipated once the US entered, liberals sought to prevent the revisionism that had discredited World War I. The government funded academics to justify the war and silence prominent anti-intervention scholars.[82] Less prominent Americans were tried for sedition.[83] Whereas Nazi torture focused on race and Soviet torture extracted ridiculous and humiliating open confessions to terrorize the public, liberals preferred indirect character assassination, protracted affairs meant to destroy the defendants' reputation and livelihood. Squeamish about physical torture, they hid it under legal fictions and red tape. Judge Edward Van Roden, appointed to investigate the torture of German prisoners, reported that American "investigators would put a black hood over the accused's head and then punch him in the face with brass knuckles, kick him, and beat him with rubber hose. Many of the German defendants had teeth knocked out. Some had their jaws broken," and many "had been kicked in the testicles beyond repair. This was Standard Operating Procedure with American investigators."[84] Interrogators extracted Germans' confessions with torture and upon threats of destroying their family or handing them over to the Russians. US scientists had already participated in unethical medical experiments, and in Operation Paperclip the US Army and CIA rescued notorious Japanese and Nazi scientists (Shiro Ishii of Unit 731 and Kurt Blome), who had performed horrific experiments on prisoners in concentration camps, to advance their own knowledge of biological weapons. In 1946 the US Army established Camp King to torture and perform experiments on German POWs.

The war never ended for liberals; only their enemy changed. After fascism's defeat, liberals set about undermining the remaining British and French colonial empires and Soviet satellite states. James Burnham, a former Trotskyite who edited William F. Buckley's *National Review* and advocated an elite-run managerial state, warned that America was in a *Struggle for the World* with the Soviets. "A World Government," he wrote in 1947, "would be the best solution to the present crisis," but it would require "political unity."[85] The US must create a new myth to mobilize the West and unify the world, "the doctrine of common humanity and the brotherhood of man." And it must grow out of its naïve isolationist republicanism and use its monopoly over atomic weapons to build a *"democratic world order,"* a "World Empire" (albeit with a nice name like "World Federation"). Despite the ideal world state, political theory lagged in the proper techniques: "the world today is a community as geographically intimate as a county a thousand years ago." He concluded, "The administration of the world, or most of the world, as a single state is now technically possible. There is no longer any insuperable technical obstacle to a degree of integration in armed power, police, courts, finances and economy sufficient to constitute a unified world state." The US must train experts in foreign affairs to enable it to seize power in foreign nations and implement democratic ideals.

The Cold War was a liberal consensus. Truman criticized Stalin for squashing free elections in Poland, canceled lend-lease payments to the Soviets, and blocked Russia's role in governing postwar Japan. To his left, Henry Wallace proposed "fair play" for Russia; to his right, Lippmann (now a conservative) warned that war would force the US to rely at incalculable cost on "satellites, puppets, clients, agents about whom we know very little."[86] Liberals pushed a global ideological struggle, institutionalized in a new military establishment, including the National Security Council and metastasizing CIA. After warnings of Soviet influence in Greece, Turkey, and Iran, Truman promised military aid to nations fighting communism. The CIA used Marshall Plan funding to wage covert war against the Soviets around the world. The Soviet blockade of Berlin was a response to a CIA scheme to change German currency. The US responded with a sensationalized airlift and the first permanent peace alliance, NATO, which quadrupled the defense budget from $12.9 billion to 50 billion. Moral indignation and fear drove the liberals, who accused the USSR of betraying the postwar international consensus. McCarthyism, with its frightful stories of Soviet espionage, was the correlate to liberal internationalism, convincing the American public that intervention in Europe and all over the world was necessary.

The Marshall Plan, denounced by both Wallace and Taft, spent $13 billion to build up a military presence in noncommunist countries. It mostly failed to revitalize war-torn Europe. Support for the so-called Economic Cooperation Act was gained in a hostile Republican Congress by buying it off. The economic planners of a postwar liberal order worked with US corporations and unions to secure billions in corporate welfare and bribes to foreign leaders. US administrators in Europe maintained the ineffective policies of price controls, production quotas, conscription of resources, and rent controls. The plan created a structural adjustment program to encourage the creation of a Eurozone under the influence of Pax Americana. The myth of its success gave rise to another that the US could, with the aid of covert operations, export democracy to Asia and Latin America. Economist Walt Rostow argued that if the US increased investments 5–10 percent in poor countries like Vietnam, it would accelerate the primitive capital accumulation to push them over the communist bump. Only $4 billion could buy sustained economic growth in Asia, the Middle East, Africa, and Latin America. The US signed agreements with thirty-four countries in three years, at an annual cost of $155 million, to sponsor popular movements. It remained unclear whether economic growth would lead to democracy or the other way around: liberals sponsored both—USAID for the former, the CIA for the latter. Sometimes the two met, as when USAID was used to instruct foreign secret police forces in methods of torture.[87] In 1951 the CIA built a "torture house" at Villa Schuster in Kronberg, followed by black sites in Japan, where it tortured and murdered "expendable" prisoners.

Thus liberals birthed the contradiction between idealism and realism. National Security Council Paper NSC 68, which defined US policy for the next forty years, described a world conflict between freedom and slavery. American freedom now depended on the freedom of other peoples, thus its necessary expansion around the globe. Freedom meant resisting appeals to any grand ideology or competing utopian vision (except liberalism). And it required unending guardianship: "For a free society there is never total victory, since freedom and democracy are never wholly attained, are always in the process of being attained." Realism accepted that world hegemony required vast evil. In the words of George F. Kennan, morality could never become "a general criterion for the determination of the behavior of states and above all as a criterion for measuring and comparing the behavior of different states.... Here other criteria, sadder, more limited, more practical, must be allowed to prevail."[88]

The Postwar Liberal Domestic Order

The domestic liberal postwar political order was not inevitable. In 1946, Republicans, on the slogan "Had Enough?", won both houses of Congress. But liberal Republicans, defeating Taft's attempt to downsize the New Deal, forged a "liberal consensus" to institutionalize the administrative state. Liberal Democrats had defended economic regulatory agencies modeled on the NLRB: congressional delegation of lawmaking authority to publish general regulations and issue cease and desist orders to violators in industry given due deference by appellate courts. But criticism had mounted over agencies' unchecked powers, subpar performance, and mediocre appointments. Industries captured the agencies that should have regulated them. Administrative tribunals ignored evidence and reversed the burden of proof. Once appointed, experts were unaccountable, and it was naïve to suppose they were truly detached from partisan or economic interests. Thus, Republicans and southern Democrats argued that agencies should follow a judiciary or prosecutorial model: investigation, hearings, and fact-finding reported to the Department of Justice and adjudicated by an Article III court. They united to pass the 1946 Administrative Procedure Act, which required agency transparency in organization, procedures, and rules, (limited) public participation in the rulemaking process, and uniform standards for formal and informal rulemaking and adjudication to define the scope of judicial review. The "Big Six" regulatory boards continued to handle questions of monopoly, restraint of trade, price-fixing, labor abuse, market entry, and rates. They engaged in "vertical agency surveillance," dealing with only a few industrial managers and establishing clientele relations with industry. Their main sanctions were disapproval and cease and desist orders. In trial-like hearings, they issued yes or no verdicts in accordance with their formal rules. The following year Congress passed Taft-Hartley to weaken the NLRB's mandate for closed shops. Even UAW President Walter Reuther agreed with the act's anti-communist provisions.

In what Berle called the American Economic Republic, Congress created the institutions of state capitalism, the 1946 Council of Economic Advisors, Joint Economic Committee, and Bureau of the Budget, which worked with regulatory agencies to coordinate economic policy in the separate branches. It prioritized government control over industry by breaking up domestic and international business concentrations. The fight against cartels as promoting fascism was intensified by the discovery, after the bombing of Pearl Harbor, that Standard Oil had secretly agreed to stay out of the chemical business, including producing synthetic rubber, if IG Farben stayed out of oil in foreign markets. The US experienced a rubber shortage and had to accelerate synthetic rubber development. The DOJ convicted Standard Oil and six subsidiaries, along with many executives, for criminal conspiracy to restrict trade. It continued a vigorous antitrust policy against mergers between large corporations for decades. The Supreme Court upheld the prohibition of mergers even where there was little threat of monopoly.[89]

Liberalism rose to ascendancy in the 1948 presidential campaign. Moderate Republicans, supporting Thomas Dewey, sacrificed their conservative wing as the "radical right." In the Democratic Party, liberals combatted progressive Henry Wallace, who lambasted "lukewarm liberals" for turning away from economic redistribution and toward a corporate-friendly warfare state. Cold War policy, he said, had heightened tensions with the Soviet Union. He ran on a platform of full civil rights, against military expenditures in the Truman Doctrine and Marshall Plan, and for a new world order secured by an international police force. He accused the "party of war" and "the Wall Street–military team" for betraying its commitment to new economic rights, including universal health care. Defeated in the primary, Wallace formed a Progressive Party ticket endorsed by the Communist Party. His defeat marked the beginning of the Democrats' war on communism, both in the party and public office. The House Un-American Activities Committee hounded progressives and communists in public trials, and Truman required loyalty oaths for federal workers. Over one hundred college professors lost their jobs or were denied tenure for their communist affiliations; the Supreme Court in *Dennis v. United States* (1951) upheld the Smith Act, which required the registration of Communist Party members.

The manifesto of postwar liberalism, Arthur Schlesinger Jr.'s 1949 *Vital Center*, presented a horseshoe model in which liberalism, in its rejection of absolutes, marked the vital center between opposing socialist and fascist dogmas, which meet at the opposite center in totalitarian government. Economic liberalism was "democratic, regulated capitalism—the mixed society."[90] Liberals would cautiously effect "piecemeal" changes that would not "disrupt the fabric of custom, law, and mutual confidence upon which personal rights depend." In pluralistic management of interest groups, liberals claimed they prevented business, the most powerful group, from destroying itself by its own greed. The welfare state was the best weapon in the Cold War. It smothered the ideological fires of the right and left by both eliminating the instability of the business cycle and peaceably redistributing wealth. Sociologists and political scientists proclaimed "The End of Ideology" and the "exhaustion of political ideas" in the West (both capitalist and socialist), and they warned their readers about the peddlers of dogmatic systems.[91] As Eric Hoffer wrote in his 1951 bestselling *The True Believer*, these mass movements were sparked by failures, men of low self-esteem who "use the slime of frustrated souls as mortar in the building of a new world."[92] Liberalism, the antithesis of mass man and mass movements, was "intolerable for the true believers."[93] Ensconced in academia, liberals wrote histories in which America was pragmatic from its conception. The "continual, potential threat to liberalism" was millennialist faith, which "often hides behind a rationalist façade."[94] In his 1962 Yale University address, John F. Kennedy later preached Schlesinger's words: "The central domestic issues of our time...relate not to basic clashes of philosophy or ideology but to ways and means of reaching common goals—to research for sophisticated solutions to complex and obstinate issues." In "economic decisions" America did not need "grand warfare of rival ideologies which will sweep the country with passion, but the practical management of a modern economy."

Eisenhower, a Republican, cemented the liberal consensus. Making peace with the New Deal, his "dynamic conservatism" combined fiscal responsibility and anti-communism with expanding social security. He appointed businessmen to his cabinet and built a new base of suburban support. Returning war veterans and the northern migration of hundreds of thousands of black workers fueled a housing demand. Borrowing a twenty-seven-step mass production model from the navy Seabees, Abraham Levitt created the model suburb of Levittown on Long Island. Twenty million Americans, subsidized by FHA loans and the 1944 GI Bill, trekked to the suburbs, whose population equaled that of the cities by 1960. Federally financed slum-clearance, urban renewal, and development aided the expansion. Governments built more than eight hundred thousand public housing units in sprawling ghettoes like Chicago's Cabrini-Green. In what E. Michael Jones has called "ethnic cleansing,"[95] the FHA barred blacks from loans and pushed them into white ethnic neighborhoods, from which Irish, Italian, and Polish residents fled. Stripped of their traditions, they became "middle class." The GI Bill sent a record number of students to college, creating a new managerial class. While income distribution did not change, the economy boomed. Civilian wages rose 29 percent, with increased savings. As adolescents filled vacated cashier and food service jobs, businesses marketed products to youth, teenyboppers with extra spending money for clothes and records. To get his suburbanites to work, and fast, Eisenhower claimed that national defense required a highway system, which birthed entire industries in motels, fast food (Jack in the Box, 1951; Kentucky Fried Chicken, 1952; Burger King, 1954; McDonalds, 1955; Taco Bell, 1962), and frozen "TV dinners" (Swanson, 1950). The American Heart Association and margarine companies preached the goodness of margarine and other trans-fat products over butter and saturated fats as well as the starch-heavy food pyramid. Sugar consumption skyrocketed. As an alternative to high-cost sugar, high-fructose corn syrup was invented in 1957. An industry of drugs helped Americans' focus on tasks in office work. "Since the war," noted *Time* magazine in 1951, "the coffee break has been written into union contracts."[96] By 1955, almost one-quarter of women and more than half of men were "active smokers"; annual per capita cigarette consumption had risen from 54 in 1900 to 4,345 in 1963.

American morality during the 1950s, its "Happy Days," was that of the "permissive society." Divorces and separations spiked during and after the war. Nonsupport and desertion were higher than believed, though low compared to today's numbers: the 1960 census reported eighty-one million married, three million divorced, and five million separated. Desertion, the "poor man's divorce," was reported a crisis. Always high among blacks, it had increased among whites in the "professional classes," with 44 percent of cases.[97] Thomas Monahan of the Philadelphia Municipal Court reported that separation and desertion constituted between 5 and 10 percent of married couples.[98] In 1948, New York state devised a way to collect the earnings of fugitive husbands. States could mutually enforce husbands' financial support, making extradition for nonsupport unnecessary. Local courts affirmed support orders against the father or husband in his state of residence. Seeing the opportunity to ease public spending for dependent women and children, from 1952 to 1957 all states enacted laws based on the Uniform Reciprocal Support Law. By 1958 the divorce rate (21 percent), family desertion, and nonsupport had leveled off (and in some places declined).[99] In 1963 illegitimacy was 3.1 percent among whites and 24.2 percent among blacks. Liberals had instituted what Max Rheinstein called the "democratic compromise," in which fault for divorce was seldom genuinely proven in court but attempting to do so was an effective inconvenience.[100] Lawyers advised clients on how to collude with their spouses to produce evidence for fault. Accepting the legal penalties for guilt, the misbehaving party agreed to arrange photographs with a third party as proof or spouses pled "cruelty," the basis for 60 percent of all divorce cases. The compromise both discouraged divorce by making it more difficult and rewarded fidelity by making the unfaithful party pay.

Addicted to television, families gathered around the tube over TV dinners to watch ideal families interact. Shows like *I Love Lucy* and *Leave It to Beaver* depicted the "democratic" family model, in which women maintained their domestic roles but with greater power and status. Television introduced interracial marriages and challenged religious prejudice. In 1955 there were more than forty shows featuring pioneers and cowboys; in 1957 Westerns were one-third of prime time shows. Advertising soared with the increase in discretionary income (from $40 billion in the 1940s to $100 billion). Walt Disney's rendition of *Davy Crockett* drove up the price of coonskin (ten million caps sold). Competing against TV, big-budget films mythologized the war and promoted a new war against communism while subtly warning about McCarthyism. On screen, American icon John Wayne embodied liberal realism: a rugged individualist who saw the need for "a welfare work program" and a loner removed from civilization who introduced order by violence. Off screen, he was an outspoken anti-communist who helped to blacklist writers, a thrice-married Christian who stood for family values, and a man of three Hispanic wives who said, "I believe in white supremacy until the blacks are educated to a point of responsibility." Wayne was a self-proclaimed liberal who criticized irresponsible liberals—permissivity with limits. "Healthy, lusty sex is wonderful," he told *Playboy*, but *Midnight Cowboy* was just "a story about two fags."[101] In 1957 he reprimanded Kirk Douglas at a party for agreeing to play Vincent van Gogh. "We got to play strong, tough characters. Not these weak queers."[102]

Rising secularism *and* religious identification defined religion in the 1950s. In the universities, the older faith waned as science replaced it, yet religion peaked in culture (with 68 percent church attendance in 1960).[103] In a second deal with the devil, religious leaders joined the elite by redefining their traditions in liberal terms. Ministers compromised on dogma in ecumenical and psychological platitudes. Norman Vincent Peale's *The Power of Positive Thinking*, based on the ideas of psychoanalyst Smiley Blanton, remained on the bestseller list for 186 consecutive weeks. Priests, rabbis, and pastors seeking credentials in pastoral counseling baptized methods of secular psychology, borrowing psychoanalysis and the new client-centered therapy as neutral tools. In truth their aim, "normality," was an alternative moral standard. They traded the "doorbell image" of pastoral visitation and exhortation for the "interview image" borrowed from "clinical psychology."[104] Protestantism and Catholicism, formerly *Christendom*, became "Judeo-Christianity," a new identity opposite Soviet atheistic communism. Congress added "under God" to the pledge of allegiance in 1954, and millions in Christian organizations, such as Reverend Carl McIntire's American Council of Christian Churches (1.5 million members) and the National Association of Evangelicals (growing from one million in

1945 to ten million in 1952), supported elements of the postwar order and its interventions against communism.

In the "triple melting pot" theory, noted Will Herberg in his book *Protestant, Catholic, Jew*, immigrant whites from distant villages had assimilated into a "great community" of three religions.[105] In this new social structure, the Anglo-Saxon type remained the "American ideal"; others transmuted into it. Protestants (66 percent of the population) were disproportionately rural, but most resembled the average American. Jews (3.5 percent) were urban, highly educated, and wealthy (almost none were working class). Catholics (26.5 percent) were largely urban and working class. Each played a role in the liberal order. Educated urban and suburban WASPs, formerly an exclusive lot, celebrated their Christ-like sacrifice in denouncing Anglo-centrism (likened to Nazi racism) to usher in a diverse society. They leaned toward pro-business policies, begrudgingly conceded to unionism, and denounced southerners as racists and small businessmen as fascists. Safe in the suburbs, they used urban blight to appropriate city property for administrators while bisecting Catholic Irish, Polish, and Italian neighborhoods with highways and integrating them with blacks.[106] Catholics, representing unionized laborers, pushed for economic social justice, while Jews became the face of racial social justice.[107] Placing Holocaust victimhood at the center their identity, Jews celebrated ethnocentric exclusivity, opposing interracial marriage for themselves but demanding it for others, resurrecting forgotten religious rituals, and promoting compensatory treatment for racism.[108] Jewish interest groups abandoned socialism to combine support for an ethnostate of Israel (supported by evangelical Protestants) with non-assimilation at home.[109] In numerous court cases, liberals excised Christian prayer and symbols from schools and public life, replacing it with a common faith in a new international order.

Considering citizenship, liberals called the US "a nation of immigrants."[110] The presence of diverse ethnic and religious groups in American history was an underwhelming fact, but liberals celebrated pluralism as its *goal*, America's founding and *essence*. In 1951 Oscar Handlin rejected a distinction between settlers and immigrants, writing in his popular book *The Uprooted*, "Once I thought to write a history of the immigrants in America. Then I discovered that the immigrants *were* American history."[111] The US had a duty to import refugees from communism: the president's 1952 Commission of Immigration and Naturalization stated the "belief that the United States had not yet fulfilled its obligations to suffering humanity." Aside from the four hundred thousand Europeans brought to the US under the displaced persons program, "existing emergencies abroad demanded further efforts on behalf of refugees, expellees, escapees, remaining displaced persons, relatives of those who had reached safety in the United States, and other categories of people whose living conditions and constant dangers are a reproach to our civilization."[112]

Qualitative Liberalism and the Great Society

Eisenhower so successfully coopted institutions for liberalism that conservatism afterward meant conserving liberalism. Liberal intellectuals chafed at their loss of status. Mocked as eggheads, they embraced the term in opposition to an ungrateful, consumerist middle class. They became bitter and cynical even as they, in the words of liberal Harvey Breit, "loafed on beaches and in television rooms. How sad for most of us."[113] Needing to distinguish themselves from Republicans, Democrats embraced a new "qualitative" liberalism. Keynesian popularizer John Kenneth Galbraith argued that the old questions of economic inequality and insecurity lacked meaning in a post-scarcity society. Liberals had rendered the capitalist business cycle obsolete. The Phillips Curve, which represented the New Economics, a political commitment to economic expansion, inversely related the rate of inflation to unemployment. The government could use fiscal policy to maintain high levels of demand to continue high sales volume, business investment, and profits. If the economy slowed, the central bank would print more money, raising prices and lowering unemployment. The *new problem* was that of the "affluent society": Americans had lost a sense of purpose because they accumulated money for private consumption. The solution was a greater role for government: spending tax dollars on public projects that would renew the sense of national purpose. Qualitative liberals promised to create large government programs that would finally achieve, with the aid of science, a color-blind society, the end of poverty, and a peaceful international order.

While the FEPCs were viewed as weak, civil rights groups' criticism faded after 1950 as blacks made vast economic and social gains. From 1940 to 1960, the percentage of blacks living in poverty fell from 87 to 47 percent. Blacks made gains in labor unions, constituting 20–30 percent of automotive workers in Detroit. At the Dodge assembly plant, black workers constituted an estimated 60 percent of the work force.[114] Blacks took industrial jobs in cities like Chicago, whose black population rose 77 percent during the 1940s and another 65 percent in the 1950s (an increase from 278,000 to 813,000). Non-white median annual income had risen faster than that of whites, almost quadrupling from 1939 to 1951, a fact not lost on American business, which estimated a black market of $15 billion.[115] The dramatic rise of the "black bourgeois" correlated to the institution of the black church and its class stratification. The largest denomination was the six-million-member National Baptist Convention. Its president, Joseph H. Jackson of Chicago's Olivet Baptist Church, argued that civil rights meant celebrating American ideals, thus *civil obedience*, or legal change. He, along with black congressman William Dawson, supported Richard Daley's Democratic machine and its pluralistic compromise with community leaders and vote hustlers to peacefully separate races into ethnic enclaves.[116] Chicago's "Silent Six" black aldermen opposed integrated housing. But civil rights had been a part of both parties' platforms for years, and liberals claimed that science proved racial equality (even where scientists argued that the data did not).[117] A change took place with *Brown v. Board of Education* in 1954, which mandated desegregation of elementary schools. Instead of overturning *Plessy* and mandating a color-blind policy, the Court, allowing states to delay implementation, subordinated the injunctive relief of the individual to the progress of the group. In the 1957 recession, black income fell and unemployment rose to twice that of whites; without union seniority, black employees were laid off first. If racial equality required integration, civil rights advocates began to argue, there was a need for group rights, for disparate treatment. Just as the courts had recognized group labor rights, they must apply "benign" or "benevolent" quotas for blacks.[118]

While Keynesian economists celebrated the expansion of the economic pie, liberals niggled over the size of the pieces. Michael Harrington, who worked among the poor, argued for their moral reform—hard work, frugality, and sexual restraint would accompany economic reform—and, politically, he attacked the barriers that impeded assimilation to the middle class. His 1962 book *The Other America*, which "sparked the War on Poverty," revealed that the poor, especially blacks, had an entirely different culture that shaped their perceptions and choices. The failure to assimilate blacks caused "profound institutionalized and abiding wrong that white America has worked on the Negro for so long."[119] Unemployment led to "mass enforced idleness." Denied assimilation, blacks turned to the "commotions" of religion and demagogic politics, which pandered to "the laughing, child-like, pleasure-loving Negro who must be patronized and taken care of as a child." The greatest discrimination was not legal but psychological. White stereotypes colored "the 'natural' character of the Negro: lazy, shiftless, irresponsible." The "pessimism" of the poor led to an inferior "personality of poverty": "the fact that they do not postpone satisfactions, that they do not save. When pleasure is available, they tend to take it immediately." As part of the "massive action against the culture of poverty," Harrington recommended reforms in housing, education, medical care, and a restoration of the nuclear family. Gunnar Myrdal famously argued that America could only achieve racial equality when blacks adopted middle-class virtues, which correlated with socioeconomic advancement. Assuming that "American culture is 'highest' in the pragmatic sense," he wrote, "it is to the advantage of American Negroes as individuals and as a group to become assimilated into American culture, to acquire the traits held in esteem by the dominant white Americans."[120]

Qualitative liberalism included escalating the Cold War. JFK's exhortation to "bear any burden...because it is right" turned the Third World into a battleground for "freedom," whether using the new Green Berets or the new Peace Corps. He sent military advisors to South Vietnam and increased foreign aid from $2.7 to $3.6 billion. Having refused to sign the Geneva Accords in 1954, the NSC planned to create "a viable and increasingly stable democratic society." The US backed Ngo Dinh Diem all the while threatening him to reform or else face "unpredictable consequences," like his assassination in November 1963. A series of failed puppet dictators led to direct US involvement. Mocking the old military establishment, Robert McNamara promised an efficient "social scientists" war, where experts would "model" South Vietnam using computer simulations. Vietnam was the first war the US fought not to win but to buy time to implement civilian social programs. Counterinsurgency or "grand tactics" borrowed from colonial empires spearheaded military objectives. The CIA and USAID were simultaneously charged with building South Vietnam's economy and winning over its people.

Lyndon B. Johnson carried out liberal foreign policy with gusto. He compared Vietnam to the Alamo. But he was full of bluster. Fearing traditional war, he opted in March 1965 to carpet bomb the Vietnamese into submission. A meliorist, he promised to export the Great Society to Vietnam: "Our foreign policy must always be an extension of our domestic policy." He had a grand vision of uniting the countries of Southeast Asia in a cooperative developmental effort. He asked Congress for $1 billion to enrich the lives and educations of one hundred million people—to bring the war on poverty to Asia.

The Mekong River economic development program was compared to the TVA: "Old Ho," he said, "can't turn this down!" The social scientists tallied irrelevant statistics: supposedly pacified villages, body counts, rice yields, and school attendance. According to one US Marine Corps Special Film, "Our success with the military action of patrol and ambush backed up by an expansive civic action program continues to win the trust of the people in Vietnam." At the 1966 summit in Hawaii, LBJ pushed for victory not just over aggression but also hunger, disease, and despair: "Have you built democracy in the rural areas?" It would be a "social revolution" for "free self-government." But his assumption that development would bring peace was flawed: the US military, which fed inflation and anti-Americanism, actually hindered economic growth, and South Vietnam never came close to becoming a self-sufficient state. When America left in 1973, the economy collapsed, followed by the fall of the country two years later.

In the wake of JFK's domestic New Frontier, in 1964 LBJ proposed a Great Society, one "where the meaning of our lives matches the marvelous products of our labor." It would bring equal opportunity for all, black and white, rich and poor, to every area of the nation: classrooms, countryside, and city. It promised beauty and purpose to every life, free from boredom and full of opportunities for self-realization. Northern Democrats and Republicans compromised to punish the Jim Crow South with the 1964 Civil Rights Act, which prohibited discrimination for reasons of race, color, religion, sex, and national origin. Sixty-eight percent of northern whites supported civil rights initiatives to end segregation without mandating racial quotas. The federal government already hired a disproportionately larger number of blacks than whites, and unions already integrated blacks without violating whites' promotions under the seniority system. But under the new law, the Office of Federal Contract Compliance mandated "affirmative action" policies for all federal contractors. Title VI created the Office of Civil Rights in executive departments to oversee discrimination claims for all government contractors. It delegated agencies the power to issue "rules, regulations, or orders of general applicability" to delineate discriminatory behavior with the power to terminate money to any particular program. Title VII created an Equal Employment Opportunity Commission (EEOC), modeled on the state FEPCs, to hear individual complaints of discrimination against private employers. It would investigate and write letters recommending conciliation to the offending company, which would then have to document its practices. If the company refused arbitration, then the EEOC could refer the case to the DOJ, which could prosecute. To prohibit racial quotas—Hubert Humphrey promised to eat any of the bill's pages that sanctioned them—Section 703(h) approved impartial employer hiring tests, even ones that led to disproportionate hiring outcomes; 703(j) explicitly banned, and many legislators denounced, any attempt at racial balancing as itself reverse discrimination in "violation of title VII"; 706(g) required showing intent to discriminate and not just statistical proportions. And quotas had been rejected by civil rights leaders and the courts.[121] Moreover, the administrative process under the Administrative Procedure Act constrained rulemaking in the new agencies.

The 1964 CRA was the culmination of the liberals' assault on private freedoms in business and association to deracinate illiberal opinions on race. The right of private association by definition must allow one to exclude, but now under the commerce clause, Congress moved beyond citizens' rights to public accommodations to prohibit discrimination in all private business. Most liberals mistakenly assumed that the bureaucrats administering the bill would respect the legal stops they included, yet the liberals' own changes in the theory of law, marked by pragmatic balances, would undercut this position. Activists had already marked other areas of private right for regulation. Will Maslow, General Counsel of the American Jewish Congress, argued, "the discrimination attacked by the [NAACP] has largely been governmental action—the acts of school boards, of jury commissioners, of state legislatures. The anti-Semitism that vexes the Jew...is that of private groups, or personnel managers, resort owners, admissions committees, or rabble-rousers, almost entirely nongovernmental and hence not subject to the majestic provisions of the Fifth and Fourteenth Amendments. Although these may be 'private governments' in the power they wield...their acts do not fall within the accepted categories of legal wrongs. Before these groups can be sued, *new laws have to be created making their conduct unlawful.*"[122]

The "unconditional war on poverty" began by defining poverty as the bottom 20 percent of the population, whose elimination was a statistical impossibility. Fighting poverty had little to do with providing basic needs in an industrial society. LBJ's advisors knew this, but they found it quite easy to justify any program so long as the economy was strong. The broad Economic Opportunity Act (1964) funded programs like Volunteers in Service to America (sending young people to do service in the cities), Job Corps (training the poor with basic job skills), Community Action Programs (local agencies created to administer federal money with the goal of empowering the poor), and Head Start (preschool for low-income children). It had an abysmal record. In Job Corps, by 1965 three hundred thousand people applied for ten thousand slots. Young applicants were bussed 1,200 miles from home to learn basic job skills. Costs exceeded $8,000 per student. In its first decade, two-thirds of enrollees quit. After six months, 28 percent of graduates were unemployed; only one-third had jobs related to their training. It was unrealistic to take poorly educated youth and train them for good jobs. Courses prepared students for unskilled entry-level positions, where a large pool of applicants already existed. In the greatest of all programs to defeat poverty, LBJ signed the Social Security Amendments of 1965, creating Medicare and Medicaid to provide health insurance for the elderly and poor. These programs were more popular but, as we shall see, far more pernicious in long-term costs.

The Great Society in the cities, country, and classrooms was a liberal windfall. Members of Congress used programs such as the $2 billion Appalachian Regional Development Act (1965) and Urban

Renewal for graft. The Demonstration Cities and Metropolitan Development Act (1966) promised to abolish ghettoes, improve urban transportation and landscaping, plant parks, and provide other urban amenities. Cities jumped at the free money. The 1968 Fair Housing Act was a "Magna Carta to liberate our Cities." It authorized 1.7 million subsidized housing units over the next three years. Section 235 of the bill provided FHA bank loans for low-income buyers. Section 236 increased the supply of rental housing to the needy. The Brooke Amendment (1969) later mandated that low-income families pay no more than 25 percent of their income for rent. The Great Society in the countryside was spurred by Rachel Carson's bestselling *Silent Spring* (1962), which warned of the effects of pesticides on animals (spring was silent because the birds had all been poisoned) and humans. The Wilderness Act (1964) allowed only a "Minimal human imprint" in wilderness areas, which would be controlled by four federal agencies. The act banned development in more than nine million acres of public domain. The act's uniqueness was not conservation but its explicitly religious language—nature "untrammeled by man" was a good in itself.

In the classroom, the Higher Education Act of 1965 aimed to "strengthen the educational resources of our colleges and universities and to provide financial assistance for students in postsecondary and higher education." It increased federal university funding, scholarships, low-interest loans, and "financial assistance" to students (Title IV). It established a National Teacher Corps and Upward Bound, which provided individual grants to low-income high school students to attend college. The Child Nutrition Act (1966) appropriated monies for state milk, breakfast, and student lunch programs. The most extensive federal statute affecting education was the 1965 Elementary and Secondary Education Act; it has been, under various names, reauthorized every five years since. Its $1.3 billion to fund elementary and secondary education emphasized equal access and established accountability standards. It funded professional development, instructional materials, and resources for educational programs. Education in its highest sense meant enriching the soul with culture. To free children from corrupting corporate influence, Congress created a National Endowment for the Humanities, National Endowment for the Arts, and the Corporation for Public Broadcasting (PBS/NPR).

The 1965 Immigration and Nationality Act had the greatest consequences. LBJ proclaimed that it overcame the "the twin barriers of prejudice and privilege."[123] It rejected the "harsh injustice of the national origins quota system" that entitled 70 percent of immigrant visas to residents from three countries: Ireland, Germany, and the United Kingdom. Abandoning the logic of cultural unity necessary for republican government for that of balancing plural interests, it gave priority to families, not nationalities, with the rhetoric that it would preserve the present citizenry's makeup—"more Italians, Greeks, Poles."[124] In a twisted logic, LBJ declared that because soldiers dying in Vietnam "were all Americans," their difference in origin must be celebrated as a unifying strength: "Our beautiful America was built by a nation of strangers.... The land flourished because it was...nourished by so many cultures and traditions and peoples." The bill indeed initially brought more Greeks and Poles but soon almost exclusively Asians and Latin Americans. But this was what the Jewish lobbying groups and sponsors had long had in mind, a "cultural pluralism" that discriminated against northwestern European immigrants to weaken the Anglo majority.[125] On the one hand, their goal was "inclusion in a pluralist democracy that would value Jewish participation and protect the rights of its minority citizens."[126] But on the other hand, adds David Verbeeten, "In this sought-after, end-of-history, pluralist America...the locus of accommodation was not conceived as the Jewish community, but the Anglo Protestant or white Christian majority, which was required...to suppress its own hegemony, out of a sense of 'obligation and guilt,' so as to make way for the cultural expression or ethnic assertion of various minorities."[127]

The Great Society was the climax of the liberal welfare-warfare state. With total fiscal spending in 1969 at $183.6 billion, spending on education increased from $1.5 billion (1963) to $8.6 billion, on health from $2.6 to $12.1 billion, on defense from $52 billion to $83 billion, and on "income security" from $9.3 to $23 billion. From 1964 to 1970, federal transfer payments for social insurance and public assistance programs more than doubled from $24 to $52 billion. In 1971, the federal government for the first time spent more on welfare than on defense. From 1949 to 1979, total housing, education, and welfare spending rose from $10.6 to $259 billion (more than one-half of the budget, and 11.5 percent of GNP) even as defense spending rose from $11.5 to $114.5 billion (4.5 percent of GNP). The liberals had not just increased the debt but initiated a new policy of permanent debt financing (there were no balanced budgets from 1970 to 1979). They concealed those deficits with the unified budget, in which the government loaned payroll surpluses to itself to spend on the discretionary side of the budget.

Liberalism's implosion forms the subject of the next two chapters. Angered by liberal hypocrisy on race, class, sex, and foreign war and faced with the financial crisis of the welfare-warfare state, a generation of young elites, both *radicals* (chapter 4) in the liberal arts and bureaucracy as well as *neoliberals* in finance and technology (chapter 5) challenged the liberal regime of scientific adjustment and economic planning. They rejected the middle-class mores and economic policies that had secured the liberal democratic order.

4

===

RADICALISM

The liberals' promises for a color-blind society, the end of poverty, sex fulfillment, and a peaceful international order divided their coalition along class lines. The identity politics of the "New Left," a phrase coined by sociologist C. Wright Mills in 1960, challenged the liberal consensus and the old middle class. The 1960s radicals who broke with liberalism had an alternative conception of human flourishing and effected institutional changes to achieve it. They created a new constituency of identity groups, directing their loyalty against the old American nation and toward the distant project of a global order. In many academic fields, radicals exposed the hypocrisy and failures of the 1950s political order and its claims to scientific authority, which, they argued, perpetuated the very evils it claimed to remedy. They pushed an identity politics of race and gender to uproot the traditional institutions of family and private association.

The Radical Critique

World War II, the period of liberalism's triumph, ironically set the stage for its collapse. Plagued by knowledge that the world's most scientifically advanced nations descended into genocidal barbarism and living under the shadow of nuclear war, philosophers began clearing the old ground. Almost as a rite of passage, thinkers wrote critiques of Dewey and pragmatism. Liberals had proudly rejected all absolutes, yet the four hundred thousand American deaths in the war had required, they claimed, a "fighting faith." *In what* was unclear. The Office of War Information's research of army draftees showed that "fewer than a tenth of the men surveyed in August 1942 had a 'consistent, favorable, intellectual orientation toward the war.'... Over a third of a 3,000-man army sample had never heard of [the Four Freedoms] and only 13 percent could name three or four of them."[1] Moreover, modern science, defined as constructing tentative hypotheses for action, uprooted its European, Christian foundations that sought permanent truth. Scientists were now knowledge pimps who peddled their wares to the highest bidder. Outside of a few stalwarts like Sidney Hook and Ernest Nagel, who argued that the rejection of pragmatism was a new "failure of nerve," liberalism was philosophically bankrupt by 1950. For Morton White it was "the end of an era.... These are days in which Dewey's views are being replaced by Kierkegaard's in places where once Dewey was king."[2] Vernon Parrington had noted, "Liberals whose hair is growing thin...are likely to find themselves today in the unhappy predicament of being treated as mourners at their own funerals."[3] Émigrés from Nazi Germany oddly led attacks against liberalism. They often felt ambivalent about the US. Preoccupied with the collapse of Weimar's liberal democracy into fascism and disdainful of vulgar American culture, they warned of the crisis of "modernity": relativistic liberal democracies could not sustain themselves, and thus they decayed into totalitarianism.

Criticisms of liberalism began with its fundamental philosophy. Despite Dewey's attempt to preserve social criticism in philosophy, the dominant analytic philosophy proceeded in imitation of the natural sciences, stressing logical and linguistic analysis, syntax and semantics, and scorning the old questions of justice as topics for therapy. But few liberals had Dewey's or Freud's intelligence. Many openly praised relativism, even taking an absurd pride in the indefensibility of their moral opinions, which they viewed as a sign of maturity. Liberals were thus the first to be chewed up by totalitarian regimes. Some suggested that faithless grown-ups should not reveal relativism to commoners who needed their religious myths. But even so, they encountered the rhetorical problem: If all politics were systemic, even theological, in forwarding a teaching of justice, then anti-systemic thinking would ever require an exoteric gloss, a logical defense of moral and political systems. Liberals themselves taught faith in democracy, which permeated their behavior outside the lab, but it now seemed a blind hope in an atomic future in which scientific management would subvert democracy itself.

German philosopher (and Nazi sympathizer) Martin Heidegger's phenomenology challenged the liberals' claim that metaphysics had died. Humans, he argued, are temporal animals, born into and perceiving objects through a tradition, against which they can know themselves. If one confronted this authoritative tradition, then he could know the very structures of being, a primordial way of experiencing that revealed the possibility for an authentically human way of life.[4] Liberals who rejected essences outside of time really smuggled it back in via their own dehumanizing technological worldview, which presented all nature, including man, as objects for scientific manipulation or "standing reserve."[5] By its logic, all thought could be reduced to calculation. Technology uprooted peoples from tradition and subjected them to greater control, and thus it threatened to annihilate meditative thinking. The US and USSR were both liberal, or metaphysically the same, and while Nazism had begun as a traditionalist movement, it too had assimilated technology in its attempt to win the war. "Only a God can save us now," said Heidegger; the philosopher must turn to poetry and develop a new language, the sprouts of tradition that could form a true culture. In American universities William Barrett, Marjorie Grene, Walter Kaufmann, and Hubert Dreyfus popularized existentialism, challenging scientific authority. Barrett's *Irrational Man*, assigned as a college text, pointed out that scientists unquestioningly adopted an authoritative moral code. In Dewey's thought, "man [is] essentially *homo faber*, the technological animal. This belief is still a supreme article of the American faith."[6] Grene called Dewey's pragmatism a "new dogmatism, less precise in outline but just as dogmatic as those it replaces."[7] Feeling inferior, humanities professors had abandoned a useful holistic philosophy to imitate the quantitative physical sciences; social science departments had become knowledge factories cranking out useless information. But in an urgent time, when atomic war could vaporize human life, ethical decisions could not wait on the slow scientific accumulation of evidence. Barrett said that liberals diagnosed existentialism as psychological morbidity, but they failed to recognize that it expressed a failed, morbid liberal society. Appealing to the ancient Greek conception of philosophy as "a passionate way of life," existentialists returned to "great questions" of anxiety in the face of death, the essence of justice, the origin of evil, and the good life. Man's confrontation with nothingness was a prerequisite to his decisions about technology's use that threatened to objectify, even destroy, the world and himself.

The Frankfurt School, which included polymath Marxists Max Horkheimer, Theodor Adorno, Herbert Marcuse, and Erich Fromm, critiqued liberalism from the perspective of social justice. State capitalism, they argued, used technological language and logic to aid an oppressive ruling class. It had even absorbed Marxism, now an abstract Western orthodoxy used to justify Stalin's tyranny in the USSR. All wrote critiques of Dewey. Pragmatism, said Horkheimer and Adorno, was mere scientific positivism, which, distinguishing facts from values, could no longer question its own ends and unreflectively offered obedience to power.[8] The scientific promise to predict and control nature necessarily turned the world into a laboratory, where scientists manipulated humans at tyrants' bidding. Scientific rationality had become a myth, in which reason was equated with authority, thereby losing its critical function.[9] Dewey's assault on a priori ideas, wrote Marcuse, had a priori foreclosed the inquiry into universals such as justice. By denying systemic oppressions in order to focus on particular grievances to be solved by experts, the scientific method became a religious ritual confirming unwarranted assumptions and impeding systemic change. Dewey, said Marcuse, had "cover[ed] up the chasm between 'empirical values' and Reason."[10] The Frankfurt School's "critical theory" sought to revive reason's critical activity by inquiring into liberalism's unquestioned dogmas that both undergirded the positive sciences and defended the status quo. Recovering dialectical thought, in which the identity of an individual and a society is inseparable from its *other* (that which it is not), it would uncover the contradictions between historical societies and their normative claims.[11] As the culmination of Western philosophy, liberalism imposed a "logic of domination," positing "laws of thought" as "techniques of calculation and manipulation."[12] Despite their promise of liberation, scientists sought to conquer nature, both human and physical, by subduing human pleasure and the environment. It brought neither equality nor freedom. Western reason universalized white males and justified the oppression of their other, women and minorities. Adorno uncovered a systemically racist, patriarchal society, the genesis of the fascist personality that used technology to oppress and not liberate.[13]

Psychologists rejected the liberal view that individuals were infinitely malleable and could be adjusted to any system. Liberal "adjustment" meant personal deformation that rejected human nature.[14] Obsessed with conformity, the liberal mind was calculating, consumerist, or neurotic at best and at worst a fascist personality: racist, sexually repressed, and obedient to state authority. The nation state provided not an identity but an anti-identity. In his bestselling *Growing Up Absurd*, Paul Goodman argued that liberalism lacked conditions for human growth: students molded as acquisitive cogs for the materialist machine; families uprooted from community and isolated in the suburbs; emasculated men flipping hamburgers; caged housewives hiding whiskey in laundry hampers. Americans worked all day and, too exhausted to get frisky, zoned out to the TV; their erogenous zones were mechanized to crank out both widgets and children in boring monogamous marriages. The new Third Force Psychology studied questions of man's identity and completion: Erik Erikson's Life Cycle, Carl Rogers's Person-Centered Therapy, Maslow's Hierarchy of Needs. Maslow wrote, "It is possible to study this inner nature scientifically and to discover what it is like—not invent—discover."[15] Leading psychologists and cultural icons adopted Wilhelm Reich's Freudo-Marxism, which sought to create a society without repression. Reich had called morality a "sickness in which the person has to act according to the criteria of an established norm outside himself," an "insoluble conflict between instinctual needs and moral inhibitions."[16] Healthy humans could engage in the "affirmation of pleasure and the loss of sexual guilt." They were by nature social and constructive and only made the contrary by political and religious authorities.

The psychological claim to know human nature became the basis for an ethics. Freudian revisionists applied Freud's methods to a normative study of character, or natural right. The nature of an individual would set the parameters for self-actualization in a harmonious soul, or "orderliness in man's inner nature or in his outer behavior."[17] "Intrinsic guilt," wrote Maslow, "is the betrayal of one's own inner nature or self, a turning off the path to self-actualization."[18] Rogers rejected Freud's political analogy: "Consciousness, instead of being the watchman over a dangerous and unpredictable lot of impulses, of which few can be permitted to see the light of day, becomes the comfortable inhabitant of a richly varied society of impulses and feelings and thoughts, which prove to be very satisfactorily self-governing when not fearfully or authoritatively guarded."[19] Marcuse celebrated the erotic soul and a "logic of gratification" opposed to domination: "Being is experienced as gratification, which unites man and nature so that the fulfillment of man is at the same time the fulfillment, without violence, of nature."[20] Conversely, the "sadism" of traditional morality perverted human nature. The new virtues included magnanimity, the ability to stand free from and against the herd mentality, and the courage to question authority, fight oppression, and reflect on one's own death. An existential investigation into the fundamental mood of angst toward nothingness, or death, could show humans how to live authentically by incorporating the imminent possibility (of death) into all of life's decisions. But only a few could achieve Maslow's self-realization. He believed in top-down education, while Rogers believed in spontaneity on the part of group members. Reflecting this divide, humanists championed an aesthetic education for an elite (to both subvert the old authoritative communities and provide a sense of meaning) and a vulgar morality of self-creation for the many. At their most radical, elites built hedges around transgressive acts of liberation and tabooed pleasures in sex and drugs to manage authentic experiences for a new birth into new communities while celebrating the release of "id" to better manage the lower classes (particularly blacks, said Maslow).[21]

For the elites, authenticity became a personalized faith complete with a theology and varieties of religious experience, perfect for a leisured class with the luxury of existential crises. Rituals included a conversion and new way of life that rejected conformity, listened for the authoritative "call" to authenticity, and lived with resolution. Sacred confrontations with the "other" could also provide meaning and purpose. The "other" could include individuals (employing sacred terms like *I* and *Thou*) or "other" minority communities, where one could leech a sense of purpose from true believers. Finally, it taught a new metaphysics of "life" that sanctified ecological science to reunite humans with physical nature. Facing both the threat of secular liberalism and their own crisis of belief, Christian theologians made their final deal with the devil by incorporating existentialism and dialectical theory. Equating their own private alienation (the product of any liberal education) with a social crisis, they set to destroy their own communities. Despite the religious boom in America in church attendance and in religious orders, they condemned religion's rigidity and shallow moralism, which lacked existentialist trembling and zest. American churches reflected bourgeois, liberal, "atomized" society and "radical individualism." Rogers's *Counseling and Psychotherapy* became the second-most popular textbook for pastoral counseling. It applied the nondirective approach of unconditional acceptance: "The client has the right to accept his own life goals, even though these may be at variance with the goals that the counselor might choose for him."[22] Paul Tillich's systematic theology redefined sin from transgressing God's law to "tragic estrangement from one's true being"; the term *demonic* referred not to "sinful men" but to alienating "structures which are stronger than the good will of the individual."[23] *Revelation* meant an experience that put one in a new situation as a self or person. The key to *salvation* was the self-acceptance necessary to experience grace: "Acceptance of the unacceptable, is the very necessary precondition for self-affirmation." *Acceptance* was superior to *forgiveness*, which supposed a moral superiority. Thus faith required the "courage to be," transcending all theisms (or authorities) in unconditional self-acceptance: "It is the accepting of the acceptance without somebody or something that accepts. It is the power of being-itself that accepts and gives the courage to be."[24] Catholic theologians introduced existentialism with new sacred terms, teaching authenticity as personhood. With paeans to ecumenism, Vatican II destroyed the old liturgy.[25] Masses abandoned Latin, the priest turned away from the tabernacle, and Protestant hymns and campy sing-alongs replaced sacred music. The Land O'Lakes statement of Catholic universities, signed by Notre Dame's president Father Theodore Hesburgh, pushed the "ecumenical goals of collaboration and unity." Catholic students were invited "to participate in and contribute to a variety of liturgical functions, at best, creatively contemporary and experimental."

White ethnic enclaves had been the source of American Catholic tradition and strength, but Catholic elites searched for religious meaning in integration and racial harmony, in programs involving "inner-city social action" and "aid to the educationally disadvantaged." Facing scrutiny from the civil rights movement, the United States Conference of Catholic Bishops condemned "discrimination based on the accidental fact of race or color" and ordered that "parish and diocesan societies" be "common meeting grounds" to discuss racial injustice, thus condemning the insular ethnic parish.[26] Hesburgh, a member of the Civil Rights Commission, marched with Martin Luther King Jr. in 1963 and later testified before Congress in favor of forced busing to integrate schools. Actively destroying the ethnic parish, the center of community life, the new churches became volunteer organizations ceaselessly talking about "community."

Religious leaders, evangelicals in 1960 and then Catholics in 1966, partnered with humanists to develop encounter groups, sensitivity training, and alternative modes of charismatic worship that allowed parishioners to express themselves. To be saved, preached Robert Schuler, is to be "changed from a negative to a positive self-image—from inferiority to self-esteem."[27] With Pope Paul's encouragement, some Immaculate Heart of Mary convents were given "full license to experiment with the liturgy" in ways that desacralized the sacraments. In one example, the Mass was celebrated at a dinner table and followed by a meal, at which the priest swept the crumbs from the consecrated host into the salad bowl. Religious orders like the Immaculate Heart Nuns hired psychotherapists Rogers and Adrian van Kaam to lead encounter groups for their novitiate. On special retreats, democratic procedures replaced traditional rules, and initiates voted on wearing habits or attending Mass. Rogers knew that releasing sexual and aggressive energy would subvert the authoritarian hierarchy. At the end of the experiment, more than half the nuns requested release from their vows except a small group of radical lesbian nuns. Jeanne Cordova reflected, "They promised me monastic robes, glorious Latin liturgy, the protection of the three sacred vows, the peace of saints in a quiet cell, the sisterhood of a holy family. But I entered religious life the year [Paul VI] was taking it apart: 1966. The fathers of the Holy Roman Catholic and Apostolic Church were sitting in the Vatican Council destroying, in the name of Change, my dreams. Delete Latin ritual. Dump the habit. Damn holy obedience. Send nuns and priests out into the Real world."[28] Cordova disavowed Catholicism for a new "vocation" of "lesbianism" and "social justice." As Catholic elites conflated social justice with anti-racism and integration, they became disgusted with parishioners and often left the church. And insofar as Catholic radicals succeeded, they weakened their own churches and ethnic traditions by integrating once-Catholic neighborhoods with black Protestants. Jones described Irish historian Dennis Clark's "transition from being an Irish Catholic to becoming an anti-Catholic Irishman": "Like most Catholic liberals at the time, [he] made integration synonymous with social justice and then went on to judge the Church by this criterion. When the Church failed this test in Clark's eyes, he abandoned the Church and became an embittered opponent of religion whose main self-identification was Irish ethnicity."[29]

Sociologists, diagnosing Americans as morbid materialists, reserved special hatred for the new suburbs, the "apotheosis of pragmatism," which molded Americans into conformity.[30] Extensions of corporate growth, the metastasizing suburbs lumped together large numbers of rootless, interchangeable strangers without any collective goal higher than moneymaking. In his bestseller *The Lonely Crowd*, David Riesman wrote that suburbanites, having lost their social institutions, lost on the one hand the necessary socialization for an authoritative sense of self required to resist conformity and, on the other, the traditions against which an autonomous individual derives a sense of purpose. Desperate for community and seeking meaningful ties, the residents grew shallow roots—bridge clubs, canasta, and bowling leagues—that were just enough for the bare minimum of communal life. There was much social activity but little real civic or political activity. Friends were chosen for convenience, and new associations, led by tiny, unspectacular leaders, produced brief, ephemeral traditions. Surrendering to the fleeting opinion of the group, the residents placed a premium on "adjustment"; indeed, the best-adjusted were the ones who were constantly adjusting. Examining the "character structure" of these suburbanites, Riesman announced the decline of the "inner-directed personality," which follows the demands of conscience, and the rise of the "other-directed personality," which is anxious to receive the approval of others.[31] Toleration of others became the premiere social virtue: residents did not tolerate those who were intolerant. Such toleration produced greater conformity because it leveled all opinions, leaving nothing sacred. But suburban society was not just soulless. Riesman applied Fromm's characterology to assess middle-class, other-directed, "herd man," who, isolated and afraid of his own freedom, sought shelter in fascist dictators.

Sociologist C. Wright Mills, seeking to revive a Left demoralized since Wallace, provided the most trenchant critique of liberalism. Dewey's social theory, wrapped in the scientific jargon of the "biologic-adjustment model of action," had confused adjustment for the end of mere survival with the social ends of a historical culture—thus allowing him to posit certain values under the authority of science.[32] While Dewey had pointed out the historical origins of competing values, he ignored his own. Pragmatism grew from Progressive Era nationalism, which minimized social divisions by locating "all problems between *man and nature*, instead of between *men and men*." Its function was "to assimilate all value, power, or human problems to a statement of the function of intelligence" and to defuse social problems that required radical solutions with calls for "more education." But the rule of scientific experts had led to an incompetent "crackpot realism," where supposedly brilliant strategists invented idiotic schemes like mutual assured destruction.[33] Liberals prided themselves on achieving the rational society, but the liberal "end of ideology" was itself an ideology: their claim to neutrality with aloof or sneering skepticism was but a political tool to defend the status quo. The liberal conception of reason was a narrow empirical science placed unquestioningly into the service of power, making nuclear weapons and napalm or predicting and controlling the populace. It also resulted in injustice. By deriding abstraction and focusing on "the particular situation" with incremental reforms, liberals dissolved the racial or class identities that could mount effective group opposition. Liberal paeans to democracy only masked the rule of a "power elite," a privileged class that circulated through the halls of power, engaging in piecemeal interventions and balancing group interests in a distributive game that impeded structural change. The battles between the presidents and Congress over control of supposedly impartial agencies revealed the fraud of liberal expertise.[34] The term "iron triangle" was coined in 1956 to describe the corrupt partnership between members of Congress, bureaucrats, and special interests to award contracts that benefitted industry more than the public good.[35] Leading scholars, and finally Landis himself, questioned the integrity of administrative rule, which had become characterized by a backlog of cases, an absence of general laws, and ineffectual appointments. But Landis's liberal solution was more bureaucratic oversight, new bureaucrats with more power to oversee bureaucrats.

Mills focused on what Eisenhower called the military-industrial complex. In 1950, military expenditures accounted for $12 billion (30 percent of the budget); by 1955, it was $40 billion (65 percent). JFK added $9 billion based on the spurious "bomber" and "missile gap," warning that the US was falling behind in nuclear superiority. By 1970, the military budget was $80 billion, making fortunes for producers and investors. Two-thirds of the $40 billion spent on weapons systems went to fifteen corporations; six-sevenths of those contracts were not competitive. A Senate report showed that one hundred defense contractors held 67.4 percent of contracts and employed more than two thousand former high-ranking officers of the military. A veritable "double government" had formed. Truman had ordered the CIA disbanded, but the agency continued to operate in the Pentagon, sending thousands of poorly trained insurgents to their deaths in ill-conceived, hare-brained insurrections. Resurrected in 1947, it, along with the FBI, spied on US citizens, worked with the Ford Foundation to secure information, and funded numerous liberal front groups like socialist Norman Thomas's Congress for Cultural Freedom. The

FBI wiretapped dissidents on both the Right and Left, the John Birch Society and the civil rights movement.

Radical intellectuals sought to both rescue the life of reason and imagine an alternative political order, as revealed by the utopian city in speech. Marcuse presented three conceptions of freedom in the character types of the philosopher, the artist, and liberal, middle-class man. Finding the philosophical attitude, born of natural curiosity, opposed to liberal asceticism, he constructed a rhetoric for the New Left. The higher ranks of soul, philosophic and poetic, must ally in "solidarity" with women, minorities, and the colonized "wretched of the earth" against the conformity of mass man that threatened life itself.[36] The elites must turn away from "the conservative popular base" to "the substratum of the outcasts and outsiders, the exploited and persecuted of other races and other colors, the unemployed and the unemployable."[37] Marcuse called for revolution to end "surplus repression" and found the "aesthetic state," a political order providing material goods and the conditions for self-actualization.[38] "Polymorphous sexuality" would liberate society from the "innerworldly asceticism" of the capitalist work ethic. Modern man would fully detach sex from monogamy and reproduction and accept as good what he formerly viewed as sexual perversion. The human body in its entirety, the whole personality, would become an instrument of desire and pleasure, no longer bound as an "instrument of toil." The workday would be dramatically altered; as scarcity had been conquered, work itself would become erotic, jobs being a form of expression and satisfaction, experienced as play. A healthy society would recognize the many unique manifestations of erotic desire and grant sexual rights to both explore and express one's discovered identities. Individual growth and self-esteem also required the end of liberal color-blind assimilation and the affirmation of cultural group identity, by which one could develop a sense of purpose in relation with others.

In Mills's own formulation of the possible relations between political philosophers and power, intellectuals must lead a new revolutionary class. But unionized blue-collar laborers were reactionary, bought off by higher wages and benefits. White-collar workers, isolated in their cubicles, focused on private hedonism and lacked class consciousness. The key to creating a New Left was identity. Sociological "craftsmen" must construct symbols to connect personal problems to structural injustices and thereby mobilize new "publics" for systemic change.[39] Liberated from "false consciousness," individuals would revolt against the oppressive system that destroyed their capacity for rationality and freedom. The new proletariat would combine the "young intelligentsia," minority groups, and Third World revolutionaries.[40] In Mills's ideal world, intellectuals would receive funding and special international privileges to travel, study, and advise political leaders, and the US would devote 20 percent of its GDP to advance industry in developing countries.[41] "The American working class," said Stokely Carmichael, "enjoys the fruits of the labours of the Third World. The proletariat has become the Third World, and the bourgeoisie is white western society."[42] Fromm, agreeing with the duty to aid developing nations, envisioned a global order in 1960: "The aim of socialism is the abolition of national sovereignty, the abolition of any kind of armed forces, and the establishment of a commonwealth of nations."[43]

The New Proletariat

In the elites' aesthetic revolt against middle-class mores, intellectuals knew the popular morality of self-creation was "silly," but they preferred it to the old liberal asceticism.[44] The youth picked apart their parents' hypocrisy on race and sex. Icons James Dean and Jack Kerouac, having no objective force to struggle against, were "rebels without a cause." Norman Mailer's "White Negro" fled repressive liberalism to embrace the danger, purpose, and thus authenticity of black culture.[45] Viewing themselves as carrying Beat culture to the New Left, Ken Kesey's Merry Pranksters traveled the nation by bus in 1964–65, reveling in acid trips. One of them, Paul Krassner, started the yippies with Jerry Rubin and Abbie Hoffman. They lampooned traditional culture with provocative, racy slogans and obnoxious pranks: bringing a shaman to exorcise the Pentagon, tossing money onto the New York Stock Exchange floor, and nominating a pig for president. Vulgarity and pornography became staples of New Left art. Hollywood discarded the Hays Code by using the Holocaust to exempt itself from the prohibition on showing nudity in the 1964 film *The Pawnbroker*—criticism of it would be racist. In 1969, best picture went to the X-rated *Midnight Cowboy*. Televised and cinematic treatments of abortion increased, from once in the 1950s to twenty-five times in the 1960s, and culminated in the 1972 episode of *Maude*, in which Bea Arthur conquers her irrational guilt to have an abortion. A series of court cases made obscenity legally nonexistent for ten years. Educated elites, the Court ruled, and not legislatures, should decide whether sexual speech had "social value."[46] The newfound right to privacy brought a legal sexual revolution in contraception for both married and unmarried couples as well as women's right to abortion.

Goodman and Mills's call for radicalism motivated the student Left. Finding that liberals had few answers, students soaked up their professors' warnings about technology and their critique of scientists' inability to defend their own way of life. The most ambitious of the baby boomer generation, unlike the Beats, converted their existentialist angst to activism. The first generation to go en masse to college, it turned its noses at sloppy sots like Kerouac, instead directing its energy toward political change in civil rights and the antiwar movement. Christian youth groups traveled south to test their faith in marches and sit-ins. Catholic Michael Novak preached a "theology for a radical politics." Tom Hayden wrote his master's thesis on Mills, romantically entitled *Radical Nomad*. In "A Letter to the New (Young) Left," he helped create a radical movement among college students. The 1962 Port Huron Statement called for "participative" democracy, a politicization of personal and cultural "modern problems": nuclear war, racism, meaningless work, nationalism, American affluence, world hunger, overpopulation, limited world resources, and government manipulation. As the civil rights movement moved from southern segregation to northern ghettoes, student activists, finding themselves thwarted by campus authorities, protested against the restrictions; the university was part of the liberal machine. The Berkeley Free Speech Movement began when police arrested CORE activist Jack Weinberg (who coined the phrase "Don't trust anyone over thirty") for violating university policy in setting up a display table on campus. A mob blocked the police car, and Mario Savio, taking off his shoes, climbed atop to rally the crowd. In his Sproul Hall address, he attacked the corporate liberal machine and exhorted students to throw their "bodies upon the gears and upon the wheels, upon the levers...to make it stop!"

Black identity politics initiated a revolt of white and black elites against the "black bourgeoisie" like Joseph H. Jackson. In 1966 most blacks favored integration and disapproved of violence and Black Nationalism. Jackson supported economic boycotts against segregation in Baton Rouge and Montgomery, the latter led by Martin Luther King Jr. By these means, blacks could gain power within the democratic process. But he broke with the revolutionary King, who wanted to use the pulpit to promote sit-ins and political demonstrations. Progressives' sit-in over Jackson's leadership at the 1960 Baptist convention was followed by a 1961 march-in—storming the stage. In the struggle, rioters shoved Reverend A. G. Wright off the stage, breaking his neck. In the following schism, the majority of Baptists voted for Jackson, while the King faction started a separate Progressive Convention. Jackson, supported by many black ministers, railed against civil disobedience and the use of schoolchildren in marches. King's *nonviolence*, he said, required violence and intimidation to be effective, not just the police beatings to draw media coverage but the increasingly aggressive sit-ins that trashed stores and cowed business owners and their employees; so, too, it undermined respect for the law and democratic negotiation. When King came to Chicago to march for urban reform in 1966, Jackson worked to squash his Soldier Field rally; planned for a hundred thousand, it only drew twenty thousand. Jackson argued that *he* was the true civil rights leader because he supported the legal progress of black communities and families into the middle class. Distinguishing between racial *preference* and *prejudice*, he argued against legal prejudice while leaving citizens to their own race preferences. The right to preference, including the right to marry, befriend, and associate with whomever one wishes, he argued, "is a sacred right that each individual must enjoy.... No powers of government must usurp or destroy it."[47] By preference, Jackson first meant blacks' preference for themselves. Progressives, he argued, were really a coalition of white elites and privileged blacks who did not love, respect, or want to live with their own people but promised to deliver the votes of a dependent black lower class using welfare.

King's vision of the "beloved community" rejected Jackson's view on preference. He prophesied a spiritual unity with whites that transcended race. While praising American ideals, King faulted the country for failing to uphold a "higher law," thus justifying civil disobedience. Desegregation and integration were insufficient; affirmative action was needed in public and private as well as full employment and economic redistribution, a $50 billion "Marshall Plan" for blacks.[48] Whitney Young's 1964 plan included preferential hiring and accelerated promotions for black workers, government-subsidized housing and forced integration in schools and neighborhoods, appointing "qualified Negroes...to all public and private boards and commissions," funding for "preventative and remedial programs," and "dramatic, aggressive intervention by social workers at all levels."[49] Considering integration, Young said, "I hope that we will be able to create the kind of society wherein people will have to apologize for sameness—for an all-white school or neighborhood or church—because this would be an indication of their immaturity, their lack of sophistication." New laws would create a society where "people will boast of diversity."

But King found himself quickly outflanked on the Left by young blacks over leadership of the northern black underclass, which had begun to riot. King, declared Malcolm X, belonged to the black bourgeoisie and white liberals; he was a "twentieth century...Uncle Tom," whose job was to keep blacks defenseless against whites.[50] In 1966 Stokely Carmichael, rejecting the Great Society and the black bourgeoisie, proclaimed the failure of civil rights and called for Black Power. Huey Newton called the "pro-administration" black bourgeoisie "house Negroes."[51] The "bourgeois Negro," declared the SNCC (Student Nonviolent Coordinating Committee), "has been force-fed the white man's propaganda" and "cannot think for himself because he is a shell of a man full of contradictions."[52] Black sociologist E. Franklin Frazier had long argued that black middle-class integration into American economic life betrayed a neurotic desire to assimilate to a racist system. The black bourgeoisie, he said, accepted a groveling position that allowed it to look down on poor blacks.[53] But the white middle class offered a soulless image to imitate. Blacks must turn to African intellectuals like Frantz Fanon, who taught liberation from the "systematized oppression" of colonialism. Trinidad-born Carmichael had attended the Bronx High School of Science, in the uncomfortable position of being the lone black welcomed by affluent white liberals, where he winced at their need to collect black friends. He found purpose in the civil rights movement and a mentor in the writings of his "patron saint" Fanon.[54] Carmichael's rhetoric laid out the tenets of identity politics: systemic racism, capitalistic oppression, consciousness raising, black solidarity, white allyship. Black power meant becoming conscious, or "woke," to blacks as an identity group, a prerequisite to the "process of mutual recognition" in negotiating as equals for power, not mere liberal welfare.[55] Though the West is "uncivilized," he charged, "'modern-day missionaries'... come into our ghettos—they Head Start, Upward Lift, Bootstrap, and Upward Bound us into white society."[56] In an irredeemably racist society, an "unconscious racism" infected whites, while incarcerated blacks were "political prisoners."[57] Black separatists argued they did not hate white radical allies, only white liberal oppressors.

Caught between the black bourgeoisie and separatism, King moved to the Left. Breaking with LBJ, he called Vietnam a racist war and, while preaching nonviolence, threatened that more riots would follow if whites did not adopt his economic platform: "A riot is the language of the unheard," caused by unjust conditions.[58] In King's new logic, the moderate position between "submission" and separatism was "direct action" in "militant massive non-violence," teaching unconscious racism and identity politics as a means to topple the system and achieve universal brotherhood. "Most Americans," he said, "are unconscious racists," and the only solution was "a reconstruction of the entire society, a revolution of values."[59] He now demanded racial hiring quotas and an *international* Marshall Plan for blacks as repayment for colonialism. Of whites' opposition to programmatic change, he said, "The arresting of the limited forward progress by white resistance revealed the latent racism that was deeply rooted in U.S. society."[60] Whites were moved by the "doctrine of white supremacy." Rejecting any distinction between preference and prejudice, King remarked that despite a white woman's support for full civil rights, her confession that she "would not want [her] daughter to marry a Negro" betrayed unconscious racism: "The question of intermarriage is never raised in a society cured of the disease of racism."[61]

By 1968, King's theology of anti-racism shared much with James Cone's *Black Theology of Liberation*, which reinterpreted Christianity through the lens of systemic racism as a struggle against oppression, or "whiteness." "What we need," Cone preached, "is the destruction of whiteness, which is the source of human misery in the world."[62] Black power was God's message for a white supremacist America. God especially loved and favored the "wretched of the earth" as the chosen vehicle for its liberation from whiteness, the antichrist; whites were by definition unconscious of their oppression of blacks. Blacks denigrated themselves when they adopted white Christianity. *Black,* the word capitalized for a chosen people, became a new religious identity; borrowing from Tillich, Cone argued that truth arises from the existential situation of oppression, requiring the construction of a new language of traditional terms, such as God. Revelation was "God's self-disclosure" of historical liberation; the black community was God's divine presence, thus only it (and not whites) could understand sin and salvation.[63] Blackness is a measure of righteousness, while "sin is whiteness," and salvation required one know that he cannot "affirm whiteness and humanity at the same time." Cone defined sin "for black people" as "a desire to be white and not black," a "loss of identity." Salvation must be political, in the "liberation of the oppressed" and in the "destruction of whiteness," both America and Christendom.[64] Blacks must make whites conscious of their racism and offer them a chance to seek atonement by allying with them in the struggle against oppression. This struggle would not necessarily culminate in integration, nor would it be nonviolent.

Black elites adopted white elites' ethic of authenticity in a radical chic of race solidarity, a secular, therapeutic substitute for Christian community that traveled back from North to South. Mocked as Uncle Toms, bourgeois blacks like Jackson as well as the black nuclear family (like the white nuclear family) became the bête noire of black intellectuals, who shook off middle-class restraints on sex and violence and postured as revolutionaries, styling afros, leather jackets, and berets. Blacks, it was said, had different standards of art and morals.[65] Blaxploitation films of the early 1970s used stars like Ron O'Neal to teach a generation of underclass blacks that empowerment meant sexual virility and brutal violence. King himself was a transition to this. References to his dream that children would be judged by the content of their character and not the color of their skin often omit both King's own character and his support for policies based on skin color. Under FBI surveillance, King met with other Baptist ministers at the Willard Hotel for one of his many orgies in 1964. There they "discussed which women among the parishioners would be suitable for natural or unnatural sex acts. When one of the women protested that she did not approve of unnatural sex acts, the Baptist minister immediately and forcibly raped her. King looked on, laughed, and offered advice."[66] King *justified* his forty-plus extramarital affairs and use of prostitutes and orgies. He viewed sex, particularly when interracial, as more than bravado; it was a form of transcendent spirituality to achieve a society without repression. "I'm f---ing for God!" he told one woman. To a white prostitute he said, "I'm not a Negro tonight."[67] The night before he received the Nobel Peace Prize, "King's group was running naked, drunk white prostitutes up and down the halls of the hotel."[68] He used a logic of sexual liberation: "F---ing's a form of anxiety reduction"; "Every now and then you'll be unfaithful to those that you should be faithful to."[69] In the FBI report, "When one of the women shied away from engaging in an unnatural act, King and several of the men discussed how she was to be taught and initiated in this respect. King told her that to perform such an act would 'help your soul. It will help you.'" King echoed black nationalists, who envisioned a "black lobby" to redistribute white wealth, in his demand for reparations. In May 1969 James Forman barged into New York's Riverside Church and demanded $500 million "from the Christian white churches and the Jewish synagogues...fifteen dollars per n-----."[70] Black leaders abandoned the labor coalition with whites to become leaders of a dependent black underclass. By 1969, Democratic and Republican strategists had rejected the rhetoric of liberal assimilation for that of group identity.

White bourgeois radicals, the children of liberals, revolted against their upper-middle-class parents. Students called the university a training ground for corporate jobs and refused to be molded for them: they would transcend the establishment. Cut off from power yet believing in their merit, white youth felt "themselves to be underprivileged."[71] SDS president Greg Calvert applied Mills's personal politics to organizing whites. Through consciousness raising, alienated youth would awaken to see they were not alone but part of an oppressed proletariat. Young

radicals must organize "a truly radical, an authentically revolutionary movement for change," a white "revolutionary class" allied with
minority youth to destroy the older "white America."[72] If unsuccessful,
they must "orient themselves toward Third World revolutions" to help
"peasant-based revolutions" against "the American imperialist monster,"
a "dehumanizing system." Guilt motivated white *liberals*, he added, but
white *radicals* recognized their duty to change the system and remove
oppressive conditions. A new proletariat of students, social workers,
and teachers in universities and government could achieve a radical
consciousness. Students must reject liberal free speech as repressive:
true "liberating tolerance," said Marcuse, "would mean intolerance
against movements from the Right, and toleration of movements from
the Left."[73] All speech must connect to political conditions. Defining
violence as the "cause of the difference between the potential and
the actual," Johan Galtung argued that speech, even if indirect and
unintended, was "structurally violent" if it led to unequal power and
outcomes.[74] Eldridge Cleaver's 1968 *Soul on Ice*, hailed by white radicals
as a masterpiece, argued that, unlike blacks who now celebrated their
heroes, it would be young whites who would experience the psychic
pain of identity politics, demoralized by the death of "the American
way of life" and its heroes.[75] The same year Charles Levy observed a
pattern among young whites in their identity crisis. Wishing to gain
black trust, they first became conscious of their whiteness and sought
to reject it by exempting themselves from their race, even proclaiming
whites as the enemy.[76] They then attempted to convert to blackness,
confessing their privilege and performing humiliating tasks, only to
find that the endeavor must fail—blacks still viewed them as ineluctably
and suspiciously white. They finally reconciled to their whiteness but
now with a higher consciousness of the need to support blacks as allies
in their struggle for justice, united against other whites who were still
unconscious of their racism and privilege. In this new rite of passage,
privileged whites wrapped their egos in a new identity of cosmopolitan
humanism, often with the hipster trappings of forgotten but oppressed

European ethnicities: Hayden was "Irish on the Inside"—*Irish* a synonym for fighting oppression.

Ambitious leaders of other "oppressed" groups saw the advantage of race politics: new Chicano parties like Action in Mathis, Texas, attributed the poverty of migrant workers to racism while demanding government money from the war on poverty. Rejecting the "old-style" liberal coalition for a "third-party" tactic, radical groups like La Raza encouraged Chicanos to vote in a bloc. Activist Armando Rendón noted, "The concept is quite new to the Chicano and reflects the overall revolution that is occurring within the Chicano community against Gringo ways."[77] A new party realignment based on race identity, an "undisguised assertion of Chicano nationalism" working for race representation, must replace the old division between the "haves" and "have-nots." Brown power meant rejecting "middle aged" Chicanos "still too tied up with making it as Anglos" and achieving empowerment through the decline of the gringo and the rise of the Hispanic race. The Anglos, wrote Rendón, were an imperial, dehumanizing force, "a cultural milieu which desensitizes man and woman into profit-producing machines, devoid of humanity and soul." Whites "gringoized" "the best talents and minds of our people" and enriched themselves at the "expense of the poor and minority peoples." The goal of La Raza was "to fulfill our people, Chicano; To reclaim our land, Aztlan." At the same time Chicano activists argued for the takeover of federal agencies, Nixon appointed Hispanics to high administrative positions. Registered Democrat Martin Castillo became director of the Civil Rights Commission. At his swearing-in, Castillo affirmed that he and the thirty Chicanos present were "neither Democrats nor Republicans" but "all fighting for one cause, la raza." He promoted the agency, established its budget, and replaced most of the former personnel.

But Brown Pride had several problems, the first of which was that Hispanics were legally white.[78] For that reason, said the Ninth Circuit Court, Hispanic children, unlike "Indian" and "Mongolian" children, could not be segregated into Spanish-speaking schools.[79] Thus the League of United Latin American Citizens (LULAC) and La Raza in states like Texas fought for civil rights by arguing that Mexican Americans were not white but "other" in order to fight de facto race distinctions. The federal government abandoned the category in 1971 and recognized Hispanics as a protected minority group under the Fourteenth Amendment.[80] The second problem was that there were few Hispanics—in 1960 only 4.7 percent of the population. In 1966 Hispanic congressman Edward Roybal had only 11 percent Chicanos in his district. Organized labor and the American public demanded sanctions against employers hiring illegals—Cesar Chavez famously supported the "wet line" at the border, where his United Farm Workers patrols beat up illegal Mexican labor scabs. But radicals saw that by importing more "disadvantaged" immigrants, legally or illegally, they could swell their constituency. The solution was using the 1965 Immigration Act, whose family unification provision opened up a massive *legal* loophole. By giving priority to relatives, any family member could receive privileged status in visa applications, launching a never-ending system of chain migration. Entire clans entered the country. The bill's immigration caps were swamped by double the number of family members, such as brothers and sisters, now given the right to enter. The civil rights lobby worked with big business, which wanted cheap labor, to import a new electorate. In 1952, Congress had inserted the "Texas proviso," exempting employers who hired illegals from the very penalties the law imposed. Enforcement bills that passed in the House in 1972 and 1973 failed in the Senate, where Senator James Eastland chaired the Committee on Immigration. Laxity in enforcement encouraged more *illegal* immigration. In 1965 the Border Patrol in San Diego picked up 4,000 illegals; in 1986 it reported 421,000. In total, more than one million illegal aliens were apprehended in 1976.

By the mid-1970s, the Chicano movement had shifted from seeking farmworker rights and union wages to celebrating illegal aliens as a form of racial power. Leaders in the Mexican-American Legal Defense Fund and LULAC opposed employer sanctions and the enforcement of immigration law as discriminatory: "A check of one's legal status" was "an act of degradation and oppression."[81] While the NAACP and the Urban League had initially supported employer sanctions to protect black laborers' wages, by the early 1980s civil rights groups had allied with immigrant, agricultural, and big business interests to oppose them. Unlike the liberal importation of refugees from communist countries, the "human rights" of migrants were recognized as a form of reparations for systemic racism. Within the bureaucracy, the Immigration and Naturalization Service constantly impeded attempts by the conservative Border Patrol to enforce the law. The de facto position was simply not to enforce it or even to increase the number of illegal immigrants. Thus, the Civil Rights and Immigration Acts constituted a demographic revolution. Civil rights groups had won legal recognition of non-white groups, in categories of black, brown, yellow, and red, and they increased their power by securing entitlements and affirmative action preferences for millions of migrants who had never faced discrimination under Jim Crow.

Radical feminism began as a revolt within the civil rights movement by young women who identified with those whom they sought to liberate. In 1965, Casey Hayden and Mary King argued that women, like blacks, were a caste, a colonized people; Gloria Steinem said they were chattel.[82] Feminists analyzed the "gender roles" associated with biological difference to reassess their identities as wives, mothers, and citizens. In Carol Hanisch's 1969 formulation, "The personal is political": in consciousness-raising sessions, women could connect their personal problems to systemic injustices.[83] Incidents like a husband's failure to pick up the house revealed systemic gender oppression. Patriarchy, some argued, transcended race or class. Two millennia of systemic oppression had reduced women to servitude.[84] With a newfound sense of "sisterhood" or community, women could achieve both new personal relations and a sense of meaning by participating in social progress. Men also needed consciousness-raising groups "to admit their vulnerability and fears." Warren Farrell made a career teaching men how to overcome the "male mystique."[85] In 1970 Shulamith Firestone declared war on female biology itself as oppressive. The feminist revolution entailed not just "the elimination of male privilege, but of the sex distinction itself."[86] Liberation could come only when technology enabled women to transcend sex altogether: children would be born artificially, and "professional foster parents" would replace mothers and fathers.[87] Some radical feminists in 1970 demanded unisex bathrooms or "an end to...segregation in the bathroom."[88] But most feminists did not go so far as to aspire to a gender fluid society. As part of a new elite class, they wanted freedom from the old gender roles of wife and mother.

Feminism portrayed itself as a battle between the sisterhood and patriarchy, but this is a myth. It was really a battle over honor *between* female elites and the old middle class. As Betty Friedan noted, the most ambitious women sought careers but often at personal sacrifice; they were the subject of ridicule by other women who claimed the honor of being superior wives and mothers. Women's journals painted careerist women as sexually frigid and domineering, plagued by neurotic desires stemming from daddy issues. Feminist elites successfully inverted the hierarchy: homemakers became languid, caged birds, not fully human, infantile, parasitic subordinates. Motherhood must be subordinated in status to economic production. The "ultimate myth," Steinem said, was that "children must have fulltime mothers, and that liberated women make bad ones."[89] The new family, an elite model built upon the ashes of the old, would include cohabitation or serial monogamy between two sexually experienced, economically independent partners. Equity required new political rights: equal pay, free contraception, abortion, and universal daycare. By the mid-1970s, organizations like the National Organization of Women (NOW) changed their focus to political lobbying for "career advancement for elite women" and their "sexual and reproductive rights."[90]

Forgotten lower-class, middle-aged women raced to keep up. "I'm short, fat and forty-five!" began Susan Jacoby's 1973 "The Flatbush Feminists," which chronicled working class homemakers' crises of the loss of sexual allure and vocation after children had left the nest.[91] Jacoby describes how, instead of looking to religious authorities, these women turn to *Ms. Magazine* for advice about starting a consciousness-raising group. By the end of the piece, they take jobs outside the home, spice up their sex lives, and start preaching contraception in their parishes (in one 1971 study, only 10 percent of sexually active young women between fifteen and nineteen said they were "on the pill"). They warn their daughters *not* to follow in their footsteps. Black feminist lesbians of the Combahee River Collective argued they resided at an intersection of a "whole range of oppressions. We do not have racial, sexual, heterosexual, or class privilege to rely upon."[92] They were the navel of the enslaved body of oppression: "The most profound and potentially most radical politics come directly out of our own identity, as opposed to working to end somebody else's oppression." Thus, "If black women were free, it would mean that everyone else would have to be free since our freedom would necessitate the destruction of all the systems of oppression." Freedom would mean "access to resources and power" that privileged groups possess, followed by a new consciousness or autonomy.

Elite males *promoted* feminism, and not just womanizers like Ted Kennedy who liked de facto polygamy. Birch Bayh drafted and sponsored Title IX, and Republicans Ronald Reagan and Nelson Rockefeller signed abortion and no-fault divorce bills. In 1971, Congress passed the Comprehensive Child Development Bill, which would have funded day and afterschool care centers and provided nutrition, counseling, and medical and dental care (Pat Buchanan pushed Nixon to veto the bill). It supported the Equal Rights Amendment (ERA) in 1972. In 1977 it appropriated $5 million for the National Women's Conference, a ratification rally in Houston that resolved in favor of gay rights, government child care, and federal funding for abortion (including for minors). The Stop ERA movement was led not by men but by Phyllis Schlafly's coalition of homemakers, who saw their status as wives and mothers threatened. The 1979 White House Conference on Families, funded with $3 million, selected thirty-nine radicals and one conservative to make proposals to "strengthen families." Steinem crusaded to use the word *families* by way of including alternative families, both homosexual and extramarital.

Liberal psychologists had labeled homosexuality a mental illness until 1973 but had long argued for its decriminalization. Radicals argued that sexual deviations in "gender identity" were *natural*, both statistically and ethically.[93] The sexual revolution had lifted strictures on freely consenting adults and recognized gender identity as a source of group oppression. In 1966 Lars Ullerstam penned "a sexual bill of rights for The Erotic Minorities." He appealed to exhibitionists, pedophiles, homosexuals, and voyeurists: "Erotic minorities of all categories, unite!"[94] Goodman listed gays as a civil rights group: "My homosexual needs have made me a n-----."[95] In the new formulation, "chick equals n----- equals queer."[96] It was a question of "self-affirmation of minorities," the denial of which was oppression.[97] While Gore Vidal had argued that humans were bisexual by nature, with homosexuality describing certain acts, Marcuse viewed homosexuality as part of one's identity: homoeroticism was natural in an ethical sense, parallel with the philosopher's narcissism (self-love and examination) and freedom from convention. Both drew the murderous hatred of heterosexual moralists. Marcuse influenced Carl Wittman's 1969 *Gay Manifesto*, which connected sexual repression to reproductive taboos: "Nature leaves undefined the object of sexual desire. The gender of that object is imposed socially."[98] Dennis Altman applied Marcuse's concept of liberation to discover the "polymorphous whole": "Liberation...will come only with a new morality and a revised notion of 'human nature.'"[99] Healthy identity requires liberating "that part of ourselves...that we have repressed," achieving a harmony with the repressed homosexual desires that are the source of hyper-masculinity.

One's sexuality is part of "his total concept of identity, and...it is almost impossible to eradicate it without doing damage to the whole personality." Oppression, or the "denial of identity," took the form of persecution, discrimination, or liberal tolerance. The last was worst, living with difference without fully validating it. "Coming out" was a political statement, requiring the aid of a community, or "gayworld," that created its own countercultural mannerisms and behavior. Gay liberation did not equilibrate the older morals but inverted them; it was an "attack on conventional morality." Wittman wrote, "Exclusive heterosexuality reflects a fear of people of the same sex, it's anti-homosexual, and it is fraught with frustration." In 1967 George Weinberg introduced the pathology *homophobia* for those who could not overcome their "prejudice against homosexuality."[100] The "guilt and self-hatred" homosexuals struggled with would someday be reserved for white heterosexuals. Like blacks, homosexuals disagreed over whether to form their own separate communities or push for broader liberation, achieved in the eradication of all strictly heterosexual or homosexual identities. By 1973, the gay bathhouses in New York had become "radical chic" for heterosexuals.

In transgenderism, one's sex does not align with socially prescribed gender roles. John Money, who pioneered hormone therapy, theorized that sex was determined by multiple variables, including genetics, hormones, genitalia, and gender identity, and the last took precedent over genitalia in shaping a patient's mental health. In 1965, Johns Hopkins started the first US sex change program, the Gender Identity Clinic for Transsexuals. Doctors told reporters that transsexuals were "physically normal people who are psychologically the opposite sex."[101] In the words of plastic surgeon Dr. John Hoope, "If the mind cannot be changed to fit the body, then perhaps we should consider changing the body to fit the mind."[102] Psychiatrist Jon Meyer, who joined the program in 1969 (before he went on to oppose it), noted that patients "would start out talking about their wish for sex reassignment but would very rapidly get into anything people would talk about in therapy," such as loss, abandonment, and grief; Hoope recalled of the applicants, "We had quite a number of patients from The Block, transvestites, gay men, strippers, just a bizarre group of people." Still, the procedure was called a success. Reported the *Boston Globe* in 1972, "Statistics have also shown that many transsexuals are indeed happier afterward, relieved of their frustrations, and able to lead lives of greater fulfillment"; "change-of-sex operations," related *Jet*, were "a necessary ingredient to a dynamic society."[103] Some feminists saw a threat. Janice Raymond argued that transsexuals were "*not* women" but "*deviant males*," the byproduct of a patriarchal society that constructed binary genders to oppress women.[104] Instead of accepting their sexuality, "all transsexuals rape women's bodies by reducing the real female form to an artifact, appropriating this body for themselves." But transsexuals responded that Raymond had *also* proceeded from binary identities: her attempt to define the word *woman* oppressed men who identify as women by imposing trans-exclusive categories.

In foreign policy, radicals rebelled against the popular support for the Vietnam War. They destroyed the liberal myth of the so-called "triumph and tragedy of Lyndon Johnson," which praised his domestic policy and lamented that it had been torpedoed by his unnecessary foreign war. The two were in truth inseparable. Liberal containment bred militarism and bankrupted the treasury. Liberals had claimed to bring democracy to the world, but they could never tease apart realpolitik—dictatorial rule and economic interest—from their supposed benevolence. Whether propping up a reactionary monarchy in Greece, boosting the Shah's secret police in Iran, protecting Guatemalan banana investments, or whacking the Ngo brothers, the split between realism and idealism only expressed the contradiction of rejecting American principles when dealing with other nations. The liberal war against communist "ideology" instead of concrete nations for reasons of national interest had a dehumanizing effect. In the 1960s, the US greatly increased its aid to foreign police forces as concerns grew about communist insurgents in the developing world. By 1968 it was spending, mostly through the USAID Office of Public Safety, $60 million a year in thirty-four countries to train police and security forces in torture and execution. Told they were fighting a war against ideological enemies, US soldiers were thrown into concrete civil conflicts with the task of pacifying entire civilian populations. Lieutenant William Calley, convicted in 1971 for massacring 109 Vietnamese at My Lai, defended his actions: "When my troops were getting massacred and mauled by an enemy I couldn't see, I couldn't feel, and I couldn't touch...nobody in the military system ever described them as anything other than Communism." For his crimes, Calley was placed under house arrest for three years until Nixon commuted his sentence.

Liberalism's halfway house between nationalism and globalism, spreading American ideals, fed a backlash of resentment: the US subverted European colonies with nationalist movements, but it alone possessed the rights, privileges, and wealth it promised to universalize. For radicals, America was "a nation built upon inhumanity," imperialism, even "genocide."[105] The Vietnam War, reflected Todd Gitlin, "was symptomatic of a rotten system or even an irredeemably monstrous civilization." It was a "racist war" waged by "a technologically superior, white-led juggernaut against a largely peasant Asian society."[106] America's tyranny abroad mirrored its tyranny at home, a "seamless economic and cultural system characterized by white supremacy, murderous technology, and irresponsible central power devoid of justice." "First of all," explained Hayden, "we were internationalists," siding with Bobby Seale and the Vietnamese people against "a decadent and super-rich American empire": "We want to join with the new humanity, not support a dying empire."[107] "The American pie," said Carmichael, "means raping South Africa, beating Vietnam, beating South America, [and] raping the Philippines."[108] Thus he called for solidarity with the oppressed on a global scale. Radical elites, not peasants, led Third World revolution in Cuba; the Cuban "middle class as a whole," wrote Theodore Draper in 1960, "has been marked for destruction."[109] Radical feminists called "worldwide Women's Revolution the only hope for life on the planet."[110] "Women and girls in the U.S.," said one group, "are being oppressed, raped, and this has been going on since 1776, when Amerikka arose as a 101% capitalist nation."[111] Progressive white, Black, Brown, Red, Yellow, and gender identity groups formed a "rainbow coalition" against the liberals' pseudoscientific rule at home and "imperialism all around the world."

The war between liberals and progressives came to a head at the 1968 Democratic National Convention (DNC), which voted for LBJ's policy in Vietnam. Unions supported the war, and hardhats dependably showed up to beat protestors. AFL-CIO President George Meany worked with Mayor Daley to suppress protests at the convention. A thousand Americans were dying in Vietnam each month, and radical protestors gathered outside the amphitheater to shout insults and hurl bags of feces; in turn, the blue-collar Chicago PD beat their own feces out of them. Polls showed the public sided with the police, but influential Democrats concluded that the party center must represent the radical base. They made a principled, practical, and prescient decision to incorporate identity politics. Strategist Fred Dutton, perceiving changes in the electorate, noted a growing divide between the upper and "working classes."[112] College graduates had voted Democrat for the first time in 1964, but the socially conservative, blue-collar "Catholic vote"—ethnic Poles and Irish—held the power. Yet there was room for a new Democratic Party. The tremendous increase in federal spending offered "political opportunities" to provide graft for a new constituency, "minority groups, young people and women."[113] The meaning of representation changed from voter choice to a "demographic theory," in which a new activist elite would represent oppressed groups designated by race and gender traits. These elites organized protests to maintain solidarity. In a party takeover, even called a "heist," the McGovern-Fraser Commission changed the rules to overrepresent those groups among delegates and to underrepresent local and state leaders that represented average voters. Its author, Rick Stearns, said, "The function of conventions is not to overthrow the elites, but to choose between competing elites."[114] And the new elites were "cultural elites."[115] The radical 1972 convention opposed the war and affirmed "cultural identity."[116] The party ate huge losses (McGovern lost 60.7–37.5 percent) in the face of what Kevin Phillips called an "emerging Republican Majority." It was the end of a long-standing labor alliance: Meany and Jimmy Hoffa refused to endorse McGovern, and Reuther sided with the antiwar platform. Alienated blue-collar workers voted for Nixon. But the party built a new coalition. McGovern won 87 percent of the nonwhite vote, did 13 percent better among working women, and increased support from educated elites and skilled professionals.

The Long March through the Institutions

The "new constituencies" of race and gender groups and the goal of achieving the new idea of nature required institutional devices. Marcuse repeated Italian Marxist Antonio Gramsci's theory that orthodox Marxism's focus on materialism failed to grasp the crucial role of the superstructure of ideas. Rejecting the working class as the agents of change, Gramsci promoted the takeover of state institutions, whereby a minority of radicals could change society by changing its culture. This march would take place in education, bureaucracy, social regulation, and civil society. Radical activists ensconced themselves in federal agencies and programs, where they secured government funds for community organizing at the grassroots level. Liberals had marked the Great Society's community action programs for graft, but radicals coopted funding for the National Welfare Rights Organization and ACORN and, to liberals' dismay, programs like the "Hate Whitey Liberation School" in Nashville.[117] They secured forty thousand dollars for LeRoi Jones's Black Arts Theater, which produced Black National-ist dramas on Harlem's streets. In one, a parody of the radio-TV *Jack Benny Program*, Benny's black valet, Rochester, robs and conquers his white oppressors; in another, black teens beat up a white teen for his homosexual advances. Jones told *Negro Digest*, "The Black Artist's role is to engage in the destruction of America as he knows it. His role is to report and reflect so precisely the nature of the society... [that] white men [will] tremble, curse, and go mad, because they will be drenched in the filth of their evil."[118] When James Farmer, who launched the 1961 Freedom Rides, proposed an adult literacy program, President Johnson personally axed it and demanded an end to "kooks and sociologists" in the Office of Economic Opportunity.

The liberals initially used the 1965 Elementary and Secondary Education Act for graft. To get support from local school districts, the bill gave them primary responsibility for conceiving and administering compensatory programs, and they siphoned Title I funding into their regular budgets. School administrators defined educational deprivation as low achievement, not poverty. A 1977 survey reported that two-thirds of students funded by Title I were not poor and that more than one-half were low achievers. Forty percent of recipients were neither poor nor low achievers. But radicals saw how the act could achieve federal control over educational standards and new programs. They began to publish a vast literature attacking the "hidden curriculum" of "sexist beliefs, attitudes, and values" in public schools, including "Christian doctrine," "heterosexual bias," and "speciesism."[119] Mere consciousness raising did not lead to resistance; rather teachers must engage in multicultural methods to reveal students' prejudices and liberate them from "institutional racism," sexism, and nationalism.[120] Paulo Freire's 1970 *Education for the Oppressed* introduced multicultural education to make "oppression and its causes objects of reflection by the oppressed," who will then engage "in the struggle for libera-tion."[121] From 1970's Earth Day and programs like Spaceship Earth to global citizenship, Leftists used powerful images to transcend "eth-nocentrism" and nationalism to achieve "diversity," "cosmopolitan sensitivity," and "global awareness."[122] In 1968 educators James Becker and Lee Anderson promoted "a global or planetary society—that is, a world social system."[123] Globalists needed to displace the old myths of American identity with new myths that, teaching the injustice of the West, undermined its authority for a transition to a global identity. In 1974 the Office of Education announced that it would publish rules for the "Ethnic Heritage Studies Program," with grants of $2.7 million, under its Title IX authority.

Racism awareness training paid. Multiple groups, from the National Education Association and state level education associations to the US Navy, YMCA, and New Perspectives on Race, Inc., began to use racism awareness training programs for white children. By the early 1970s, a codified dogma taught that racism was primarily systemic and structural, not individual. All whites were by definition unconsciously racist as they participated in the system. In 1970 Pat Bidol defined racism as "Power + Prejudice," meaning that minorities could never be racist nor women sexist because they lacked power.[124] Racism awareness training promised to make whites conscious of their privilege, not because they could cease to be racist but to obligate them to join as anti-racist allies. In 1971 the National Education Association put together "antiracism activities" for children, published in *Education & Racism*, "to raise to consciousness within the student an awareness of white racism, to identify its forms within the culture, institutions and individual behaviors of our society, and to enable him to actively engage in social change."[125] All whites bore guilt: "All white individuals in our society are racists. Even if a white is totally free from all conscious racial prejudices, he remains a racist, for he receives benefits distributed by a white racist society through its institutions. Our institutional and cultural processes are so arranged as to automatically benefit whites, just because they are white. It is essential for whites to recognize that they receive most of these racist benefits automatically, unconsciously, and unintentionally." Some white students might be "triggered," meaning resistant, defensive, or angry, and deny their complicity in racism.[126] Thus, teachers instructed children to make a "whiteness collage," search for the "rightness of whiteness" in advertisements from popular magazines, form racial castes in the classroom ("serfdom simulation exercise"), watch movies about white racism, make confessions about their "new racial identity awareness," and "try out new antiracist" behaviors ("New Behaviors for Whites") in controlled settings.[127] All this required ample feedback from "Third World people."

Public schools became a battleground as the federal government funded both educational initiatives and community organizers who disrupted education. In 1971 Albert Shanker, president of the 73,000-member New York City American Federation of Teachers, complained to Congress that government-funded anti-poverty groups like United Bronx Parents (which received $3.2 million) bussed in parents from other school districts to "stimulate violence."[128] The new federal "legislation and court decisions tend[ed] to make everything that happens to a student in a school an adversary proceeding." Instead of learning, students were conscripted in political fights. When students were punished or suspended, they believed it was a fight against oppression. With little disciplinary action, misbehaving students returned to classrooms. Teachers found themselves blamed for theft and violence. With only half the violence reported, violence (even rape) escalated against teachers. Public officials had propagated the theory of systemic racism to condone school violence as "merely a symptom of the injustices of our school system." Instead of calling students "criminals," they portrayed them as "romantic figures fighting for a cause when they steal from somebody or when they push a teacher down the steps." Predictably, teachers left to take jobs at suburban schools. Whites, Shanker said, were not withdrawing their children from city schools because of racial integration but because their children had become victims of violence.

At university, radicals became an increasingly ensconced priesthood, articulating a serpentine catechism of diversity. They offered a visionary political regime with cosmopolitan campuses as the nexuses of a new global order born of collective efforts to solve problems that racist, sexist, capitalist nation-states could not solve. University researchers turned to quantitative social science and ignored liberal arts as the realm of irrationality. Group identities secured new studies that combined metaphysical identity parsing with ethical, social, and political commitments. A growing student population required hundreds of thousands of professors and administrators to peddle identity and monitor compliance with federal regulations. After the first black studies program launched in 1968, white elites donated to support more than five hundred programs by 1971. Women's studies programs climbed from 150 in 1975 to 300 in 1980. Hispanics demanded funding for Chicano studies. The federal government and corporate foundations sponsored a proliferating number of "global" and "international studies" programs. Universities began to implement anti-racism training, anti-discriminatory policies, and new speech codes on campuses. Judy Katz's "White Awareness" anti-racism training (for which she received a PhD) began, "Racism is a white problem"; more specifically, citing the US Commission on Mental Health, it was "the number one mental health problem in the United States."[129] White racism caused "the psychological, sociological, and physical genocide of Third World people." Moreover, the dissonance between whites' espoused ideals and "living a personal lie" that denied their role as oppressor was "extremely damaging to white people's psyche" and made them empirically ignorant, "unable to experience themselves and their culture as *it is*. This inability for experiencing reality keeps white people from confronting and seeing their true selves and results in individuals and a society that is less than fully human." Whites are then in a state of "confusion around their identity"; they universalize whiteness as the norm but avoid coming to terms with the guilt of their whiteness by not seeing themselves as white and thus claim some European ethnic heritage: Italian, Irish, or Jewish. As the "disease of racism runs deeply through every white citizen," Katz's training program combined readings with "white-on-white encounter groups" to aid whites in "becoming a fully developed and whole person": "Whites must identify with the culture and their whiteness, not as a luxury but as an integral part of who they are." Jane Moosbruker's Internal Racism Project at Boston College in 1969 had a goal of "'reeducation' of the university staff, faculty and student populace to the problems that blacks encounter with the white majority." It would "generate changes in the recruiting of faculty and students, in the hiring of staff, and in the curriculum of the university," but "only if the whites involved...were willing to 'face the facts.'"[130] It presented racially tense films with "real shock value" to produce a "'moving' and 'emotional experience.'" The poor response from students, reported Moosbruker, "indicated a negativism which further illustrates the need for such a program."

Securing a constituency of minorities and women, the radicals outflanked public opinion by taking over the agencies that implemented the 1964 Civil Rights Act. They overturned its mandate of equal opportunity to institute preferential treatment. Implementing Title VI, the new progressive coalition simply circumvented the APA's required standard rulemaking procedures, subject to judicial review. When its decisions were challenged, friendly progressive judges upheld the radicals' new standard of equitable relief despite the lack of a statutory provision. In what R. Shep Melnick calls "institutional leap-frogging," "The courts or federal agencies take the initiative on a race- or gender-related issue. The other branch adds to the regulation and sends it back to the first, which in turn makes the regulation a bit more demanding."[131] Praising the expertise of agencies in formulating guidelines, courts added their power of injunction to their rulings cooking up statutory or constitutional legitimacy. The Office for Civil Rights (OCR) issued *informal* guidance documents to recipients of federal funds that it expected the courts to uphold. The courts in turn deferred to the OCR's "interpretive memos," "clarifications," and "guidelines." Thus "civil rights regulation contains few clear-cut, publicly proclaimed rules. It rests instead on layer after layer of administrative guidelines, interpretive memos, suggestions included in enforcement handbooks, judicial interpretations of statutes and of agency rules, and even more esoteric judicial doctrines on burden of proof." Average Americans were clueless about the arcane methods of regulation. The most radical proposals entered into law without congressional debate and were even antithetical to the agencies' originating statutes.

The 1965 education acts had given the OCR authority to oversee billions in federal spending. But instead of cutting off funding for discriminatory practices, the OCR used its rulemaking authority to work with sympathetic federal judges. It issued advanced advice, including broad rules and concrete directives, to those receiving federal funds, which courts, deferring to agency expertise, enforced in detailed structural injunctions. Violating school officials would be arrested for contempt. While the CRA mandated that desegregation "shall not mean assigning children to particular schools to achieve racial balance," the OCR wrote rules for racial balance anyway with quotas for proportional representation of black students. The Fifth Circuit Court deferred to the agency's expertise on civil rights and directed district courts to do the same. In 1970 the OCR ruled that bilingual education, which few school districts had implemented, was an educational requirement. It had little force until 1974, when the Supreme Court recognized the OCR's authority to mandate support for "national origin-minority group children." The next year the OCR used that ruling to justify extensive regulation requiring classes and support for ethnic minorities. It made consent decrees with various state and local school districts, extracting concessions based on political expedience.

It was not so simple with affirmative action in government contracts. In 1968 the Office of Federal Contract Compliance (OFCC) devised the Philadelphia Plan that would require preferential hiring for federally funded construction contracts. The plan's obvious quota goals, to be monitored by federal compliance officers, conflicted with both Section 703(j) barring quotas and long-established bidding procedures already in place. Comptroller Elmer Staats squashed the program as a violation of competitive bidding. But in one of the great ironies of the period, it was resurrected by Nixon's labor secretary George Shultz, who took it up with vigor. In his typical petty fashion, Nixon believed that by embracing affirmative action he could court both blacks and labor while turning them against one another. With its new mandate, the OFCC not only implemented affirmative action, but its 1969 Order No. 4 extended preferential hiring to all federal contracts, which accounted for one-third of the American labor force.

Congress denied the EEOC, which implemented Title VII, both broad rulemaking authority and cease and desist powers. Many considered the EEOC a "toothless tiger." It was understaffed, and the first commissioner, Franklin Roosevelt, Jr., began conservatively. Samuel C. Jackson ended his term proclaiming that the "case method" had been "ineffectual," but he affirmed that the law could "increase the rate of hire and promotion of Negroes and Spanish-speaking Americans."[132] Embarrassed by criticisms of the ineffectiveness of the EEOC, Johnson appointed Clifford Alexander, who supported a more radical agenda. Typical of the new radical staffers in the commission was Timothy Jenkins, former SNCC member, Howard University professor, and future lawyer for communist Angela Davis. Calling EEOC policy a failure in 1969, he called for "legal" remedies such as enforced quota hiring, compulsory training programs, and yearly governmental and private requirements for the creation of new jobs.[133] The EEOC used the voluntary forms it requested from companies to build a statistical case for systemic racism, and the courts simply adopted the broad EEOC standards that violated its originating statute and granted the commission full rulemaking authority. In *Griggs v. Duke Power Co.* (1971), the Supreme Court overturned a competence test that fulfilled all legal requirements; it used the EEOC's theory of systemic racism that expanded its domain from intentional individual discrimination to "disparate impact," weighing the effects of a company's impartial policy on protected groups. The 1972 Equal Opportunity Act granted the EEOC enforcement powers to prosecute cases of discrimination in the federal courts that had granted it deference. In a massive shakedown, large corporations in the 1970s paid out millions in settlements. In 1977, Jimmy Carter appointed as chair Eleanor Holmes Norton, signer of the 1970 *Black Woman's Manifesto*, which began, "Racism and capitalism have trampled the potential of black people in this country and thwarted their self-determination." After probing analyses of "adverse effects," in 1978 four agencies adopted the "four-fifths rule": a company's "selection rate for any race, sex, or ethnic group which is less than four-fifths... of the rate for the group with the highest rate will generally be regarded... as evidence of adverse impact."

White students could not be made aware of unconscious racism if they remained in segregated environments. Instead of symbolically admitting a few blacks to white schools, forced busing aimed to integrate schools fully. Title IV of the 1964 Civil Rights Act explicitly affirmed color-blind desegregation. It did not mean forced integration: "'Desegregation' shall not mean the assignment of students to public schools in order to overcome racial imbalance." But, the Supreme Court ruled, "The Constitution does not prohibit district courts from using their *equity power* to order assignment of teachers to achieve a particular degree of faculty desegregation."[134] *Brown v. Board* could be interpreted not as an order against segregation but as an order to integrate. If a judge found no constitutional mandate to integrate, civil rights groups found another judge until the Supreme Court, looking to social science as a precedent, ruled in 1971 that forced busing was constitutional.[135] Judges' structural implementation plans focused on large, ethnically diverse school systems, requiring elaborate gerrymandering schemes to bus black children to white schools outside the city center. Social scientists and elites crusaded for busing; neither white nor black parents supported the policy, nor did it lead to academic success. In 1973 the Supreme Court, applying adverse impact to "de facto" segregation, found that the Denver School District had violated equal protection by not implementing a forced busing program.[136] Because intent to discriminate could not be proven, ruled Justice Brennan, "the burden is on the school authorities" to prove non-racist motives. In Massachusetts the NAACP sued the Boston School Committee in 1972 for its failure to comply with a state integration law requiring further integration of any school with more than 50 percent minorities, and federal district judge Wendell Arthur Garrity issued an order to implement it.[137] Everywhere around the country, whites left the city or sent their children to new private schools. Working-class Irish Catholics in South Boston and Charlestown resorted to protests. In the North, the change in the percentage of integrated schools remained minimal, but the white ethnics' neighborhoods and social fabric were marked for destruction. As for southern schools, they could make no defense of preserving a way of life because they, unlike white ethnics, were merely white.

The nation abandoned the legal standard of equal opportunity for equitable relief, or applying race inequality to achieve race equality. The courts upheld preferential treatment for minorities in voting, employee and union seniority, education, hiring and promotions, and job testing. The goal was no longer punishing actual acts of discrimination but in directing future behavior to achieve a vague racial justice. In his review of the Civil Rights Commission's three-hundred-page *The Federal Civil Rights Enforcement Effort* (1970), Nathan Glazer pointed out, "*There is scarcely a reference to any single case of discrimination by anybody in this enormous report.... It uses a new measure—the achievement of full equality of groups.*"[138] He noted that blacks accounted for 15 percent of federal employees but constituted only 11 percent of the population. The notion of transitional inequality on the way to equity covered for the fact that the civil rights agencies had become special interest groups entrenched in bureaucratic infrastructure—defending their entitlements and delivering privileges to their constituents. Every civil rights agency grew in personnel and budget. In 1967 the EEOC employed 570; by 1973 it had grown to 1,500; its staff increased from 314 in 1966 to 3,746 in 1980; over the same period its budget grew from $2.3 million to $125 million. As it grew more powerful, the EEOC hired fewer whites. In 1966 it employed 40 percent blacks, which increased to 49 percent in 1971. And it lowered standards to do so. Glazer noted that in order to further black representation in federal jobs, the "arithmetic and algebraic components of the Federal Service Entrance Examination...have largely been eliminated." The list of victim groups expanded with the civil rights lobby's power to regulate all employers concerning jobs, promotions, appointments, and admissions; it grew to include women, Hispanics, Asians, Indians, the elderly, the disabled, and (later) homosexuals.

The civil rights bureaucracy published tracts to justify its expanding power. *Racism in America: And How to Combat It* (1970), with a cover portraying a white stick man sitting on top of a black one, affirmed racism as not just historical but embedded in "long-established institutional structures and practices."[139] "White racism" subordinated "negroes, Puerto Ricans, Mexican Americans, Japanese Americans, Chinese Americans, and American Indians." It caused black poverty and violence and indeed every minority problem, where they "live, their incomes, their self-images and degree of self-confidence, the nature and stability of their families, their attitudes toward authority, their levels of educational and cultural attainment, and their occupational skills." And whites were "guilty" of racism even if they did not intend it because racism is a "matter of *result* rather than *intention*." "Almost every white American supports some form of institutional subordination"; thus "they are all 'unintentional racists.'" Though most racism lost its overtness, it continued invisibly in institutional "mechanisms indirectly related to color," such as "'merit employment' programs," white flight and self-segregation, arguments for decentralization, and resistance to race-integration busing. Yet nonwhite groups should also retain their identities. Race separation is only racist if whites choose it because then it involves subordination. *Whiteness* must no longer be universal, rendering minorities either invisible on television or only visible in ways to hurt their self-esteem. First whites must become aware of racism "in their own behavior and in the institutions around them" and then their privilege, "how racism provides benefits to whites" psychologically, economically, and politically. This requires not just self-examination but a confrontation; only nonwhites can reveal racism. Next is to empower nonwhites, building up their capabilities with large public welfare spending programs led by minorities, who possess "sensitivity to human values." These programs must extend to local and state policies, both public and private. Americans must become aware that "overcoming the burdens of racism will cost a great deal of money, time, effort, and institutional change." To "develop alliances of nonwhites and whites" in order to combat racism, a strategy of integration must provide jobs for minorities in predominantly white institutions in business, the suburbs, and public schools. This must go beyond equal opportunity to equal representation so that "the minority-group...exercises power and influence at least proportional to its numbers."

In sex discrimination, the EEOC began conservatively. It exempted jobs where sex was a "bona fide occupational qualification" and allowed discrimination between men and women in newspaper classified ads. By 1968, commissioners Aileen Hernandez and Richard Graham had vacated their seats in frustration to found the National Organization for Women. But new appointees to the commission pushed a radical agenda. In 1971 the EEOC quietly extended preferential treatment to women in Revised Order No. 4. The 1972 Title IX Education Amendments, which prohibited discrimination in federally funded education, were a Trojan horse for activism. Birch Bayh had written it with girls' sports in mind, and Nixon's signing statement only mentioned school busing. But Title IX followed the same relationship between the courts and agencies. Even though it focused on sex discrimination in education and lacked Title VI's constitutional right of private suit against discrimination, the Supreme Court decided that right existed anyway. Activists within the Department of Health, Education, and Welfare (HEW) applied "adverse impact" to every facet of education:

recruiting, admissions, financial aid, student rules, housing, health care, student hiring, curriculum, and women's studies programs.[140] Agencies redefined sexual harassment to include underrepresentation in medical and law schools. A regulatory morass of graft for myriad well-paid compliance officers developed at every school and college. In 1975 HEW passed rules requiring "equal athletic opportunity" for male and female intercollegiate sports, arrogating to itself the authority to inspect a college's selection of sports. Attached to a three-year limit for compliance was the vagary that unequal expenditures did not necessarily mean noncompliance. In 1979, the Department of Education established a three-pronged test to determine compliance: whether male and female participation levels reflected their proportionate enrollments, whether schools could prove the expansion of such programs, and whether the "interests and abilities" of the underrepresented sex had been accommodated.

The New Left created an entirely new social regulatory regime in federal agencies and in administrative law. Its assault on state capitalism and focus on participatory democracy fed the explosion of grassroots and citizen-lobbyist movements in the late 1960s and '70s, in civil rights, environmentalism, consumer protection, and worker health and safety: the Environmental Defense Fund (1967), the Consumer Federation of America (1968), Friends of the Earth (1970), the Center for Auto Safety (1970), Environmental Action (1970), Public Citizen (1971), and the Children's Defense Fund (1973). The liberal regulatory boards and commissions had worked to protect industries, setting price and entry restrictions. They blocked standing for those seeking deregulation and competition-increasing waivers. Radicals rejected the liberal presumption that elites given broad mandates to experiment could balance private industry and the public interest. Agencies had been captured by the interests they regulated. "Uncle Sam," said Ralph Nader in 1973, was a "Monopoly Man."[141] Moreover, the radicals rejected the liberal concept of the transcendent "public interest" for that of "distinct interests of various individuals and groups in society."[142] Society consisted of competing groups, so administration must include competing social interests. Elites must mobilize unorganized and thus underrepresented groups to affect agency policy. A new public interest law would represent the interests of consumers, environmentalists, and the poor. Nader published books on vanishing air quality and unsafe automobiles designed for profit at consumer risk. Nader's Raiders publicized corporate activities that hurt the public and funded the formation of other advocacy groups.

Given the change in elite social climate, Congress found a new model of response. In the 1973 Subcommittee Bill of Rights, the Democratic Party revoked the seniority principle to strip chairmanships from liberal southerners and distribute them to its more progressive members. The so-called Watergate babies elected in 1974 rejected the liberals' pluralistic compromise rooted in local politics for divisive grandstanding on national issues. Touting reform and transparency, they introduced televised proceedings and a new politics of posturing and soundbites. They no longer saw their primary task as lawmaking. Upon news of an emergency or disaster publicized by activists, Congress created a new agency or program to implement broad rules to control for it. Interested in casting the widest possible net to prevent an adverse event in the spectrum of risk, it maximized agencies' freedom to make quick, detailed, far-reaching decisions without paying the cost of extensive hearings, detailed investigation, decisions, and revision of specialized issues. While Congress had passed eleven consumer protection laws during the New Deal, it passed sixty-two from 1960 to 1978; where it passed five occupational and worker safety laws before, it passed twenty-one. Thus Congress could claim credit for the goods of broad legislation while blaming bureaucracy for unpopular implementation. If the agencies made decisions too unpopular or hurt business in their districts, congressmembers could then openly condemn them in hearings for bureaucratic overreach and demand they alter their standards.

While some scholars suggested a revival of nondelegation doctrine (which rendered the whole administrative state unconstitutional[143]), radicals saw an opportunity to bend the older regulatory scheme toward a new theory of justice and administrative policy, to secure new goods and services, and to make corporations pay for the externalities of industrial production. The new social agencies included the Council on Environmental Quality (1969), the Environmental Protection Agency (1970), the National Highway Traffic Safety Administration (1970), the Occupational Safety and Health Administration (1970), and the Consumer Product Safety Commission (1972). Moving away from the protection and regulation of private business, the new social regulation would protect clients, whether the oppressed or consumers, by regulating business with vast, intrusive regulation. In the new command-and-control regulation, agencies no longer adjudicated whether or not a regulation had been violated but directly regulated an industry by providing detailed standards for permissible and impermissible actions, and not just within an industry, but by *economy-wide standards across industries*, with the addition of timetables to prevent agency capture. The new agencies undermined corporate autonomy by extending agency controls over decisions formerly reserved to corporate managers.

The judiciary expanded social regulation by reversing decisions of Congress and the agencies. The courts' new function of judicial review had shifted from the protection of private rights to ensuring "the fair representation of a wide range of affected interests."[144] The presumption was no longer that of impartiality, nor of scientific management—that scientific experts would work with interested business to regulate markets—but that of agency capture, or designing ways to represent underprivileged groups against decisions made on behalf of industry. In the "due process revolution," they extended rights to new goods and services: a "property interest" in welfare rights, tenancy in low-income housing, possessing a driver's license, and government employment. Procedural protections were extended to students, parolees, and prisoners. The courts further diminished the older property rights; administrative agents no longer needed to obtain warrants to search a "closely regulated industry."[145] Judges extended legal standing to sue to millions of formerly unrepresented individuals and groups, including those indirectly, even minutely, affected by agency actions in areas of health, safety, consumer protection, the environment, and racial discrimination. Public interest lawyers specialized in suing corporations within agencies on behalf of their disadvantaged constituencies. Moreover, Congress had even authorized funding of "intervener programs" to do so. Groups could now sue the FCC if harmed by racist content. The FCC muzzled conservative talk-show hosts like Dan Smoot and denied licenses to radio stations that challenged civil rights.[146] The courts interpreted the APA to give advocacy groups greater participation in agency proceedings. Agencies would give *notice*, or propose guidelines, regulations, and standards published in the *Federal Register*. They also received *comment*, or held hearings, and revised rules, which were promulgated in technical detail. In multiple layers of review, the courts forced agencies to justify the rationale for their rules in order to limit corporate influence.

The most important institutional change took place in the family. Intellectuals by the late 1960s firmly supported no-fault divorce. The modern era had changed the incentives for marriage, they argued, and families were separating anyway. Lawyers and judges objected to the legal fictions used to bypass statutory requirements for fault. Forcing unhappy couples to stay married, they pleaded, was unethical. In truth it reflected the growing class divide. Elites, tantalized by sexual liberation in new gender roles, wanted freedom from the traditional duties of the institution even as 60 percent of Americans polled by Gallup in 1968 wanted to make divorce "more difficult." Feminists like Herma Hill Kay, who shaped the Uniform Marriage and Divorce Act, supported no-fault divorce as a way to destroy the patriarchal family and liberate women. Reagan supported and signed the first no-fault law in California in 1969. Forty-nine states had passed similar laws by

1983. Where liberals had used bureaucracy to prevent divorce, radicals used it to alter marital and parental roles. The new laws overturned the liberal "democratic compromise," in which proving fault forced the misbehaving party to pay. Now divorce was unilateral, regardless of the misbehaving party. Women initiated most divorces because they held an advantage in custody (90 percent) and child support. In the family courts' secretive labyrinth, litigants with no due process rights to speech, to religion, or to confront their accusers were subject, by capricious tests like "best interest" and "imputed income," to arbitrary decrees, fines, and incarcerations that unequally affected poor men, especially minorities.

Finally, the counterculture provided a new concept of business. It rejected the old middle-class mores for those of authenticity, or maximizing experiences for an elite class, best captured in two 1970 bestsellers, Charles Reich's *The Greening of America* and Alvin Toffler's *Future Shock*. The first described a cultural revolution in consciousness, habits, music, dress, and sex and the second a libertarian age in a computer-savvy tech world. Those united by the new consciousness transcended country and religion. The industrial age and working class resided in the past; the heroic future human would embrace transience in relationships with other people, things, ideas, places, and institutions. Both books captured an ethos of elites who required years of education before starting a career and who wanted relaxed sexual strictures, extended adolescence, and self-exploration without boundaries. The counterculture provided the mores for Silicon Valley, which arose in the atmosphere of freedom and genius: libertarianism as a personal and political philosophy. Steve Jobs traveled to India to meditate with a guru, and he devised the idea of personal computers from a homebrew club. After a decade of self-introspection, Jerry Rubin reinvented himself as a socially aware capitalist. Providing authentic experiences for elites, noted Toffler, was both a powerful marketing tool *and* good business. From 1971 to 1984, more than one million people underwent Werner Erhart's EST training to liberate their self-potential in hotel conference rooms. Describing EST in "The 'Me' Decade," Tom Wolfe noted that self-dissection has ever been the pastime of elites. Education and media would be packaged for the new individualists with content tailored to their preferences. There was money in "cultural diversity," providing exotic stewardesses for businessmen's peculiar tastes.[147] Technology in the computer revolution accentuated individualism. The new businessmen, hard at work and play, embraced entrepreneurism over liberal state capitalism. Bill Gates pointed out to computer hobbyists in 1976 that they had all purchased their computers but stolen his software, destroying the incentive for innovation. By 1978 "yuppies" (young urban professionals) had appeared in major cities all across America; it was the image of a generation socially liberal and economically conservative. The word was a play on yippies like Rubin, whose lucrative investments in Apple led him to view finance as a vehicle for activism. Rubin went on the road with Hoffman, putting on debates between yuppy and yippie for college students. In this moral hierarchy, neither those who "sold out" *nor* those who became bureaucrats lived among or like the poor they were supposed to save. The criticism of "selling out" was a virtue signal and justification of privilege, not by those who remained true to the movement against those who did not but by those who found jobs in government bureaucracy against those who took jobs in the private sector. The latter celebrated technology and capitalism as a better way to solve the old problem of exploitation. Large corporations, hating uncertainty, responded to demands for equality in race and gender; they worked with federal agencies to implement "equal opportunity" and even invented their own more vigorous affirmative action policies.

It was the end of the old, embedded liberalism with its concern for class and protection of "whole industrial sectors."[148] Both parties had turned against the middle class of the industrial economy. Socially conservative and economically liberal laborers conflicted with both the new Democratic base and with Republican business interests. And so arose two antagonistic populist constituencies: one Christian, white, and traditionalist, and the other an underclass of minorities and single females. Meanwhile, privileged elites held both parties' leadership, but they shared increasingly less with their bases. Republicans embraced the new libertarianism and neoconservatism, while privileged white and minority Democrats justified their affluence in bureaucracy and education by claiming to help the disadvantaged. Over the next three decades, the 1960s radicals would retain their influence and perfect their systems of thought in university humanities departments. And among centrists, a new school of thought called neoliberalism replaced the older liberalism in finance and bureaucracy. In the new knowledge economy, a new struggle of orders began among college-educated baby boomers, between these radicals and neoliberals. Their tensions, ideas, and their eventual marriage under Barack Obama will be the subject of our next two chapters.

5

NEOLIBERALISM

The liberal welfare-warfare state faced a crisis: the industrial economy could not fund the growth in both entitlements and military expenditures. The Nixon administration planted the seeds for a neoliberal political order, an oligarchy that enriched itself through finance capitalism and funded a growing dependent class through deficit spending. The neoliberal system of thought, forwarding a new ethics and economics, justified the marriage between monopoly capitalism and the administrative state. It ascended under Reagan and peaked in the 1990s under Clinton, bringing an era of globalization, mass immigration, and foreign intervention. But it reached an impasse under George W. Bush, whose presidency exposed the corruption of America's military and financial empire.

Great Society Implosion and the Nixon Transition

Supported by a white middle-class backlash, Nixon defeated McGovern in a landslide, but he continued the war on poverty, the sexual revolution, and the growth of the social regulatory state. He charged the Environmental Protection Agency (EPA) and the Occupational Safety and Health Administration (OSHA) with implementing the most expensive and expansive regulations in US history. The EPA's impossible mandate was to set ambient air quality standards within 30 days for particulate matter and pollutants that have "an adverse effect on the public health or welfare" and to issue within 120 days final standards, with all regions in compliance by 1975. The Clean Air Act required automakers, under threat of massive fines ($10,000 per car), to reduce carbon monoxide and hydrocarbons emissions by 90 percent by 1975. For stationary sources, the EPA worked with states to create State Implementation Plans to (by 1972) identify pollutants and set emission limits and reduction schedules for the two hundred thousand polluters in its jurisdiction. The Clean Water Act aspired to zero pollutant discharges by 1985. The EPA must promulgate standards by 1973; by 1974 it would issue effluent permits for all waste discharges into waterways as well as for municipal sewage treatment plants. It could enforce its rules with civil injunctions, criminal penalties (up to $25,000 per day and one year's imprisonment), and even closure of facilities that failed to meet its 1983 guidelines. The secretary of labor and OSHA had to "assure so far as possible every working man and woman in the nation safe and healthful working conditions and to preserve our human resources." They had to promulgate and enforce standards for all private-sector employees "to the extent feasible," an assessment of risk with no clear threshold or mandate. By 1974 OSHA had identified forty-two thousand chemical substances used in industry, including two thousand possible carcinogens.

Congress gave the agencies an unprecedented political mandate for risk management under the name of health. Regulators appealed to the authority of natural science, though Congress tasked them with integrating both scientific *and* social science data, both "unquantified environmental amenities and values" and "economic and technical considerations." The courts further expanded the agencies' responsibilities and admitted new suits that challenged their rules and standards. These rulings required the agencies to produce substantive bodies of evidence and held them to strict timetables for review.[1] But they also narrowed the category of formal rulemaking procedures required by the APA while increasing deference to agency decisions over the substance of their policies.[2] And in the name of health, agencies could appeal to the APA's "good cause" emergency exemption, a provision that permitted them to forego the normal rulemaking process. However, the agencies' task was illusory. First, to manage the risks of chemical hazards and meet optimistic regulatory timetables, Congress charged regulators to develop entirely new technologies. Second, scientists made moral tradeoffs disguised as technical calculations. Chief Justice William Rehnquist noted that scientists were choosing "whether the statistical possibility of future deaths should ever be disregarded in light of the economic costs of preventing those deaths."[3] Regulators thickened this technical veil by using impenetrable vocabulary about invisible, ambient air quality standards and occupational safety thresholds for dangerous toxins, which were measured in parts per million or billion. They assessed the probability of injury by using statistical models based on incomplete data and tenuous assumptions extrapolated from limited evidence. Moreover, most regulators using such language were not scientists at all but lawyers and compliance officers.

Social regulation was a model of inefficiency and injustice. Tasked with setting unachievable standards but seeking to avoid blame, the EPA and OSHA made worst-case scenario assumptions requiring the costliest implementation. Businesses routinely filed lawsuits against OSHA's interpretation of "feasibility." In 1977 OSHA used its emergency power to lower the exposure threshold for benzene, a chemical ubiquitous in petroleum and petrochemical industries, that would have been "prohibitive" for the industries.[4] Facing rebuke from both industry and Congress, OSHA exempted the 795,000 gas station employees exposed to the highest levels of benzene but applied it to the remaining 35,000 workers, most of whom worked in the rubber-manufacturing industry. OSHA estimated that compliance costs for the petroleum refining industry would reach $24 million in capital costs and $600,000 in first-year operating expenses to protect three hundred workers ($82,000 per employee), all of which it expected industries to absorb or pass on to consumers. In that case, the Supreme Court ruled that OSHA's ruling had not been "reasonably necessarily or appropriate" and remanded it to the agency, but the courts did uphold OSHA's stringent standard for asbestos and cotton dust.[5]

Costs ballooned. In 1969 Congress required agencies to complete environmental impact statements (EISs) for major federal actions; in 1971 agencies filled 2,000 EISs. To fulfill the new tasks, bureaucratic work became one of the fastest growing occupations in the 1970s. From 1970 to 1977, full-time positions in federal regulatory agencies grew from twenty-eight thousand to eighty-one thousand. When limited by hiring freezes in the 1970s, the federal government farmed out services to state and local governments, which increased their personnel 40 percent, some four million hires. From 1936 to 1977, the number of pages of federal regulations grew from 2,599 to 65,603; it sextupled from 1969 to 1974 and tripled during the 1970s. By 1972 the EPA had expanded to more than fifty laboratories, with two thousand experts in sixty different fields. Within the agencies, constant hearings exhausted resources; the EPA's lengthy rulemaking process was subject to layers of review and oversight. Lawyers and program managers concerned with practical research and legal mandates conflicted with scientists, who wanted to direct funds to career-advancing pure research. Agency decisions exacted ongoing relief, strained the economy, and soured the once-friendly relations between agencies and industry by imposing new costs for business that were often uncertain in scale, timing, and compliance. Regulations blocked smaller firms from market entry. Large corporations passed their costs on to consumers and often found lobbying and litigation cheaper than compliance. As legislators introduced numerous bills and riders to either exempt small firms from regulation or to restrict OSHA's jurisdiction, economists debated the impact of the new regulations. One estimate blamed them for 16 percent of the industrial productivity slowdown from 1972 to 1975, and another held it responsible for "about 30 percent of the decline in productivity growth in manufacturing during the 1970's."[6]

Liberals had taken for granted the economic growth necessary for entitlements. The "Great Inflation" of the 1970s, along with the oil embargo, crop shortages, and rising unemployment, followed the Great Society. Stagflation (stagnation + inflation), which included high oil prices *and* high unemployment, challenged Keynesian liberal economic assumptions. The future for entitlement programs looked bleak. Medicare and Medicaid caused major price inflation. They reduced the net price of hospital services at the time of consumption and thus removed the chief motive for cost restraint. Doctors recommended the most expensive care, and health care costs soared. People paid more out of pocket in total dollars, though the percentage they paid fell. Medicare costs quickly surpassed estimates, rising from $3.4 billion to $18 billion in ten years; the number of Medicaid recipients surged from four million to twenty-four million. By 1976, Medicare and Medicaid financed medicinal services for one-fifth of the population at a cost of $32 billion. Social Security, by 1981, teetered "on the edge of bankruptcy."

At the local level, Democratic mayors circumvented the labor coalition by promoting entitlements, administered by an army of bureaucrats and social workers, that destroyed black families and communities. Radicals organized the inner-city poor for welfare rights. In "tin-cup" urban policy, mayors like Detroit's Coleman Young, elected in 1973, stoked racial animosity, driving out middle-class whites and blacks. For revenue, he turned to state and federal grants, which by the late 1970s paid up to one-third of the city workforce. The Federal Housing Act had disastrous effects.[7] Section 235 had provided mortgage subsidies for 400,000 housing units by 1972. With the cooperation of appraisers, realtors, and bankers, speculators bought cheap homes in the slums, made cosmetic repairs, and then sold them for inflated prices to government-backed buyers. Under Section 236, which provided 593,000 more units, the government subsidized 90 percent of construction costs. While profits were capped, construction investments became a tax shelter for the rich. The Housing and Community Development Act of 1974 created the Section 8 program, in which tenants paid no more than 30 percent of their income for rent, with federal money paying the difference. Poor residents who could not pay their mortgages walked away. The chronic housing oversupply brought abandoned homes, reduced property values, and white flight. Businesses fled and crime surged. National homicide rates doubled, driven by black crime, from 4.5 per 100,000 in the early 1960s to 9.0 in 1978; in Chicago, from 10.3 in 1960 to 25.0 in 1975.[8] The rate of aggravated assaults, robbery, and forcible rape tripled. The tremendous gains blacks had made in voter registration, income, school integration, college attendance, and employment came at the expense of a large class divide. In 1978 black sociologist William Julius Wilson noted that race mattered less than class: affirmative action had secured a new class of black elites in bureaucracy and business, while welfare had mired a black underclass, some 30 percent, in permanent dependency. From 1960 to 1985, black illegitimacy increased from 21.6 to 61.4 percent.[9] Families headed by women rose from 24.4 to 56.7 percent, with 40 percent of children on public assistance. Poor blacks had a 40 percent dropout rate and committed 40 percent of all murders. Programs like school busing ended once they affected white and black activists themselves; none of the prominent Democrats sent their children to integrated schools.

The sexual revolution subsidized the destruction of the middle-class family. Under no-fault laws, divorce spiked, doubling from 1960 to 1980. Only 11 percent of children born in the 1950s experienced divorce, compared to 50 percent of those born in the 1970s. Illegitimacy skyrocketed among the poor. Social workers went door-to-door advertising welfare benefits, which were only paid out to unmarried single mothers, encouraging broken families by substituting fathers with payments. The city riots had driven out manufacturers, destroying the jobs black males needed to start families and gain self-respect.

Physical and sexual abuse rose as children were separated from their biological parents. Progressives blamed the nuclear family and instituted a new regime of abuse *prevention*, including restraining orders and mandatory educational programs on sex relations.[10] Domestic violence, which gained its contemporary meaning in 1973, recast spousal abuse, a criminal act, as a social problem. In the muddied area of sexual consent, which depended on a woman's subjective feelings, Susan Brownmiller in 1975 abstracted from concrete incidents to define rape as power, a form of systemic oppression. Studies reported a crisis of "date rape." Educational programs focused on preventative care and communication instead of safety with the goal of changing attitudes about sex. In 1974, Congress passed a child protective services law for social workers to replace the fragmenting family. For the elites, divorce eventually levelled off as couples developed new ways to interact. For the poor, a vast bureaucracy replaced the traditional family's functions.

The new divorce laws were designed to shame and deprioritize homemakers and force all women into the workforce. Herma Hill Kay saw it as a problem that "mothers of young children are consistently the most underemployed": "It is critical that major governmental planning be undertaken to devise ways of facilitating labor market entry and job continuity for these women."[11] With industry shrinking as a share of the economy and the concept of "family income" destroyed, women entered the workplace en masse, driving down wages. Their income rose throughout the 1970s and '80s, nearing that of male high school graduates, while the wages of working-class men steadily declined. Service and retail trade contributed more than 70 percent to private-sector job growth from 1973 to 1980, with 40 percent of those jobs concentrated in food, health, and business services, which grew at sixteen times the rate of industry. Restaurants created more new jobs than existed in the automotive and steel industries combined. Economist Emma Rothschild summarized the new "women's work": "Waiting on tables, defrosting frozen hamburgers, rendering 'services to buildings,' looking after the old and the ill.''[12] Those women made up 89 percent of workers in nursing and personal care facilities and made on average $3.87 per hour in 1979, compared with $6.69 in manufacturing and $6.16 in the entire private economy. Women dominated part-time, low-paying, dead-end service professions (56 percent of workers in restaurants, 81 percent in health services). The new labor-intensive industries were structurally different from manufacturing in that they purchased inputs mostly from suppliers within services and trade and not from other industries. Their expansion would not necessarily boost American manufacturing.

As the US proportion of global GDP declined, neoliberals challenged the justice of union pay compared with low-pay service jobs. The older industrial capitalism, which had made the US a leading manufacturer, prioritized public investment in infrastructure and industrial protection, which subsidized basic services, thereby lowering the cost of living and doing business. Wealthy entrepreneurs took risks by investing in factories, employing unionized workers, and making goods to sell at a profit. But most trade unions, it was now said, were inefficient in terms of wages and working conditions. And the most successful represented not unskilled workers but high-income workers like airline pilots and craft unions in carpentry, plumbing, and electricity. Trade unions were really cartels that increased their wages by monopolizing labor and depressing employment. Milton Friedman calculated, "The effect of the higher pay of unions [10–15 percent] is [4 percent] lower pay for all other workers." Unions had negotiated for extravagant health care and pensions, which made their companies less competitive and ultimately their own jobs less secure. Municipal unions for garbagemen, teachers, police, and firemen negotiated with city officials who paid their wages with taxes. They grew in power in cities that faced both a decline in manufactures and middle-class flight to the suburbs. By 1975 New York faced bankruptcy, with only $34 million to cover a $453 million debt. It borrowed money against city pension funds to operate busses and the subway and pleaded successfully with Albert Shanker to use teachers' pensions to buy city bonds.

Nixon was the last economic liberal. He liked balanced budgets but famously admitted in 1971 that he was "now a Keynesian." Believing economic recession had cost him the 1960 election, he opted, with only 3.5 percent unemployment and 5 percent inflation, for a "full employment" budget that he thought would reduce unemployment by deficit spending without increasing inflation. He later wrote, "Philosophically...I was still against wage-price controls, even though I was convinced that the objective reality of the economic situation forced me to impose them."[13] A Democratic Congress had given Nixon the authority to fix prices in 1970, but none thought he would use it; Schultz called it "a political dare." Nixon-appointed Fed chairman Arthur Burns had already declared his conversion to price controls, admitting the need for government to balance business and labor with a wage-review price board. At Camp David, Nixon and his aides agreed to a ninety-day wage and price freeze (they spent more time discussing whether a speech during the popular TV show *Bonanza* would hurt him in public opinion). The decision to fix prices was a hit: Wall Street had its then-largest single day increase. But by the time Nixon reinstated price controls in 1973, they stopped working. Gene Healy recalled, "Ranchers stopped shipping their cattle to the market, farmers drowned their chickens, and consumers emptied the shelves of supermarkets."[14] The price hikes of the oil embargo, leading to the long gas lines of the 1970s, made it politically unfeasible to lift the price control on gasoline.

Nixon became the first neoliberal by scrapping the Bretton Woods system. American dollars had returned to Europe by military expenditures, which skyrocketed during the Vietnam War. In August 1971, the British ambassador requested that the Treasury Department convert $3 billion into gold. In his Camp David meeting, Nixon agreed to remove the US from the gold standard, closing the Gold Pool (halting convertibility of the dollar) and introducing floating exchange rates, a Friedman idea. This violated the Bretton Woods Articles of Agreement, ending the postwar financial order. No longer buying gold, foreign central banks used their balance-of-payment surpluses from US military spending to purchase US Treasury debt, which financed rising US deficits. In what Michael Hudson called *Super Imperialism*, the US could spend without borrowing from US investors, while the presence of US military bases reminded foreign nations of the meaning of "full faith and credit."[15] While it was a safe investment for foreign elites (the US had the world's largest economy), it crippled their own nations' economic development when they sold their profitable industrial sectors to US investors and borrowed from US financiers. If nations did not buy dollar assets and US Treasury securities, then their currencies would rise against the dollar in world markets, slowing their exports. But oil-producing nations saw their holdings in the devalued US dollar depreciate. They increased the price of oil 870 percent in the 1970s (from $4.31 in December 1973 to $10.31 in January 1974 alone) to keep its parity with the value of gold, which rose 1,200 percent in the 1970s. This, combined with oil-exporting nations' defeat by a US-backed Israel in the October 1973 Yom Kippur War and the rise of terrorism, threatened to upend US–Middle Eastern relations.

Secretary of State Henry Kissinger negotiated the petrodollar system to end the oil embargo and secure global demand for the dollar. The Saudi royal family agreed to price oil sales exclusively in the dollar, refuse other currencies as payment for oil, and keep its massive profits in dollar assets. The US agreed to protect Saudi oil fields and provide $2 billion in military contracts. By 1975, all OPEC nations had agreed to price their oil in dollars and, amassing huge surpluses, to invest petrodollars in US securities and in the financial markets of major industrial economies. Oil-importing countries had to keep dollar reserves and pay higher prices for oil, incurring long-term debts; debt among the top one hundred oil-importing developing countries increased 150 percent from 1973 to 1977. Private investors and governments discretely invested billions through major commercial banks.

Brazil, Argentina, and Turkey accepted economic restructuring in return for loans from the International Monetary Fund (IMF) and American financial institutions. Thus the US secured the dollar as the world's reserve currency by making political arrangements with oil-producing countries and introducing a web of financial services. Nations' economies depend on the dollar's value, which determines the price of their domestic goods and services. To facilitate financial exchanges, the Society for Worldwide Interbank Financial Telecommunication (SWIFT) was established in 1973, supported by 239 banks in fifteen countries (and monitored by the NSA). The US could use the dollar's monopoly currency status as a weapon by restricting access to dollar markets. Defiant nations faced US subversion or even military intervention. By 1981 all foreign central banks demanded dollars. They were easily exchanged, underwritten by US taxpayers, and relatively well managed by macroeconomic policy.

The Neoliberal System

As the American elite separated from its middle-class moorings, two thinkers defined its sense of justice. Milton Friedman and John Rawls, often viewed as antitheses, both expressed the neoliberal consensus. *Neoliberal* in part comes from the "classical liberal" or free-market policies of Nobel Prize–winning Friedman, who warned that the liberals' state interference, such as price controls intended to benefit low-income workers, would cause inflation. Only the free market, Friedman argued, self-regulated to correct prices and wages for the right amount of goods. Thus central banks must privilege anti-inflationary monetary policies over fiscal policies, such as taxation and redistribution by "big government." The free market was predicated on *homo economicus*, a rationally choosing individual who (if free to choose) maximizes his preferences and thereby wealth creation, benefiting consumers: "People in pursuing their own self-interest would also promote the general interest." There was no need for governmental constraints on corporations. Monopolies, he argued, could not exist under free-market conditions that provided incentives to cheat and avoid cooperation; cartels became unstable, could only work with few players, and soon faced market competition (ignoring the Fed's cartel over the money supply). Monopolies actually depended on government interference in licensing, tariffs, and regulation. To secure cartel prices, industries captured agencies that were supposed to regulate them and then used those agencies to bar entry to competitors. Thus antitrust laws did "far more harm than good" by impeding market competition and efficiency. Alan Greenspan agreed with Friedman: "No one will ever know what new products, processes, machines, and cost-saving mergers failed to come into existence, killed by the Sherman Act before they were born."[16] Robert Bork argued that antitrust laws violated "original intent" jurisprudence.[17] What appeared to be monopoly in industry was really greater "efficiency." Antitrust, said Friedman, should only be used to smash labor unions. Neoliberalism included a theory of public management and policy. Government must nurture innovation and enhance productivity in a competitive marketplace by deregulation, liberalization of trade and industry, and privatization of state-owned enterprises. Globally Friedman advised removing controls on finance and trade: "Eliminate all tariffs and all restrictions on foreign trade, and…enable the world to come in as competition to prevent domestic monopoly."[18] Democratic institutions posed a problem as national self-determination could impede market efficiency in a global division of labor. US intervention, suggested Friedrich Von Hayek, may be necessary to "allow American financial institutions to operate unhindered within [foreign] territory."[19] Thus neoliberals displaced the liberals' concept of the democratic subject with that of the consumer—economic concentration would promote "consumer welfare."

John Rawls's 1971 *Theory of Justice* amalgamated neoliberalism with redistributive politics. To make his theory friendly to quantitative social science, he inserted *homo economicus* into a new theory of the social contract. Claiming to abandon metaphysics, he would apply only "the notion of pure procedural justice" in a new theory, the "original position."[20] In this hypothetical social contract, persons (both "rational," or pursuing their own conception of the good, and "reasonable," understanding that they must limit their actions by agreement with others), prior to any political order, agree to represent another individual in choosing the principles of justice that will order the society he will live in.[21] Historically, societies have been founded to protect particular interests. But Rawls introduced a "veil of ignorance," behind which one must choose the basic principles of justice without knowing "his place in society, his class position or social status; nor...his fortune in the distribution of natural assets and abilities, his intelligence and strength and the like."[22] Given the possibility that one might be poor, he would choose the outcome of the greatest wealth for the least advantaged. He would select freedoms to follow his personal view of the good (religious toleration), legal protections against discrimination, and welfare programs that give him an equal opportunity to succeed. Rawls thus defended both "basic liberties" *and* distributive schemes that would help the disadvantaged to compete.[23] Basic goods, he argued, *must* be protected in a certain "serial order."[24] First came basic liberties (the right to vote and hold office; freedom of speech, thought, conscience, and association; the right to hold property; freedom from arbitrary arrest and seizure). Second, "social and economic inequalities are to be arranged" for "the greatest benefit of the least advantaged," with "offices and positions open to all under conditions of fair equality of opportunity." The "least advantaged" was an abstract economic group that varied from society to society. Rawls had in mind "the working class," but his theory justified different legal treatment according to race and gender. Once groups had equal opportunity, their members would possess "self-esteem" as individuals, alleviating envy over inequalities. Thus Rawls promoted market efficiency, but he defined justice as prior to and ultimately consistent with it. He also defended bureaucratic rule under social regulation. Indeed, a "hierarchical class structure" could justly embody the "right form" of government. Constitutional interpretation would conform to a "traditional idea of democratic government," but judicial review would amend it by appeals not to "basic (or natural) rights" but to "conceptions of the person and of social cooperation most likely to be congenial to the public culture of a modern democratic society." Administrators would have greater discretion to act in particular cases as the veil of ignorance diminished.

Friedman attacked the liberal regime as inefficient; Rawls attacked it as unfair. As to the source of injustice, Friedman blamed government constraint on individual liberty, and Rawls blamed chance. But the two were more similar than supposed, and their rival ideas formed the two pillars of the neoliberal welfare state. They both offered abstract theories of the free market or original position to forward a new theory of justice that promoted centralization in monopolies and bureaucracies. Beginning from the abstract individual, stripped of all ideological preconceptions, both represented two ends of a spectrum, from risk-taking to risk aversion, that sought to harness self-interest for the public good. Justice for Friedman meant securing freedom for equal opportunity and rewarding risks, which best produced equal distribution of property: the innovative capitalist hero creates wealth, protects consumer rights from government, and redistributes wealth to the disadvantaged via low prices. Justice for Rawls meant securing basic liberties while distributing property to elevate all individuals in equal opportunity to take risks: the caring bureaucrat justifies his privileges by working for the least among us. Both agreed on unequal outcomes born of natural differences, hard work, and benefits for those disadvantaged by chance of birth. Friedman was sensitive to the claim that he promoted callousness, Rawls to the claim that he impeded risk-taking.[25] Friedman insisted that private associations better handled charity. And Rawls wrote, "The difference principle permits indefinitely large inequalities in return for small gains to the less favored," but income and wealth inequality "should not be excessive."[26] Equal and free competition, Rawls said, meant scrapping the minimum wage and allowing the free market to determine wages but then supplementing wages with government subsidies, tax credits, and employment. Thus, both believed in fair wealth distributions, but they disagreed about the best trickle-down scheme: corporations or bureaucracies. And both redirected esteem away from the practice of industrial virtues to honor and reward the elites who help the disadvantaged.

Friedman and Rawls both spoke the language of liberty and employed a rhetoric of relativism that promoted individual freedom from government and denied that a free people needed to share a common conception of the good. But this concealed a certain vision of the good life disguised by Friedman's "equality of opportunity...to promote the full use of our human resources" and Rawls's "contract conception of justice [that] supports the self-esteem of citizens generally."[27] Both taught government nonintervention in the private realm. Friedman supported the individual right to choose without state interference, and Rawls claimed that the liberal state should be confined to matters of public procedural justice because it could not determine matters of private good. Friedman called for the legalization of drugs (including heroin) and sex (prostitution, abortion, and homosexuality) as matters of individual choice, meaning the state would no longer support the traditional family. Rawls rejected the shaming of permissive "sexual relationships" and called for the state to provide equal services for those who could not afford them, meaning the state would intervene to destroy the traditional family.[28] Let citizens be as irrational as they please so long as they do not harm others or take reserves from the less-advantaged. Yet, as it turned out, Rawls said, "Not all reasonable balances are the same." Opposition to first trimester abortion, for example, was unreasonable.[29] For both men, education should teach these possibilities but in reality encourage them as experiments. Thus, by means of *homo economicus*, both justified a new morality for *homo biologicus*. Both led to state control in private affairs by encouraging state interventions. Friedman's rhetoric on sexual freedom was inseparable from Rawls's bureaucracy that would have to raise bastard children. Friedman's free trade, outsourcing, and turning infrastructure and industry over to rent-seeking corporations required Rawls's interventionist state to provide unemployment, welfare, and health care for dislocated workers. Friedman diffused the race issue by arguing for its inefficiency under free markets but a possible choice of corporate diversity, and Rawls embraced affirmative action under the difference principle. Friedo-Rawlsianism created the neoliberal consensus between elites in business and bureaucracy to support the least advantaged and erode the old middle class.

Neoliberalism, focusing on economic efficiency and compassion for the disadvantaged, was a win-win for centralized industry. Friedman argued that the end of business was profit, and he rejected the idea that business had a responsibility to promote social justice, help the poor, or support the traditional family. Instead of firms paying males family wages, broken families would offer two workers for the price of one and a half while also paying bureaucrats to raise their children. And those laborers would now compete with millions of legal and illegal immigrants. Elite feminists took token positions in corporate America, receiving competitive pay and honor, while working-class women worked low-paying jobs fed by the promise of raises that were funded by decreased wages to their prospective husbands. Homemaking mothers were dishonored as parasites. Despite declining self-reported rates of happiness since 1970, facilitated by the ruin of family, kin, and purpose, women now took pride in expendable jobs; in the name of race solidarity, minorities welcomed cheap labor that further depressed their wages.

Political theorists praised Rawls for single-handedly reviving the field and constructing a new liberalism preserved from Leftist radicalism. Legal scholars, celebrating Rawls's new "center-left practical consensus," applied his views to Fourteenth Amendment Equal Protection, in which disadvantaged groups received special treatment or "welfare rights."[30] The Supreme Court cited the "new property," the right of the disadvantaged to government largesse, forty times from 1968 to 1978.[31] Friedman became policy advisor to Barry Goldwater. The courts adopted his ideas on antitrust and mergers, think tanks—the Heritage Foundation (1973), Cato Institute (1974), and the Manhattan Institute (1977)—popularized them, and politicians endorsed them, including Ronald Reagan, Margaret Thatcher, and Deng Xiaoping.[32] Deng introduced "socialism with Chinese characteristics" after the death of Mao Zedong in 1976; Westerners called it "neoliberalism with Chinese characteristics."[33] Neoliberal economists displaced Keynesians in research universities and business schools, whose students returned to their home countries of Chile, Argentina, and Mexico as well as to the World Bank, IMF, and UN.

Economists and activists found common cause in questioning Keynesian economics on unemployment, the Phillips Curve, the business cycle, inflation, and government intervention. They opposed inefficient government programs with poor oversight, cronyism, and mismanagement. Both Ralph Nader and Chicago economist George Stigler attacked the ICC's cozy relationship with industry. Stigler influentially argued that regulation, rather than advancing the public interest, created a cartel benefitting regulators and the regulated industries. It stifled competition with barriers to entry, price controls, direct subsidies, and regulatory burdens on firms seeking innovative alternatives. Regulators exchanged policies for votes and campaign funds, while the public paid the cost in taxation, higher prices, and limited choices. Political costs were few because voters lacked organization, information, and common preferences. The "most damning" indictment of the ICC, wrote Thomas McCraw, was that it had "worked to impede economic efficiency": it "prevented market forces from allocating traffic according to the individual modes of transportation—whether rail, highway, or water—best suited for particular kinds of freight."[34] At first by ignorance, then through the "misguided attempts to be 'fair,'" liberalism had led to noncompetitive, subpar outcomes that often hurt the industry itself. Mark Green, director of

Nader's Corporate Accountability Research Group, agreed: "Competition is to the economy what political freedom is to our polity: both oppose unchecked power and both value diversity in the contest for solutions." The solution, "where there would be a viably competitive market but for economic regulation," was that "industry should be freed from regulatory restraint."[35] Restructured agencies, wrote Richard Stewart, could *both* encourage competition *and* redistribute income.[36]

The influence of business and activist groups exploded in a new era of lobbying. From 1971 to 1982 the number of companies with registered lobbyists in D.C. rose from 175 to 2,500. On the one hand, the Great Society had brought a scramble over untraceable billions in taxpayer dollars. McGovern's ally Gerald Cassidy started one of the first lobbying firms using the connections he had made in politics to peddle influence. Consumer advocacy and civil rights groups as well as churches got in on the action: by 1980, 50 percent of Catholic Charities funding came from government. On the other hand, new industry compliance costs mobilized business groups, which expanded their membership, budgets, and D.C. staffs. Under the Federal Election Campaign Act of 1974, organized interests began creating political action committees (PACs) to channel campaign contributions. By 1984, the number of PACs had grown from 608 to 3,371. In 1980, 72 percent of organizations in D.C. represented corporate and trade associations, which accounted for 62 percent of all PACs and 59 percent of all PAC contributions ($32.4 million). Business interests successfully used campaign finance for congressional acquiescence and connected neoliberal critiques of regulation with stagflation, a key issue in presidential elections.

The Efficiency Regime

Facing blame for stagflation, presidents appointed fiscally minded directors, threatened budget cuts, and demanded cost-benefit analyses in review processes. President Gerald Ford consistently attacked

OSHA for the inflationary effects of regulation. The 1975 Report of the President said deregulation "could save billions of dollars by releasing resources for other uses, helping combat inflation, and making the economy more efficient and more productive in future years."[37] As inflation hit 12 percent in 1974, Ford created the Council on Wage and Price Stability to monitor private-sector inflation and review the inflationary impact of government programs. Executive Order No. 11821 required agencies to perform inflation impact analyses on all major regulations and rules. They became an important part of the review process and included both the Office of Management and Budget (OMB) and the Council of Economic Advisors (CEA); without clearance, regulations could be killed. And they forced crucial institutional changes within the agencies, which needed to create cost-benefit offices and hire economists to help them plan and evaluate implementation. Carter continued these reviews in the Regulatory Analysis and Review Group, which prioritized cost-effectiveness and scrutinized significant rules. In the 1980 Regulatory Flexibility Act and the Paperwork Reduction Act, Congress required regulators to consider policy alternatives that reduced the burdens on small businesses and the amount of information they must report. The OMB reviewed these business requests, making it a regulatory watchdog.

With the new economic constraints on regulation, neoliberal economists changed agencies from within by pushing for deregulation and regulatory reform. Under the Carter administration, the EPA introduced market solutions: offsetting pollution from new sources by reductions in existing sources, bundling together sources to increase competition, and introducing saleable emissions credits to incentivize greater emissions reductions, not just within a firm but among them. By putting a price on emissions, the EPA created financial incentives to develop new control technologies and encourage corporations to work together to lower pollutants. Following the 1975 Senate hearings into the Civil Aeronautics Board's (CAB) industry capture—it had allowed overpriced long flights and denied entry to all proposed new trunk lines in its first forty years—CAB initiated its own deregulatory polices in 1976, lowering barriers to entry and beginning price competition. Appointed to chair the CAB in 1977, economist Alfred Kahn, who called himself a "good liberal Democrat," created the Office of Economic Analysis within the agency, staffing it with deregulation supporters. Kahn's reforms increased the number of passengers by 10 percent in a year while almost doubling the industry's profitability.[38] Congress eliminated CAB in 1984 and transferred its duties to the Transportation Department. In the face of the Teamsters Union, the ICC began deregulation in 1975 by prohibiting rate bureaus from challenging the rate filings of its members, allowing carriers to defect from the regulatory cartel. To encourage competition, it expanded commercial zones without rate regulations, deregulated all shipments under government contract, and reduced barriers to entry by refusing to consider the impact of new entrants on current carriers. The Motor Carriers Act of 1980 authorized and extended many of the ICC's deregulatory policies, setting in motion its future elimination.

The new "efficiency regime," which applied an incentive-based approach, replaced the enforcement patterns under "command-and-control" regulation. A regulatory authority must now apply economic analysis to determine whether the social benefits of regulation outweighed corporate compliance costs; the market became the new standard for policy. Agencies mixed deregulation with regulatory reform, both reducing process to revive a stagnant economy (with incentives to produce and invest) and introducing new economic criteria into the regulatory decision-making process. Agencies turned to economic analysis to find rules for administrative policy and to gauge whether decisions maximized efficiency or mimicked the market under ideal conditions. If a regulation failed the cost-benefit assessment, then agencies considered it for deregulation.

Greater centralization in *both* the economy *and* bureaucracy characterized the efficiency regime, under which democratic institutions declined. Deregulation led to mergers in finance and industry. The agencies, which now made far-reaching decisions for the entire society, excluded those without postgraduate training in specialized languages and methods. Congress demanded standards that scientists themselves could not accurately provide but that few could understand except the regulators and regulated groups. Subjecting their decisions to technical questions of their underlying analyses and alternatives, policy makers forged tighter relationships with corporations and trade associations. Large firms had the means to negotiate with regulators, buy them off, or evade their rules. The expertise in agencies outpaced politicians, populist groups, trade associations, and major advocacy groups. Judges were ignorant of the standards they had to rule on, and Congress increasingly turned to staff and counsel to draft bills. In this double government, officials who won televised elections and oversaw high-profile hearings provided a veil of constitutionalism, legitimacy for a permanent bureaucracy to carry out the new tasks of government under the new notion of democracy. They turned away from traditional party politics rooted in local constituencies to run on national issues. Under the premise that social regulation was the new form of representation, interest groups created huge coalitions that intersected the older liberal regime of autonomous state and local governments, private industry, and commerce. Despite the neoliberals' explicit rejection of a public good, they really identified it with two groups: utility-maximizing consumers and the disadvantaged. Monopoly capitalism maximized consumer welfare, while the "underrepresented" groups in civil rights, pollution, consumer protection, and workplace safety received special representation in regulatory agencies. Regulators identified environmental, racial, and gender-based violations even as they developed close relations with agricultural and pesticide producers or civil rights advocacy groups.

Neoliberalism crushed the industrial economy and began a new finance economy, in which experts manage currency and wealth for returns on investments, subject to rules that few understand and that are often removed from tangible results. Technology and finance drove innovations in services, creating worlds of mathematical abstraction and statistical probabilities. "A coalition of academic lawyers and economists, state officials, bankers, and managers," notes Gerald Berk, shared a "common institutional project, which subordinated production to trade and finance. Concentration, in that project, has served diverse purposes for the members of this coalition. For government regulators, it provided a logic for American competitiveness. For retailers, it has provided an instrument to take transactional rents. And for bankers, it has expanded access to tradable assets."[39] The new finance capital aimed to make money from money through lending and stock market speculation. When factories moved to foreign countries, the profit, instead of being reinvested in those plants, could purchase stock buybacks to bid up the stock price or be paid out as dividends. As finance became the principle means of sustaining the regime, government supported financial capital itself by bailing out the instruments of finance instead of production. The US focused on short-term profits by using debt leverage on developing countries and isolating and even destabilizing countries that attempted to leave the dollar.

In foreign policy, neoliberals rejected the older liberal support of institutional democracy, central planning, and antitrust. Corporate governance and humanitarian aid followed US military deployments. In a 1973 CIA-backed coup, Augusto Pinochet assassinated Chilean president Salvador Allende and, advised by Friedman's "Chicago Boys," instituted free markets, which is to say, sold state-held assets to wealthy investors. Plutocracies supported by military might terrorized political opponents in Central and South America, bringing economic implosion and chaotic migrations. Seeking to apply Rawls's view to global inequality, Charles Beitz argued that the US should take a cosmopolitan view of resources and trade with an eye to caring for the developing world's laborers and consumers. Jimmy Carter embodied this neoliberal contradiction between capital controls and humanitarianism. He pledged to both trim the military and increase foreign aid. The US provided billions in loans and subsidized wheat exports to the USSR in the name of détente. McNamara, now director of the World Bank, called for a "new world economic order" to bring "social justice."[40] Carter's 1977 Notre Dame speech redirected focus away from an "inordinate fear of communism" to international human rights. Where the US had formerly traded with South Africa to resist the spread of communism, Vice President Mondale, whose Air Force airliner was called "an international version of a freedom riders' bus," threatened to boycott the apartheid system.[41] But the new balance between "human rights" and "American interests" was plagued by more demoralizing hypocrisy: support for dictators, revolutions, and torturers in Nicaragua, El Salvador, and Iran. Mondale lectured Philippine president Marcos on "the return of democracy" while negotiating for a military base, Clark Airfield. Carter proclaimed Vietnam a failure but now demanded homes for refugees fleeing communist rule in Indochina. He sent the Sixth Fleet to rescue migrants on boats; at the UN, he pressured other nations to do the same. Factions in the White House simultaneously supported the PLO and Israel. But both the new humane empire and the old anti-communist one swallowed up the autonomy of nations. In 1981, interest on the debt owed by poor countries exceeded the sum of new aid they received. The golden apple of China, with its billion cheap laborers and customers, ever tempted US investors. The US, teasing a rift between the USSR and the People's Republic of China (PRC), even promised to selflessly build up the Chinese economy. Given the choice between chest-beating imperialism and selfless Americanism, conservatives chose the former and liberals the latter.

Carter, facing the pressures of securing economic growth to maintain the welfare-warfare state, failed in his experiment with neoliberal economics. Inflation hit 13 percent and unemployment 7.7 percent. The price of oil rose from $14.85 in January 1979 to $39.50 in April 1980. Confronting stagflation and national malaise, Carter's solution was balancing budget cuts with deregulation of the airlines, trucking, and railroads to spur economic growth. To head the Federal Reserve, Carter appointed Paul Volker, whose high interest rates brought a flow of capital into the US. The strengthened dollar crippled exports and devastated manufacturing, a key union stronghold. From 1979 to 1985, unionized workers fell from 23 to 16 percent of the working population. Carter had run on a platform of pulling the Democratic Party and the nation together, but his fiscal policy dissatisfied both party elites who wanted the old liberal spending and the middle class disgusted by inflation and his focus on race, gender, and the Third World.

Ronald Reagan: Neoliberalism Ascendant

In 1981 Reagan, who had listed Friedman among his influencers, announced his own Program for Economic Recovery to combat ten years of stagflation and high unemployment. His solution, captured in the famous Laffer Curve, to Carter's crisis of balancing the entitlement state with economic growth was to decrease taxes on the rich, who would actually pay lower tax rates instead of sheltering their income. Reagan claimed that the government itself caused stagflation: "Government regulation...has increased production costs," high taxes have reduced "incentives...to work, save and invest," and "transfer payments" for welfare, unemployment, and social security "reduce employment of the poor and of older workers."[42] With increased savings and investment, the rich would innovate and take risks, creating jobs and wealth that would trickle down to all. The poor would work longer hours, leading to overall economic growth and increased federal revenues, thus paying for entitlements and balancing the budget: defunding the government would pay for it. The Great Communicator's rhetoric glossed over the divide between the old conservatism of small business and the new conservatism of finance capital, unfettered free markets, world interventions, and massive deficits.

The conservatism of the 1980s, a new intellectual system, contained more than Reagan's promise to fix the economy. In what *National*

Review editor Frank Meyer called Fusionism, conservatism blended free-market libertarianism, interventionism, and traditionalism. Little of it was republican, and all of it was William F. Buckley, who, unlike older conservatives, had found a polemical way to use the liberals' media against itself. In *National Review*, his column *On the Right*, and on PBS's *Firing Line*, he defended entrepreneurs and financiers who labored in white collar jobs: they, and not envious, lazy social activists and trade unionists, were the heroic and deserving creators of wealth, which consisted less in production than in ideas. In social policy, he was joined by "neoconservatives" Nathan Glazer, Irving Kristol, and Daniel Bell, Jewish ex-Trotskyites who preached personal responsibility against liberal victimhood and condemned liberalism's failure to defend individuals against Soviet collectivism. They pushed for "pragmatic" US interventions that favored Israel and opposed communism. But Buckley was no pragmatist; he faulted liberalism above all for its relativism. Moved by Whittaker Chambers's *Witness* and Russell Kirk's *The Conservative Mind*, he wrote, "back of all political institutions there are moral and philosophical concepts, implicit or defined."[43] Also an editor at *National Review*, Kirk rooted conservatism in a forgotten British aristocratic tradition that had opposed both rationalism and relativism. The magazine attracted political philosopher Leo Strauss, who, warning of the "crisis of liberalism," argued that liberals had totally abandoned rationalism: conservatism required reclaiming the pursuit of truth by returning to its origins in ancient Greek philosophy. Buckley appreciated this elitism. He was an internationally educated Yale man who spoke in a strange accent and crossed the Atlantic in a yacht. The problem with civil rights, he argued, was not that there were too few Negroes voting but too many whites. Meeting with Kirk and presidential candidate Barry Goldwater in 1962, they agreed on purging the "irresponsible right," populist John Birchers, from the party as conspiracists and antisemites. Reagan did the same.

Reagan's presidential posturing, beginning with his Time for Choosing Speech at the 1964 Republican Convention, incorporated

Buckley's fusionism. He rode the wave of American resentment against stagflation and the New Left by promising to redistribute wealth from welfare recipients to workers. He campaigned, noted Rothschild, for "an economy of industrial workers, male, white ... to 'get working again.'"[44] Celebrating "basic manufacturing values," he promised "to kick the poor by eliminating social programs." Reagan had been libertarian on social issues like abortion, no-fault divorce, and gay rights but had seen an opportunity to court the religious right, now alienated from government, in his 1976 campaign against Ford. Betty Ford had disappointed many evangelicals by saying that she would not be concerned if her daughter smoked marijuana or had premarital sex. Reagan began to make conservative and patriotic pronouncements for "bedrock values of faith, family, work, neighborhood, peace, and freedom."[45] He praised traditional families, pro-life policies, and opposed gay rights and "welfare culture." And Reagan had long made neoconservative, patriotic appeals to strong defense and interventionism, which played well against Carter's foreign policy humiliations.

Reagan connected regulation to unemployment and declining wages, and he wanted stronger methods to direct agency reform. His new director of the OMB, David Stockman, warned that regulations from the 1970s were a "ticking regulatory timebomb" that would "sweep through the industrial economy with near gale force" unless there were a "series of unilateral administrative actions to reduce the regulatory burden." It was an "Economic Dunkirk."[46] Murray Weidenbaum, chairman of the CEA, said, "No longer will we tolerate the view that economic issues are necessarily on a lower rung of the ethical ladder than some regulatory issues."[47] In 1981 Reagan created the Task Force on Regulatory Relief, which reviewed proposed rules and existing regulations to determine whether they yielded net social benefits, targeting the most burdensome regulations for elimination. He called for a sixty-day freeze on new regulations, followed by Executive Order 12291, which required cost-benefit and Regulatory Impact Analyses for all new regulatory proposals. Stockman's OMB could now delay the rulemaking process as agencies labored to file their RIAs, subject to review, consultation, and denial. Agencies strained to hire in-house personnel or outside contractors to perform reviews. Using the OMB, Reagan constrained and cut the budgets of regulatory agencies like the EPA—25 percent in 1981–82, with 22.6 percent reduced staff. The number of full-time employees in the major agencies had declined 16 percent by 1984, decreasing their annual number of new regulations by one-fourth. To direct OSHA, Reagan appointed Thorne Auchter, whose family construction company had been cited for numerous violations. Auchter implemented reductions in budget and staff (one-sixth from 1980 to 1982), hence in inspections, violations, and fines. He pushed cooperation with business, which would engage in voluntary self-inspections, and replaced federal with state-level inspectors. By 1982 the number of cases referred to the DOJ had dropped 50 percent. Reagan also deregulated communications and transportation. With competitive bidding for routes, airline services expanded while federal funding for infrastructure was slashed.

The Reagan years culminated in even greater centralization of regulatory authority in the White House and OMB, which were matched by the agencies' own evaluation offices that were created to comply with the demands and to develop independent databases to defend their policies. The Supreme Court confirmed the agencies' independence in 1984 when it crafted the two-part "Chevron Test." Because the agency must have rulemaking and adjudicatory flexibility, the courts should give the agency deference, or the weight of law, if its decision did not exceed statutory authority and if it were permissible and not "arbitrary and capricious."[48] By 1988, economic professionalization and the growing reliance on planning and evaluation in agency offices meant that a neoliberal framework dominated the policy process, from reform-minded administrators to regulatory staffs, making executive reviews redundant. Regulations without economic rationale were left unenforced, and economic approaches were used for implementation, removing some of the regulatory burden and reducing the economic impact of regulation. Pollution became, for example, "an economic problem to be worked out by business firms rather than a moral or political problem to be worked out by political institutions."[49]

Reagan preached the public choice theory of the New Federalism: voters, responding to local government policies, would vote with their feet. Smaller, decentralized government improved market efficiency. Using block grants, he turned social welfare programs like AFDC, school lunch programs, and Medicaid over to states. The federal government would manage only major entitlement programs like Social Security and Medicare. But Reagan, adopting Friedman's views, did not apply decentralization to large firms. To head the DOJ Antitrust Division, he appointed William F. Baxter, who immediately changed merger guidelines to consider only "economic efficiency" and not market share. It was, Jonathan Tepper and Denise Hearn write, "a revolution by unelected bureaucrats. The Department of Justice…changed the nature of antitrust without a new law, public debate, or vote."[50] The office expanded and recruited top economists, assigning them to work with prosecutors, where they routinely refused to support cases on their economic merits even if they could proceed under legal precedent. The caseload applied almost universally to horizontal restraints, "thus ending for all practical purposes many of the standards established under antitrust laws" and even against the intentions of attorneys general who wanted enforcement.[51] Under the new burden of proof in antitrust cases, the government only considered the price of goods. Corporations could justify any merger by promising to keep prices low and markets "contestable" to new entrants. "Every single Merger Guideline since has only made it easier for firms to completely dominate their industry and gain greater market share through acquisitions."[52] AT&T's division into seven companies was an exception to the rule. Reagan presided over a series of mergers, acquisitions, and leverage buyouts among some of the largest corporations. In the Wall Street–driven bull market of 1984–87, corporate raiders initiated takeovers, sold assets for huge profits, then laid off work forces. In the Black Monday crash of 1987, the stock market lost one-third of its value overnight.

Reagan's rhetoric of fiscal responsibility did not match soaring deficits. The original trickle-down theory presumed expenditure cuts, but Reagan retained the welfare-warfare state model. Without decreasing entitlement spending, he increased defense spending. Defense Secretary Caspar Weinberger said that defense spending actually generated increased revenue. Federal revenues eventually fell so far that Reagan had to sign tax increases, which he called "revenue enhancements." To keep the "nation's ironclad commitment to social security," he signed the 1983 Social Security Amendments, taxing up to half of pensioner benefits and increasing the retirement age (sixty-five in 1983, sixty-seven by 2022). He quickly backtracked on disability reform, leading to increased disability rolls. Reagan's second-term outlays averaged 21.7 percent of GDP, outspending both Carter and LBJ. His deficits brought total government debt from $965 billion in 1981 to $2.74 trillion in 1989, doubling again by 1993. The next thirty-four of thirty-eight years ended in budget deficits.

Nor were Reagan's tax cuts, in 1981 and 1986, along with a decreased capital gains tax, truly (as claimed) "a 25 percent across-the-board reduction in personal tax rates."[53] The top tax bracket plunged from 70 to 50 percent (and to 38.5 percent in 1986) while the lowest from only 14 to 11 percent. Real disposable income increased slightly for average Americans to consume a bit more, but not enough for savings and investment—unlike the wealthy, whose investment tracked dramatic stock market gains. Reagan disparaged a social safety net for the poor but provided one for the rich, who were encouraged to speculate, most infamously in the savings and loan (S&L) industry. To boost the flagging industry, the 1982 Garn–St. Germain Act deregulated S&Ls and allowed banks to write adjustable interest-rate mortgages. It lifted the requirement for S&Ls to fund residential home mortgages at fixed interest rates. Now they could invest in commercial real estate, speculative land deals, business ventures, and junk bonds. Regulators at the Federal Loan Home Bank Board were poorly trained and understaffed: hundreds of S&Ls escaped the most basic examination for years. They reduced the amount of funds S&Ls had to keep in deposits, from 5 to 3 percent in January 1982, freeing up capital for further investment but making them vulnerable to downturns. They also abandoned the older shareholder standards, which required 125 of every 400 to be from the local community, with no individual owning over 10 percent of the total stake. Now a single individual could be the shareholder. S&Ls could now choose to have federal or state charters, so states began competing for them to relocate to benefit from fees. California S&Ls could invest 100 percent of their deposits in anything they wanted. Depositors cared little as their insurance grew from $40,000 to $100,000. In the speculative frenzy, S&Ls went from losses of $4.6 billion in 1981 to $3.7 billion in gains in 1985. In 1984 private banks were allowed to securitize mortgages, contributing to the subprime mortgage crisis. Reagan introduced "Too Big to Fail," a social safety net for the rich, in 1984 with the massive bailout of Continental Illinois National Bank. To ease the risk to financial speculators, the Fed introduced the "Greenspan Put," lowering interest rates to ease market corrections, following Black Monday in 1987.

Reaganomics devastated the middle class, which shrank 20 percent from 1980 to 1991.[54] Middle-class Americans falling into poverty outnumbered those rising into affluence. The total share of income of the 0.1 percent had risen from 1.8 to 5.4 percent in 1988 and 7.3 percent by 2000. While productivity paralleled real wages from 1947 to 1970 and doubled over the next twenty-three years, the crack that formed between them under Nixon became a fissure. Reagan had campaigned on reigniting the industrial economy, but he saw "Reagan Democrats" as remnants of big labor. After he fired eleven thousand PATCO workers, union membership and strikes plummeted. His response to Americans' demand for higher wages was to import cheap labor. In 1977, pointing to the dearth of apple pickers in New England, Reagan asked, "Are great numbers of our unemployed really victims of the illegal alien invasion or are those illegal tourists actually doing work our own people won't do?"[55] The *Wall Street Journal* editorialized in 1984, "If Washington still wants to 'do something' about immigration, we propose a five-word constitutional amendment: There shall be open borders."[56] Reflecting the neoliberal civil rights–business alliance, the *New Republic* and *The Nation* joined the call for open borders. In 1986 Reagan signed Simpson-Mazzoli, which legalized 2.8 million undocumented workers while shielding business from prosecutions for hiring millions more. US corporations and the *Wall Street Journal* also promoted the myth of a *skilled* labor shortage: "As long as we don't train enough scientists, engineers or software designers ourselves, immigration is a saving grace.... Come to think of it, with jobs available why have a quota at all?... Our view is, borders should be open."[57] The 1990 immigration bill included H-1B visas to import cheap foreign workers in science, technology, engineering, and mathematics (STEM) fields. An industry of immigration lawyers rose up to exploit the family loophole, doubling the number of immigrants entering under the legal cap from 264,000 to 570,000. Unskilled American men suffered most. The hourly wages of men in the bottom fifth of the income distribution fell about 1 percent per year from 1979 to 1989 and those in the second fifth fell by more than 1 percent. Women's labor force participation increased, undercutting men's wages throughout the decade. Following the 1981–82 recession, unemployment among those without a high school diploma reached 18.3 percent.[58] Americans did not work, save, or invest more than before. Personal savings, which had been 11.4 percent since 1951, began to decline in 1981, sinking to 8.5 percent in 1988 and 3.2 percent in 2005. Investment slowed or declined, and the middle class kept pace in consumption by taking on debt. Household debt surged after 1984; credit card debt almost quadrupled from 1981 to 1988. Reagan reappointed Volcker in 1983, who reduced inflation by 50 percent with high interest rates but also made financing near impossible for low- and middle-class families.

The Reagan Doctrine promised military support for democracies and free trade with allies against the Soviet bloc. Neoliberalism was never free trade but neo-mercantilism. In the early 1980s the IMF and World Bank, in return for loans, demanded that Latin American and African nations implement "structural adjustment programs" that required production for export rather than meeting national and local needs, reduced social programs, and pushed for privatization and deregulation of transnational corporations. To be sure, lenders prioritized payment because of the rampant corruption in these countries. Reagan used economic warfare against the "evil empire" in the arms race to stop the spread of Soviet influence in the Third World. He covertly sponsored anti-socialist puppet regimes, sent steady shipments of arms to the anti-Sandinistas in Nicaragua and the mujahedeen in Afghanistan, and propped up the unstable regime in Grenada. The Soviet Union was already plagued by economic stagnation, perennial shortages of essential consumer goods, waste, bureaucratic inefficiency, and the Communist Party's declining legitimacy. When it collapsed, the Soviets were spending 40 percent of their budget to fund the Afghan War.

Reagan's nationalist rhetoric serviced his internationalism. He sponsored global free trade and open markets as part of his 1980 campaign. His selective tariffs on steel, semiconductors, cars, and motorcycles were exceptions to his rule of globalization; he vetoed textile quota bills in 1985 and 1988. He pushed the 1982 GATT negotiations to liberalize agriculture and services, and he initiated the Uruguay Round of multilateral trade negotiations (1986–93), which lowered global tariffs and concluded in the World Trade Organization. In 1988 he supported the US-Canada Free Trade Agreement, forerunner to NAFTA. Trade deficits rose. Between 1981 and 1989, American investors doubled spending on imported goods, services, and foreign investment (from $334 to $663 billion). Increased interest rates strengthened the dollar, and nations with dollar-denominated debt went bankrupt and flooded the US with cheap goods, undercutting domestic manufactures. Patriotic appeals still had power: clothing "Made in the USA" featured Hollywood celebrities, and Miller Beer advertised beer "Made the American way." Ironically, Walmart used the publicity campaign Crafted in America to sell American-made clothing and package itself as an American-friendly retailer while cutting off most American suppliers by demanding they slash prices. Residents in textile communities even celebrated the arrival of Walmart stores. Textile manufacturer Fieldcrest Canon CEO Frank Larkin praised the "close relationship between Wal-Mart and Canon products" in a ribbon-cutting ceremony in Concord, North Carolina.[59] Many Fieldcrest workers took jobs at Walmart when their plants closed in 2003.

Reagan's nostalgic rhetoric for working-class whites and New Right religious conservatives did not match his policy. While lavishing praise and confidence upon his supporters, he gutted their moral and economic status: divorce and abortion skyrocketed, and music and cinema celebrated liberation from traditional mores. Reaganomics had plenty of detractors, who pointed out that it relied on a kind of faith, but they failed to appreciate its source. Rothschild declared that Reagan's "America no longer exists," neglecting the part that *did* exist, and responded to his vision of a great Christian nation set against Soviet communism. Reagan appealed to the old American work ethic; the entire affirmative action regime was to white middle-class Americans a source of resentment. Kevin Phillips, who had predicted the new Republican majority, directed his ire at Buckley's ("Squire Willy") elitism. In 1982 he predicted a split between populist and ideological Republicans: "People are going to become angry with the small group of people at the top with the capital skills and education. It's the Europeanization of American politics, a more class-oriented politics."[60] Two populist bases emerged, each seeing the other's victory as defeat. Family and patriotism meant conservative indoctrination; social services and education meant liberal indoctrination. For each angry minority taught that disadvantage sprang from white racism and that America owed him reparations, there was an indignant white from a middle-class hardworking household who resented the charge that he had not earned what he had. Meanwhile, both elite camps now embraced a globalist view of American values. For Reagan, hardworking immigrants were more American than union members; for the Left, immigrants were morally superior to American racists.

How the Democratic Party Became the Party of the Rich

Neoliberalism was *also* adopted by the young elites in the Democratic Party, McGovern supporters and the Watergate babies elected in 1974 who admitted the failure of economic planning. Independents found Democrats' policies outdated and ineffective. Liberal and minority gains for Democrats were dwarfed by a growing white Republican vote, which had moved from the cities to the suburbs and Sunbelt to get away from liberal rule in crime-ridden, poverty-stricken cities. The rising class of educated young professionals combined social liberalism with free-market conservatism. After spending the 1970s establishing themselves in business and education, young professionals began their move back to the cities, part of a "regentrification," a reconquest of cities from poverty and crime and an "urban renaissance."[61] On the *CBS Evening News* in 1977, Eric Sevareid exulted the new "flowback of people from suburbs to inner cities." Chicago's Dan Rottenberg reported on the twenty thousand new units built "within two miles of the Loop over the past ten years to accommodate the rising tide of 'Yuppies'—young urban professionals rebelling against the stodgy suburban lifestyles of their parents. The Yuppies seek neither comfort nor security, but stimulation, and they can find that only in the densest sections of the city." Good riddance to smoky factories; the goal was the cosmopolitan city. But Rottenberg had doubts: the yuppies were singles, but cities needed families to revitalize, transmit values, and grow roots. The answer, he prophesied, was blending good business management and countercultural innovation: tear down poor housing projects like Cabrini Green and build incubator spaces and neighborhoods that link "a high density of sophisticated population and affluent population" with "low overhead, low property values." Culturally elite blacks had a premium; poor blacks did not.

Bill Clinton, Gary Hart, Paul Tsongas, and Dick Gephardt were called "neoliberals" for their plan to promote deregulation, relax antitrust laws, end rules against financial concentration, and lift price regulations.[62] Lester Thurow's 1980 *The Zero-Sum Society* was called "the economic Bible" of the movement. Macroeconomics, Thurow argued, was a zero-sum game: the government must balance free-market profits for upwardly mobile Americans with economic stewardship to solve inflation, sluggish economic growth, and pollution. Certain members of society must bear the brunt of taxation and government programs. The key was cooperation between government and business to organize institutions for efficiency and growth. It meant further concessions by organized labor in the face of declining industrial capacity. In 1982 *Esquire* featured "The Neoliberal Club." Timothy Worth, Gary Hart, and Bill Bradley, after the Democrats' devastating loss in 1980, turned against "bleeding hearts": it was the "end of the New Deal," and the "Great Society had been rejected by American voters."[63] Hart said that "too much concern not for central social issues but fringe social issues" had devastated the Democrats and the nation. The neoliberals wedded centralized bureaucratic oversight to deregulation and entrepreneurship. Hart championed fiscal restraint, lower taxes, profitable risk, free trade, and welfare-work reforms. Clinton supported "workfare" as governor of Arkansas. They conceded to "Reagan Republicans" on deregulation and leaving markets "as unfettered as possible to create wealth." They supported the repeal of the Glass-Steagall Act with the goal of "stimulating growth *first* and hastening the creation of new jobs, new products and new wealth." They differed from Republicans by balancing entrepreneurial incentives for risk-taking with limited welfare and sound environmental regulation.

Political theorist and Mondale advisor William Galston saw the need to appeal to both "cultural" and "economic" populists to attract a "reasonable proportion of the white vote."[64] Americans, he warned, correctly believed the Democrats' Rainbow Coalition of identity groups splintered any unifying vision. Mondale's 1984 speeches praised "free market incentives" and getting tough on crime as well as "fairness."[65] The "New Democrats" formed the Democratic Leadership Council in 1985; it included centrists like Al Gore, Dave McCurdy, Ed Kilgore, and Joseph Lieberman. They celebrated the neoliberal principle of "individual responsibility" in place of the liberals' "collective welfare." It had three principles: promoting opportunity for all, demanding responsibility from all, and fostering a new sense of community. After Dukakis's defeat in 1988, Galston wrote "The Politics of Deception," which argued for a new Democratic Party that rejected tax-and-spend policies for balanced budgets, while Republicans, endorsing supply-side economics, became the party of low taxes and large deficits.

The Democrats' opportunity came with the 1991–92 recession. The real estate bubble burst in 1991, followed by the collapse of over one thousand S&Ls. The federal bailout cost taxpayers $132 billion. Americans' approval of George Bush further plummeted with his decision to raise taxes to shrink the deficit. Clinton pinned the recession on the failures of the Reagan-Bush era; his strategist reminded campaign workers, "It's the economy, stupid!" Moreover, the fall of the Soviet Union in 1991 took communism off the table, important for Democrats viewed as weak on defense. Ross Perot's populist campaign won 19 percent of the popular vote, giving Clinton a plurality of 43 percent. Embodying the "New Democrat," Clinton gained a foothold with both the older generation and independents. He publicly criticized Sister Souljah, who had said of the LA riots, "If black people kill black people every day, why not have a week and kill white people?" Democrats extended the neoliberal social and economic agenda. Clinton proposed gay rights at the national level and instructed the attorney general not to prosecute for obscenity. He affirmed the family values of the new elites and attributed the high crime rate among blacks to the destruction of the family. He worked with Republicans to reform welfare and get tough on crime. Hillary called repeat offenders "super-predators." The 1996 Welfare Reform Act required work in exchange for assistance and capped benefits at two years, after which a parent must work or go to job training. Clinton supported an earned income tax credit as well as increases in the federal minimum wage. He eased rules and requirements for student loans, providing higher limits to borrowers. Tuition costs continued to rise 7 percent per year, twice the average rate of inflation.

In what John B. Judis and Ruy Teixeira called "McGovern's Revenge," the "growth of professionals" spearheaded a new "Emerging Democratic Majority." While factory employment decreased 4.4 percent during the 1990s, the number of skilled professionals increased 30 percent. They had doubled their numbers in the workforce from 1950 to 2000, from 7 to 15.4 percent, while factory workers had fallen from 26 to 14.3 percent. The Labor Department projected that professionals would be the fastest growing occupational group until 2008. Their labor devoted less to producing goods than ideas and services, and they prized authenticity and status in their jobs more than profit: "Software programmers worry about the 'coolness' of their code; architects about the beauty and utility of their buildings; teachers about whether their pupils have learned; the doctor and nurse about the health of their patient."[66] Still they had more in common with the top 1 percent in centralized finance capital. Unlike small business owners interested in low taxes and deregulation, they desired and depended upon the credentials and status provided by the system. From 1990 to 2000, the percentage of Americans with four-year degrees rose from 22 to 26 percent. In 1991, Saskia Sassen noted a "new social aesthetic" in "global cities," in which "the consumption capacity represented by high disposable income...is realized through the emergence of a new vision of the good life."[67] Financial centers used taxes for sports stadiums and attractions for elites, gentrifying old minority neighborhoods. David Brooks noted the rise of the "bourgeois bohemians" who united Friedman's economics with Rawlsian compassion; it was a "meritocracy," and he could see no end to its rule.[68]

The Democrats became the party of upper-middle-class values of fiscal responsibility and economic growth. The 1990s brought a Democratic and Republican neoliberal consensus. To Schlesinger's annoyance, Clinton stole his term "vital center." Clinton declared in 1996 that "the era of big government is over"; he worked with Republicans to balance the budget. His advisers—Alice Rivlin, Lloyd Bentsen, Robert Rubin, Larry Summers, and Leon Panetta—had ties to Wall Street and were "deficit hawks"; deficits would raise interest rates and deter private investors. Greenspan supported the program of decreasing the deficit $500 billion over five years. The policy brought the deficit to zero, lowering long-term interest rates without weakening the dollar. Investors from Asia and Latin America purchased US bonds and tech stocks in the booming Silicon Valley. Clinton signed capital gains and estate tax cuts in 1997 and 1998. CEO compensation reached new highs, while wages stagnated or grew marginally. Clinton also worked to further deregulate finance: "antiquated regulatory policies" curtailed entrepreneurial initiatives aided by technological breakthroughs in telecommunications and new financial instruments. He oversaw the 1999 Financial Services Modernization Act that removed legal divisions between commercial and investment banking and between insurance companies and brokerage houses. The Telecommunications Act of 1996 led to a spate of mergers and allowed Bell companies to compete in long-distance services and cable TV delivery. Supermergers in banking (and increased service fees) reduced the number of commercial banks by one-third, while the average bank size nearly doubled. More mergers and bailouts further concentrated finance by giving the largest institutions borrowing and lending advantages. Supermergers in "big oil" brought dramatic gasoline price spikes in the early 2000s.

Clinton worked with Congress to pass acts to promote regulatory efficiency, require executive agencies to submit annual performance and budgeting plans, and prohibit unfunded mandates for private business and state and local governments. In his strategy of "government reinvention," regulatory agencies would become negotiating grounds for finance capital and social justice interests. The new partnership would lower compliance costs and save resources in litigation and enforcement. The EPA and OSHA provided greater regulatory flexibility and assisted corporate experimentation in pollution control. Firms would provide technical support for regulatory innovation and use the agencies as a clearinghouse for information. The EPA's Common Sense initiative stressed compliance over enforcement: it would cooperate with corporations and their stakeholders and create a task force to help smaller businesses lacking resources for fulltime compliance staffs.[69] OSHA also formed partnerships with business in consultation and technical assistance, while firms that refused faced increased regulatory scrutiny.[70] Social justice groups found that corporate centralization let them best advocate broad policies for their constituencies in civil rights, pollution, or consumer safety. And corporations pushed for federal oversight, where they could maximize their influence, seek special privileges and exemptions, and discourage competitors with a labyrinth of requirements. Thus the incestuous relationship between government and corporations renewed—between the EPA and DuPont, the Minerals Service and oil companies, the Pentagon and Halliburton, the FDA and Monsanto.

In foreign policy, Clinton initiated the "second wave" of neoliberalism," the "Third Way" between the Keynesian Left and the neoconservative Right. Neoconservatives argued that the USSR's fall had vindicated interventionism and that US power and democratic regime change no longer had limits. In 1995 Bill Kristol launched *The Weekly Standard*, whose writers pressed for US world hegemony, a Pax Americana. Following Clinton's disastrous appeal to the progressive base on health care and his attack on Chinese imperialism in Tibet, he "triangulated" to the center on neoliberal policies. Clinton and UK prime minister Tony Blair "agreed on the necessity of ridding

first-wave neoliberalism of its neoconservative accretions—hyper-
patriotism and militarism, attachment to antiquated 'family values',
disdain for multiculturalism, and neglect of ecological issues."[71] The US
must embrace its role as the world's lone superpower and implement
a "socially conscious market globalism" to "propel the entire world
toward a new golden age of technological progress and prosperity."
Official US policy was the Washington Consensus: using the World
Bank and IMF to implement "structural adjustment programs" (loans
to developing countries in the "Global South"). Clinton wanted the
US to lead using "soft power" (the term of Clinton official Joseph Nye
Jr.) or "cultural and ideological appeals" rather than neoconservative
"hard power," military and economic "carrots" and "sticks." Market
globalism really fostered US international hegemony; it was not
about promoting "multilateralism" and "global democracy." Clinton
and Blair converted NATO from a Western military alliance to limit
Soviet expansion into a global, multipurpose organization to enhance
international security, protect human rights, and carry out peacekeep-
ing missions, such as the 1999 intervention in Kosovo. Clinton was
the first president to deploy troops without the support of Congress.
He justified bombing Serbia on the humanitarian grounds of "moral
imperative," not national interest.

The elites of both parties endorsed free trade policies that would
liberate the developing world by creating a single global market. On
signing NAFTA in 1993, Clinton said that it would "permit us to create
an economic order in the world"; free trade embodied the "symbolic
struggle for the spirit of our country...in a rapidly changing world."[72]
Hardly free trade, the 1,200-page agreement removed capital controls
and protected intellectual property. It protected US financiers and
flooded Mexico with American corn, displacing two million farmers, whose children migrated north. The death of antitrust combined
with billions of new consumers put American farmers in cutthroat
competition, where only the largest growers and slaughterhouses
survived with such tight margins. From 1991 to 2000, the US trade

deficit surged from $66 to $450 billion, 5 percent of GDP. The price for small gains at the grocery store, like cheaper avocados, was the devastation of American rural communities.

American inequality under Reagan exploded with Clinton's outsourcing. Hourly wages of non-supervisory employees in private non-farm jobs rose from $5.34 to $8.12 from 1950 to 1975 in 1982 dollars but stagnated from 1980 to 1997, $7.78 to $7.66. One hundred and twenty countries joined GATT, whose eight rounds of tariff negotiations eliminated tens of thousands of tariff concessions and fueled tens of billions of dollars in international transactions. In 1995 the new WTO reduced trade barriers on goods, liberalized services, clarified "unfair trade practices," and promoted international agreement on "intellectual property rights"—where the US had a major advantage. Clinton also balanced economic claims with social justice and international labor and environmental standards. He sent dozens of economic advisors to the former Soviet Union to direct Russia's transition to capitalism. US investment in Asian nations as well as liberalized capitalization law meant that they accepted large amounts of investment, subjecting their economies to the destabilizing effects of US finance. To stabilize its currency, China pegged the yuan to the dollar in 1995 (undervaluing it by an estimated 40 percent). The Asian financial crisis of 1997 required an international bailout package and sale of Southeast Asian commercial assets to foreign corporate investors at rock-bottom prices. By Deng's death in 1997, the Chinese compromised "to buy popular legitimacy by means of global economic integration that would raise the living standards of most Chinese people."[73] The Chinese Communist Party (CCP) invited a flood of investment in "special enterprise zones" that offered incentives, including tax breaks and secured-risk arrangements, in which foreign investors profited first.

Globalization referred to the worldwide expansion of markets facilitated by transnational corporations and technological developments in information, communication, and transportation, a digital revolution in the rise of personal computers, the internet, satellite

TV, standardized shipping containers, fiber optic cables, electronic barcodes, and global supply chains. Neoliberals constructed a myth of globalization's inevitability to justify the new world order: the global economy existed prior to political orders and grew according to an unstoppable rational economic process that furthered individual freedom and material advancement for all, lifting entire regions out of poverty. Cultural differences should bow to a single global free market in goods, services, and capital. Academic "democratic peace theory" preached that democracies were less likely to go to war with each other. Francis Fukuyama proclaimed the "end of history," a "new world order" of peacefully trading liberal democracies. For Thomas Friedman, free-market capitalism ("democratizations of finance, technology, and information") had blown away the alternatives of communism, welfare statism, and crony capitalism and given "birth to a new power source in the world ... the Electronic Herd"; global investors stampeded across a world whose terrain had been flattened by an information-based revolution.[74] The golden straitjacket, the fifteen "golden rules" of free-market capitalism, punished those who did not comply. Every nation must make "the private sector the primary engine of its economic growth" and shrink "the size of its state bureaucracy, maintaining as close to a balanced budget as possible, if not a surplus, [while] eliminating and lowering tariffs on imported goods." These "market forces" were inevitable and logical. Friedman supported Clinton's "third way" as the only way: "Globalization isn't a choice. It's a reality." In 1999 Friedman cheered the new securitized subprime housing mortgages, invested with maximum leverage. William Greider wrote about the coming "one world" in 1997: "The nation-state faces a crisis of relevance. What remains of its purpose and power if authority over domestic social standards is yielded to disinterested market forces? If governments are reduced to bidding for the favors of multinational enterprises, what basis will citizens have for determining their own destinies? If commerce and finance are free to roam in the borderless world, why should people be restricted by the mere geography of their birthplace? Political leaders are weak and unstable at present because they lack coherent answers to such questions."[75]

George W. Bush, Compassionate Conservatism, and Cracks in the Neoliberal Order

George W. Bush ran on a "compassionate conservative" (comcon) platform. Doug Wead, a self-professed "bleeding heart conservative," coined the phrase in 1979; it was used to describe Bush I's views and pushed by Bush II and his adviser, Marvin Olasky. Domestically, comcons would use free-market means to aid the disadvantaged, women, and minorities. Republicans reenacted fast-track trade authority (under which Bush signed eight more free trade deals) while promoting Rawls's theory of justice to help the least among us. "Comcons like immigrants," said Myron Magnet as a way of promoting racial equality.[76] "Third Way Conservatism" would "build cars, train mentors for children and treat AIDS in Africa."[77] Faith-based initiatives, with government aid, would now work with private industry to solve the "problems of the urban underclass." Government would sponsor civil society and families for urban renewal. It would promote home ownership for high-risk minority buyers—with adjustable-rate mortgages, packaged and sold in CDOs for wealthy investors. Church charities from every denomination would implement nonreligious community programs such as helping youth, after school education, family centers, single-mother programs, financial management, job training, senior day programs, literacy programs, and food pantries. To this Bush supposedly added tough love: workfare, stigmatized illegitimacy, and paternalistic homes for single moms. Bush rejected "quotas" but "strongly support[ed] diversity of all kinds, including racial diversity in higher education"; he promised to "actively promote diversity and opportunity in every way that the law permits."[78] Cooperating with private drug companies, Bush signed Medicare Part D to provide prescription drugs in one of the largest entitlement programs since the 1960s. Those who wrote the bill simultaneously negotiated jobs as lobbyists for pharmaceutical companies, for which they left to work after the bill's passage. Bush also promoted privatized education and charter schools. He signed No Child Left Behind, which, in order to implement strict testing standards, micromanaged teachers' time and made classrooms large study sessions for state tests.

The US had successfully fought for China's admission into the WTO in 1999; China was, said David Gerson, now a "democracy." Bush oversaw the greatest outsourcing of US manufactures. "Outsourcing is just a new way of doing international trade," said the Council of Economic Advisors.[79] Finance capitalism, looking to short-term gains rather than long-term economic growth, pressured CEOs to outsource all major industries for quarterly profits. US manufacturing, which had remained stable from 1970 to 1998 (never falling below 16.5 million workers), lost 5.7 million manufacturing jobs, principally to China and Mexico, from 1998 to 2013. Automation did not sustain the same output with fewer workers. Controlling for value added in computers, economists calculated a 30 percent decline in output from 2000 to 2010.[80] Nor did the US service economy compensate for the decline in manufactures; from 2001 to 2003, the trade deficit rose 37 percent, from $358 to $489 billion. Technology followed production. US businesses complained about technology theft to the Department of Commerce but dared not go public lest they lose their profits from Chinese production. Bush unsuccessfully lobbied for *more* outsourcing, to extend NAFTA to Central America and the Caribbean, in a Free Trade Area of the Americas (FTAA). Neoliberals repeated slogans of "creative destruction" of capitalism and the benefits of cheap migrant labor; US workers, it was promised, would receive welfare payments while they learned to code.

The terrorist attacks on the World Trade Center, a product of lax immigration policy and poor intelligence, did not derail Bush's compassionate conservatism. To his neoconservative advisors, the

"Vulcans," the end of the Cold War marked another step toward US world hegemony. Despite Bush's earlier criticisms of "nation building," his administration saw an opportunity for "an expansion of the philosophy of compassionate conservatism": building democracy for the least advantaged in the world, including regime change in Iraq.[81] In his own articulation of democratic peace theory, he said, "Democracies don't go to war with each other."[82] The War on Terror was unending, unbounded, unjust, and incompetent. The US demanded compliance from any nation suspected of harboring terrorists. Bush re-implemented counterinsurgency (COIN), the "grand tactics" of warfare used in Vietnam. COIN dominated among the officer corps and military experts, and it became a religion of winning the hearts and minds of the people. But US soldiers in Afghanistan, believing they had entered a war against terror, had really allied with the Northern Alliance against the Taliban in the Afghan civil war. Supposed terrorists, in reality tribal enemies, were rounded up by the thousands; some were tortured at CIA-funded black sites in foreign countries. Corporate war was not only, as one Afghanistan veteran called it, a "big money funneling operation" that depended on patriotic appeals to whites (who comprised most combat units), it was particularly incompetent. Billions of dollars in government contracts with American corporations poured into Iraq. The special inspector general for reconstruction in Iraq reported that as much as $8 billion of $60 billion was simply wasted. While construction crews botched hospitals, wastewater treatment, and bridge projects, the State Department sent cosmopolitan Ivy Leaguers ("male, pale, and Yale") to cook up programs: Arabic translations of *Tom Sawyer*, organic chicken farms, art shows.[83] Regime change was not limited to open military force. Under the new strategy of "color revolution" (so-called because of colors attached to each coup) the US and corporate interests, aided by the media, funded "democratic protests" and opposition groups to overthrow numerous governments, including in Georgia, Ukraine, and Belarus.

Homeland Security funding traveled home, where mustached police officers were replaced by head-shaven SWAT teams, who now occupied American instead of Afghan cities. Billions of dollars in surveillance equipment—Humvees, armored personal carriers, and M-16s—went to local law enforcement (and some just went missing), which in return collected information for the FBI, the beginnings of a truly national police force. Key to the new surveillance state was removing the encryption of metadata collected by the NSA and creating new programs to spy on American citizens. Constitutionally (as if it mattered), multiple provisions were used to justify surveillance. The government had always worked closely with the telecommunications industry; in Room 641A in the SBC Communications building in San Francisco, it installed a beam splitter to monitor all internet traffic under the "business records" provision of the 1978 Foreign Intelligence Surveillance Act. The Ninth Circuit Court dismissed a privacy suit after Congress granted all participating telecommunications companies retroactive immunity. Under Section 215 of Bush's PATRIOT Act, the NSA and FBI demanded that third parties, like banks and telephone companies, hand over private information "relevant" to international terrorism. The NSA's PRISM network, giving it access to leading internet companies Google, Facebook, Skype, and Apple, was justified under Section 702 of the FISA Amendments Act, allowing the government to surveil non-US persons "reasonably believed" to be outside US borders. For all others, there was Reagan's Executive Order 12,333, which allowed intelligence agencies to collect information from foreign cables. US citizens' information on offshore servers was stored in massive billion-dollar facilities.

While neoliberals called national self-sufficiency a myth, outsourcing of production and technology made the US dependent on foreign nations. Aspirin, tennis shoes, silverware, Vitamin C—entire industries were shipped overseas. China produces 96 percent of all antibiotics used in the US. Beginning in 2000, every American producer of telecommunications equipment was outsourced to China. Matt Stoller writes, "First, in the 1980s and 1990s, Wall Street financiers focused on short-term profits, market power, and executive pay-outs over core competencies like research and production, often rolling an industry up into a monopoly producer. Then, in the 2000s, they offshored production to the lowest cost producer. This finance-centric approach opened the door to the Chinese government's ability to strategically pick off industrial capacity by subsidizing its producers."[84] Formerly the world's leader in the rare-earth metal industry, especially rare-earth magnets, the US financial sector sold the companies to China, who shipped them back home. Xiaoping's sons-in-law, using banker Archibald Cox Jr.'s hedge fund as a front, bought the US rare-earth magnet enterprise, then moved "the factory, the Indiana jobs, the patents, and the expertise to China. This was not the only big move, as Cox later moved into a $12 million luxury New York residence." J. P. Morgan and Goldman Sachs created programs to hire Chinese "sons and daughters" for lucrative positions in their companies.

Neoliberalism had become a national security threat. Companies like TransDigm not only overcharged the Department of Defense for its products, it outsourced systems vital to US defense. Despite the fact that the US spends more on defense than any other nation, its contractors, focusing on creating monopolies, use the money to outsource technology and production to China, which steals the technology (surpassing the US in 5G technology and hypersonic missiles). The US imports aluminum from China for its aircraft carriers and is losing its submarine fleet. Because it has outsourced production of high-quality fasteners and castings, it cannot build as many ships per year as it retires. The US now depends completely, 100 percent, on nations like China for the materials (like specialty chemicals) for its advanced weapons systems. When confronted with the Chinese threat, neoliberals only proposed to undercut China with cheap labor from India, for whom the US would build nuclear power plants and enact a Trans-Pacific Partnership to offshore business to other countries besides China.

With outsourcing, immigration, and imperial policy, neoliberals concentrated political and economic power. In 2005, three analysts at Citigroup noted the "rise of the global elite": "the World is dividing into two blocs—the Plutonomy and the rest."[85] US CEOs rejected American identity altogether. They called themselves a meritocracy, not inheritors but creators of wealth, best fit to rule undifferentiated global consumers, to whose money they had more allegiance than to Americans. Despite receiving taxpayer benefits and subsidies, ninety-nine of the top one hundred largest corporations, including the Ford Motor Company, refused to say the Pledge of Allegiance before their annual stockholders' meetings because they were "multinational," not American. They had become, reported Chrystia Freeland, "a transglobal community of peers who have more in common with one another than with their countrymen back home. Whether they maintain primary residences in New York or Hong Kong, Moscow or Mumbai, today's super-rich are increasingly a nation unto themselves." It was, wrote Roger Kimball, a regime "of the privileged, by the privileged, for the privileged."[86] Yet the global elite still depended on the American nation to protect its speculation, which brought the 2008 collapse of the US housing market and threatened an "economic Armageddon." Bush signed the first Troubled Assets Relief Program (TARP) spending bill, almost $1 trillion in corporate bailouts. Rallying to protect the order, neoliberals found an ally in presidential candidate Barack Obama, whose articulate leadership at the White House emergency talks outshined John McCain's incompetent platitudes.

Bush represented everything duplicitous about neoliberalism. The Iraq War and 2008 Great Recession exposed the corruption of the US military and economic empire. The Iraq War, at first widely supported, became an unmitigated, uncomfortable mess and Iraq a failed state. Weapons of mass destruction never materialized. Republicans defended the supposedly successful "surge," or rewarmed

COIN, but Bush's conservatism rested on now-vacuous ideologies peddled by think tanks and educated elites. Libertarians pushed for open borders and cronyism called free trade; neocons supported bloated military budgets to slaughter forgotten youth on the altar of global corporatism; traditionalists peddled agrarian poetry to white upper-class conservatives, teaching the evils of the nation-state and modernity. The 2008 campaign was a watershed moment for Republicans: intelligent young conservatives supported Ron Paul, and the base could not vote for John McCain, a neocon supporting another immigrant amnesty. The party placated the base by selecting Sarah Palin for a running mate. Palin had made a reputation challenging Alaska's oil and gas companies, and she made her message national: the corporate oligarchs were destroying the American middle class. The *National Review* crowd clutched its pearls. William F. Buckley's son Christopher wrote, in his endorsement of Obama, "Palin is an embarrassment, and a dangerous one at that.... America ought, really, to be governed by men like John McCain"; David Brooks called her "a cancer on the Republican Party."[87]

The populist revolt on the Right accompanied one on the Left, a "New, New Left" that reasserted the identity politics that had percolated in academia since the 1960s. Faced with a crisis of legitimacy, neoliberals sided with the Left, the subject of our next chapter.

6

———

IDENTITY POLITICS

B y the 1990s radicals in the academy had completed a system of identity politics to educate young cosmopolitans. They provided a moral framework for the "bourgeois bohemians" who had tried to balance the benefits of globalization with Leftist criticism and would unite in opposition to Bush's neoconservatism. Barack Obama's own neoliberal policies were opposed by both populists on the Right *and* Leftist groups fortified by new economic and violent revolutionary theories. Neoliberalism could not last long without religious sanction. In the "Great Awokening" of Obama's second term, the oligarchs, fearing the nationalist threat, kissed the ring of the identity politics priesthood. After the surprising election of Donald Trump, they applied their own foreign policy of destabilization to subdue the American people at home.

The 1990s Cosmopolitans

The neoliberal oligarchs worked to destroy the remaining ties and images of American middle-class mores. Hollywood and cable television singled out white males and the traditional family for mockery while peddling new cosmopolitan images, transitioning from shows like *Dallas*, *Magnum PI*, and *The A-Team* to *Seinfeld*, *Friends*, and *ER*.

Cable television offered outlets like C-SPAN, CNN, and Fox News as an alternative to the dominant Washington press corps. They featured socially permissive programing; as the channels came in a package, viewers could not isolate the former from the latter. Developing its own shows, MTV entertained its audience (two-thirds of which was between 18 and 34) with the stupid *Beavis and Butthead* and the cynical *Daria*. To keep up, ABC's *NYPD Blue* first aired partial nudity and gritty language. Politicians responded to cable TV by changing their strategies for approval ratings and pushing policies. They avoided the intense questioning and distorted soundbites of the press by creating their own performance art. Clinton played the saxophone for Arsenio Hall and answered the question "boxers or briefs?" on MTV, which promised to "rock the vote."

Where academics celebrated the new technological "civic engagement" in the information age, Robert Putnam observed the decline of social capital and trust.[1] The new "communities" were internet boards: "virtual reality" helmets individuated and separated citizens, removing them from older associations. Saturated with media images, young people became detached from reality, narcissistic, and self-ironic. His thesis reevaluated the 1950s suburbs; far from spaces of soulless detachment described by elites, they had provided civic engagement that did not drop off until 1965. Putnam attributed the decline to the breakup of families, individualist media, and generational change. And the cost was existential. "Social capital," he reminded, "makes individuals—and communities—healthier, wealthier, wiser, happier, more productive and better able to govern themselves peaceably."[2] While pioneers from Silicon Valley had promised authenticity in creative workspaces, young adults found servitude in a corporate hierarchy. At best it involved performance or creating shallow art of one's own personality with no experience other than conventional education and consumer products. At worst it was Patrick Bateman, a horror show of conformity, distrust, and cutthroat competition.

Gen Xers and millennials (the most educated generation in US history—39 percent went on to receive bachelor's degrees) were far more likely than their parents to earn a college degree. But for most it meant dumbed-down education with remedial classes and courses useless for living, and for the elites it consisted of niche specializations and hoops for status-promotion. Despite the financial boom and material comfort, young adults resented their own regime as it ripped them from natural relations and the rites of passage that gave them a sense of identity and purpose. They delayed or forewent marriage, formed their own households more slowly, and more frequently lived at home with their parents and for longer stretches of time. Young women, who entered the workforce far more frequently than their mothers, criticized the old feminist promise that they could have careers and families. As women outpaced men in education and previously male fields, men began to drop out altogether, leaving to form their own private armies in paintball, video games, and in mixed martial arts, which became the fastest growing sport in America. Brooding alternative music and angry Nu metal replaced the spirited rock of the 1980s. Films like *American Beauty*, *Fight Club*, *The Matrix*, and *Office Space* featured white male protagonists in dead-end office jobs, obsessed with consumerism, who leave to find meaning in new rites of passage. "We're a generation of men raised by women," said Tyler Durden. "I'm wondering if another woman is really the answer we need." Not just fatherlessness but the lack of father figures left children without order. With no tradition to confront, young men and women failed to internalize an authoritative sense of self, a confidence in proper boundaries separating the private and public spheres.

The oligarchs promoted hedonism to control the private sphere. Sexual images saturated American life more than ever before. Dating decreased. By the mid-1990s, sexual hookups and fleeting, emotionally unsatisfying relationships characterized college campuses and cosmopolitan life. Clinton's refusal to prosecute for obscenity, along with the launch of the internet, brought a perfect storm of pornography. Sex comedies for both adults and teenagers, *Sex in the City* and *American Pie*, went mainstream. While politicians still defended their populist constituencies' opposition to homosexuality—Clinton signed the Defense of Marriage Act in 1996—millennials broke with their parents on homosexuality and gay marriage. Hit shows *Friends* and *Will and Grace* portrayed gays as bubbly, harmless, and persecuted, lesbians as beautiful and chic. The media seized on reports that twenty-one-year-old Matthew Shepard had been murdered by a stranger for making homosexual advances. He became "the new poster child for gay rights."[3] The *New York Times* reported a "homophobic epidemic of '98."[4] A play about Shepard, *The Laramie Project*, became one of the most produced theater pieces in America. It was all a fabrication (he had been murdered in a robbery by a fellow meth addict), but the murder fueled new "anti-hate-crime" legislation to punish homophobic intentions.

New technologies accelerated hedonism. Science, or *scientia*, is properly the love of wisdom, rooted in human experience. It includes human health, that which is vibrant and flourishing. But now the authority of science, detached from human good, meant servicing corporate profits with technologies of control to degenerate human health, diet, mind, and reproduction. US manufacturers, responding to farm subsidies that brought excess corn and falling prices, developed high-fructose corn syrup, a cheaper substitute to sugar and by the mid-1980s a staple in most soft drink beverages. Americans consumed more fast food (and larger portions) and fewer vegetables while living sedentary lifestyles at the office and at home, where they zoned out to thousands of media stations, internet videos, and video games. They became fat and depressed. To maintain this unhealthy lifestyle, scientists invented drugs, with side effects requiring more drugs, to regulate every aspect of human life. Total spending on prescription drugs rose from $40.3 billion in 1990 to $121 billion in 2000 (Medicaid spending alone increased to $20 billion). From 1992 to 2000, prescriptions increased from 7.3 to 10.8 per person. To treat their depression,

Americans became addicted to Prozac and Zoloft. Doctors administered Ritalin, followed by the more effective Adderall, to ADHD-diagnosed children. The number of children taking stimulants grew from six hundred thousand in 1990 to 3.5 million in 2013. In 1991 the Department of Education ruled that an autism diagnosis qualified a child for special education services. The government broadened the category and worked with drug companies to treat skyrocketing cases, from 1 in 1,400 children in 1987 to 1 in 150 in 2000. College students and adults became addicted to Adderall (five million prescriptions in 2000), which altered their personalities, allowing them to function in monotonous or high-stress settings while giving them a euphoric feeling. Doctors prescribed Adderall-like stimulants fifty million times in 2011, a 40 percent increase from 2007.

And science sterilized Americans. After 1984 legislation changed the system of drug approval, facilitating competition from generics, pharmaceutical companies stopped marketing birth control as a contraceptive; manufacturers in the 1990s promoted oral contraceptives to doctors and teenagers as "lifestyle drugs," medications "designed to improve a person's quality of life."[5] Birth control would reduce acne and premenstrual dysphoric disorder. From 1985 to 2000, its use among sexually experienced women increased from 56 to 76 percent. Most oral contraceptives used synthetic estrogen (EE2, an endocrine disruptor), excess exposure to which disrupts infants' reproductive hormones and development. As American women's fertility rates shrank, they daily ingested and excreted millions of doses of synthetic estrogen into wastewater, rivers, and lakes. Male fish developed female biomarkers like ovaries and became less fertile across generations. A greater threat to fertility were the phthalates used to make plastic for food manufacture, processing, and packaging. Mimicking sex hormones, they disrupt human hormone production and inhibit female and male fertility.[6] Around two million tons of plastic enter the ocean each year from rivers, accumulating in the 617,000-square-mile Great Pacific Garbage Patch.

Agricultural and pharmaceutical companies waged war on male biology, not just sedating boys in classrooms and exposing them to phthalates that stunted their genital development but in contaminating their food with Atrazine and feeding them soy (containing phytoestrogen) that reduces testosterone and lowers sperm count, all making them docile and manageable. For the high yields to supply the world corn, exhausting the soil, farmers relied on chemicals and pesticides. The widely used Atrazine, an agricultural weed killer, disrupts hormones, inducing "complete feminization and chemical castration" in African frogs—"ten percent of the exposed genetic males developed into functional females."[7] It contaminated tap water and wells of millions of Americans.[8] Soy food sales rose from $300 million in 1992 to $4 billion in 2017. Working women, with no time to nurse, fed their babies infant formula, 25 percent of which is soy-based.[9] In one study, soy-fed babies had thirteen thousand to twenty-two thousand times more estrogenic compounds in their blood than milk-fed babies.[10] Pediatricians labeled new syndromes for boys, who from high estrogen levels had delayed puberty or developed breasts. Testosterone levels declined significantly between 1987 and 2004, creating men with shrunken genitals, impaired sexual function, feminine traits of higher voices and passivity, and less muscle tone and hair.[11] They became transgender.

And science stupefied and exterminated humans. For pain, California first legalized medical cannabis in 1996; seven more states did so by 2000. Pharmaceutical companies used partial studies to aggressively promote opioids as "a safe, salutary and a more humane alternative" to surgery, and this, they claimed, without addiction.[12] From 1990 to 1995, opioid prescriptions increased by two to three million each year. In 1995 the USDA approved Oxycontin, made by Purdue Pharma, which began aggressively marketing the addictive drug for the treatment of chronic pain, particularly to primary care physicians; according to the DOJ, Purdue Pharma paid physicians to prescribe it.[13] From 1997 to 2002, annual Oxycontin prescriptions increased from 670,000 to 6.2 million, and the total number of opioid prescriptions increased by forty-five million. "From 1999–2019," reports the CDC, "nearly 500,000 people died from an overdose involving any opioid, including prescription and illicit opioids."[14] To compensate for population destruction, the elites imported new people by immigration.

Diversity, Multiculturalism, and Political Correctness

As the oligarchs promoted diversity and globalization, the national and violent crime rates peaked in 1991, and racial hatred flared in the 1992 LA riots.[15] Race tribalism was entertaining, and good business. Where black and white viewers shared fifteen out of the top twenty shows in the 1985–86 season (*The Cosby Show* ranked first), stations in the 1990s ran programs to appeal to black identity and barrage whites with anti-racism. Marked for scorn was the liberals' white savior narrative, in which heroic white allies protect people of color against white racists. It was a weakness for whites who had adopted the religion of racial equality yet depended on affirmation by minorities. Scorning the image of impotent whiteness, young whites purchased black music, affected black manners, worshipped black athleticism, and romanticized the violent black masculine gangsterism in "urban jungles." Mailer's "white negroes" became "wiggers" and "wannabes" who wanted black saviors and courageous rites of passage packaged in white rappers by music corporations. Clinton's impeachment was part of the *culture wars*; more than a Republican power play, it expressed the dissolution of white middle-class morality. Black support for Clinton soared to 90 percent during the hearings. Toni Morrison called him the "first black president": "Clinton displays almost every trope of blackness: single-parent household, born poor, working-class, saxophone-playing, McDonald's-and-junk-food-loving boy from Arkansas."[16] White middle-class America was hypocritical and contradictory, but Clinton was the ideal white, flawed politician, candid about his prejudices and thus morally superior to whites who concealed their racism and sexual urges.

On the matter of racial diversity, the media preached a distant loser. According to the 1990 census, "the browning of America" would bring a white minority. The Hispanic portion of the population had doubled since 1960, from 4.7 to 9 percent. *Time* reported, "Someday soon . . . white Americans will become a minority group. . . . The presumption that the 'typical' U.S. citizen is someone who traces his or her descent in a direct line to Europe will be part of the past."[17] Americans had long supported immigration restrictions and penalties for hiring illegals, but the alliance between the business and civil rights lobbies had secured an increase in the number of unskilled and skilled immigrants in the 1990 Immigration Act while giving immigrants of color special recognition and privileges as oppressed, an absurd argument for those who had never lived under Jim Crow. It was anti-democratic and treacherous for elites to import a new electorate. Responding to public outcry, Clinton created the Council on Immigration Reform. Its findings led to 1996 legislation that simplified deportation proceedings and financed two border walls. In 1994 California governor Pete Wilson successfully campaigned against illegal immigration. Proposition 187, which established a state screening system to prevent funds from going to illegals, passed with a 60 percent majority. The next year the California Board of Regents prohibited preferential hiring in university admissions, employment, and contracts. Proposition 227 ended the state's bilingual education system and replaced it with English immersion. But this only showed that whites had lost moral confidence. Afraid to be called racists by outspoken Leftists, noted Victor Davis Hanson, "Embittered Californians decline to challenge the therapeutic bromides offered to Hispanics in their schools and state agencies—but then go quietly to the polls to vent their rage by ending what they see are special concessions to those who broke the law in coming here. It is not a very healthy state of affairs to have a voting population of millions thinking privately what they would never express publicly."[18]

By the end of the 1990s, given the supposed inevitability of a white minority nation (Hispanics were nearing 13 percent of the population), Democrats saw a decreasing need for unity. In 1998, Clinton celebrated "a new wave of immigration larger than any in a century, far more diverse than any in our history.... Within five years there will be no majority race in our largest state, California. In a little more than 50 years there will be no majority race in the United States. (Applause.) No other nation in history has gone through demographic change of this magnitude in so short a time."[19] Clinton presented an intentional policy as inevitable, and young, educated, white progressives in Portland cheered the demographic demise of working-class whites in Ohio. Paul Starr, followed by John B. Judis and Ruy Teixeira, foresaw an "emerging Democratic majority"; growing Hispanic majorities and declining white birthrates constituted a demographic revolution and endless Democratic victories.[20] In 1999 California's Democratic governor Gray Davis refused to defend Proposition 187 in federal court. As America was destined to be a majority-minority country, multiculturalism took center stage and with it a new morality of "political correctness" fraught with the empirical fact that racial groups, while promised equal opportunity, reached different outcomes.

Conservatives began to explain disparities in race and gender by publicizing long-held scientific evidence of biological differences. Charles Murray's *The Bell Curve* argued for recognizing the difference in intelligence between humans (including whites) and more controversially, between race groups. Government policies since the 1960s had both unjustly promoted underskilled applicants and undermined the morals that allowed minorities to get ahead. Murray affirmed equal opportunity under the law as well as the older morality that preserved the family. Race differences, argued Jared Taylor, caused the plight of blacks and the "catastrophe" of diversity that had destroyed civic trust. Yet 90 percent of new immigrants were nonwhite; and one could not challenge policies privileging minorities because systemic racism had become an orthodoxy. Pat Buchanan and Lou Dobbs opposed neoliberalism for eroding Anglo-American culture; they supported an economic nationalist platform against NAFTA and the WTO, opposition to which had fueled Perot's presidential candidacy. Buchanan, himself a candidate in '92 and '96, proclaimed a "great betrayal": "American sovereignty and social justice," and republican freedoms, had been "sacrificed to the gods of the global economy." Previously a "militant Milton Friedman free trader," he now called "free trade...a betrayal of the country." Peter Brimelow and Steve Sailer proposed a moratorium on immigration. Multiculturalism attacked the very idea of preserving a cultural West and its priorities of reason and science. But the term *West* was *historical.* Rather than mere abstract principles, it meant either the ethnicities that had developed certain intellectual, political, and moral habits or a demand for assimilation to them, presuming their superiority. And those habits, argued Sam Francis, corroded under what he called neoliberal *anarcho-tyranny:* "the combination of oppressive government power against the innocent and the law-abiding" with "a grotesque paralysis of the ability or the will to use that power to carry out basic public duties such as protection or public safety." In this "managed pacification and manipulation of the citizens...Americans are increasingly habituated to an entirely passive role in government, economy, culture, and now even basic social functions such as childrearing and health care."[21] Governments used infractions and regulations to raise revenue from middle-class whites while leaving them unprotected from crime. He proposed recognizing a white identity to resist it and moreover, given the inability for whites to restrict immigration, called for a leader to smash the bureaucracy. These intellectuals became pariahs to mainstream conservatives (neoliberals), but paleoconservatism had left its mark.

Neoliberals, who celebrated racial diversity and globalization, argued for culture's primacy. They debated whether children should learn one American culture or coexisting plural cultures. Center-right intellectuals argued that Hispanics were socially conservative future

Republicans, provided a net-economic benefit through cheap labor, and had a more American work ethic than natives. The white middle class had only itself to blame; it wanted protectionism instead of hard work and selfishly complained about its declining standard of living while corporations were saving the world's poor from starvation. Cheap labor was the *American people's fault*; they refused to do migrant work yet benefitted from the lower prices. Disturbed by the rising identity politics on the Left, prominent centrist liberals like Schlesinger and even Todd Gitlin criticized multiculturalism and warned that Americans were losing their common vision. Charles Taylor proposed a middle way between liberalism (a fighting faith for women's rights and free speech) and multiculturalism: mutual recognition required an honest engagement with other cultures, presuming each had something important to say, and whose validity would be demonstrated concretely by the change in the horizons of Western values. A vigorous debate about the meaning of nation and patriotism followed Martha Nussbaum's call to make "world citizenship, rather than democratic or national citizenship, the focus for civic education."[22] A volume of scholars challenged her words, but none defended patriotism removed from global moral obligations. Whether idealistic or pragmatic, they were globalizers all: the rational scholar must agree to international cooperation and be *open to the possibility* of a global order.[23] Third-way neoliberals promoted this vision in education by adding a "sense of global citizenship" to national and ethnic identity: a "cosmopolitan outlook is the necessary condition of a multicultural society in a globalizing order."[24] But even as corporations repackaged 1960s radicalism for consumption—flare jeans, Woodstock '94 and '99, a new Volkswagen Bug—progressives united against neoliberalism for failing to achieve social justice.

In the 1990s, progressive systems of thought that claimed a monopoly on personal identity permeated the universities and became the moral authority for the postmillennial generation. Leftists in education had abandoned the framework of class for multiculturalism.[25] Race and gender did not exist (groups were fluid, with no permanent essence), but they mattered as political constructs. Unequal outcomes confirmed systemic white racism; neoliberal appeals to universal humanity were actually racist and sexist. The "denial of difference contributes to social group oppression," wrote Iris Marion Young, who forwarded "a politics that recognizes rather than represses difference."[26] Thus the Left denied group essences but made them essential in practical cultural assessments. In the words of Cornel West, liberalism forced those who never chose to be black to assimilate to a social order of Whiteness.[27] Ensconced in research universities, the growing fields of women's and Afro-American studies required new claims of expertise in convoluted jargon, conflicting schools of interpretation, and endless metaphysical disputes among privileged tenure-track professors. To advance their fields, feminists and black studies professors debated "environmental sexism" and anti-racist math. As each field became secure, questioning its fundamental assumptions on patriarchy or systemic racism became heresy. The Left celebrated the demise of *whites* and *the West* as a racial *and* cultural standard and offered a religious and salvific vision of diversity, a new heaven on earth brought about by a new consciousness. The West was "dominant but dead." But the culture must die, too, else its moral presumptions remained. If one were to imagine the West as a great empire, defined by proximity to its center, then the farther removed one was, the more other he became. Transcending otherness required a dialectical confrontation with the identity of oppressive Whiteness as defined against its oppressed other. Any defense of the West was white nationalism, the subject of a growing body of scholarship.

Whiteness could never have remained an abstraction removed from actual white people, thus Leftists demanded that whites diminish their populations, admit their privilege, and champion race-based structural reforms. Centrist liberals who questioned the orthodoxy were branded racists, even historian Gary Nash, who had helped to found ethnic studies. Clinton's welfare reform, Leftists charged, had channeled single mothers away from school to low-paying service jobs. Angela Davis continued the fight against systemic racism in black incarceration, low graduation rates, and the increasing use of "stop and frisk." The defeat of Whiteness as evil included the end of Western hegemony abroad. Progressives both attacked neoliberal colonialism and crusaded for globalism, transcending the nation state. Universities created degrees in global studies, and globalism became elite orthodoxy. Noam Chomsky's critique of American imperialism was printed in comic book form and recorded on CDs. US free trade agreements had allowed "stateless" corporations to offshore jobs, and WTO rulings allowed the US to overrule other nations' environmental regulations as unfair trade barriers. Challenging corporate deregulation, radicals focused on ecology and global warming and pushed for an international regulatory regime, such as the 1997 Kyoto Protocol on Climate Change. The dispute peaked in 1999 when tens of thousands of protestors disrupted the WTO's convention in Seattle. The Right and Left—Pat Buchanan, Ralph Nader, and James Hoffa—representing labor and environmentalist groups converged in opposition to globalization as it undermined economic security, environmental protection, and national sovereignty. Holding up the five-hundred-page GATT agreement, Nader said, "This is not free trade. These are who makes the rules, and it isn't the people. It's concentrated corporate power utilizing the governments of the world against us." Rioting anarchists, who Clinton called "creeps," accompanied them. Foreshadowing the future alliance between the oligarchs and identity politics, state-funded academics divided the coalition by race. The problem with the protests, they said, was that labor and environmentalist groups were "too white" and must include minorities in leadership positions.[28]

The System of Identity Politics

Identity politics is a system that any minimally intelligent person can learn. It begins with a critique of Rawls's neoliberalism, whose scientific, empirical pretense and supposed rejection of metaphysics conceal an authoritative view of "public reason." In this critique, Rawls uses a Western "logic of identity," which reaches beyond order and comparison to the construction of its own totalizing system. This logic searches "to find the universal, the one principle, the law, covering the phenomena to be accounted for" and then classifies concrete particulars as inside or outside this essence so that its categories may be stable and its operations certain and predictable.[29] The search for universals (that which is the same) logically requires an either/or, a binary referent other (that which it is not). Thus, it creates authoritative categories and replaces normative questions with absolute narratives that deny and suppress difference.[30] As the Western logic of identity seeks to homogenize all differences, it turns the merely different into an absolute and inferior other, creating dichotomy instead of diversity. It entails oppression because its teaching of human nature as defined by reason, which obligates one to universal categories of moral impartiality, only expresses a particular white male morality. It excludes women and people of color—the realm of ambiguous and sensuous experience—as immoral. Deemed inherently inferior, they are barred the rights of citizenship. Both at home and abroad, Western colonialism generates exploitative categories of race and gender, to which the other is forced to assimilate. Yet the colonial project necessarily fails because this totalizing movement always leaves a remainder in repressed gender fantasies and oppressed peoples, who become conscious that they cannot assimilate. Thus identity politics both attacks and quietly embraces essences. On the one hand, it claims to reject universal claims to nature used for political authority, and, on the other hand, it promotes a vision of human nature that informs the good society. The "politics of difference," recognizing identity groups, was a tool to challenge white nationalist identities and then "transcend those very differences" and "leap to humanist liberation theory."[31]

In psychology, progressives challenged the neoliberal denial of a comprehensive good and the abstraction *homo economicus* and taught authenticity as individual excellence in light of a global political order. They provided a comprehensive teaching of human virtues grounded in enduring personality traits. Rejecting "ethical relativism" and appealing to "human nature," the new positive psychologists sought to reconcile science with virtue ethics as informed by happiness: "Six virtues... are endorsed across every major religious and cultural tradition": wisdom, courage, humanity, justice, temperance, and transcendence.[32] Ivy League schools had higher IQ scores and claimed to have better moral virtue than their WASP forbearers. Graduates furthered technologies like renewable energy and space exploration, and they exercised prudence in furthering global initiatives and courage in fighting fascism and white supremacy. Progressive elites declared themselves a meritocracy, grounding their right to rule on both excellence and helping the disadvantaged. They championed a "politics of authenticity" to create an environment where all humans could actualize their potential, where "ideals of individual achievement are actually realized, where talent, motivation, ambition, and hard work actually do pay off, where race, class, sexuality and gender predict very little about [one's] economic and social life."[33]

Through self-examination, identity politics teaches a group identity that includes one's moral duties to others and a sense of entitlement for entitlements. The Left had long debated who was most oppressed: blacks, women, or homosexuals. In Kimberlé Crenshaw's 1989 theory of intersectionality, oppression compounds with the accumulation of disadvantaged identities, such as black and female. She reviewed legal cases in which plaintiffs could not claim disparate impact on the basis of race or gender alone but could if the courts affirmed that the intersection of traits creates a new identity category more than the sum of its parts. As black females had no protected, intersectional category, corporations could avoid discrimination suits by hiring only black males and white females. But black women were neither: they had unique experiences, practiced different morals, and faced unique discrimination. Crenshaw provided a social theory in the allegory of the basement. If the first floor of the house is the equal playing field for individual competition, privileging "whiteness or maleness," the disadvantaged are in the basement with a single hatch granting access.[34] Those with one oppressed trait are closer to the hatch, climbing atop those with multiple traits and pressing them down. She advocated a new bottom-up theory, which placed "those who currently are marginalized in the center" instead of a top-down theory that privileged black males and white women. Theorists debated how to assign status without prioritizing one category of oppression over another, for example, by ascribing each identity trait a privilege score to assess one's sum advantage or disadvantage. But this Oppression Olympics, it was alleged, tended toward virtue signaling without political change.

Patricia Hill Collins wanted to *politicize* "a new vision of race, class and gender." Concerned about the dichotomous thinking in oppressor/oppressed and a simplistic "additive analysis of oppression," she wanted to reconceptualize "oppression by uncovering connections among race, class and gender as categories of analysis."[35] Identity categories themselves must remain but could be transcended. She offered the "matrix of domination": "Everyone is affected by the same interlocking set of symbolic images" in institutions, symbols, and individuals. Thus all in the matrix, especially white Christian males, must accede to its systemic oppression, which is concealed (often unconsciously) by a language of objective merit, or "equality of opportunity." Because all institutions ("schools, businesses, hospitals, the workplace, and government agencies") participate in this matrix inherited from slavery, they must become a battleground. The university is a "modern plantation" that must become a center of political activism, a place to study the self in order to change the world. "Widespread, socially sanctioned ideologies" have justified "relations of domination and subordination" reinforced by dichotomies in either/or language. Binaries like masculine/feminine reinforce gender hierarchies by making opposites of their others or, worse, by dehumanizing others and making them invisible. Professors must promote "diversity in our scholarship, in our teaching, and in our daily lives," overturning the "controlling" or "seductive images" that affirm the status quo. They must provide a new "vision on interpretations of reality thought to be natural, normal and 'true.'" Because "each of us carries the cumulative effect of our lives within multiple structures of oppression," they must become the focus of all individuals; all choices become political acts.

Identity politics guides students in self-examination by recognizing the importance of group identity for individual growth. Academics revived consciousness-raising and identity-parsing, becoming "woke" to one's own unconscious racism and sexism. The sexual revolution required self-exploration in order to answer questions of the good life. Progressives did not deny sex differences among homosexuals and transgenders, but they challenged the value of essentialist categories used for universal gender roles. Sex was one characteristic along with gender identity, gender expression, and physical and emotional attraction. Stuart Hall argued that the end of Blackness as an essence meant the "end of innocence" and a new conception of politics that redefined oppression and violence to include the unconscious judgments of others in a social hierarchy.[36] Thus the public benefits from recognizing, affirming, openly supporting, and reinvigorating diverse communities that assist identity formation. "Assimilation" is a "cardinal sin against the ideal of authenticity."[37] The individual cannot develop without tradition and bonds of affection, intimacy for self-exploration, and self-realization. A politics of difference secures those traditions, with and against which one discovers and articulates an identity. Laws must give positive cultural enforcement for minorities and women in the sciences and the workplace and prohibit cultural appropriation that reinforces negative stereotypes.

In every regime the elite send their children to the priests for education. Identity politics, funded by the state, became a substitute religion for agnostics and atheists. The number of Americans claiming no religious preference barely rose from 1971 to 1991, from 5.1 to 6.7 percent. But as the percent of those with four-year degrees rose (22 percent in 1990, 26 percent in 2000, 30 percent in 2010, 33.4 percent in 2016), so did those professing no religion, from 6.7 percent in 1991, to 14 percent in 2000, to 18 percent in 2010, to 22.8 percent in 2014.[38] By 2021, 43 percent of millennials professed agnosticism or atheism. Television shows proselytized diversity to urbane cosmopolitans. Identity politics channeled the varieties of religious experience into numerous race, gender, and environmental religious orders. The search for authenticity guides elites' spiritual experiences, while active faith is directed to morals and politics. Identity politics proffers all-encompassing explanatory systems of justice, thus a gnostic sense of insight. A class of priests, peddling redemption, promises unity once racists, sexists, and hubristic polluters atoned for their original sins; white elites could then feel at one with the other, the humanistic and globalist promise. By a horrific recounting of a select past (slavery or the Holocaust), students emotionally confront existential questions and channel indignation to contemporary inequalities. The system provides moral clarity, meaning, and catharsis of atonement for guilt through various penances. One born Christian, white, or male publicly confesses his privilege to a priest, owns his group's sins, and strives to change his behavior. Peggy McIntosh's "Unpacking the White Knapsack of Privilege" listed the ways she had unconsciously transgressed by *not* reflecting on her sin of racism. The religious rituals of ethical ecology unify humanity to "save the planet" and harmonize man and nature, or else the people reap damnation. Prophets scare children with horrors unless their message is heeded. They preach scarcity from overpopulation, mass extinctions, a fiery judgment of global warming and the floods of climate change accompanied by super volcanoes, asteroids, and flash tidal waves.

Because all sacred values strive to become absolute, identity politics did not create a new equilibrium but transvaluated the old morality into evil and blamed individuals' suffering on the macrostructure of oppression. The oppressive stigma that blacks, women, and homosexuals fought now belongs to white Christian heterosexuals, who must experience guilt. The phrase "toxic masculinity," coined in 1994, referred to the ways that an education in masculinity *deformed* one's unique identity.[39] Colleges funded "Check Your Privilege" campaigns for white, male, upper-class, Christian, heterosexual, cisgender, and able-bodied students. Because these groups' claims to rights merely affirmed privilege, their confessions of privilege removed their claims to rights. Straight, white males, "member[s] of several oppressor groups," may be injured and pained, but they cannot be *oppressed*.[40] Oppression became a structural claim, rendering the word meaningless. Similarly, because race is about power, blacks cannot be properly called *racist* nor women *sexist*. All must recognize their benefits in the structure and remedy its injustices. One who admits his white privilege cannot reject his identity, nor should he wallow in guilt. The confession is no mere call to subordination; it is a call to service. Michael Kimmel writes, "Refusing to be men, white, or straight does neither the privileged nor the unprivileged much good.... [Privilege] is embedded in the social architecture that surrounds us. Renouncing privilege ultimately substitutes an individual solution for a structural and social problem."[41] Whites must renounce the privilege of being unnamed and invisible, the presumed universal group. Whiteness must be studied to reveal and relativize whites' absolute group status. According to Richard Dyer, "We may be on our way to genuine hybridity, multiplicity without (white) hegemony," but "we won't get there until we see whiteness, see its power, its particularity and limitedness, put it in its place and end its rule."[42] Abandoning "race neutrality" for a theory of race oppression will achieve a fair society, with group empowerment as the basis for individual authenticity. The idea of empathy or equal individual worth remains, but whites' claim to *absolute* empathy, or to fully understand the suffering of the other, inhibits universal inclusion and participation.

Because there is no neutrality—one fights for or against oppression—elementary classrooms adopted identity politics. "Culturally responsive teaching," respecting each child's diverse cultural contribution, viewed children as "colearners" with a premium on self-esteem.[43] At elite universities, the identity politics confession became a moral temporizing gateway for positions of power, wealth, status, internships, and entry into the ruling class of bureaucracy, corporations, and finance. By condemning the sins of middle-class whites, white male elites demonstrated their moral superiority, thus justifying their own privilege and their right to rule for the disadvantaged other. The progressive ritual promises to bring a ruling class together across race and gender differences. It provides moral affirmation to anti-racist whites and justifies affirmative action for minorities. This university model of affirming difference necessitated censuring contrary arguments. Over three hundred university speech codes were in place by 1991.

Progressives affirmed democratic socialism. Where neoliberals had focused on redistributive justice for past injustices in welfare payments, token hires, and forced integration, progressives challenged the Rawlsian liberal contract itself as a racial contract or a sexual contract: it was an agreement between whites and males to secure rights to themselves and domination over minorities and women. The Rawlsian "veil of ignorance" disguised white systemic racism. Moreover, it was a "global contract." "White supremacy," wrote Charles Mills, "is the unnamed political system that has made the modern world what it is today."[44] Whiteness is literally ignorance, a defective prism of perception that makes whites cognitively stunted and oblivious.[45] Mills writes, "It is not merely that Rawls and Rawlsians have not addressed the issue of racism, but that the apparatus itself hinders them from doing so adequately."[46] Whites seldom profess racist views but now "downplay the impact of the racist past on the present configuration of wealth and opportunities (another type of ignorance)."[47] Rejecting liberalism's "ideal of impartiality," progressives instead supported a politics of group empowerment and esteem, which justice demands and cannot be distributed in any meaningful sense. Justice, or who gets what, is determined by how individuals advance the progressive order. Genuine democracy, as opposed to the liberal "ideal of justice...as transcendence of group difference," would mean not just payments to minorities but recognizing oppressed groups, renegotiating concepts of fairness, and redistributing decision-making power to minorities and women in politics and the workplace.[48] Policy should treat groups differently to elevate them and correct for structural oppressions.

Identity politics *broadly* construes politics. To correct for structural injustices, it politicizes "vast areas of institutional, social, and cultural life in the face of the forces of welfare state liberalism."[49] This means rejecting the Rawlsian liberals' focus on public procedural justice and breaking down its barrier to "local justice," or private associations and the family, to free women and children from hierarchies of power.[50] Identity politics required a "democratic" restructuring of the family: alternative forms of family, sexual experimentation, and lengthier periods of higher education. "Blue state" models touted lower divorce rates and family-friendly legislation. Modes of expression in private life must be freed from shame, meaning "equality as acceptance" of "a male, female, or androgynous lifestyle according to their natural inclination or choice."[51] Traditional opinions must not be tolerated but shamed as unacceptable. It also meant politicizing the bureaucracy, subordinating "meritocracy" to identity politics in public policy implementation, in race-based hiring and diversity training. Critical legal studies, seeking "to break up entire areas of institutional life and social practice," challenged legal neutrality as a social construct that legitimized white supremacy.[52] It would use equal protection to both protect and empower minorities. Individual rights must balance with group recognition. Liberalism only limits speech or expression that leads to bodily injury. But a progressive society will both regulate hate speech as injury (if uttered by whites) and integrate predominantly white male associations.[53] Free speech, for example, cannot be used to attack the sacred values of Muslims or to defend racism or sexism.[54] Oppressed groups may claim property in symbols essential to their identity. They must have power to control positive representations of themselves in media and prevent cultural appropriation, such as negative portrayals of Arabs and blacks.[55] Christopher Lebron argued for a "variety of policies wherein the polity is nudged, or ... actively compelled ... by being exposed to specially crafted public service announcements, or by suppressing unfair news coverage in which blacks are overrepresented in crime segments."[56]

Promising to convert neoliberalism's profiteering to moral ends, progressives rejected nationalism for a new political ideal that weds the municipal and global communities in a transnational grid. Frank Garcia wrote, "Globalization is creating new normative possibilities for international relations by developing the social basis for a truly 'global' justice."[57] Young looked to the "normative ideal of city life," which is broad enough to include all groups yet also retains face-to-face relations and creates "*pockets* of community," to transcend national identity.[58] City life, which embodies the virtues of "social differentiation without exclusion, variety, eroticism, and publicity," contrasts with small town American life, with its stifling nationalism, which Lebron called "medieval America."[59] Still, large cities are proportionately underrepresented in supposedly democratic systems. Because liberal notions of local autonomy exacerbate injustices in American cities (poverty, segregation, suburbanization), "city life would be better realized through metropolitan regional government founded in representational institutions that begin in neighborhood assemblies."[60] The world's great cities are the nexuses of an emerging global order and should have greater control over their outlying provinces.

The rejection of the Rawlsian liberal "international order" for a "global order," Singer argued, required a correlate change to a globalist ethics rooted in the "moral intuitions" of "our evolved human nature": "Ethics appears to have developed from the behavior and feelings of social mammals. It became distinct ... when we started using our reasoning abilities to justify our behavior to other members of our group. If the group to which we must justify ourselves is the tribe, or the nation, then our morality is likely to be tribal, or nationalistic. If, however, the revolution in communications has created a global audience, then we might feel a need to justify our behavior to the whole world."[61] As nations "move closer together to tackle global issues like trade, climate change, justice, and poverty...national leaders need to take a larger perspective than that of national self-interest."[62] Common hopes for and duties to future world generations will create "one world" born of collective efforts to solve global problems that nation states have failed to remedy. US interests demanded that it pay disproportionate dues. So too with global poverty: "In the global village, someone else's poverty very soon becomes one's own problem: of lack of markets for one's products, illegal immigration, pollution, contagious disease, insecurity, fanaticism, terrorism."[63] Thus Singer added the additional incentive of fear: resource scarcity, environmental destruction, atomic and biological war, genocide, terrorism, overpopulation, and species extinction.

The mechanisms were already in place to convert neoliberalism to political globalism. Progressive legal scholars proffered standards of international law arbitrated by global courts of justice for UN interventions. It must extend, writes Singer, to "the inhabitants of the most remote mountain valleys of the farthest-flung countries of our planet."[64] Michelman argued that US constitutional interpretation must be informed by international courts and a "global consciousness" that is "receptive to influence by the norms and practices of a broader community of constitutional-democratic jurisdictions and tribunals."[65] To enforce international law, organizations must take on a truly global function. Singer and David Held argued, "States [must] give up, to a world federation, a monopoly of the use of force. The world federation would possess the moral authority of a body that was established by mutual agreement, and reached its decision in an impartial manner. In the modern world, that means a reformed United Nations, with adequate force at its command, and impartial procedures to decide when that force should be used."[66] The UN must become more democratic by revoking the veto from the privileged nations of the Security Council and eventually apportioning nations' representatives by population. Powerful nations, including the US, must facilitate these radical changes. To achieve a truly global community, national leaders must recognize the basic rights of global citizens. Nations must abandon, Singer reminds, the "absolute idea of state sovereignty."[67] The nation-state will continue to exist as a tool for its own destruction. Nations will accept limits to their own sovereignty, whether economic, cultural, or territorial, and become sources of "personal identity."[68]

Barack Obama and the Neoliberal Dilemma

"Barry" Obama attended the wealthiest school in Hawaii, followed by Columbia and Harvard Law. He held neoliberal economic and foreign policy views.[69] After the 2008 housing market implosion, the wealthy came, hat in hand, to the White House, expecting a lashing, but they found a compliant abettor. In March 2008 the federal government, moved by Hank Paulson and Timothy Geithner, secured a merger between the failing investment bank Bear Stearns and J. P. Morgan Chase by financing $29 billion for its assets. In September, the Treasury promised up to $200 billion in capital to rescue mortgage agencies Fannie Mae and Freddie Mac. Attorney General Eric Holder declared the banks central to the economy and therefore not prosecutable for selling worthless assets to unknowing buyers. The financial risk was global; the Fed created $29 trillion to bail out banks, including $500 billion for foreign banks. As congressmembers preened in hearings, CEOs received million-dollar bonuses, and Congress passed Dodd-Frank, which further centralized the financial establishment. To avoid deflation, Congress passed two rounds of TARP spending, and in what was called quantitative easing, the Fed purchased assets from select companies. This central planning, argued Paul Krugman, prevented global recession in the tradition of Milton Friedman. The Fed, keeping interest rates at 0 percent for almost ten years, loaned central banks and corporations money, which would in theory trickle down to the people in the form of record levels of private debt. But instead of spending money to circulate in the economy, the wealthy held onto some $4.9 trillion in cash, which they used to purchase and inflate the price of their own company stocks, which the Fed in turn bought back to finance public deficits. Monopolies formed in almost every industry. Tepper and Hearn reported, "Two corporations control 90% of the beer Americans drink. Four airlines completely dominate airline traffic.... Many states have health insurance markets where the top two insurers have an 80–90% market share. When it comes to high-speed internet access, almost all markets are local monopolies."[70] In 2015, three companies controlled 70 percent of the world's pesticide market. Four companies controlled 66 percent of US hogs slaughtered, 85 percent of the steer, and half the chickens. And four companies controlled 85 percent of US corn seed sales, up from 60 percent in 2000, and 75 percent of soybean seed, from about half.[71] By 2018 Amazon controlled 49.1 percent of all online retail spending (eBay had 6.6 percent, Apple 3.9 percent).

Wealth inequality skyrocketed under Obama, who made Bush's tax cuts permanent. Since 1989 the net worth of the wealthiest 1 percent in America had increased $21 trillion, while the bottom 50 percent lost $900 billion. Household and credit card debt reached record levels. Elizabeth Warren and Charles Murray both chronicled the decline of the American middle class. Blacks suffered most: they fell out of the middle class more than whites as their ownership of real property plummeted. But Murray focused on rising "cultural inequality." To make his point, he excluded race as a confounding variable and treated the growing inequality between the 20 percent of whites in the upper class (labeled "Belmont") and 30 percent of whites in the lower class (labeled "Fishtown"). "We have developed a new upper class with advanced educations, often obtained at elite schools, sharing tastes and preferences that set them apart from mainstream America. At the same time, we have developed a new lower class, characterized not by poverty but by withdrawal from America's core cultural institutions."[72] Since

1960 the common culture had come apart. Where 94 percent of those in Belmont and 84 percent in Fishtown had been married, marriage rates had stabilized in Belmont at 84 percent in 2010 but plummeted in Fishtown to 48 percent. Illegitimacy among whites (2 percent in 1960) by 2008 had increased to 44 percent in Fishtown, while it was less than 6 percent in Belmont. The number of prime-aged males "out of the labor force" had increased in Fishtown from 3 percent in 1968 to 12 percent in 2008, while among Belmont's college-educated white males, it was only 3 percent. From 1960 to 1995, the violent crime rate in Fishtown had increased sixfold while remaining static in Belmont. And while those professing either no religion or attending a worship service at *most* once a year grew in Belmont from 29 to 40 percent, those in Fishtown had grown from 38 to 59 percent.

Educated whites, with a sneering contempt, had pulled away from middle-class Americans in the foods they ate, the shows they watched, the beers they drank, the vacations they took, the elite schools they attended, and the neighborhoods they lived in. And here, said Murray, the inequality got even worse: "A subset of Belmont consists of those who have risen to the top of American society. They run the country, meaning that they are responsible for the films and television shows you watch, the news you see and read, the fortunes of the nation's corporations and financial institutions, and the jurisprudence, legislation and regulations produced by government. They are the new upper class, even more detached from the lives of the great majority of Americans than the people of Belmont—not just socially but spatially as well. The members of this elite have increasingly sorted themselves into hyper-wealthy and hyper-elite ZIP Codes that I call the SuperZIPs." Eleven of the thirteen D.C.-area ZIP codes, placed in an index of education and income, were in the ninety-ninth percentile for income and education. And the bubble that they lived in thickened as their children knew nothing of the world outside of privilege. The wealthy caste limited access to power via educational degrees that increasingly determined one's future. Even as student debt surged, college tuition costs rose 1,400 percent since 1978, or fifteen times the increase in the Consumer Price Index.[73] Elite schools accepted 77 percent of the children of wealthy parents, ensuring little social mobility. Scott Galloway pointed out that universities, no longer aspiring to be public servants, had adopted "a strategy of artificial scarcity to create irrational margins," boasting their exclusivity as "the luxury brands of tomorrow."[74] Their profit margins of 90 percent were far higher than that of any business. At Ivy League schools, "there are more students whose parents are in the top 1 percent of the income distribution than the entire bottom half." While the Ivies are "clubs for the elite, they are taxed as charities." Alumni donations are tax–deductible, both growing endowments and creating an enormous public subsidy: more than $100,000 per student at Princeton, compared with $12,500 at Rutgers. Those graduates *transform industries* to favor exactly the kind of fancy education that they have." The top two careers for Yale and Harvard students are finance and consulting.

As a neoliberal in foreign policy, Obama attacked Bush's war in Iraq but tried to appear strong by escalating the war in Afghanistan. Obama rarely mustered the courage to challenge the military establishment, and the rule of elites again resulted in cronyism and incompetence: a $335 million diesel power plant for which the Afghans had no fuel, $200 million for failed literacy programs for Afghan soldiers, $2 billion on roads to nowhere, $6 million to breed cashmere goats, $486 million for scrapped cargo planes, and $6 billion for poppy eradication. Even worse, Obama believed in overt, shallow displays of goodwill and social justice. He bowed in apology to Egyptian Muslims for American chauvinism. Secretary of State Hillary Clinton called for economic sanctions against countries for gay rights violations. As no one could believe US soldiers were fighting for "freedom," neoliberals peddled romantic brotherhood narratives (soldiers were fighting for each other), and they increasingly turned to fighting for social justice—rights for women in Iraq and Afghanistan against their own peoples. Obama repealed "don't ask, don't tell" and depleted military standards (purging 197 dissenting officers in five years) to show progress in diversity.

Deft at PowerPoint presentations and memorizing talking points, US elites failed to appreciate the dexterity of tyrants who could pacify warring tribes. They extended the "color revolution" by destabilizing nations in the name of democracy. Nonmilitary means elided into force, using private contractors, rebel insurgents, and US Special Forces. In the Arab Spring, the US backed the overthrow of ally Hosni Mubarak in Egypt by the "democratic" Muslim Brotherhood. As part of "corporate social responsibility," American companies sponsored Egyptian programs for "social transition and democracy building."[75] With chaotic weapons drops, the US funded competing militias in Libya to topple Muammar Gaddafi, who was brutally sodomized and executed. Clinton laughed after watching the video: "We came, we saw, he died." Failing to secure the embassy in Benghazi, the US peddled misinformation to cover its incompetence. In the ensuing anarchy, oil production fell and chattel slaves were auctioned off on the coast for $400. In Syria, Clinton said Bashar Al-Assad had "lost legitimacy," and Obama urged him to "step aside," promoting rebel insurrection and bloody civil war. In Ukraine, the US sponsored "pro-democracy" agitators to oust democratically elected President Viktor Yanukovych. While plotting which Ukrainian puppets the US should install, Assistant Secretary of State Victoria Nuland gave civil rights slogans to the protesters: "[Yanukovych] knows what he needs to do. The whole world is watching." The new regime was courted to join NATO (for US military protection), sell its natural gas industry to foreign investors, and enrich US politicians. The Russians intercepted Nuland's communication planning a US puppet government. Anxiously watching the video of Gaddafi, Vladimir Putin determined not to share the same fate. He invaded Crimea and waged proxy war against US troops in Syria.

Democratic peace theory, the staple of neoliberalism in universities, had brought the nation's longest and most expensive wars while failing to bring either peace or democracy abroad. China continued forced abortions, the occupation of Tibet, and organ-harvesting of Uighur prisoners. Iraq, Afghanistan, and Libya were failed states.

After US troops withdrew, the four-hundred-thousand-strong Iraqi National Army folded to ISIS in months. To avoid US casualties, Obama ordered insurgents and even a US citizen murdered in drone strikes without due process. US imperialism abroad undermined democracy at home. Liberals like Galston distinguished elites "working through bureaucracies" from the plural dependencies they managed.[76] Western nations, he said, were governed by a "bargain" between the elites and subjects: in exchange for "public support," "popularly elected governments would deliver economic growth and rising living standards; social protections for health, employment, and retirement; domestic tranquility; and the abatement of international threats." By 2011 journalists affirmed the "rise of the global elite," who extended the war on terror to US subjects.[77] Obama increased Bush's surveillance, made government less transparent, and prosecuted more whistleblowers than any other president. After Edward Snowden's revelations, NSA director James Clapper denied under oath that the agency collected US citizens' information, a lie for which he was never charged.[78] The FISA Court rubber-stamped FBI surveillance requests, granted warrants for little cause, and combined mass surveillance with sloppy detective work. In the "rise of the warrior cop," young war veterans adopted a new aggressive military policing.[79] Armored SWAT teams served search warrants with violent, no-knock, early morning raids.

Administrative rule lost any semblance of law. Responding to the increase in informal rulemaking, in 2001 the Supreme Court attempted to limit *Chevron* deference to an agency's formal decisions and documents, or regulation promulgated under "notice and comment," but not informal letters.[80] But this presumed a functional Congress that monitored the bureaucracy, not Congress as *cursus honorum*, no longer concerned with lawmaking. Congress routinely failed to update old statutes and correct agencies that controverted its legal provisions. "Law" consisted of thousand-page bills, written by staff in convoluted, incoherent legalese that demanded agency rulemaking and expected courts to sort out the mess. Max Baucus sponsored the Affordable Care Act but never read it. Nancy Pelosi said, "We have to pass the bill to find out what's in the bill." Staffers routinely "cashed out" to take lucrative jobs with corporations for which they secured benefits. Intervals of legislative silence were punctuated with comprehensive bills that contained "big waiver" provisions, granting agencies broad authority to waive regulatory requirements for special interests. In this rule by legal exception, agencies routinely operated without formal APA rulemaking.[81] One government study of agency rulemaking from 2003 to 2010 concluded that agencies invoked the good cause exception (skirting a proposed notice of rulemaking) in 77 percent of major rules and 61 percent of nonmajor rules.[82] Despite the Court's prompting to legislate greenhouse gas emissions or net neutrality, Congress left these to the EPA and the FCC, which changed with incoming administrations. Congress no longer bothered to correct statutory drafting errors, such as its failure to exempt uninsured US branches of foreign banks in Dodd-Frank or the ACA's failure to secure tax credits for those in states without health care exchanges. The courts then fabricated law by presuming to rule according to what Congress *would have wanted*. Given the vast amount of regulation, few court cases, ambiguity of statutory terms, and industries' preference for interim rules to none at all, agencies freely rewrote statutes and improvised procedures. They perfected the arts of manipulating procedural orders to evade judicial review and passing review by "parroting" statutory language in a regulation. This rule by "nonbinding" guidance documents allowed agencies to avoid promulgating formal regulations while extorting individual companies to pay settlements rather than litigate under such uncertainty.

The Rise of the New, New Left: Modern Monetary Theory and Revolutionary Violence

Growing inequality angered Americans. First the conservative Tea Party, then progressive Occupy Wall Street (OWS), attacked neoliberalism. Both opposed the bailouts. The first demanded the failure of the banks, and the second demanded government takeover. Obama was, said Cornel West, a "puppet for corporate plutocrats and a mascot for Wall Street oligarchs." Chomsky agreed. The ACA did not require negotiations with pharmaceutical companies for drug prices, and it guaranteed profits for insurance companies.[83] Adopting the slogan "We are the 99%," OWS gathered in September 2011 in Zuccotti Park to demand greater wealth distribution from the 1 percent. They adopted the "consensus decision-making" methods of anarchist thinkers along with civil disobedience tactics to *occupy* various institutions.[84] They were animated by desperation, born of massive student debt and crumbling expectations to remain in the upper-middle class. New ideas also fortified them. The first was a new economic doctrine called Modern Monetary Theory (MMT), and the second was a new revolutionary theory of violence as a way to achieve democratic socialism.

Economists like Warren Mosler developed MMT, a "post-Keynesian economics," in the late 1990s. It attacked neoliberal orthodoxy as an abstraction from reality, stood it on its head, and pioneered a new economics for a free-floating currency. Clinton's concern for balanced budgets and deficits was a remnant of a bygone fixed exchange currency (the gold standard). Balanced budgets, noted L. Randall Wray in 1998, normally unleash deflationary forces, which impede economic growth. So do concerns about deficits, debt-to-GDP ratios, or interest on the debt. Fiscal "unsustainability" is a myth; it does not exist for a sovereign government with a central bank that controls monetary policy. Understanding the monetary monopoly offered the solution. A currency-issuing government can never go broke. To finance deficits, the Fed need not raise taxes or borrow money in bond sales (where a lack of investors will lead to crisis); it is making it up. Rather, "taxes are required to give value to money, while bond sales are a part of monetary or interest rate policy."[85] As the monopoly issuer of currency, government defines money by choosing what it accepts for payment, the terms for obtaining money, penalties for not paying, and its purchases of goods, services, and assets from the public. Thus *government does*

*not need the public's money to spend; rather, the public needs the govern-
ment's money to pay taxes.* Citizens must labor or produce to obtain
money from the markets or the government itself. Government sells
bonds not to fund itself but to prevent interest rates in the private
economy from falling too low, and it sells higher interest Treasury
bonds to banks to raise overall interest rates.[86] Nor does the market
constrain the Fed in choosing its own interest rates, which determine
payments from the government to the private sector. Deficits do not
take money out of the economy; loans create deposits; assets are public
or private liabilities, adding to dollar deposits in the economy. Most
importantly, MMT argued for a return to fiscal policy, promising
"both full employment with enhanced price stability."

Hitherto, government had responded to inflation by raising interest rates and forcing slack, or unemployment, in the private sector to
keep prices down and maintain price stability, but MMT economists
like Wray claimed that it was "possible to have truly full employment
without causing inflation."[87] Inflation (whether public or private
consumption, or trade surplus) had nothing to do with balanced
budgets or the Fed's failure to adopt "money targets" to control
the "quantity of reserves" and everything to do with managing the
amount of currency in circulation by "an overnight lending rate at
which reserves are supplied." All this required close regulation of
banks' capital and assets. Thus MMT assessed deficits and surpluses
not as goals in themselves but as tools to be used in relation to the real
economy. Surpluses, for example, hurt the economy during periods
of recession and high unemployment. If there is too much saving,
there is a need for spending. Government issues debt to private bond
markets in corporate welfare, giving corporations a risk-free asset to
hedge uncertainty and creating wealth for the corporate sector, or it
increases spending for employment and public infrastructure. The
risk of hyperinflation is small; it only accompanies plummeting production. Rather than simply printing money, the government would
ensure full employment. It would provide a "job guarantee" to pay

those who would have been unemployed (with "no market demand for their services") to "produce socially useful goods and services" and "promote feelings of self-worth."[88]

MMT's "novelty," wrote Wray, was the government as employer of last resort (ELR), its use of labor as a "buffer stock" to enhance price stability. While government can set all prices, it is preferable for it to create a price anchor, to fix only one important price, with the market then establishing all other prices relative to it (the alternatives are for government to attempt to fix all prices or to accept market-determined prices for what it buys). Governments have used buffer stocks like gold or oil to control for inflation. Oil buffers well because it enters into the production of most other commodities. During inflationary periods government sells oil at a set price; during deflation it buys oil, whose relative price rises, supplying more currency and inducing greater use of resources in oil production and refinement. But labor is the supreme buffer stock. Not only is labor "a basic input into virtually all conceivable production processes," its opposite, unemployment, is the worst evil because it decreases production and corrupts habits.[89] Given the government's monopoly on force, it always sets the unemployment level. "'Employer of last resort' workers act as a 'buffer stock' of employable labour, available for hire by the private sector at a mark-up over a known, fixed wage (the government's stated wage). This serves to anchor wages and, thus, prices."[90] To end unemployment, the government agrees to buy all labor at a fixed price by hiring workers for public projects until private employers can buy them back at a slight mark-up. The unemployed show up for ELR, receiving a wage and job training. The growing and shrinking ELR pool will anchor prices and reduce business cycle fluctuations: when private markets are depressed, ELR workers will flow into the pool, increasing government spending and the currency supply while helping maintain consumption. When the private economy booms, businesses will hire workers from the ELR pool, shrinking government spending.

MMT shrugged off the conservative bogeyman of hyperinflation to redirect focus on deflation. It combined the reality of a free-floating currency with globalization and its seven billion potential new consumers. As the US yielded its position as the largest industrial power to become the world's financier and currency manager, US financiers vastly increased the global money supply and captured a larger share of it. The BRICS nations (Brazil, Russia, India, China, and South Africa) had an inexhaustible amount of cheap labor that would both supply manufactures and increase the demand for dollars. By promoting foreign development, the US increased foreign dependence on the dollar. Foreign nations pegged their currencies to the dollar, keeping them weak, to ensure endless US trade deficits driven by US demand for cheap goods. Elites from developing nations built up their own manufactures and infrastructure and purchased US real estate and commodities (and degrees from elite American universities). *MMT was thus a factual expression of the increasing demand for dollars* formulated in an accounting identity: Domestic Private Balance + Domestic Government Balance + Foreign Balance = 0. With massive US trade deficits, the government must fund huge spending sprees and run large deficits to protect the private sector from monetary contraction. Budget surpluses or small deficits during periods of low business borrowing create deflation, and in the global economy, dollars in circulation dwarfed the US deficit.[91] To control for monetary shocks, the US uses sophisticated models that stop inflationary pressures, with the Fed intervening in foreign currency exchanges.

Politically, MMT exposed the fraud of deficit financing, especially among conservatives. It was no accident that Congress had not passed a budget since 1997 and now passed continuing resolutions. Politicians could no longer understand market-tracking tools, but many understood that the old economics was a myth. Under MMT "conservative" meant favoring the rich—lobbying for corporate welfare policies in tax cuts and quantitative easing, and "liberal" meant spending on the bureaucracy for social welfare programs. The Republicans' vapid fiscal responsibility rhetoric merely pleased its base. By the late 1990s, deficit spending in the private sector had driven the dot-com boom. In such an instance, Clinton's federal surpluses helped. But if the private sector does not spend, then the government should run deficits either by tax cuts or spending increases. In 2003, companies were not borrowing and spending, even with interest rates lowered to 1 percent. Mosler was invited to present MMT to Andy Card, Bush's chief of staff and former GM executive. Mosler advised a then-shocking $700 billion deficit (6 percent of GDP) in loans to the private sector. Bush agreed. He signed massive tax cuts, along with *additional* spending on prescription drugs. By the third quarter, the deficit hit $200 billion, replacing the spending lost by the private sector. Asked about the deficit, Bush replied, "I don't look at numbers on a piece of paper, I look at jobs."[92]

The greatest shock of MMT is not its redefinition of economic terms but its political implications. Whereas a fixed-exchange currency is understood as a medium for trade for free laborers, MMT argues that money is the creation of debt, or forced human labor. Mosler explained, "The whole point of the monetary system…is to provision government…to move…real resources from the private sector to the public sector." To get an army or a legal system, the government must "slap a tax on something that nobody has, and then in order to get the funds to pay that tax," subjects must "come to the government for them, and then…the government can spend its otherwise worthless currency to provision itself." He compared MMT to creating demand for worthless business cards by making the cards requisite to leave the room guarded by a man with a 9mm handgun. Employment is the creation of a government that must coerce its subjects to labor in order to get the money to pay their taxes. Taxes do not generate revenue but help regulate subjects and the economy (to control inflation and keep prices low). But MMT hinted at far more. Subjects do *not* pay money created by government. *The government is an armed force to collect dollars created by private bankers.* This is, by definition, plutocracy, with government as the executive arm of private wealth managing dependent subjects. Moreover, if technology has destroyed the preconditions for market capitalism, with repetitive jobs easily replaced by software, then the political order has invented ways to tame and control people who produce little but need something to do. Thus it has *determined* the distribution of wealth, where corporations, especially tech firms, hold large amounts of cash, using it for buybacks and recoveries without middle-class wage increases.

MMT empowered democratic socialism. It revealed how neoliberals exploited people, created crises, and then broke their own rules with deficit spending and quantitative easing by giving money to bankers and financiers. In 2012 Wray attacked the Fed for distributing money to Wall Street and not to average Americans. Bill Mitchell called politicians of the Right "deficit terrorists," making taxpayers suffer in austerity for Wall Street speculation. "Representative government," said Mosler, means a populace of consumers informed that default cannot occur. If people knew there was no default risk and understood the minimal inflation risk, they would never support representatives who cut spending or rejected full employment. The only true policy option, using fiat currency to fight deflation, meant choosing either corporate or public welfare. Numerous Democrats, supported by leading economists, adopted MMT. The *Nation* attributed it to Bernie Sanders's "rock star appeal."[93] It later justified the Green New Deal and Medicare for All without matching tax increases. MMT also recalibrated the old question of unfunded liabilities. Social Security funds consisted not of pensioner investments but were a matter of currency management. The massive entitlements promised to the elderly were really a form of intergenerational redistribution. And as government policy constructed debt, more people called for debt forgiveness. As private debt weakens the economy—consumers make interest payments to the wealthy—economists revived the ancient concept of the jubilee year.

The protesters in Zuccotti Park were also visited by Leftists such as Slavoj Žižek, who had revived the concept of violent revolution. The neoliberal turn since 1976 had been a "bitter betrayal" of 1960s radicalism.[94] Leftists rejected the liberal idea that one could objectively distinguish between legitimate revolution and revolutionary terror. Jacques Lacan had called this obfuscation of emancipatory force the "Big Other," a concept of some "collective will" used to claim both religious legitimacy for the state and legal confinement of its critics, who think they need to get permission from the state for violence. Žižek defended "revolutionary terror" and "divine violence" as "the heroic assumption of the solitude of a sovereign decision. It is a decision (to kill, to risk or lose one's own life) made in absolute solitude, not covered by the big Other."[95] In such acts, "one should accept the revolutionary act not covered by the big Other—the fear of taking power 'prematurely,' the search for a guarantee, is the fear of the abyss of the act."[96] Alain Badiou reunified Robespierre's "humanism *and* terror," where liberals had construed the two as opposites. The revolutionary refuses to shelter from violence in excuses that the state or the law legitimates it, and instead he heroically commits himself to the cause and leaps into the void. Badiou advanced a "metapolitics" of fantasy that restructures reality *against* what exists, not the politics of compromise over a plurality of interests.[97] Militant activists thus played a crucial role in providing models for a future politics.

The Great Awokening and the Globalist Conversion of Neoliberalism

By 2012 the nation was divided by class, and the neoliberal gods that held it together were dead. No political order can subsist without religious myths, and the oligarchy needed legitimacy. Populist revolts, with neither side understanding the financial system, challenged both political parties. On the Left hand, the identity politics elite did not make decisions based on neoliberal sympathies, and every CEO and politician would need to fear heresy trials. Investors feared that activists would use MMT to push for large, unconstrained social spending projects. On the Right hand were conservative nationalists, who wanted to end the nation's commitment to globalization, which would depress global trade, inflate the dollar, and even incentivize nations to leave it as the world's reserve currency. Nationalism guaranteed neoliberalism's suicide. Deciding that there could be no profitable return to an industrial economy, the corporate elites planned their future with the billions of non-American consumers around the world. They endorsed identity politics, one of their most vehement critics. It had been years in the making. Thomas Friedman, responding to the Tea Party's resistance to big fiscal policy in health care and climate change, concluded, "There is only one thing worse than one-party autocracy, and that is one-party democracy, which is what we have in America today. One-party autocracy certainly has its drawbacks. But when it is led by a reasonably enlightened group of people, as China is today, it can also have great advantages. That one party can just impose the politically difficult but critically important policies needed to move a society forward in the 21st century."[98] Thus, he concluded, "The need to compete in a globalized world has forced the meritocracy, the multinational corporate manager, the Eastern financier and the technology entrepreneur to reconsider what the Republican Party has to offer. In principle, they have left the party, leaving behind not a pragmatic coalition but a group of ideological naysayers."

The means to achieve this one-party rule came from observing Occupy Wall Street, where race and gender appeals moved protesters more than economic redistribution. In the "revolutionary progressive stack," or venting procedure at Occupy protests, intersectionality provided the rules, encouraging "women and traditionally marginalized groups [to] speak before men, especially white men."[99] In "consensus-based organizing," the "'progressive stack'... disrupt[s] the kinds of hierarchy and domination that routinely reproduce themselves in our spaces of discussion."[100] The chaos of the movement was its appeal.

OWS's power was in its religious fervor, thus moral superiority; intimidated by threats of open violence, local governments did not enforce curfews or warrants and only intervened to stop looting and sanitation crises. Radicals aptly used social media; Facebook and Twitter became disproportionately radical platforms for ideas and coordinated violence. OWS, a class-based movement launched by educated whites, easily morphed into a movement for race and gender equity against the white middle class—from a movement against global oligarchy into an identity politics movement. Activist Cecily McMillan said, "Black and brown people came down and said, 'Listen, you're not doing anything for us.' It turned into a practice that has led us to have a conversation about what is the white role in black oppression."[101] For little cost, neoliberals could provide prerogatives for privileged minorities and revive social welfare programs. OWS became, in media and corporate America, Black Lives Matter. The anger of radicals and minority elites, educated in the ethics of authenticity and globalism, could be shifted away from wealth inequality and toward the white middle class.

Democrats had long claimed the ascendance of a new majority of elites, women, and minorities. Insulated in their urban bubbles, confident of their moral superiority, and increasingly intolerant of dissent, progressives asked why liberals, having won the "culture war," had compromised thus far. Harvard professor Mark Balkan recommended denazification for conservatives. A pragmatist by temper, Obama had run on a unification platform. He bemoaned "identity politics," calling it "an enormous distraction" from important issues while courting it on the side, such as in his nomination of Sonya Sotomayor.[102] But Republicans, influenced by their populist wing who "cling to their guns and religion," controlled the House and promised to sabotage Obama's legacy. Obama had had enough. His second term has been called the "Great Awokening," when neoliberals took a hard turn Left, adopting views that had only circulated in the universities before. Zach Goldberg and David Rozado have chronicled how The *New York*

Times's use of Leftist terminology, such as "patriarchy," "mansplaining," "toxic masculinity," "whiteness," "nonbinary," and "racism" tripled from 2011 to 2015. It did not use the word "intersectionality," a pillar of 1990s diversity theory, until 2015. Indeed, most Americans did not think racial inequality was a serious problem in 2014.

Concerning gender, Obama now supported gay marriage, which he had opposed. He instructed the US attorney general not to defend the Defense of Marriage Act. *Newsweek* labeled him the "First Gay President." In the military, he repealed the prohibition on women in combat and secured transgender persons' right to select bathrooms. Discrimination against transgender persons, said Joe Biden, was the "civil rights issue of our time." To implement identity politics, the OCR added detailed guidance in 2014 with the goal of changing "the culture on the college campuses." Schools must institute new programs to prevent a "hostile environment" or face costly public investigations. The OCR required that schools use the lenient "preponderance of the evidence" standard in disciplinary hearings, in which the accused had no right to confront his accusers. Demanding belief in female accusers, the new policy led to many false accusations and suspensions of male students without due process. By 2016 Harvard employed more than fifty Title IX coordinators (Yale had thirty); in one estimate, from 2011 to 2015 colleges spent more than $100 million on compliance, most of it for the salaries of coordinators, who now constituted academic departments of state agitprop. Sensing the change, in 2015 the Supreme Court followed by finding same-sex marriage constitutional. Homosexuals successfully sued wedding web designers and photographers who refused them service. The next month, the EEOC interpreted "sex" under Title VII to include sexual orientation *and* gender identity.[103] Employers could not restrict a transgender woman from a common female restroom or misuse a transgender employee's new name or pronoun, and they must update records to include gender changes. Sex orientation and gender identity claims began to flood the EEOC, which in 2015 resolved 1,135 LGBT charges, including voluntary agreements awarding $3.3 million in monetary relief. In 2016, the Departments of Education and Justice jointly sent the first "Dear Colleague" letter, informing education workers of the new gender identity regulations. The DOE threatened to remove funding from high schools unless they allowed biological males to shower with teenage girls. OCR required health care providers to comply by 2017.

Following the 2012 killing of Trayvon Martin, Obama faced scrutiny from the Left for downplaying racial tensions. His political instincts now told him to play to race division. He told the nation, "If I had a son, he'd look like Trayvon," an absurd statement given Obama's own privilege. Black Lives Matter, founded in 2013, connected police brutality to systemic racism and "white nationalism" and crusaded to defund the police, release minority prisoners, fight segregated schooling, and destroy the patriarchal family. As the product of Leftist academic orthodoxy connecting race and transgenderism, BLM was an instant sensation among college students. The death of Michael Brown brought riots in Ferguson, then in Oakland and Baltimore. In this scripted narrative, media outlets, following social media, would report a case removed from all context as another example of racial violence, further escalated by social media. White cops, the story went, were hunting black men for sport, a theme of Ta-Nehisi Coates's bestselling *Between the World and Me*. Privileged revolutionaries initiated violence against riot police while underclass blacks looted stores. Facebook and Twitter provided a platform for nobodies to post heroic violence against fascism. The media refused to cover black crimes against whites (90 percent of all interracial crimes), such as the 2012 knock-out game (where black teens tried to knock out victims with one punch, resulting in multiple deaths), violent flash mobs, and outright racial murders, such as the 2014 murder of Zemir Begic with a hammer in front of his fiancée.

Neoliberalism's crisis year came in 2016. Its quintessential candidate, Hillary Clinton, was rejected by Sanders's democratic socialists on the Left and Donald Trump's economic nationalists on the Right, which, unlike the string of Republican losers, constituted the first real threat to the neoliberal order. Trump rejected the exhausted ideological schools of conservatism, now derisively called "Conservative, Inc." Republican candidates, though supported by Fox News, failed to defeat Trump in the primary as academics wrung their hands about the end of the postwar liberal order. Supported by *Breitbart News's* Steve Bannon, Trump ran against the bedrock issues of Washington special interests. He promised to end illegal immigration and build a border wall. He promised to scrap or renegotiate trade deals like NAFTA and the Trans-Pacific Partnership, a five-thousand-page bill written in secret by special interests and marked for fast-track congressional approval. He promised to end foreign wars. Finally, his promise to "drain the swamp" clearly threatened the oligarchs. While Republicans had increasingly fought rearguard actions, such as gerrymandering districts to secure victories, Trump audaciously fought to win the white vote in the "blue wall," the Democratic-leaning states in the Midwest. Democrats had counted on winning votes from Midwestern whites until immigration made them irrelevant. Trump's platform was common sense to half of Americans but an existential threat to the elites. In this moment of clarity, he simply reflected the growing class divide: the Democratic Party was the party of the rich, and the Republican Party the "deplorables" of the declining middle class. Democratic money, mostly from rich small donors, rose from 54 percent in 2012 to 76 percent in 2018. "Never Trump" corpses like Bill Kristol and David Frum voted for Clinton. But fewer than 80 percent of Sanders's primary supporters voted for Clinton, and fully 12 percent of them voted for Trump in his narrow victory.

Trump's election began the openly declared "resistance," or opposition against him and his supporters within the judiciary and by thousands of bureaucrats on the federal payroll. Federal judges thwarted Trump's attempt to limit immigration and asylum seekers. "Senior officials in [Trump's] own administration," reported an anonymous bureaucrat in the *New York Times*, "are working diligently from within to frustrate parts of his agenda."[104] The FBI had refused to prosecute Clinton for her illegal deletion of thirty-three thousand emails (she had an aide destroy two devices with a hammer), yet it lied to the FISA Court, using the corrupt Steele dossier (paid for by Clinton) to frame those who had helped Trump as well as Trump himself. Baseless claims of Trump's collusion with Russia in the election led to the fruitless two-year Mueller investigation, followed by manufactured scandals and two impeachments. The Pentagon outright lied to Trump about its troop levels in Syria. Ambassador Jim Jeffrey, one of dozens of Republican national security officials who signed a "Never Trump" letter in 2016, said, "We were always playing shell games to not make clear to our leadership how many troops we had there." It was "a lot more" than the two hundred Trump agreed to leave there in 2019.[105] Well-paid bureaucrats in universities and law schools (in open partisan affiliation the professoriate is 95 percent Democrat, with administrators even *more* partisan) wrote opposition statements and endorsed impeachment.

Government agencies and universities aimed at Trump's support-ers, mandating race sensitivity training to shame whites as uncon-sciously racist and forcing them to undergo ritual humiliation. As college presidents used diversity funding to build private fiefdoms of diversity compliance, social scientists in psychology endorsed the Leftist agenda; those who voted for Trump suffered from "identity fusion." Progressivism no longer consisted of psychological traits balancing conservative traits; it had taken on its own traits of loyalty, authority, and holiness, establishing an entirely different political order. Secular liberals, not understanding sacred values, felt shocked that the overthrow of one religion would lead to another. Promoting the victory of atheism, when humans would evolve out of their religious sentiments, they found themselves forbidden from discussing scien-tific studies that confirmed race and sex differences. Geneticists were forced to communicate esoterically or to openly profess the opposite of what their research demonstrated. Professors like Brett Weinstein, Bo

Weingard, and Jeffrey Poelvoorde, who spoke out against the diversity regime, were threatened, harassed, and fired.

While culturally responsive teaching had taught black children to have higher self-esteem than other children, multiculturalism and diversity had not achieved equality, leading to an intensified focus on "inclusion" and "deep equity." The first meant eliminating marginalization by creating "soulful spaces," where each individual brings a unique story or narrative that enriches the group. White educators are "profoundly insulting" when they pretend to be color-blind, ignoring systemic racism. The second meant measuring outcomes "distributed equitably across different demographic and identity groups." White children should be taught about systemic racism and their complicity in it at the age of three. And teachers should challenge boys to question their genders but not to tell their parents. Inundated with gender fluid messages, young girls showed significant interest and were fast-tracked for gender transition. Those who sought traditional alternatives to the educational cartel were a threat. Despite homeschool children outperforming public school children 30 percent in national testing, in 2020 educators gathered in closed conference at Harvard to discuss how to destroy homeschooling, which, they claimed, prevented students from learning democratic values.[106] Still, 20 percent of public school teachers send their children to private schools (in Philadelphia, 44 percent).

In the new woke capitalism, the neoliberal establishment courted and funded progressives to receive legitimacy. Democratic strategist David Shor noted the "host of incredibly powerful institutions— whether it's corporate boardrooms or professional organizations— which are now substantially more liberal than they've ever been."[107] "Democratic elected officials," he said, were "to the left of 90 to 95 percent of people." Neoliberals promised economic growth, and progressives would use their monopoly on nonwhite voter identity to deliver electoral majorities, for which they received large salaries, esteem, and special privileges. Corporations had long celebrated diversity and compliance to justify monopolies—for the small cost of token hires, they could remove competition from businesses unable to navigate labyrinthine regulations. But now they honored progressive leaders and endorsed statements demeaning both whites and the West. Behind faces of color on university stages and glossy corporate pamphlets hid lily-white executive boards. Technology firms fought oppression by calling their Asian workers minorities. The identity politics priesthood preached a formulaic narrative: blaming the failure of the globalist dream and the world's evils on white nationalism and justifying the rule of the elites. Corporations pulled out the stops, restricting speech and punishing any who showed support for Trump, especially white women, who lost victimhood status after securing Trump's election. Progressives boasted that demographic change would achieve final victory. Between 2010 and 2020 all US population growth had come from minorities. The US government flooded rural white areas with refugees and illegal immigrants.

Following the 2018 midterms, progressive Democrats like Alexandria Ocasio-Cortez became the moral voice of the party, and Nancy Pelosi struggled to hold ranks by becoming more progressive herself. They stoked racial hatred, blaming black underachievement, a product of solidly Democratic cities and schools, on rural middle-class whites, the key Republican demographic. Privileged progressives now openly demanded minority reparations and free health care for immigrants. They used urban black homicide rates to justify taking AR-15s from law-abiding rural whites with low crime rates. Democratic candidates in the 2020 primary promised to naturalize twenty-two million illegal immigrants, open the borders, dissolve Immigration and Customs Enforcement (ICE), do away with the Electoral College, stack the Supreme Court, and add new states to the Union. With a booming economy and dismal prospects for the 2020 election, Democrats selected Joe Biden to attract white voters in the blue wall. Fifty-one intelligence experts publicly lied to cover up the corruption found on his son Hunter's discarded laptop, including that the "big guy" used his political connections to obtain millions in payoffs from Chinese and Ukrainian oligarchs.[108]

Facing the threat of Trump's reelection, in 2020 the ruling class seized on the novel COVID-19, likely created in a Chinese lab with US gain-of-function research funding, to unify its claims to authority over human health and identity and disrupt the fabric of American life. Klaus Schwab, founder of the World Economic Forum, had formerly predicted "a true global civilization," and he saw COVID-19 as an opportunity to return to the project of a world order. He called this "The Great Reset," a chance to steer nations back on the track to globalism. Biden campaigned on Schwab's slogan "Build Back Better." COVID-19 justified the ruling class's emergency powers to deprive Americans of their rights, punish them until the election, and control them. It was, argued Darren Beattie, a new color revolution at home formulated by the same bureaucrats who had deployed it abroad. Seizing on the death of George Floyd, corporations funded "democratic protests," in which revolutionaries attacked, humiliated, and even murdered Trump supporters. In this war to subjugate the American people, the ruling-class rejects their founding, destroys their monuments, renames their landmarks, and honors those who mock their traditions. The 1619 Project, winner of the Pulitzer Prize, is a refounding myth to subvert the American founding as colonialist—an inversion of the truth. Thus the supposed fight against colonialism justifies the colonization of Western populations. It is an old tactic of colonial rule to use race and gender divisions to distract from the class divide, which is maintained by pointing to more impoverished people who are not citizens, the "global village." The ruling class expands its allegations of the crimes of middle-class Americans to include global colonialism to justify importing a new populace—including two million illegal immigrants in 2021 alone—to defeat the last remnant of republicanism at home.

7

DESPOTISM

This book has attempted to provide an objective basis for understanding the American regime. But now, in its treatment of today's regime, it must exaggerate, albeit based on real features, to show its most striking and problematic tendencies. This chapter, focusing on the crises of 2020–21 that should never fade from American memory, will assess the US kleptocracy and what it has in store for its subjects in the future. While not every member of the neoliberal order, which still employs well-intentioned bureaucrats, has agreed to support a despotic agenda, the regime's character forces one to draw certain conclusions. Many neoliberals had aspired to a global aristocracy, magnificent men and women flipping quarters to grateful peasants. Oligarchs brokered the outsourcing of US industry in return for financial control under the dollar even as they engineered technologies for a new information age. But today's globalist American empire is a kleptocracy filled with princelings of the political and corporate elite who inherited—and now drain—the wealthiest and most powerful empire in history. It consolidates market share and outsources its technologies to foreign companies for its private benefit. It despotically introduces a permanent state of exception to the law to rule in its own interests. In fear of the subjects off whom it feeds, it assigns legal identities to groups to determine their privileges. In this civil war between Western whites, the kleptocrats claim science's authority to subdue the populace, and they enlist an identity politics priesthood to stoke racial hatred against middle-class whites, who suffer indignities, humiliations, and loyalty tests. Following the COVID lockdowns and unlawful 2020 election, the last vestige of legitimacy has collapsed, and the kleptocracy has revealed itself as an incompetent, corrupt class of degenerates. In their palaces at the center of a rotting kingdom, the despots surround themselves with harems, catamites, and vicious eunuchs to administrate a world of performance rituals and sadomasochistic fantasies even as their people and world hegemony decline.

The Globalist American Empire and the Kleptocracy

One can assess the globalist American empire using a classical framework. To be self-sufficient and thus unify a people and secure its happiness, a political regime requires agriculture (farmers), industry (engineers, artisans, and laborers), defense (soldiers and police trained in the arts of war), taxation (wealthy bankers and financiers to plan revenue and monetary policy and to fund public projects, private business, and war), care of religion (priests to manage the sacrifices, counsel the rulers, and educate the youth), and institutions for determining justice (political leaders to determine the public interest and what is necessary and expedient). As the US abandoned republicanism for the welfare-warfare state and then began outsourcing its production, government-sponsored oligopolies assumed these functions. Agencies manage and work with private business in each fiefdom, for example, in agriculture, food, and manufacturing (15.8 percent of GDP, 22 million jobs). The regime is guided by finance, which, along with insurance and real estate (8.8 million jobs), constitutes 20 percent of GDP. It is defended by a warrior class (military and intelligence agencies, spending one trillion per year, 4 percent of GDP, 2.8 million jobs). The priests of body and soul—health care (19.7 percent of GDP, twenty million jobs) and public education (5 percent of GDP, 11.2 million jobs)—claim the authority to define life and instruct the youth in "equity." Finally, a ruling class uses the federal government (including contract and grant employees, 9.1 million jobs, 6 percent of the nation's workforce), which provides 30 percent of state and local governments' revenue (employing 7 million). The information, media, and entertainment industries (6.9 percent of GDP, 1.87 million jobs) supply its propaganda and censorship and direct the leisure and moral indoctrination of subjects and their children. Depending on other nations for its consumption, the empire must expand its control over the world at the cost of faction at home and endless wars abroad. As the producing nations become self-sufficient, the empire must increasingly rely on openly coercive financial and military measures.

The upper echelons of the ruling class come from wealthy *cosmopolitans* (as opposed to the rich in rural areas), those in the top 0.01 percent (about twenty-three thousand individuals, or 0.007 percent of the population worth over $10 million) who control each fiefdom, limit access to its ranks, and jockey for political influence and benefits. Almost 25 percent of those in the Forbes 400 derived their wealth from finance—especially hedge funds and private equity—which grows faster than the economy, while 15 percent came from technology companies and 10 percent from food and beverage. While the Rothschild, Walton, Koch, and Mars families manage and maintain their wealth, a significant number of the Fortune 400, such as Elon Musk, Mark Zuckerberg, and Jack Dorsey, rose through skills in the technologies that have globalized and enhanced business growth. But one cannot simply look at profits. Wealth guarantees political influence but not political power—it is necessary but not sufficient. The wealthy seek to retain control of their fiefdoms by funding political initiatives, buying off politicians, and developing and maintaining close ties with the decisionmakers who craft and enforce the rules they agree to play by.

They must participate in the political framework shaped by a narrow class of insiders, the ruling class properly speaking, which uses wealth to gain and maintain political power.

While each fiefdom helps preserve the order and negotiates for its privileges, at the center are the 3,000 Tyrants, a ruling class of kleptocrats who ally with, stroke, tax, or intimidate the monopolies they secure. It controls more than half of the nation's industrial and banking assets and more than three-quarters of its insurance assets. These few thousand individuals, writes Thomas Dye, control the media and investment firms and "over half of all the assets of private foundations and two-thirds of all private university endowments. They direct the nation's largest and best-known law firms in New York and Washington, as well as the nation's major civic and cultural organizations. They make the largest political campaign contributions. They occupy key federal government positions in the executive, legislative, and judicial branches."[1] The ruling class is best understood as the hub that uses gatekeeping power to connect segmented fiefdoms. Those at the top are driven by ambition and rise by charisma, manipulation, and duplicity. Some, like George Soros, Jeff Bezos, Michael Bloomberg, Mark Zuckerberg, Charles Koch, Tom Steyer, Larry Fink, and Warren Buffet openly purchase political influence for both profits and policies like open borders and outsourcing.[2] Billionaires like Zuckerberg, Koch, Soros, and Bloomberg have created "new activist models of political involvement that combine electioneering, issue advocacy, and philanthropy. They pursue influence through interlocking networks of foundations, grassroots organizations, tax-exempt groups, and super PACs."[3] Political elites (Barack Obama, Mitch McConnell, John Kerry, the Clinton and Bush families) often depend on wealthy donors for their rise to power but when powerful enough gain independence from them.[4] "Annoyed and bored" with Soros, who gave economic lectures but little money, Obama told his campaign organizers, "If we don't get anything out of him, I'm never f---ing sitting with that guy again."[5] To strengthen their power, the kleptocrats intermarry, guard their connections, and nepotistically secure positions for trusted friends and family, for whom they broker billion-dollar deals (the McConnells in China, the Bidens in Ukraine), often with foreign oligarchs, and hide the money in offshore accounts. Their greatest secret is each fiefdom's internal operations: not just buying off bureaucrats and public officials but accomplishing *anything* in a nebulous fiefdom like the Pentagon or evading or passing investigations by the SEC or accessing and using political operatives in the intelligence agencies.

The ruling class wields executive force to protect, milk, and extort the rest of the top 0.1 percent and offer it the cover of legitimacy. It secures billions in government contracts with pharmaceutical and defense contractors, from which it taps profit and influence. Every industry regulation provides kleptocrats information for insider trading (even while banning it). Using the myths of free markets and private corporations, kleptocrats spy on enemies and launder political favoritism through *interconnected government monopolies*. "Three companies control about 80% of mobile telecoms. Three have 95% of credit cards. Four have 70% of airline flights within the US."[6] Amazon controls more than 50 percent of online retail, while it receives a $1.46 subsidy from the federal government per package and more than $3.7 billion in government subsidies.[7] The internet "mediates modern life, like a giant, unseen blob that engulfs the modern world."[8] Google holds 92 percent of the global search market. Facebook receives 77 percent of the social network ad revenue, and Facebook and Google receive about half of all internet ad revenue. Google and Apple provide 99 percent of mobile phone operating systems, Apple and Microsoft 95 percent of desktop operating systems.[9] Monopolies crush attempts to start alternative social media websites; they are barred from the Google Play app store and deplatformed by Amazon Web Services. Amazon *is* the government—it provides cloud computing for the CIA and the Pentagon. Google *is* the government—the US military and intelligence agencies are its biggest clients. The Pentagon uses Google's servers to store critical information and to surveil billions of people while manipulating the information they can access. Six firms control 90 percent of media, down from fifty in 1983. Kleptocrats choose headlines and argue for fact checking in news in order to silence dissenting media. Google blacks out conservative websites from searches. Facebook limits circulation or removes certain accounts as spam, destroying years of content for "inauthentic behavior." Twitter deplatforms users or limits viewership. To secure these monopolies, the rulers bar market entry by blocking financial access to bank loans and credit card services. The banks *are* the government, public-private partnerships in the most regulated industry. The DOJ instructs Chase, Bank of America, Wells Fargo, and Citibank to lock out political dissidents marked as "high risk"; Visa blacklists companies and persons for "hate speech."[10] The IMF recommends that one's "history of online searches and purchases" be used in assigning credit scores.[11] PayPal cooperates to shut out online purchases. Periodically the kleptocrats *extort* industries and billionaires to make them fall in line.[12] They use regulations to threaten or smash key industries, which their friends, families, and financial backers then purchase for pennies on the dollar.[13] They used a Facebook whistleblower to threaten Mark Zuckerberg with regulation for not censoring dissident speech. Jack Dorsey was forced to step down from Twitter.

Aided by its cosmopolitan managerial minions in the top 1 percent (with incomes above $500,000), the ruling class monopolizes the gateways to power and congeals its influence in the top 9.9 percent (incomes above $158,000) in an ooze of bureaucrats and corporate toadies. Access into the higher ranks of these fiefdoms, which dispense honor and wealth, depends on birth, wealth, and education. This pseudo-aristocracy "has mastered the old trick of consolidating wealth and passing privilege along at the expense of other people's children."[14] Each fiefdom plays a function in maintaining the regime and thus requires some competence to work in (skills in econometrics, technology, or pharmaceutical research). Goldman Sachs, J. P. Morgan, and leading law firms, while hiring for elite connections, toss meritorious applicants into a stressful grinder. Whereas the US used to draw its best and brightest into physics and engineering, now it draws them into finance, where they make more convoluted instruments for the hucksterism of the kleptocracy. The corporate structure remains the same across industries, blending cutthroat competition with sanctimonious statements promoting diversity and worker authenticity. HR departments manage humans as resources, and PR departments display ruling-class mores. The function of elite universities is to instill an education in both ruling-class mores and diversity. The orthodoxy both weakens allegiances that might undermine loyalty to the corporation and teaches a jargon of racial and gender inclusion, equity, and integration that befits diversity in both the workplace and global markets. Wealth and status accompany one's climb up the corporate ladder: cosmopolitans take breaks from corporate pressure to sample luxury brands, exclusive resorts, and exotic vacations.

Every regime needs religion for both legitimacy and sacrifices. The ruling class does not wake up each morning believing its success has come from the parasitism of its own people. It launches global foundations—the Ford Foundation, Rockefeller Foundation, George & Barbara Bush Foundation, Clinton Foundation, Obama Foundation—that combine power, wealth, and moral causes. It turns to moralistic priests to sanctify its power and indoctrinate its own children as well as to give subjects an identity and sense of meaning. The priests of identity politics explain race and gender identity, attaching each individual to a group with certain rights and duties. They provide the ambitious with a sense of purpose in fighting evil (Whiteness) and in improving the world by social and environmental justice. At Alphabet (Google), where the mean income in 2019 was $258,708, the workers union fights not for higher wages but for greater social activism and censorship.[15] Google fires employees for hate speech and polices their social media accounts. The therapists of authenticity hear the cosmopolitans' private confessions and prescribe cures, in counseling and psychotropic drugs, for their disordered souls. They spin parables of authenticity, simpler ways of life, and love and freedom in a modern world. Using Thomas Friedman's terminology, they point out the dead olive posts to Lexus drivers.

The ruling class claims a right—by birth, wealth, and education—to rule others without their consent. It speaks of vague ideals like "democracy," the "Constitution," and "the rule of law" while staging the hoax of popular government in ritual public elections and televised press conferences. For the bottom 90 percent who cannot afford therapy, the ruling class uses media and entertainment to provide self-esteem and moral superiority for having the right opinions on climate change, transgenderism, anti-racism, or gun control. Increasingly it assigns legal privileges based on group identities. The media manufactures crises and sham opinion polls, and Netflix and YouTube fixate viewers' attention to monopolize their perceptions of reality and eliminate competing stimuli so that they ignore reality all around them. For a growing and increasingly degraded, ignorant, and dependent class, the kleptocracy peddles democratic socialism: leaving monopolies intact while socializing consumption for peasants—EBT cards, free clean needles, and pornography for their stupefaction and sterilization.

The 3,000 Tyrants are not statesmen. Statesmen are patriotic, attaching their ambition for immortality to the love of a people. The tyrants only benefit themselves while enslaving the lower class they claim to liberate. As the kleptocrats bask in their power, they are cut off from the problems of the people they rule, and they resent challenges to their legitimacy. As they lose legitimacy with the peoples they used to manipulate, their words become obviously hollow: their moral lectures are removed from reality, their comedians are not funny, their music and movies are repetitive and uncreative, and their poetry is propaganda. Thus they war with the old nationalist populations, the true peoples of the world, to deprive them of their rights and reduce them to servility. To disempower the American people, the kleptocrats flood their land with pliant immigrants, dilute their vote, undercut their wages, and outsource their production. They manage the people's slow decline by financing their consumption with record levels of debt, disrupting their families, and providing for their intoxication and suicide, which for US males increased more than 25 percent from 1999 to 2016.

Technological Idiocy and the Worship of… Moloch?

The 3,000 Tyrants receive legitimacy from a priestly class, the false prophets of health and diversity who scramble for simony—research money, tenure track jobs, and civil service protections. The kleptocrats' first claim to authority is "science," which is not properly science but technological idiocy. It is the use of statistical models, shorn of empirical evidence about reality, to support a power elite's official cant. Studies that challenge this teaching are discarded as unscientific, its purveyors silenced and harassed. Thus, they distort science into a source of political authority rather than use it as a method of inquiry. The *method* of control begins with wild claims (often generated from inaccurate computer models) verified by "experts" and peddled by the media as prophecy, then followed by mass hysteria. It defines climate change, overpopulation, mass shootings, and pandemics. Rent-seeking researchers produce meaningless or ambiguous statements translated by activists and the media into ominous prophecies, to which politicians respond by funding more research to justify their increasing control. With the Left's education takeover, this is all the majority of the young know about "reality." Without countervailing traditions and frightened by the end of the world in fiery judgment, they march with Greta Thunberg in a modern children's crusade (and to a similar end). Obama used the religion of climate change to smash the coal industry so that his friends and billionaire-backers like George Soros could grab millions of discount coal shares; he halted the Keystone Pipeline to secure profits for Tom Steyer's competing pipeline.[16] As Obama banned offshore drilling, the US export-import bank approved large loans for offshore drilling to Brazilian energy giant Petrobras (a Soros investment). Kleptocrats reaped billions in green energy grants to dot the horizon with windmills or solar panels, all while investing in fossil fuels, which they veil as green energy under words like *biofuel*.[17]

Pseudoscience extends to moral control under the guise of health. In what Angelo Codevilla called the "COVID Coup," politicians and bureaucrats deviously used the pandemic for political and economic control. Early COVID-19 models predicted two million American deaths within a year. Federal and state governments implemented quarantines, lockdowns, and mask mandates that would in theory slow the spread to prevent hospitals from being overwhelmed. Using their emergency powers, governors, municipalities, and state boards of health declared a never-ending emergency, a permanent state of exception to the rule of law. The rule of law, by definition universal and enforced, was replaced by changing edicts, haphazardly and unequally enforced, that denied all civil liberties: freedom of worship, speech, assembly, travel, and association (even in one's own home). Under this "new normal," state officials admitted they had "no actual plan to return to a state where all restrictions are lifted."[18] Pennsylvania justice William Stickman said, "It bears repeating; after six months, there is no plan to return to a situation where there are no restrictions imposed upon the people of the Commonwealth."[19] The courts, no longer independent, upheld these edicts despite their never-ending duration. Biden mandated a vaccine for all federal contractors, and a circuit court (later overturned) upheld OSHA's 490-page emergency order requiring vaccines for all businesses with more than one hundred employees. The CDC director even signed an order suspending the eviction of tenants who failed to pay their rent or mortgage. The Supreme Court suspended judicial review, casting aside a strict scrutiny of emergency health measures. Proper review would require assessing the reasonableness of the government's compelling interest and the actual merits of the underlying science used to deprive citizens of their core constitutional rights.

Even as the courts upheld permanent state control over sacred liberties, the underlying assessments and mandated protections proved false. Early mortality predictions proved wrong almost tenfold. COVID-19 death rates (approaching 0.1 percent overall) for children under nineteen were almost nonexistent, while deaths for those under the age of seventy were lower than the flu. The median age of death from COVID-19 was between eighty and eighty-two (which is higher than life expectancy); 92 percent of those who died were over fifty-five. Outbreaks at nursing and retirement homes constituted almost half of all deaths. According to the CDC, only 5 percent of reported COVID-19 deaths involved COVID-19 alone; 95 percent had on average four comorbidities—those racked by preexisting conditions. The mandates were based on lies: science was science fiction. The ruling class mandated masks, despite the studies showing that surgical and cloth masks would do little to stop transmission; they even recommended two or three layers and used pop-star Eminem to rap pro-mask public service announcements. The costly plexiglass barriers were not only ineffective but worsened transmission by decreasing air flow. The mandated COVID vaccines proved ineffective to stop the spread of the virus, and the Vaccine Adverse Event Reporting System listed 1.3 million cases (including 236,767 "serious" cases and 28,714 deaths) from December 14, 2020, to June 13, 2022. The most sinister mandate was lockdowns, which had killed at least 171,000 young Americans by the end of 2021. The death rate of those aged twenty-five to forty-four increased 52 percent. Assessing the net damage in terms of life-years lost, one study found that the lockdowns were ten times more fatal than COVID itself; another estimated the cost at seven hundred thousand lost life-years per month. Drug overdose deaths reached a record high of 93,655 in 2020—20,000 more than in 2019—followed by a new record of 107,622 in 2021. With people confined in their homes and afraid to go to the hospital, deaths from heart disease and diabetes spiked. Reported Dr. Scott Atlas, 40 percent of those with strokes and 40–50 percent of those with heart attacks did not call for

ambulances; half of the 650,000 Americans with cancer stopped getting chemotherapy; mandates canceled thousands of biopsies, cancer
screenings, and scheduled knee and hip replacements. For a disease
that, in exaggerated reports, killed half the number of those killed by
heart disease each year, politicians used the authority of science to
destroy the livelihoods of millions. Instead of protecting the vulnerable, such as the aged, state governors continued to confine the rest
of the populace in their homes—their jobs, businesses, and hopes
destroyed. They shuttered small businesses, gyms, schools, restaurants,
and barbershops, immiserating the population.

Those who challenged the official cant were silenced. Under the
name of *science*, Facebook and YouTube removed videos of medical
doctors questioning the severity of the virus or the efficacy of masks
and new vaccines. By August 2020 Facebook had removed some seven
million posts regarding COVID-19 and labeled 98 million others
as misinformation. Amazon refused to sell Alex Berenson's book
critical of the COVID-19 lockdowns (until Elon Musk intervened).
Twitter banned him for linking studies that questioned the efficacy
of COVID-19 vaccinations. Twitter also banned Dr. Robert Malone,
one of the founders of mRNA vaccine technology. The lockdowns
achieved political and economic control and earned $22 billion for
Big Pharma, which pushed endless booster shots supplemented
with daily pills (Pfizer expected 2021–22 COVID-19 vaccine sales
to total at least $65 billion). The government gave drug companies
immunity from personal injury lawsuits over their vaccines' adverse
effects. Public health mattered little, else gyms would have remained
open. Marijuana shops, liquor stores, casinos, and abortion clinics,
which subject the population to control and disposal, were deemed
"essential" along with corporate box stores. In this redistribution
of wealth, big business emerged unscathed, while small business
bankruptcies rose 40 percent. Quarantined people shopped with
Amazon and lived online. In April 2020, Wall Street posted its best
week since 1938 as 16 million workers lost their jobs. Almost all the

stock market gains between 2017 and mid-2020 came from five big tech companies: Apple, Microsoft, Amazon, Google, and Facebook. Airlines requested a $50 billion dollar bailout as they spent $45 billion to buy back their own shares.

Using *health* as a religious tool, the kleptocracy stokes the populace's mortal fear of the unseen, offering salvation from priests who demand obeisance. No longer believing in God, the populace clings to mere life. To this the empire adds ritual humiliations, nonsensical rules that degrade people and habituate them to servitude. They are required to remember ridiculous personal pronouns and laud new secular saints like George Floyd. During the COVID-19 pandemic and despite studies confirming its negative health effects, children were ordered to wear masks in church, outdoors, even at home. Masks stunt babies' neurological development by disrupting the normal attachment and bonding process as well as their facial recognition abilities.[20] Warped by anxiety, small children demanded sterile environments; they insisted that grandparents wash their hands before hugs.[21] Instead of civil greetings, shaking hands like equals, *people of the mask* ignored one another at the store. They nodded in muffled responses. They lived in perpetual fear, a recrudescence to mere preservation. The goal was to turn America into an Asian despotism by alienating, isolating, and dehumanizing subjects into insects without facial expressions. In "east Asian countries," reported *CNN*, "wearing face masks in public is widely accepted": "Asia may have been right about coronavirus *and face masks*, and the rest of the world is coming around." While US funding and Chinese incompetence birthed the virus and ineffective lockdowns, adulation for China's authoritarian bureaucracy increased. The *New York Times* credited it for censoring dissidents.[22] US authorities promised no end to the masks—the media early on warned of new deadly mutant strains, justifying all future lockdowns for reasons of *health*. The model was China's social credit system, which determines a subject's rights to travel and speak based on his measured docility. It included mandatory vaccination records for travel, education, and employment. Leana Wen, a Chinese immigrant, former head of Planned Parenthood, and professor of *health* at Washington University, argued that travel was not a constitutional right but only a privilege for the vaccinated. Masks had the desired effect of identifying the enemies of the state. In some parts of the country, submission was trendy. Mask-wearers signaled their virtue and sense of responsibility. Feminists who had opposed the burqa and demanded control over their bodies covered up with designer masks and lined up to be jabbed with vaccines that had no long-term studies, and they hated other women who refused to do so.

The greatest use of the authority of *health* was to harvest ballots for the 2020 election. COVID-19 justified violations of state election laws that required voting times and places and ballot signature verification. Media had long prepared the American public, reporting in September that Trump's victory on election night would be overturned by Biden's lead in mail-in ballots from the COVID-19 lockdowns. Trump held a commanding lead at midnight on November 4 in Georgia, Pennsylvania, Michigan, and Wisconsin. All four states suspended vote counts or postponed counting mail-in ballots. When counting resumed, there was a surge in Biden ballots. In Fulton County, Georgia, Republican observers were sent home for the night, after which containers filled with ballots were pulled out and counted. In Wisconsin and Michigan, counting was resumed at 4:00 a.m. and 6:00 a.m., adding over one hundred thousand votes in each state, nearly all for Biden. Milwaukee alone reported 170,000 absentee ballots, Michigan reported 3.1 million, and Philadelphia reported more than 350,000. White House advisor Peter Navarro made a case for election theft in six areas, including ballot mishandling and contestable process fouls.[23] While 77 percent of Republicans (40 percent of voters) believe that Biden won fraudulently, the threat is greater than mere fraud, long common in urban districts. It is the introduction of a new regime of casting ballots for dependents with no stake in society, used to justify making decisions for the whole country. Mark Zuckerberg bought votes in Wisconsin, violating its election laws, from his 1,600-acre hacienda in Hawaii.[24] New York passed a law allowing eight hundred thousand noncitizens to vote in local elections. For decades neoliberal Republicans agreed to import more immigrants who feed the Democratic machine while securing their own districts by gerrymandering. In thirty years the GOP has only won one presidential election by popular vote.

The state, with its established church, a priesthood of health experts and identity politics professors, may now carry out such open fraud because it has long deracinated the people from their intimate associations and traditions that promote true health and flourishing. These traditions, internalized, educate a strong sense of self that, when necessary, confidently opposes the state. But fear of the people motivates despots, so they need to disarm, humiliate, and geld them. The state attacks the remnant of the republican family (which gave independence) by encouraging divorce, illegitimacy, and sterility—the priests call it liberation. Today, most American adults are unmarried, with a 42 percent illegitimacy rate; the birth rate plummeted from 3.5 children per woman in 1960 to 1.73 in 2018. The sexual revolution, which freed elites from shame as they pursued lengthy educations, also made marriage a luxury and doomed the working class to the myriad ills of single parenthood. Only 28 percent of married American mothers say full-time work is their ideal, but their ability to escape the forty-hour workweek depends entirely on household income. Average Americans save little, teeter on financial ruin, and take on record credit card and student debt. In a return to de facto polygamy, elites encourage females to behave promiscuously with a few males and the remaining males to become porn addicts. Education, diet, and media purposefully emasculate boys to prevent them from becoming real men and to secure their docile labor. Testosterone levels, which play a crucial role in men's health, have halved since 1950. In the West, sperm counts declined 59 percent from 1973 to 2011.[25] The state forces working-class men to support women who have abandoned them and whisked away their children.

In a return to debt servitude, 13.2 percent of South Carolina's county inmates, in one 2009 study, were poor black males incarcerated for not paying child support, amounts of which need not legally correlate to their earnings. A 2007 study of nine large states found that 70 percent of arrears were owed by those earning less than $10,000 a year and expected to pay, on average, 83 percent of their paychecks.[26] Separated from their fathers and addicted to social media, today's teenagers are angry, underdeveloped, and easily controlled.

Our fathers are our models for God; the patriarchal family is inseparable from a view of the ordered universe that founded Western Civilization. In Paul Vitz's study, prominent atheists projected their own experience of fatherly neglect, abuse, and chaos out onto the world.[27] The kleptocrats' attack on the *patrias* is really an attack on the citadel of the self, faith in God. The COVID-19 coup and the houses of worship that accepted their own closure, their sacred rites moved online or canceled, showed that the real priests today are not those Christians who from a concern for the body agree to stop caring for parishioners' souls but the pseudoscientists who demand that all such care for the soul be destroyed so that they may exercise absolute control over the body. With the loss of belief in the spirit, worship threatens to return to the bodily rites of Moloch, the Canaanite god that even the Romans found too cruel. Moloch's priests, preying on the fears of a commercial philistine people, reduced life to concern for bare preservation. They demanded that parents place into the fires of Moloch their own children, whose tiny bones have been exhumed by the tens of thousands. Noblemen sent their daughters to state temples, where they were sexually groomed and prostituted to wealthy bidders, destroying the natural ties of family affection. In both ways Moloch appears to have returned.

In 2019 American women aborted 619,591 babies. In 2020 five-month-old fetuses, by consent of their mothers, were used in experiments at the state-funded Magee-Women's Hospital and the University of Pittsburgh Health Sciences Tissue Bank, called the "Tissue Hub."

There scientists graft human skin from a baby's scalp and back onto rats and mice, along with the same baby's lymphoid tissues and hematopoietic stem cells from the liver: "The images literally show a patch of baby hair growing on a mouse's back."[28] In another study, 249 California women were recruited for second-trimester abortion, the babies dissected for liver-removal, to study "racial differences in fetal exposure to flame retardants." Globally, there has long been a market for aborted human fetuses.[29] Scientists received $3 million to research the organs of babies of less than twenty-four weeks gestation. "Researchers said they needed 50 percent of the donated fetuses to be minorities and specified that 25 percent must come from black women."[30] They also requested fetuses with organs of minimized time without blood flow and listed an abortion procedure to obtain the organs. "There's the distinct possibility," Dr. David Prentice said, "that some of these babies are born alive and then their organs and tissues are removed." The FDA contracted to buy "fresh and never frozen" baby body parts from Advanced Bioscience Resources. Among the line-item prices were $685 for a set of "fetal livers and thymuses" and an "intact calvarium (baby's skull)" for $515.[31] The stem cell lines (and not organs) from aborted fetuses have long provided the basis for experimentation for vaccines and consumer products.[32] Pope Francis said that, given the "grave danger," "it is morally acceptable to receive COVID-19 vaccines that have used cell lines from aborted fetuses in their research and production process."

Political orders always extend to sexual relations. To destroy family loyalties that might challenge the state, the priesthood grooms children in sex education, creating identity confusion to subject them to new controls. Entertainment, media, and schools teach children to masturbate, question their genders, and request hormone blockers. In endless YouTube videos, self-involved teens pinpoint their place on the Gender Unicorn. Children are told to report their parents' crimes to state officials as they are indoctrinated in gender classes or even chemically castrated for the ruling class's exotic sexual fetishes and tyrannical tastes. The Me-Too Movement exposed the lusts of kleptocrat predators like Harvey Weinstein and Bill Clinton, who ditched secret service to travel on Jeffrey Epstein's "Lolita Express" twenty-six times. The ruling class recruits a sprawling harem of sterile females and catamites and places them in positions of power, where they construct and police a jargon of personal pronouns for greater compliance. Transgenderism is a more effective control than feminism. Punished or censored for making statements that are biologically correct, Americans must assent straight-faced that a male with a functioning penis is a woman even as he sexually harasses or even rapes women around him.[33] Medical school professors apologize for using the phrase "pregnant woman."[34] Formerly, transsexuals accounted for 0.001 percent of the population; in 2021 9.7 percent of high school students claimed gender dysphoria, severe discomfort with their biological sex: "Teens and young adults who did not exhibit childhood signs of gender issues appeared to suddenly identify as transgender."[35] The increase was highest among adolescent girls, previously an underrepresented demographic, with clinicians fast-tracking gender transition. Unimpressed with their flaccid male counterparts and disgusted with the sadistic sex they see on the internet, an increasing number of teenage girls declare themselves gender fluid or asexual: the share of Americans not having sex, driven by youth impotence, has reached a record high.[36] Knowing the 20–40 percent transgender attempted-suicide rate, parents alter their child's gender on the altar of identity; children, the priests reassure, have a strong sense of identity. The kleptocrats do not care about empowering women as a class—transgender athletes smash female records in wrestling, weightlifting, swimming, and track and field. The ruling class now controls formerly private spaces, forcing male and female strangers to urinate and shower with another, discarding the security of their physical space and tolerating any invasion of privacy. To counter those who might revel in their natural beauty, the priesthood celebrates *diversity*—the disadvantaged, ugly, broken, and deformed. Morbidly fat and transgender models don the cover of *Cosmopolitan* and *Sports Illustrated*.

Psychologically, the isolated, abject, craven subject—each rendered dependent and obsessive over bare preservation—is the design of all despots. The COVID regime provided a model for all future declarations of emergency rule, whether a pandemic, climate change, or white supremacy. With endless threats of new strains of death and cataclysm, the despots seek to exhaust the populace, wearing it out with permanent feelings of anxiety, despair, and helplessness. The fear of death from disease transformed many republican citizens into feeble subjects, crushing their spirits and stripping away meaning for the priesthood's administration of fear. Parents denied their own children an education or saturated their homes with cleaning agents linked to infertility. To reinforce the populace's servitude, despots demand compliance with intrusive, illogical, contradictory, and ever-changing edicts that keep subjects uncertain. They detain, humiliate, and control them with probing tools to create a biometric data system: anal swabs for COVID or forced collection by nasal swabs and retina scans.[37] They then offer sporadic small clemencies as motivations for compliance to stoke the hope for change ("if we all only followed *this* mandate…"). So degraded, resistance seems worse than compliance, and one becomes afraid of any unsanctioned freedom. Always unsure whether he is wrong, he craves affirmation by his overlords. Even those who hesitantly comply change irrevocably. Once one agrees to wear a face diaper, breathing in his own spit and farming bacteria on his face, canceling his once-sacred holidays, or abandoning his loved one to die alone, he will do whatever he is told. The abstract fear for mere life trumps the care of those dying before one's eyes. The Vatican declared a dispensation for last rites so that lifelong Catholics could die alone next to a *care*-provider wearing a hazmat suit. Elderly people fearfully assented to be locked into old-age homes. Their families watched from behind glass, from the absurd notion that crude life is better than any death. As loved ones died alone, their families were denied visits, goodbye hugs, even funeral attendance. Many who went to the hospital were killed by the sedation and ventilators that were supposed to save them.[38]

The New Jim Crow

The assault on fatherhood and God is an assault on *fatherland*, tearing apart any sense of the *res publica* and civic cooperation with tribalism. Where scientific authority and fear fail, dissidents are called racist. The priests preach global citizenship and systemic racism in every state institution. Michigan governor Gretchen Whitmer declared "racism a public health crisis," requiring "implicit bias training" for state employees. In the new Jim Crow, elites claim the moral authority of identity politics to live off the labor of a shrinking middle class, shame those who refuse to bow, and divide those who might resist. They traffic in race hatred toward whites, whom they blame for selfishly impeding globalism abroad and for domestic terrorism at home. They harass white laborers for getting uppity or showing signs of self-respect. Whites' rights to property and police protection are dismissed as "privilege." LBJ long ago identified "what's at the bottom" of Jim Crow: "If you can convince the lowest white man he's better than the best colored man, he won't notice you're picking his pocket. Hell, give him somebody to look down on, and he'll empty his pockets for you." Privileged people of color and white virtue-signaling paddy rollers sniffing for racism can justify their outrageous salaries for helping the other while, instead of economic gains, superiority to whites satiates poor minorities. Thus identity politics conceals the divide between privileged and poor people of color. Blacks who do not vote Democratic, said Biden, "ain't black," and blacks who defended Trump were ridiculed, harassed, even murdered.[39]

There is unequal treatment under the law. Elites and minorities received exemptions from social distancing at riots and funerals of black civil rights leaders and terrorists.[40] More than a thousand medical professionals published a statement that BLM protests against racism did not have to follow social distancing precautions, though protests against the lockdown did because they were rooted in "white nationalism." While New York mayor Bill de Blasio praised the BLM marchers, he welded park gates shut to prevent children from playing, ostensibly to protect them from COVID-19. A majority of millennials believe that white speech deemed hateful should be illegal; students shut down classrooms, intimidate professors, and demand safe spaces from microaggressions. Bias response teams handle anonymous complaints on 232 campuses. Those who resist are silenced by the tech oligopoly. Google removed *ZeroHedge* and the *Federalist* from its ad platform for disagreeing with BLM.[41] Reddit removed a post exposing the murder of a white woman by BLM as "trolling/satire." Dissident opinions and comments lead to ostracism, termination, and humiliating public confessions followed by requests for reeducation. To show his shame for being born white, Chick-fil-A CEO Dan T. Cathy took the stage to shine the shoes of a black rapper. Saints quarterback Drew Brees and his wife groveled for their insensitive disapproval of kneeling during the national anthem. And under the New Jim Crow, *Whites Need Not Apply*. Racism toward whites is tolerated, while whites have been terminated for supporting Trump or disagreeing with BLM. The DNC refused to hire "cisgender straight white males." A Seattle city councilmember suggested firing white police officers. City workers had to undergo demeaning racial training. They were told they must "undo their whiteness" and that they might be fired for being white.

Under the new Jim Crow, whites lose self-defense rights against the terrors of Antifa and BLM violence and must watch mobs destroy their property. Media outlets portrayed the BLM riots as peaceful while violence ensued in cities across the country. The *New York Times's* Nikole Hannah-Jones said, "Destroying property, which can be replaced, is not violence." As the Minneapolis third police precinct burned, rioters shouted, "Shoot the white people!" Dispatchers at 911 told callers that police could not respond because BLM protests were "sanctioned" events—BLM shut down one Target store for calling the police. Charleston police stood by as BLM rioters destroyed business owners' lives' work and threatened their patrons. In Louisville, BLM demanded businesses hire 23 percent blacks, purchase from black retailers or donate their profits to black organizations, require diversity and inclusion training for all staff, and place signs in their store supporting the reparations movement. All that, said one BLM activist, "so your business is not f---ed with." When the McCloskeys defended their St. Louis home, threatened by a destructive mob, by brandishing weapons, a Soros-funded district attorney charged them with felonies. Said one MSNBC reporter, "The McCloskeys...are a product of their environment, because the American environment prioritizes white people, white wealth and white land at the expense of all others no matter how many black folks, poor folks, or indigenous folks had to suffer along the way." Said another, "These cases are part of a disturbing pattern in this country of white people including some, who clearly love their guns as much as they love their privilege, threatening the lives of black people for doing the most basic everyday activities." Minneapolis City Council chair Lisa Bender said that whites calling the police for help during a break-in "came from a place of privilege." Lawmakers in Oregon, Michigan, and California proposed criminalizing "racially motivated" 911 calls. Whites must display their virtue by *not calling* the police on black thugs. Tim Wise said that if black children are not innocent, then white children "don't deserve innocence" either. Whites are told that mere "performative allyship" or tweeting support of BLM is not enough. Real allies act with their "wallets," "call out people in real life," and implement quota hiring for blacks. Whites who *do* protect themselves or their property are prosecuted by the state. Facing prosecution for the lethal defense of his own business against BLM rioters, veteran Jacob Gardner, realizing the impossibility of a fair trial, took his own life. Nebraska state senator Megan Hunt celebrated the suicide as a victory over "white supremacy."

Worse than the above violence, the new Jim Crow includes ritual humiliation of whites, who are accused of racism for their mere existence, disallowed to speak yet told "silence is violence," forced to undergo demeaning training in critical race theory, and ordered to confess their privilege and submissively kneel as a religious token of abnegation. Like a minstrel show, Jimmy Kimmel clapped and barked "black lives matter" on command. BLM members marched through university libraries and restaurants, intimidating patrons into taking oaths and performing silly, degrading acts. Students created human chains to prevent white students from getting to class or created administration-sanctioned "days without white people." Privileged blacks like Ta-Nehisi Coates, Michael Eric Dyson, and Don Lemon are rewarded for their anti-white comments. Dyson advises whites to keep individual reparations accounts, a white tax, so that they can pay people of color throughout their lives. The *New York Times* hired Sarah Jeong after publishing numerous racist posts, including, "The world could get by just fine with zero white people." Nick Cannon said white people were "closer to animals" and claimed that the "only way that they can act is evil." Robin DiAngelo's bestselling *White Fragility* argues that all whites are racist and that any denial of this constitutes emotional "fragility," a psychopathology. BLM activist Ashley Shackleford lectured, "All white people...are always going to be racist"; indeed, "White people are born into not being human" and therefore should pay "reparations" to her PayPal account. University presidents kowtowed before BLM and requested sensitivity training. One in California offered "a sincere, heartfelt, and anguished apology.... I want to ask for forgiveness...for my lack of sensitivity, lack of nuance, and lack of perspective concerning Black Lives Matter."

The fear and violence of the BLM riots supplemented the COVID-19 lockdowns in the kleptocrats' war on the Republican populist base: small businesses, working families, police unions, and Christian churches. Centralization under monopoly capitalism increased under the lockdowns: BLM riots destroyed restaurants and middling retailers while increasing market share of the largest corporations. In the first few days in Minneapolis, rioters destroyed some 1,500 businesses, mostly restaurants and retail. One *Yelp* survey reported that 60 percent of closed restaurants would never reopen. Silent about the deprivation of rights and violence toward whites, McDonald's, Cisco, Nike, and Facebook gave millions of dollars to "groups working on racial justice." Walmart pledged $100 million to fight "systemic racism." Google donated $37 million on top of $32 million in the previous five years. And corporations fund the entertainment that secures their monopolies. The NFL agreed to play the "black national anthem" alongside the white one for the 2020 season. The NBA, owned largely by Chinese investors, promoted BLM while silencing criticisms of Chinese tyranny over Hong Kong. Major League Baseball defended kneeling during the national anthem and expressed support for BLM. Even NASCAR, formerly an ethnic pride parade for poor whites, banned the Confederate flag and abetted a silly race hoax involving black driver Bubba Wallace.

Major cities resolved to "defund the police," which meant turning police protection over to mobs while hiring private security forces to protect the rulers. At least twelve police officers had been shot, some of them outright assassinated, by June 2020; by December, two thousand were injured. Demoralized and defunded by Mayor de Blasio, hundreds of New York police officers filed for retirement. When federal police were dispatched to Portland to stop Antifa mobs from burning the federal building, rioters pointed lasers at their eyes (blinding three), set fires, shot fireworks, jammed communications, and tried to cut off the water supply. Portland prosecutors refused to file charges against 91 percent of those arrested at protests. BLM and Antifa rioters, bringing carts of weapons and projectiles, injured forty-nine Chicago police officers sent to protect a statue of Christopher Columbus. Said one officer, "I have 17 years on this job. Last night was another example of how our leaders have let the radicals take over. We were outnumbered and unprepared once again. The initial officers on scene had no helmets or shields. Coppers were getting pelted with rocks, sticks, bottles and then shot with fireworks." In a final act of humiliation, Mayor Lightfoot had the statue she sent them to protect taken down. Police in Minneapolis were instructed not to wear riot gear. Thus police play a crucial role as a focal point for violence. The underclass views riots as an opportunity to loot, but the riots unify privileged Leftist mobs in the transgressive ritual of violence. The whole subsumes the individual and gives him a sense of meaning, solemnized by breaking the law under religious exemption. Democrats planned the riots as one-sided brawls, where rioters could claim victory against outnumbered and handicapped police. Like soldiers returning from war, Portland rioters will pine for the romantic days when they fought the police.

Rioters targeted white Christian churches and statues. BLM rioters desecrated St. Patrick's Cathedral in New York and vandalized and burned others. One of BLM's most visible leaders called for the destruction of all "white European" statues of Jesus and his "white European mother." Many statues of Jesus and Mary were beheaded. BLM, led by a city employee, forced its way into a Troy, New York, church, vulgarly insulting and even beating parishioners. Openly professing Christians face public denunciation. While their parishioners were degraded, many priests and pastors kneeled before the new priesthood. Chris Hodges, founder of the sixty-thousand-member Church of the Highlands in Alabama, apologized three times for following *Turning Point USA*, which an accuser said was not "culturally sensitive." Catholic integralist Adrian Vermeule advocates open borders with "immigrants from Africa, Asia, and Latin America"; those who oppose "world government" are "infest[ed]" with "racism and classism." Bishop Robert Barron preached to his COVID-19 audience that America was guilty of four hundred years of "systemic racism." Christianity, he said in a four-point homily, meant embracing "diversity," "willing the good of the Other," "inclusion," and fighting systemic racism. He was joined by the US Conference of Catholic Bishops. Bishop Timothy Doherty suspended a priest for his harsh words against BLM. The Church, demoralized by predatory homosexual grooming cults and broken by lawsuits, now serves the state. Even the word *martyr* is being redefined to include those killed for defending social justice.[42] Roughly two-thirds of Catholic Charities' budget comes from state and federal government; from 2012 to 2019, the Church received $1.2 billion in federal contracts. During the COVID-19 lockdowns, twelve thousand Catholic churches asked for federal grants and nine thousand received one. Instead of fighting for natural rights, Christian legal groups receive millions from donors to plead for grace, in *exemptions* from state regulations.

The kleptocrats use race hatred to centralize their power, monopolizing minority identity for political support. But the corporate game of self-flagellation is unpredictable. The riots exposed not just the power of identity politics to command crowds but its ability to make those in positions of influence bow to its dictates. The priesthood may issue indulgences to progressive whites for wearing blackface or faking minority status, but it may destroy those who show up in solidarity. Top Democratic data analyst David Shor apologized for suggesting that the BLM riots might benefit Trump, after which he was fired. CEOs, he said, fear the Democratic Party, which is influenced more by identity politics than neoliberalism and often acts against its own interests. The 2020 nomination of Biden, a skeletal grifter in cognitive decline, exposed the need for the kleptocrats to limit the violence they had encouraged. But the 5,500-page COVID relief spending bill, presented to members of Congress in December 2020 hours before the vote, offered further tithes: its $600 for each American was overshadowed by hundreds of billions for special interests, including Smithsonian museums for "American Women's History" and "the American Latino."

The Idols of Identity Politics and Systemic Racism

A critique of critical theory, the logic underpinning identity politics, begins with the fact that the dialectic at its center is miraculous thinking. It may be formulated: Western logic presupposes the discovery of absolute truth; the concept of absolute truth generates an absolute moral and political other; therefore, Western logic must oppress its other. Such a formulation is nonsensical when supplied concrete detail. The logical principle of noncontradiction, same and other, categorically differs from moral virtue or political citizenship and justice. The laws physicists apply to approximate nature (in engineering, medicine, and neuroscience) require neither ethical impartiality nor equal protection under the law. And it is a categorical error to say that pursuit of truth in nature necessarily leads to moral partiality or that moral impartiality leads to political injustice. A philosopher or scientist may or may not be a good man; a good man may or may not be a good citizen. The latter are educated in noble images that inspire individuals to be free from vice and to sacrifice to protect the community. One educated to a love of truth may critique, inform, and reinvigorate his traditions, but the a priori dialectical approach of identity politics magically collapses these logical categories by inserting middle terms that do not necessarily follow.

Critical theorists in identity politics do not just supply a flawed logic; they fail to be truly critical, first in their promise to use group identities to achieve a future without absolute, binary identities. Despite their claims to be rooted in experience, race and gender studies teach absolute truth behind the appearances in metaphysical systems that explain every fact, constructing entire fields of environmental racism, health-care racism, and gendered glaciology. Adherents claim to begin not from abstract essences but from an empirical "Black experience." But what they really mean is *The* Black Experience—an abstract essence requiring individual blacks to locate and reinterpret all their unique experiences within a codified system of *Blackness*. Their claim against binaries creates a binary vision of the world. The celebration of the *other* does not replace an oppressive absolute *same* with tolerance for difference; rather it absolutizes diversity itself, an oppressed *other* set against an oppressor *same, Whiteness*. It hypostatizes a few traits as absolute and then dismisses the rich complexity of experience. Projecting their own uncritical system onto the Western tradition, critical theorists ally with lesser lights who, with a degenerate view of liberty, would destroy it. Critical race theorists, from a position that moral impartiality is really white racism, undermine the teachings of universal benevolence, moral culpability, and individual merit that make a diverse society possible. Critical legal theorists, attacking impartiality under the law as racist, crusade to overturn Western individual freedoms, equality under the law, and due process protections. All these systems, affirmed by faith in dialectical necessity, are constructed in lieu of experience, which is why their adherents give mechanically predictable answers. The strength of such systems is their logical coherence with catechized answers for everything, but their weakness is a rigidity that requires adherents to double down on ideology: "This is not a debate!" Ignoring or denying empirical reality, or actual *nature*, the dogmatist preaches absurdities and joins a clown world of incompetent people and failing systems.

Psychologically, identity politics aims to monopolize the symbols by which individuals understand themselves and by this justify the privileges and duties they are assigned as group members. Empirical science that conflicts with political teachings—on health, race and sex differences, or pathology among transgenders—is suppressed. What remains is a politically driven pseudoscience that justifies tyranny over mind and identity. The ever-expanding LGBTQIA+ identity has become a fashionable way for teens, especially adolescent girls, to claim victim status. Only 4 percent of Generation X claims to be LGBTQ, but it is 11 percent among millennials and 20.8 percent among Generation Z. After professing their traumas, young people are applauded for their courage. In this inverted will to power, their claims to victimhood are really claims to have greater moral virtue and insight than others they call privileged. But Leftist activists are hardly virtuous, beginning with their physiognomy. Speakers at their rallies, like a display of Antifa mugshots, are a parade of haunted, resentful, ugly people. They passively introduce themselves by disclosing their private information—sexual preferences, stories of child abuse, neglectful parents, painful alienation—before aggressively denouncing their political enemies. They demand that conservatives not only tolerate them but openly proclaim the legitimacy of their life choices. Parents of well-ordered families must disavow claims to merit for their success. And misery loves company. Sneering at child innocence and traditional morality, broken adults give sexually explicit books and puberty blockers to children.

Confessions of white privilege reveal the nature of both confessor and priest. Only a child gelded by guilt over stories of his people's evils would accede to such ritual self-effacement, and only a gnarled puritanical soul moved by lust for power would desire to hear it. Those whites least in proximity to poor minority neighborhoods, not those who have actually experienced diversity or racism, are made to feel guilty about atrocities of whites—not even their own ancestors—and thus the need to absolve themselves and justify their privilege. Whites that have never worked manual labor jobs are easily guilted into confessing that they have not earned what they have (never mind their indefatigable CVs) to…privileged whites and minorities. To get a job one must fill out a "diversity statement," a conversion story either about one's *moral worth* in struggling against discrimination or an autobiographical story of one's coming to consciousness of privilege and the struggle to redeem oneself. It is, literally, an exercise in rewriting one's experiences through the teachings of identity politics. It is a ridiculous charade. Becoming woke to white privilege is a way of condescending to other races, like prefacing a speech by thanking indigenous peoples for taking care of the land or secularists praising burkinis. Minorities become noble savages, never tainted by the corruption of power. It is also a means to privilege. Whites who confess their privilege, displaying their humility and silence, are competing to show their superiority in abjection. In doing so they universalize themselves as the race that transcends its power, becoming savior to the world. Myriad privileged elites justify their unproductive yet high-paying jobs by their magical wisdom in the mysteries of "equity." Their "fight" against racism really means blaming the country's problems on the abstract evil of Whiteness and concretely on the middle-class whites who must be subjugated and replaced.

The problem with identity politics' focus on systemic racism begins with its definition of *racism*. Whereas it used to mean unequal treatment under the law, or prejudicial treatment in ethics, it now tautologically and meaninglessly refers to anyone who is white. Ibram X. Kendi's tautological definition is: "Racism is a powerful collection of racist policies that lead to racial inequity and are substantiated by racist ideas."[43] Because there is little evidence of racism in legal discrimination, identity politics must relocate it to the recesses of whites' unconsciousness or abstract systemic claims. If racism means racial *preference*, or affinity for that which is like oneself (the mark of any healthy human), then almost *all* Americans are racist: in 2016 only 10.2 percent of married household couples were interracial. Nor is *racism* applied consistently. Statistics that point to wealth disparities between whites and blacks ignore both the black middle class and other groups (such as Nigerians) that outperform whites. Middle-class blacks have narrowed median household income with whites in all states where they are over 5 percent of the population. American median household income ($59,000 in 2016) tracks with general disparities in IQ, education, and illegitimacy, for Asians $76,667 ($131,746 for Indians, $91,221 for Taiwanese), whites $59,083, and blacks $36,651. In 2016 Modern Orthodox Jews had a median household income of $158,000 and Open Orthodox Jews $185,000. About 77 percent of American Hindus have an undergraduate degree, followed by Jews (59 percent), Episcopalians (56 percent), and Presbyterians (47 percent). Asians lead in native-born four-year degrees with 49 percent (32 percent for whites, 26 percent for Hispanics, and 19 percent for blacks).

Systemic racism justifies the privilege of middle- and upper-class blacks by pretending they are unified with the 20 percent of blacks below the poverty line. Middle-class blacks role-play, pretending they have undergone a racism equal in pain to underclass violence and poverty. According to Charles Mills, the white *settler* state and white *colonizing* empires both operate according to the same logic. Yet Mills himself was both born into privilege and a "beneficiary of affirmative action" in a supposedly racist system.[44] Privileged minorities peddle oppression to justify their privilege as set apart from their own people: Alexandria "Sandy" Cortez grew up in an elite white suburb; Oprah Winfrey, worth $2.6 billion, says, "no matter where [poor whites] are on the rung or ladder of success, they still have their whiteness." *Black*, like *Asian*, is an ambiguous term. Lawrence Otis Graham's history of black elites starts in the 1870s. A panel on his book, attended by blacks, concluded with privileged blacks "remain[ing] silent" or "reinvent[ing] their backgrounds."[45] Black elites are conspicuously light-skinned. One 2009 study concluded that "around 10% of the African American population is more than half European in ancestry."[46] Privileged blacks are often not African American but West Indian or African, including Mills himself (Jamaican), Kamala Harris (Jamaican), and Obama (Kenyan). They fixate on the myth of systemic racism to both justify their high-paying jobs and win prestige with tokens of esteem: replacing the Fourth of July with Juneteenth; capitalizing the word *Black*; circulating race hoaxes. Black celebrities who sensationalize underclass hoodlumism and sexual promiscuity are a privileged caste. Their children attend elite universities and get jobs at elite corporations, which place a premium on minority applicants and fear terminating minorities—the EEOC handled 1.9 million cases from 1997 to 2018. Ta-Nehisi Coates vacations in Paris. Rapper and actor O'Shea Jackson's ("Ice Cube") parents bussed him forty miles away to a suburban school. Obama attended the finest prep school in Hawaii. If there were no minority privilege, biracial and multiracial Americans would not identify as black, and whites would not pretend to be of color to receive prestige. It culminates in a blackface farce: BLM's Shaun King is so light-skinned that he must prove he is black, and Rachel Dolezal colors herself to experience blackness. Yet in critical theory's own explicit teaching, denying race essence, Dolezal is blacker than Barry Obama.

After receiving their own graft, privileged minorities deliver the minority vote, promising race esteem and entitlements for poor

348 / WAR ON THE AMERICAN REPUBLIC

blacks. There is, said comedian Chris Rock in 1996, a "civil war" between black people because "black people hate black people too." There were "black people and n-----s, and the n-----s have got to go." And going they are. Black women constitute 7 percent of the population and have 30 percent of the abortions (46 percent of all abortions in New York City). Margaret Sanger stated that Planned Parenthood would require the help of black leaders—80 percent of its clinics are in minority neighborhoods. In 2015, a record 77 percent of black births were illegitimate (49 percent for Hispanics). Violence has spiked in cities with large black populations where privileged blacks have attacked the police who provide law and order. Growth in the black population comes from immigrants, which, Pew reports, "now account for 8.7% of the nation's black population, nearly triple their share in 1980." The solution, say the elites, is defunding the police, reparations (because blacks built the country but have been deprived of its wealth), and massive government interventions to help blacks achieve equity.

The claim of *systemic* police brutality against blacks has no basis. There are approximately a thousand police killings each year (out of ten million arrests), with a stable ratio of 50 percent white, 25 percent black. The vast majority of cases, 90–95 percent, are justifiable—police killed twelve unarmed blacks in 2019 (and twenty-six unarmed whites). Police use more deadly force against white people in absolute numbers but proportionately more against blacks. But police were more likely to shoot white suspects *before* they were attacked, while waiting until *after* they were attacked to fire on black suspects.[47] Black and Hispanic cops are more likely than white cops to shoot black and Hispanic suspects.[48] While blacks make up a disproportionate number of arrests, they also make up a disproportionate share of offenders. Criminologists quietly agree that there are disconcerting correlations between race and criminal behavior.[49] Blacks are more likely to be treated with force by police, but they are *seven to ten times* more likely than whites to commit violent crime. "A police officer," writes Heather Mac Donald, "is

18½ times more likely to be killed by a black male than an unarmed black male is to be killed by a police officer."[50] Blacks are 13 percent of the population but commit 52 percent of the homicides, in some cities two-thirds of all violent crime, and constitute 39 percent of all arrests for violent crime. In Chicago, blacks constitute 35 percent of the population and commit 76 percent of homicides; in New York, blacks are 23 percent of the population and commit "75 percent of all shootings, 70 percent of all robberies, and 66 percent of all violent crime."[51] Young blacks, taught that they are targets of racism, openly disrespect police at casual traffic stops. In viral videos, young black men subject white police officers, without consequence, to barrages of verbal abuse. Body cam videos have contradicted numerous allegations of racial profiling. The overwhelming majority of victims of black violence are black (95 percent), but instead of focusing on the eight thousand black deaths by black hands each year, the media focuses on dozens or fewer police shootings of unarmed blacks.

And all this while *concealing black violence toward whites*. Blacks committed 537,204 of the 593,598 interracial violent crimes (excluding homicide) in 2018 (90 percent), and whites committed 56,394 (less than 10 percent). For some perspective, the total number of lynchings of blacks in *all American history*, 3,446 (according to the NAACP), is less than the excess number of whites murdered by blacks *just* from 2007 to 2019—blacks killed 3,514 more whites. News stories routinely omit race, referring to "youths" when reporting minority riots at schools or "flash mobs" that beat whites and Asians or loot stores. Reddit notified its users that it would "no longer allow any content that shows POC [people of color] as the aggressor" because it is "considered hate speech." Media blackouts of black crime in 2020 included the assassination of five-year-old Cannon Hinnant, the murder of seventeen-year-old Veronica Baker by four black teens, and Jayvon Hatchett's knife attack on a white man because he "felt the need to kill a white male." Days later Hatchett beat his white cellmate, Eddie Nelson, to death. The *Washington Post* even justified one black man's mass murder of eight whites as caused by racism: "To those closest to him, Omar Thornton was caring, quiet and soft-spoken....But underneath, Thornton seethed with a sense of racial injustice for years that culminated in a shooting rampage." When stoking black hatred toward whites results in the murders of whites, the ruling class then conceals black hate crimes. The DOJ's Community Relations Service, which responds to "race-based tension and conflict," oversees criminal cases where race is identified as a motive. It openly promotes BLM and "Trans Power" and in the cases of white victims reaches out to local police to smother media coverage. After Darrell Brooks Jr., a lifelong criminal who had celebrated black power and spewed anti-white hatred, was released on a pittance for bail (by a black commissioner) and drove through a crowd of whites, murdering six and maiming sixty others, local police squashed the facts and then paraded religious leaders before the cameras to discuss the need for dialogue and healing. The *New York Times* did not mention Brooks's race.[52]

The claim that blacks built the country or that slaves accounted for more than one-half of US wealth is false.[53] Blacks did not "build America"; they built *some* of it. Slaves accounted for only 5 percent of GDP in 1836. While cotton was the nation's largest export, it accounted for about "4.95 percent of GDP in 1860 and 4.57 in 1850."[54] The vast increase in wealth came from innovation and industry, not the agrarian economy. And blacks have been paid Jim Crow reparations for decades. The federal government has spent $22 trillion on entitlements since the 1960s, but 70 percent of the funds have gone to a "poverty industry" to serve the poor, including administrators, social workers, and bureaucrats.[55] Reparations is a shakedown to fund privileged bureaucrats. Now government intervention defines black experience, their families planned with illegitimacy and abortion, their education diluted to embarrassing grievance narratives, and their jobs shipped overseas. Among black eighth graders, 84 percent cannot do math and 85 percent are functionally illiterate.[56] *The black underclass is not a bug, but a feature, of identity politics.* Jason Riley notes, "Black crime rates

were lower in the 1940s and 1950s, when black poverty was higher"
and "racial discrimination was rampant and legal."[57] The obvious
source of the black, and American, underclass is the breakdown of
the family and the outsourcing of living-wage jobs since the 1960s.
But the ruling class resists restoring republican economic and social
conditions because it benefits from the unequal moral standards that
create degraded subjects. They celebrate the authenticity of youthful
sexual adventures, followed by late marriage, alongside the "liberated,"
broken lives of the underclass, whose miseries they blame on systemic
racism. As BLM's founders grew rich, they attacked the "patriarchal
nuclear family structure" and recycled failed prescriptions for reparations in mass state interventions that benefit privileged minorities.
Their message breeds hatred, not just of blacks for whites but between
whites of different classes. BLM activists at rallies spoke of "white
men" as a "common enemy": "We need to get rid of them." Educated
whites joked about dreaming of "white genocide."

The Myth of Meritocracy

The American kleptocracy, which claims science and anti-racism to
justify its power, is not a meritocracy produced by equal opportunity.
The wealthy, 77 percent of whose children attend elite universities,
monopolize educational institutions as gateways to power; half of
the four thousand most powerful Americans received degrees from
just twelve universities, 20 percent from Harvard.[58] Wealth does not
translate simply into higher test scores. Legacy students at the top
thirty elite private colleges are four times more likely to be accepted.
More than a third of Harvard's class of 2020 were legacy students;
Princeton, with a 7 percent acceptance rate, admits over 30 percent of
its legacy applicants. Moreover, the ruling class must openly abandon
standards of merit to maintain the alliance between corporate elites
and identity politics. Universities increasingly drop the SAT or ACT
requirement and even the GRE for graduate school in order to admit

underperforming students. Criteria include wealth, birth, diversity, and political activism. Undergraduates have been disenrolled for posting videos that disagree with BLM, and undergrad journalists who question systemic racism have been fired, replaced by pliant token "conservative" writers. Per their test scores and overall numbers in the population, white gentiles are the most underrepresented group in the Ivy League (25 percent), meaning the most underrepresented in the halls of power.[59] White Jews are the most overrepresented group (20 percent). Black and Hispanic applicants with average GPAs and MCAT scores are accepted to US medical schools at much higher rates (81.2 and 59.5 percent) than average (30.6 percent); black applicants are four times more likely to be accepted than Asians and almost three times more likely than whites. Special diversity positions have been created for progressive educators and bureaucrats. Blacks are 13 percent of the population and hold 18 percent of civil service jobs, 50 percent in some agencies. Universities have become monolithically progressive and rife with grade inflation. One-half of tenure-track and tenured history faculty come from just eight universities; one-half of political science faculty at research universities come from just eleven universities. The future leaders are meager fare: coddled students with no real-world experience and self-entitled even in failure. They are too insulated to recognize their own privilege and too weak to rule with justice. Instead, they are honored for "enhancing race and/ or ethnic relations."

The incompetent ruling class and its priesthood clamoring for simony desires the honor of ruling without being capable of the work and thus fails to solve basic problems. Government monopolies introduce outsourcing, nepotism, and bureaucratic ineptitude, vividly exposed in the Flint water crisis. Complaints about simple incompetence, such as mailing notices of court hearings nine days after the fact, are attributed to "unconscious bias" and "institutional racism."[60] Finance capitalism no longer delivers products that work. CEOs outsource production with an eye to quarterly profits or deliver substandard goods. Boeing, once known for its engineering prowess, merged with McDonnell Douglas and put politicians and private equity icons on its board; it is now "a political machine with a side business making aerospace and defense products."[61] It outsourced its design to Indian workers at nine dollars an hour and implemented a faulty software system known as MCAS.[62] With insufficient oversight from the Boeing-friendly FFA and inadequate pilot training, the 737 Max started falling out of the sky. The US infrastructure, its roads and bridges, scored a D+ from the American Society of Civil Engineers. Infrastructure bottlenecks have been created in semiconductors, railroads, and ocean shipping. Monopolies, writes Matt Stoller, have brought "shortages in everything from ocean shipping containers to chlorine tablets to railroad capacity to black pipe (the piping that houses wires inside buildings) to spicy chicken breasts to specialized plastic bags necessary for making vaccines."[63] Cronyists used the 9-11 terrorist attacks, which could have been prevented by simple fixes (like the new reinforced cockpits), to create the Transportation Security Administration (TSA), with a budget of $8.6 billion and sixty-five thousand employees. "What the TSA is good at," writes J. D. Tuccille, "is high-visibility groping, scanning, and confiscating. Making people drop their pants, take off their shoes, and surrender their shampoo annoys people in a way that says 'we're doing something' without actually accomplishing anything."[64] While spending millions on new gadgets, the TSA has an 80–97 percent failure rate at discovering weapons.

The ruling class's incompetence extends to the military. Wall Street has outsourced components for key weapons systems to China, and American foreign policy, crafted by Ivy Leaguers, is a disaster, spending billions on corrupt dictators, cronyist infrastructure projects, and ineffective programs. Optimistic State Department talking points reflect false assessments of bureaucrats removed from failures on the ground and even intentional deception.[65] Despite spending $1 trillion a year, the Department of Defense refuses to be audited, while appropriations fund questionable programs like the F-35 fighter, M1 Abrams tank, and Littoral Combat Ship. The USS Gerald Ford, a $13 billion aircraft carrier, was so plagued by mechanical failures that by its third year (2020) it had not embarked on a single mission. A pair of deadly naval crashes in the Pacific in 2017 was caused by "total incompetence." The social justice warriors in the officer corps respond by doubling down on diversity. West Point attacks "toxic masculinity"—its cadets derisively call its required Western Civ class the "I Hate America" class. Military leaders celebrate transgenderism, and instructors are pressured to pass females who fail physical requirements. Chair of the Joint Chiefs of Staff, millionaire Mark Milley, agreed to warn the Chinese before a US attack even as the armed forces he represents have become incapacitated, debauched high schools saturated with revenge porn and rising sexual assault charges from lovers' quarrels. From 2016 to 2021 the Pentagon spent $15 million to treat 1,892 transgender troops, including $11.5 million for psychotherapy and $3.1 million for surgeries. In 2018, 66 percent of service members were "either overweight or obese." Conversely, a few highly trained combat troops are fatigued by endless, fruitless police actions. In this culture of brothers in arms, they fight not for the country but for each other and resent those back home who are unaware of their sacrifices. Twenty veterans commit suicide per day, some after serving a dozen combat tours. Delta Force has acquired a criminal reputation as some of its members, operating with impunity from the law, sold illegal drugs and committed a string of murders. And special ops units do not win wars. Despite spending over $822 billion and sending over eight hundred thousand military servicemembers to Afghanistan, with more than two thousand killed and twenty thousand injured, the US military was defeated by Taliban militiamen.

The US surveillance state, with no analytic to assess mountains of data, uses intelligence not for the public but for the kleptocrats' interests: to spy on conservative media and political enemies, including President Trump. The FBI not only peddled the fraudulent Steele dossier, it has long wasted taxpayer money for its agents to infiltrate unimportant dissident groups, entrap their members in silly plots, and then imprison them. In the farcical plot to kidnap Michigan governor Whitmer, five of the "militiamen," those who concocted the plot, were FBI agents or informants entrapping those they arrested. Prosecutors dropped the testimony of FBI agent Richard Trask, who had posted during the investigation, "If you still support our piece of shit president [Trump] you can f--- off." Unsurprisingly, the FBI payroll funded the leaders of the Proud Boys and the Three Percenters who called for violence at the January 6 Capitol riot. Homeland Security labels the riot an "insurrection" to justify its increased surveillance over political dissidents even as it declares "white supremacy," meaning Trump supporters, the country's greatest terrorist threat. Meanwhile the CIA, in another intelligence failure, could not locate its puppet president of Afghanistan, Johns Hopkins professor Ashraf Ghani, as he fled with a reported $169 million in cash while his country imploded. Overnight the Taliban confiscated $28 billion in military equipment, including Black Hawk helicopters and A-29 Super Tucano attack aircraft. George W. Bush blamed the failure on conservatives who have "disdain for pluralism." He compared Trump supporters to the Taliban, "violent extremists abroad and violent extremists at home."

Kleptocratic incompetence extends to economic mismanagement. The US has used the dollar's place as the world's reserve currency to hide growing class inequality with massive deficits that allow Americans to sustain their consumption and entitlements while outsourcing the nation's production of goods and technology. According to the Social Security Board of Trustees, the program will continue to pay out more than it collects until 2034, after which it will have exhausted its asset reserves of $2.9 trillion. The program has a present underfunding of $13.2 trillion. It estimates up to a 21 percent across-the-board cut in benefits for existing and future retirees to sustain payouts. Medicare funds will be exhausted by 2026. Entitlement spending has long enabled intergenerational redistribution, saddling the young (who do not save or invest) with debt while an average elderly couple receives $244,000 more than it puts in. In 2017 health care became the nation's largest employer, a giant cartel redistributing wealth with little long-term economic benefit to future generations. According to the principles of MMT, the problem with entitlements is not that they are "underfunded" but that they could introduce unmanageable amounts of currency into circulation. But the theory also posits that there is no real interest to be paid, only the balancing of accounts, which will justify the renegotiation of elderly whites' entitlements and pensions and "reparations" in the form of redistributive social programs to minorities and recent immigrants. MMT works best when savings are depleted, as those without a cushion immediately depend on the Treasury's monetary manipulations—a mere 40 percent of Americans have $400 saved for emergency expenses.

MMT expresses both current currency abuse and the erosion of the middle class it claims to support. Republicans secure tax cuts to the wealthy, while Democrats secure funding for green energy and bureaucratic programs. Banks and corporations that receive money first spend or invest it before inflation sets in, punishing the middle class that tries to save money. During the COVID-19 lockdowns, the financial elite wiped out middle-class businesses even as the Fed bought the bonds of companies like Apple and Verizon to support the market for investment-grade corporate debt, driving up stock prices.[66] Fed members profit by trading in stocks the agency buys. Trump and Biden initiated an unprecedented level of money-printing. From March 2020 to February 2021, the Fed created four times more dollars than existed (from $4.1 to $18.1 trillion). The great flaw of MMT is that it confuses accounting identities for real-world production. The kleptocracy bids up stock prices increasingly detached from reality in real estate, cryptocurrency, and tech start-ups, and it prints money to pay interest on its mounting debt. For the rest, wages lag behind prices. The ruling class has long promoted driving up the cost of fossil fuels and meat to force consumers to transition to renewable energy and insect-based diets. By June 2022 Biden's cuts in oil and food production brought devastating inflation and record gas and food prices. Chinese leaders have only agreed to finance US debt in order to build up their economy with offshored manufactures and technology. With the dollars they accumulate, they purchase US real estate and resources, and they secure political deals with the "Deep State" that give them monopoly status in foreign markets and allow them to expand militarily.[67] But China, like other nations, creates record amounts of money to sustain excess consumption—bringing the highest peacetime debt in world history. To keep the yuan weak, China amasses massive deficits and an estimated 300 percent debt-to-GDP ratio, driving demand by pouring money into real estate, ghost cities of shoddy workmanship, and commodities. Reserve currencies like the dollar have historically found their limits, followed by prolonged economic depression. The Chinese have long negotiated with the Saudis to price oil in yuan to destroy the petrodollar that finances US consumption.[68] With increasing demand for a stronger currency, American elites will be the first to leave the dollar to protect their wealth and blame monetary irresponsibility on the public. Klaus Schwab writes, "For quite some time now, some analysts and policy-makers have been considering a possible and progressive end to the dominance of the dollar."[69]

Most damaging to the kleptocracy is that its hypocrisy discredits its moral authority. The COVID pandemic revealed science to be an *institution*, not a *method* of thinking. Instead of a community of independent researchers who verify one another's work, it is a politically funded cartel, whose research and reporting is shaped by politics. Among scientists, there is pressure to expand funding for research, and public disagreements destroy careers. Universities own their researchers' intellectual property, patents, and publications, and their scientists punish dissidents that threaten the millions they receive in federal grants. In gain-of-function research, "Any virologist who challenges the community's declared view risks having his next grant application turned down by the panel of fellow virologists that advises the government grant distribution agency."[70] The global guild of Western university scientists has come to rely on Chinese students for tuition revenue and research for their journals.[71] For cheap labor, they outsource high-risk research to foreign labs that use minimal safety precautions. Unsurprisingly, scientists prematurely denounced the COVID-19 lab-leak hypothesis as a "conspiracy theory," attributing it to "anti-Asian" hatred, a link to the identity politics priesthood that secures the interests of a ruling class that no longer bothers to hide its hypocrisy. High-profile politicians lectured the public to wear masks and self-isolate when they themselves did not. Mayor Lori Lightfoot and Speaker Nancy Pelosi closed barbershops and salons but exempted their own hair stylists. Governor Whitmer marched with BLM protestors while attacking storeowners who remained open. Her husband opened up the family cabin and traveled to Lake Michigan to use their boat while she banned travel between homes in Michigan. Barack Obama went golfing while Michelle lectured Americans to stay home for all but essential activities. Governor Newsom closed California central valley wineries but kept his own open; despite his order prohibiting indoor dining, he dined at posh restaurants without a mask. At a Napa fundraiser, Pelosi's masked brown servants served wine to maskless wealthy white donors.

COVID only continued the discrediting drumbeat of ruling-class hypocrisy. Hillary Clinton attacked Wall Street but received up to $225,000 per speech at Goldman Sachs. Al Gore attacked the fossil fuel industry, yet he made an estimated $100 million selling Current TV to Al Jazeera, based out of oil-rich Qatar, and he spends $30,000 per year on utilities for his twenty-room estate. Obama warns of rising sea levels but purchased a $12 million waterfront mansion. Celebrities and professors demand Americans shrink their carbon footprint, yet they fly on private jets, travel to international conferences, and live in palatial homes. The politics of gender does not apply to developing countries or Muslims, the politics of race does not apply to Silicon Valley or Hollywood, and the politics of class does not apply to the Ivy League.

The pseudo-meritocracy results in Democratic one-party rule in states like California, which has the nation's greatest level of inequality. Democratic long-term rule over cities like Baltimore, Detroit, and Chicago shows the country's trajectory. Gentrifying cosmopolitans drive out middle-class voters with high rents and plan tent-cities of drug-users and street defecators. Homicides in major cities rose 44 percent from 2019 to 2020, another 5 percent from 2020 to 2021; nationwide they rose 30 percent, a sixty-year high. Even as the homeless filled cities like Los Angeles, the elites welcomed in millions more illegal immigrants, who bring the Mexican drug cartels' wars with them. As Houston reported skyrocketing homicides, the Harris County sheriff reminded deputies to share their personal pronouns in introductions. No longer prosecuting property theft, cities like Dallas and San Francisco released criminals from prison to terrorize the public and only enforced violations on citizens who could pay fines. The city of Chicago decided not to prosecute gangsters involved in a deadly public shoot-out because they were engaged in "mutual combat." White hipsters who can no longer tolerate the cost of living, filth, and crime move to more conservative cities—Boise, Bozeman, Salt Lake City, Sioux Falls—where they recreate the same failures, revealed in declining happiness among women and increasing drug use and suicide rates among men. The loss of family and private associations and their sham replacement with online identities has brought isolation, depression among the lower class, and madness among its pseudo-elites. As the middle class collapses, the US returns to an ancient politics of oligarchy and demagoguery, the "perpetual vibration between...tyranny and anarchy."

But conservatives have no reason to be pessimistic: *the emperor has no clothes.* The incompetent, corrupt, and degenerate ruling class has lost all legitimacy. Citizens no longer believe state media facts selected for political control. True science, the evidence before one's eyes, pulls back the curtain to expose the globalist American empire as a kleptocracy that has betrayed the country, outsourced its wealth and defense, and degraded its people. Progressivism is not inevitable, not on a fated "right side of history." Nor are its peddlers true believers. Most academics are status-seekers who teach anything to secure their privileges. Their intelligent students reject the orthodox myths of indoctrination necessary for graduation. Branded as *racist* or *sexist* for merely existing, they no longer care about being called either. They sit through required classes on race and gender, the global village, and climate change, calculating how to balance personal advancement with social duty. They groan at the charade of privileged professors turning their classes into awkward confessionals, pressuring students to participate in the revival, throughout which musty Pharisees sniff out every intention. Increasingly the key political demographic for any political movement, young men, has dropped out altogether.

THE CONSTITUTION, CITIZENSHIP, AND THE NEW RIGHT

Conservatives should not conclude in discouragement or despair but in ruthless and radical analysis and questioning—smashing the old idols—followed by hope. Increasingly young Americans mock the incompetent, corrupt, and degenerate cosmopolitan ruling class. And they no longer believe in the conservative lies that sold their birthright. They should openly disdain the propaganda designed to convince them that resistance is hopeless, that nothing can stop the shadows of tyranny creeping over the West. Moreover, they must awaken to the truth that they *are* the West, not a mere idea in musty books but their own flesh and blood, which they can restore when they themselves flourish. Their salvation is the salvation of the West. While it will be no easy task, if they refuse to decline, then they will begin a renaissance, recovering their long-lost religious and political traditions.

The Constitution

The New Right both exposes the false priests of the kleptocracy and smashes conservative political idols as it reassesses appeals to the US

Constitution and political ideals. *Democracy* in its current usage is a farce. Michael Bloomberg praises China as a "democracy" even as US public intellectuals and financiers openly praise Chinese despotic state control.[1] Jack Goldsmith argues in the *Atlantic*, "In the debate over freedom versus control of the global network, China was largely correct, and the U.S. was wrong."[2] According to Di Dongsheng, professor at Renmin University and CCP member, the US political system is governed by "the Establishment" or "Deep State," which "refers to the US military, intelligence, State Department, Treasury Department, Commerce Department, Office of the United States Trade Representatives, and the judiciary"—unaccountable bureaucrats in collusion with Wall Street. For the Deep State, *democracy* means importing a new populace to vote for a welfare state run by rich overlords. Legitimacy is claimed by fraudulent mail-in elections, where a "designated third party" harvests the ballots of an "underrepresented" dependent class with no stake in society.[3] In 2018 the Democratic Party in California cast 250,000 ballots (one-half of its total) in Orange County, taking every seat. But in today's parlance, democracy *does not mean majority rule*. When the majority sides against the rulers, the state overturns its will, on gay marriage, transgenderism, immigration, trade, and foreign wars. Under *democracy*, the kleptocracy plans to reduce rural Americans to serf-like status. Progressive intellectuals admit this truth but advise not to openly state the goal. National elections thus become sham forums to remove natural and civil rights, such as the right to free speech, assembly, association, and self-defense. The Democratic Party pushes race reparations, the Green New Deal, registering AR-15s, and federal management of shareholder equity but *not* private equity, which secures the wealth of the top 1 percent. It promises amnesty, naturalization for twenty-two million immigrants to secure future elections and permanent Democratic rule. Finally, *democracy* means violence at the hands of the health police or BLM mobs, forcing whites to kneel in submission and abjectly confess their privilege.

Today's references to *republic* are often a farce. Because its decaying institutions still promise resistance, Democratic candidates threaten the most radical proposals: to pack the Supreme Court, abolish the Electoral College, scrap the filibuster, and add new states to the union. While institutional reforms *could* check the unaccountable bureaucracy, the efficacy of those institutions depends on the strength of republican mores that Republican Party elites have traded for monopolies, outsourcing, and open borders—more kleptocracy and managed national decline. Prerogative has replaced the rule of law. Elected congressmembers do not read thousand-page bills filled with corporate exemptions and written by staffers who cash out for jobs as lobbyists and compliance consultants. Congress delegates lawmaking authority to administrative agencies, whose unelected bureaucrats make, enforce, and adjudicate their own rules—Madison's definition of tyranny. This growing ooze of bureaucracy is a faction with no institutional check on behalf of the people—and it even celebrates its power to lie to and resist the orders of elected officials.[4] Government now means administrative fiat with myriad exemptions; enforcement is selective and inconsistent, intrusive and violent, dependent on political connections, and often an outright shakedown. A network of unaccountable intelligence agencies spies on US citizens, while a praetorian guard of warrior cops and SWAT teams kicks in doors and throws in flash grenades for online gambling, selling raw milk, copyright infringement, or perjury.

With an absentee Congress, conservatives often look to the judiciary. Scholars love to cite precedent and case law. And at the local level in criminal and civil law, US citizens still have one of the best legal justice systems in the world. But at the federal level, the Constitution and documents like the *Federalist Papers* no longer explain how government actually works. Indeed they expose its illegitimacy. Thus *legal* appeals to the Constitution and precedent are often a farce. The Constitution aimed to protect natural rights; now it is used to subvert them. In the 1980s, "Constitutional originalism" justified monopolies;

in the 1990s it justified affirmative action.[5] Today's "judicial engagement," using the courts to constrain the other branches, is a halfway house, protecting rights under *exemptions* to regulations. Courts now uphold agencies' alterations of the wording of laws. While the progressive wing of the court makes up rulings from whatever provisions it can find, the opinions of "conservative" Chief Justice John Roberts or "textualist" Neil Gorsuch are unprincipled concessions to the ruling class: Gorsuch ruled that the word *sex* in the 1964 Civil Rights Act refers to transgender identity, and Roberts refused to hear Christians' petition for their right to worship. Roberts changes his opinions to keep things on an even keel. While Trump's appointments have shifted the court rightward, the Court's politicking shows the limitations of the conservative strategy of entrusting sacred rights to unelected lawyers.

COVID-19 and the BLM riots have revealed the breakdown of the rule of law, and Leftists now openly call organized violence an effective strategy. Professor Daniel Gillion has argued that "violent protest has a positive impact on political and policy change."[6] It brings urgency, while nonviolent protest only brings awareness. NPR featured Vicky Osterweil's *In Defense of Looting*, which presents the "strategy of looting" as a way to attack "whiteness and white supremacy." The riots, funded by corporations and abetted by Republican silence, defunded, demoralized, and overwhelmed local police. The Left seeks to monopolize the state's agents of force, purging the military and creating a national police while passing emergency decrees to create spaces for its use. Many conservatives have now become convinced that, unless they are willing to allow their churches to be desecrated, their sacred services canceled, their property and liberty taken away, and their children indoctrinated or chemically castrated, they must be willing to engage in violence of their own. One now hears it said, albeit still quietly: "Where's the New Right's Antifa or BLM?" "Who is threatening corporations that have sided against *us* in the culture war?" "If they mandate vaccines or support BLM, should their windows and properties be safe from *our* bats and bullets?" "If conservatives are harassed in the cities, why are Democrats not harassed in *our* towns and fired from *their* jobs?" "Why are we allowing a handful of officials to arrest us for not wearing masks?" "Would not our natural rights to life, liberty, and property—for all races—be better protected by a strongman than a kleptocracy?"

Citizenship

Considering the future of the American nation, there are two alternatives. The first is a return to the founders' *citizenship* revolution, a shared national identity against cosmopolitanism, with color-blind law, absolute free association, and America-First economic policies. Most importantly, it requires a border wall and an immigration freeze so that Americans can assimilate and become one people. It would end dual citizenship for the wealthy who refuse patriotic commitment. It would use long-standing antitrust laws to dissolve monopolies threatening freedom. It would boost the middle class with a return of living-wage jobs in industry and technology. It would end both the stream of millions of illegal immigrants who compete for American jobs and homes and the H-1B visas that allow companies like Disney to fire their workforce after making them train cheap replacements. It would reunite economic and moral virtues in the return of productive unions and sensible family laws that hinder divorce and strengthen families. It would return to national self-sufficiency: protecting industries and scrapping 1,200-page "free trade" deals that benefit special interests. And it would promote an "America First" foreign policy. The adoption of imperialism has meant the violation of American principles both abroad and at home.

A republican revolution would crush the state church of diversity, defunding universities that teach the divisive myths of systemic racism and global citizenship. "Well-intentioned Americans of all races," writes David Azerrad, "must understand that...powerful constituencies have a vested interest in keeping America 'racist' forever."[7] The New Right should not shy from racial discussions. An honest study of the American founders must address their view that republican freedom cannot coexist with today's diversity. After the riots of 2020, no serious person could dismiss the proposition. In today's parlance, the founders were white nationalists. Yet their preference for their own race was a force *against* slavery. The northern states and territories did not want to *exploit* black bodies, they wanted black bodies to *leave*, and they passed myriad laws to that end. At great sacrifice, millions of whites fought other whites to eradicate slavery and thereby preserve their republican way of life. But African slavery, they knew, was only one type of slavery. Multicultural empires suffocate freedoms with growing legal distinctions between subjects; they teem with disjointed populations, vast wealth inequality, and arbitrary rule. No common mind unifies the people—no *e pluribus unum*. We need to uncover these truths, not because the US citizenry will be all white again—it cannot be if it is to remain a nation—but to heed the founders' warning that great diversity threatens liberty. A historical study also provides a reply and its own challenge. *White Americans voted to include first blacks, then Indians, then Asians into the citizenry,* sharing mores, habits, and aspirations. Despite its tensions, that common way of life existed until the late 1960s. But today it is pilloried as *whiteness* even as the category *white* becomes more amorphous by intermarriage.

If America is to be one nation, it must end its racial classifications even as American culture expresses racial differences. Race is not an absolute predictor—there are greater differences within than between groups—and differences are exaggerated at the tail ends of the distribution. Still, scientific studies show group differences, such as in hormonal levels that affect physical and mental development.[8] There is a meritocracy in athletic competition, a "DNA Olympics" revealing the impact of genetic traits on physical ability within and between groups.[9] In six Olympics from 2000 to 2020, fourteen of eighteen men's marathon medalists were of East African descent, with a higher percentage of slow-twitch muscles. All finalists in the men's one-hundred-meter race were of West African descent. With better-developed musculature and a higher percentage of fast-twitch muscles, they are built for explosive energy. Black athletes constitute almost 75 percent of NFL players.[10] Eurasians, with larger, more muscular bodies, shorter limbs, and thick torsos, favoring power over speed, dominate weightlifting, wrestling, and field events (shot put and hammer). Asians, on average smaller with shorter extremities and long torsos, excel in sports with fine motor skills—diving, gymnastics, and figure skating—and fine-motor skills correlate to early mathematical aptitude.[11] East Asians and Caucasian Westerners differ in visual perception and processing, and whites seem to excel in physics and engineering but often find themselves minorities next to Asians at software companies—Asians constitute 41.8 percent of Google's workforce.[12] Bill Gates said of Microsoft hiring, "The key for us, number one, has always been hiring very smart people. There is no way of getting around, that in terms of I.Q., you've got to be very elitist in picking the people who deserve to write software. Ninety-five percent of the people shouldn't write complex software."[13] Nigerian Africans outperform Asians in college degrees and score higher than whites on IQ tests in Britain.[14] Discussing the overrepresentation of Ashkenazi Jews in "benchmarks of brainpower," Steven Pinker writes, "progress in neuroscience and genomics has made these politically comforting shibboleths (such as the non-existence of intelligence and the non-existence of race) untenable."[15] Nor does it appear that group IQ averages are immutable. Competitive pressure seems to boost IQ scores, showing why competition should not be abandoned for tribalism or decreasing expectations.[16] There are also differences in artistic ability. Coleman Hughes argues, "It's not as if white people were more open to music from black people, it's that black people were on average better at music." He adds that Germans make premier pianos and Chinese virtuosos play them. Racial generalizations may be the source of scientific interest and innocent comedy. But among

progressive whites they have become an all-encompassing explana-
tion for group grievances that both diminish the merit of individual
achievement and distract Americans from the important political
question: *the common good of all American citizens.*

Racial preference is natural, though not absolute. By any indicator,
white racism is at an all-time low. Trump's appeal to class cut into the
Democratic base; he won 38 percent of the Hispanic vote and 26 percent
of working-class black men. The current divide suggests less a conflict
between races than a civil war between whites. Progressive whites,
the most radical group, blame *whiteness* for all national problems. In
a savior complex, it is the *only* racial group to express preference for
other races above its own. To combat godless whites' religion of anti-
racism, whites (including multiracial whites) in the New Right must
recover their heritage, celebrating their own contributions alongside of
others instead of posturing as the raceless race. *Whiteness* is a vacuous
word if disconnected from Christian European traditions. Mere race
is not a positive culture, nor does it mandate religious and traditional
practices that give life meaning. Given the natural mistrust between
groups, it is a defensive bond, *a politics of the prison yard*, rooted in
biological differences that provide quick identification for survival.
Whites should find renewed inspiration in their ancestors' faith and
accomplishments instead of denigrating them while celebrating the
other. They must stop apologizing for being born white and abandon
the duplicitous reasoning that everywhere other races excel is because
of merit but everywhere they underperform is because of racism.
Building upon the Greek idea of the free citizen in the *polis*, a mean
between the tribe and the empire, Europeans pioneered the nation-
state, a republican mean between the failed city-state and the empire.
They birthed a pragmatic view of the world, the scientific method,
from a Christian vocation of uncovering absolute truth. Immigrants
from all parts of the world have experienced the benefit of and have
contributed to this order. And whites must be honest about their faults,
such as their stuffy moral officiousness that, abandoning Christian-

ity, seeks to politically convert the world to capitalism, scientism, or anti-racism. Their pride, disguised as humility, glows in saving the *other* or in overvaluing acquaintances with minorities to collect them as moral trophies. But racial brotherhood cannot form in the abstract world of a classroom; it forms in friendships while working alongside one another. Interracial friendships are not moral victories; they are their own reward.

This first alternative, economic nationalism, is unlikely without changes that amount to revolution. Returning to the principles of the nation-state would require the rule of *law*—universal and enforced. It would mean not just the end of rule by arbitrary regulation but reclaiming sovereignty from the bureaucracy. Nor are kleptocrats and their priests confused about what America is—they hate it. Stoking violent mobs, they erase its history, destroying or removing statues of Franklin, Jefferson, Washington, and Lincoln. Conservatives *own* American symbols. The kleptocrats openly proclaim their shame of them; they love the US only insofar as it immolates itself in service to a global order—they call illegal immigrants "more American" than citizens. They are intent on shaming whites whose ancestors settled here and on eradicating the Western tradition, both its natural law Christianity and the republican institutions that preserve freedom. The Smithsonian openly ridicules "*Whiteness*," the morals of the old middle class: individualism, hard work, justice, time management, delayed gratification, the scientific method, and Judeo-Christianity. Minorities who embrace these morals are called "white supremacists."[17] Public figures openly celebrate the decline and replacement of the white population. Biden demanded "an unrelenting stream of immigration, nonstop, nonstop": "Folks like me who are Caucasian, of European descent, for the first time in 2017 we'll be in an absolute minority in the United States of America, absolute minority.... Fewer than 50 percent of the people in America from then and on will be white European stock. That's not a bad thing, that's a source of our strength." Biden never would make such a statement about another race.

The alternative, civil conflict, has already begun, and it only reflects the nation's spiritual war. Asked about the American Revolution, John Adams wrote that, properly speaking, it was not the war but a revolution "in the minds and hearts of the people, a change in their religious sentiments of their duties and obligations." It occurred when the colonists realized that the British Crown was "a cruel beldam, willing, like Lady Macbeth, to 'dash their brains out.'" That revolution is occurring. Moloch worshippers rage against those who challenge their absolute authority even if it destroys the society itself. Declaring a COVID emergency, they mandated vaccines even when it decimated the labor force (including nurses) and supply chains while taxing small business. Declaring a climate change emergency, they reduced oil production to drive up gas prices. Declaring an emergency of white supremacy, they defunded police to bring record crime spikes and opened the borders to millions of illegal immigrants that lower the standard of living. Declaring a mass shooting emergency, they promise to disarm rural Americans with low crime rates. And they remove their political opponents' civil liberties and make them the objects of open ridicule, contempt, even hatred. Hollywood stokes bloodlust by romanticizing the genocide of bigoted rural whites.

The only force that can oppose this servitude is an armed citizenry with a stake in society, angry about its managed decline, and insistent upon its rights. Thus the kleptocrats' fear is an armed citizenry above all, and they seek to register, then confiscate, AR-15s to render the people defenseless against state coercion. Such tyranny could trigger open conflict—Americans own some five hundred million firearms. And while the Left celebrates revolution, its marchers have never seen the systematic ordering force of conservatism when prodded to destruction. The Left can claim control of the bureaucracy and military command, but of actual fighting forces it holds few—it has alienated local police and the 3.3 million veterans who have returned from recent imperial wars. The Right, after such a long train of abuses, must confront whether it would be willing to leap into the revolutionary abyss.

This willingness and preparedness for war may be the way to *prevent* open conflict, to force a common recognition of some table of values, of *inalienable rights not subject to negotiation.*

The New Right

If those in authority continue to tread on the people's remaining liberties and customs, then conservatives must consider the possible outcomes of our current crisis. Sitting around our campfire, our backs turned to those who might listen in, we must discuss a theory of political action. Conservative intellectuals must reconnect with their republican communities and reconsider questions concerning justice and the human good. They have too long regurgitated abstract systems of positive law or the Constitution without connecting their underlying principles to contemporary politics. Even worse, they have equated culture with aestheticism removed from the economic and political lifeblood of a community. Cultural conservatives who move to rural areas because they want to be around some of the older traditions bring with them the cosmopolitan habits that subvert them. Given the promise of tyranny, conservative intellectuals should openly ally with the AR-15 enthusiasts.

While 2020–21 exposed the despotic kleptocracy, it also showed the crucial role of state and local republican institutions. At school board meetings, parents denounced the teachers who forced COVID policies, transgenderism, and critical race theory on their children. Citizens attended library board meetings to pressure the removal of sexually explicit books and partisan employees their taxes had paid for. They signed up as school board members, precinct committee members, and election inspectors. Young conservatives went to their state capitals to learn how to change their laws. Republican legislatures in twenty-six states weakened the powers of their state boards of health. Sixteen states either limited the power of health officials to order mask mandates and quarantines or restored to themselves the authority to prevent the spread of disease. Seventeen states banned or rendered ineffective COVID-19 vaccine mandates. Seventeen states restricted the teaching of critical race theory. Fourteen states barred transgender athletes from competing in single-sex sports opposite their biological sex. Responding to the 2020 election by mail-in ballots, fourteen states passed laws to increase their management over elections and introduce stiffer penalties for election law violations. Twenty-five states passed new voter identification laws. Their next task should be to remove the legislative term limits that effectively turn political power over to unelected Democratic Party members in the bureaucracy.

There are still many jurisdictions where the rule of civil and criminal law prevails, but our current state of affairs has moved us closer to a state of nature. Democratic state and federal governments increasingly rule by emergency orders. In chaotic cities, mayors and governors have refused to protect life, liberty, and property, and the president fails to protect the nation's borders. But the kleptocracy can never legitimately take away natural rights. In these moments the New Right must remember its own superior and more ancient philosophy of revolution: an "Appeal to Heaven," for which there is no arbiter on earth. Conservatives must conserve our founders' radical claim to republicanism, defending our inalienable natural rights under the laws of nature and nature's God. We have already, during the COVID coup, led one of the largest acts of civil disobedience in American history. Under pressure, and even all alone, millions of ordinary citizens refused to wear masks, receive experimental COVID vaccines, or cover their children's faces, forcing stores, restaurants, and educators to uncomfortably become minions of the state. Against the threat of violence, by the police or by the mob, we attended church and met in our homes. Despite the tired, poor, masked masses huddling in urban apartments, life continued on as normal outside the cities and suburbs. Americans learned how to inconvenience and shame every bureaucrat sent to tyrannize over them. In the end, someone has to execute those orders, and only a few prostituted souls are willing to do so. In its inability to crush civil disobedience in the provinces, the empire, an order of degenerate schoolmarms rarely capable of concerted and direct conflict, showed how weak it truly is.

But American citizens were not alone. Some red state governors ignored or openly resisted federal mandates, and local mayors, city councils, attorneys general, and police refused to enforce or prosecute state violations. Any governor can rise to the fore of the Republican Party for a few acts of defiance against federal tyranny. What arose was a model to empower red states—a union of red state governors could collectively make business respond to decency, to control transnational corporations and regulatory agencies within their borders. It could punish Big Tech and woke corporations for their censorship; it could fire state employees for teaching identity politics. Where governors fear to sign a legislative ban on transgender players, a union of red states, including Texas and Florida, could protect women by threatening to withdraw from the NCAA and form its own athletic association. When professional leagues refuse to hold events in one red state, all red states could deny them access. The greatest test is whether red states will strengthen their national guards and protect their borders from the current invasion of illegal immigrants and laborers subsidized by the kleptocracy. While it seems impossible, someday state leaders may prioritize their citizens' freedoms over greed. The leadership of the Republican Party rests with those brave enough to force a constitutional crisis in a system that refuses to protect its citizens' rights. Leftist judges can enforce their own edicts.

Individuals only leave a state of nature by looking to ties of trust, blood, faith, and honor to form voluntary associations for the protection of life, liberty, and property. The New Right is beginning to return to education in its highest sense—reviving family and localism to form habits for a different way of life. It is either dropping out of the system or forming its own parallel systems with their own rules—charter and home-schooling cooperatives, media outlets, homesteads, farmers' markets, and independent businesses. Able-bodied men, no longer isolated, are returning to republican manliness in a culture of physical fitness and responsible weaponry. They are buying AR-15s and Glock 17s and training with their friends, not FBI-infiltrated militias or online strangers but trustworthy lifelong friends to build a community alongside. Rural Christian women are questioning the corporate, cosmopolitan harem, its cats substituting for children, and are once again becoming the centers of their societies, guiding their own children's health and morals. Only when Christians remember their long tradition of just war will mobs reconsider destroying their churches and schools.

At the core of every political regime is faith. The New Right must reflect on the Christian theology that has informed the West for two thousand years. The awakening from the soporific myths of secular priests and the failure of Christian leaders to stoke the flames of faith has forced all Western peoples to see the demonic presence before them: the vilification of whites, the open celebration of pedophilia, the puberty blockers and surgeries that irreversibly dwarf and deform young girls, the castration of young men for a new class of imperial eunuchs, the sterilization of young women and the selling of their bodies as disposable temple prostitutes, the parasitism upon the opioid addictions of broken people, the scientific experiments on human babies, and the praise of Chinese despots who harvest the organs of caged slaves. Christianity is not a mere idea but a way of life and a community in which the absolute God reveals Himself and administers His grace. It must once again become a fighting faith, the inheritance of the battles of Edington, Tours, and Lepanto. Nor is the community of saints a mere analogue but the living spirits who war against the wickedness and snares of the devil and who again urge us to battle slavery. The Christian is "bound by the law of nature and revelation," preached Simeon Howard to Boston's Artillery Company in 1773, to resist both spiritual and physical despotism, to defend his natural rights and those of his posterity. "Heaven has made us their guardians, and intrusted to our care their liberty, honour, and happiness. . . . If the present inhabitants of a country submit to slavery, slavery is the inheritance which they will leave their children."[18]

The first lesson for conservatives is the construction of a militant language necessary for a return to politics, meaning, literally, the education in beautiful speeches, and honor and shame, rather than the education in pleasure and pain. The first word we must resurrect is *evil*. It is almost impossible to overstate the evil of the globalist American empire, which trades Mark Zuckerberg's social media for real communities, Jack Dorsey's verbal vomit for communication, Jeff Bezos's virtual shopping for local business. The second word is *degenerate*, noting the global empire's deformation of souls and its education in weakness and servitude. The most degenerate are the broken souls of its priesthood who traffic in others' children and revel in their bodily mutilation. Unsurprisingly, the New Right has a monopoly on beauty, praising masculine men and beautiful women instead of the unnerved, deformed, ugly, corpulent, gender-fluid cosmopolitans. Conservatives' reclamation of their traditional monopoly on poetic beauty includes not only preserving and celebrating great works of Western art, music, and literature, but also discovering and encouraging the creation of new works. More than the failed attempt to infiltrate Hollywood and entertainment media, this means uniting the language of honor and shame with powerful and beautiful images that denounce lies, evil, and degeneracy and celebrate truth, goodness, and beauty. Such a poetic renaissance is already bristling beneath the surface and, if fostered, will flourish, bursting upon the scene with vengeance and glory.

The second lesson is that *all morality is aggression*. Morality is inseparable from demands placed upon others, by those confident they are right, upon consequence of shame. Moral aggression undergirds not just the law of fashion but all civil and criminal law, which requires the confidence to execute by force. Conservatives' past failure to practice moral shaming reflected their lack of belief. Their tolerance for degeneracy led not to tolerance by degenerates but to intolerance for decency. The Left has hitherto possessed the moral high ground, confidently shaming the Right. But the only safeguard for one's natural rights is belief that bestows confidence. The New Right must seize the moral high ground by renewing its faith. A newfound indignation will give the confidence to shame the huckster financiers who have bled our country, the incompetent Ivy Leaguers who direct clownish bureaucracies, and the cosmopolitan perverts who peddle transgenderism, pornography, and pedophilia.

The third lesson is that the Right must exercise its moral confidence in and over local and state officials by singling out and holding accountable individuals in the bureaucracy who demand compliance. There must no longer be plausible deniability. Conservatives must learn to name the culpable public health officials who abet mask or vaccination mandates, choosing to aid in destroying the livelihood of decent people, or the school officials who indoctrinate their children with perversion and anti-white racism. Those officials must be pressured to look the other way, stall, or deceive their superiors rather than to deprive citizens of their rights. Bureaucrats guilty of harassment and police officers carrying out tyrannical edicts must be made to feel lonely and vulnerable in their use of violence.

Small republican communities may have little power against an insulated national bureaucracy, but perhaps the New Right's own cultural revolution is the fertile soil for political revolution, either as autonomous islands of republican civilization in an increasingly fragmenting order or the bulwark for a Caesar. At some point in the decline of every empire, with its dissolute senators, it finally dawns on a truly great leader, one born of the family of the lion or the tribe of the eagle, "Hey, I could run this thing." The New Right now often discusses a Red Caesar, by which it means a leader whose post-Constitutional rule will restore the strength of his people. Viewing the government as a series of industrial complexes, the ambitious man who desires glory need only figure out how to pull strings in a few of them, and he will have the keys to the Washington, D.C., castle. The kleptocrats have already set the precedent of purges in the bureaucracy and military. They use the state to arrest political dissidents even as they refuse to indict their own minions for federal crimes. What they do not truly consider is that the public arrests, trials, humiliations, subjugations, and terminations they have created may be reserved for them; the deportations and mass dislocations they promise for their own enemies may be used on themselves; the corporations they use for despotism may be nationalized, redistributed, or smashed. The lengthier stalks of kleptocratic wheat may be the harvest of righteous fury.

Finally, the use of actual violence, which underlies the enforcement of all laws, including the natural law, has quickly become part of our machinations. And while I sympathize with any defense of natural right, I also fear it. Our first civil war was between states, but this new terrible war would be city against country, neighbor against neighbor, in the aisles of grocery stores, restaurants, and churches. I would not choose to live in this world, but America is fast becoming no country for old men. I still hope that we can appeal to genuine nationalism, celebrating America's principles and its remarkable achievements, rejecting a false patriotism and tribalism. But I also remind the New Right, "Those who would give up essential Liberty, to purchase a little temporary Safety, deserve neither Liberty nor Safety." I conclude with the words that one of our founding republican mothers, Abigail Adams, wrote to her son:

> These are times in which a genius would wish to live. It is not in the still calm of life, or the repose of a pacific station, that great characters are formed. Would Cicero have shone so distinguished an orator if he had not been roused, kindled, and inflamed by the tyranny of Catiline, Verres, and Mark Anthony? The habits of a vigorous mind are formed in contending with difficulties. All history will convince you of this, and that wisdom and penetration are the fruit of experience, not the lessons of retirement

and leisure. *Great necessities call out great virtues.* When a mind is raised and animated by scenes that engage the heart, then those qualities, which would otherwise lie dormant, wake into life and form the character of the hero and the statesman. War, tyranny, and desolation are the scourges of the Almighty, and ought no doubt to be deprecated. Yet it is your lot, my son, to be an eyewitness of these calamities in your own native land, and, at the same time, to owe your existence among a people who have made a glorious defence of their invaded liberties, and who, aided by a generous and powerful ally, with the blessing of Heaven, will transmit this inheritance to ages yet unborn.[19]

ACKNOWLEDGMENTS

This book was the product of a sabbatical funded by the Alan J. Kirby Center in Washington, D.C. Many thanks to Matt Spalding, David Azerrad, Matt Mehan, Michael Anton, and to the graduate students whom I was privileged to meet there. I first acknowledge President Larry Arnn of Hillsdale College. While he made this book possible, that is not to say he endorses its ideas. He is both president and scholar and will find much to disagree with. Still, he stands foremost, and very often alone, in the fight for freedom of thought where other small liberal arts colleges have conceded moral authority to those who would enslave them. Arnn came to Hillsdale College when it was racked by scandal and facing uncertainty, and he restored it by returning it to its founding principles. He protects the Western Christian heritage, which is to say the pursuit of the true, the good, and the beautiful that defines, indeed *is*, Hillsdale College. It became evident in 2020, as college after college capitulated to COVID-19 shutdowns and identity politics mobs, that the Great Books curriculum that conserves the Western heritage is *inseparable* from Arnn's political conservatism. I also thank Roger Kimball, who provides a forum for provocative ideas at Encounter Books and the *New Criterion* and has taken courageous stands on both scholarly and political issues for decades. I am grateful to Tom West, David Azerrad, and Colin Brown, who read and commented on chapters of the book, and most of all to Joshua Paladino, who painstakingly proofread the manuscript and made numerous suggestions and corrections.

While I see my own contribution in this book to be the clarification of the differences between progressivism, liberalism, and radicalism, most of its ideas are not original to me. Its thesis has been a long time in the making, forged in classes in Hillsdale College's undergraduate and graduate programs. I would be remiss if I did not thank the excellent scholars, too many to list, who made this book possible. Readers should not confuse my recognition of their scholarly excellence for their endorsement of my ideas. Thomas G. West, in his *Political Theory of the American Founding*, has connected the republican theory of the founding to concrete institutions and policy. On the progressives' regime-changing rejection of the founders' republicanism, Charles Kesler, R. J. Pestritto, John Marini, Ken Masugi, Edward J. Erler, and those at the Claremont Institute, as well as numerous conversations with Tiffany Miller, have been very influential. On American republicanism and the workings of the administrative state, I call attention to the works of Douglas Bradburn, Hugh Davis Graham, Paul Moreno, and Joseph Postell. On American foreign policy and the post–World War II order, I owe much to John Grant and Tom West's indefatigable reappraisal of postwar political institutions and history. I also thank my friends and members of the Hillsdale Politics Department: Adam Carrington, Mickey Craig, John Grant, Khalil Habib, R. J. Pestritto, Joe Postell, Kevin Portteus, and Tom West. I am most grateful for having had the privilege of agreeing and disagreeing with Tom West and John Grant for years—in a constant reexamination of the American political regime. Around them I find that I am never really sure of my opinions, and I often find that I am wrong. Most assuredly, I will be persuaded by reason to reassess many of the opinions in this book. I would respect the same of anyone else.

A NOTE ON NOTES

The original draft of this manuscript contained two thousand endnotes, some two hundred additional pages. A space-saving reduction was necessary. Where the same source is cited several times in a paragraph, I have placed the page numbers for subsequent quotations in the first note from the source. I made most cuts from the final two chapters on more current events, from which I drew largely from internet sources. I have removed almost all internet links, keeping only the author's name, title, and source. Links often go dead, and all article titles and sources are easily discovered by an online search.

NOTES

1 / REPUBLICAN CITIZENSHIP

1 Joseph Barlow Felt, *History of Ipswich, Essex, and Hamilton* (Cambridge, MA: Charles Folsom, 1834), 125.

2 Samuel Adams, in *An Oration Delivered at the State-House in Philadelphia* (Philadelphia, PA: 1776), 18.

3 Benjamin Franklin, *Plain Truth*, in *The Papers of Benjamin Franklin*, ed. Leonard Labaree, et al., 43 vols. (New Haven, CT: Yale University Press, 1959), 3:203.

4 John Adams, *The Works of John Adams*, 10 vols. (Boston, MA: Little and Brown, 1856), 2:366.

5 "Franklin on the Miracle of the Revolution," *The Papers of Benjamin Franklin*, 25:100.

6 David Ramsay, *A Dissertation on the Manner of Acquiring the Character and Privileges of a Citizen of the United States* (1789), 3.

7 James Wilson, *Collected Works of James Wilson*, ed. Kermit L. Hall and Mark David Hall, 2 vols. (Indianapolis, IN: Liberty Fund, Inc., 2007), 1:636–37; see Nathaniel Chipman, *Sketches of the Principles of Government* (Rutland, VT: J. Lyon, 1793), 172–74.

8 Ramsay, *A Dissertation*, 5.

9 "An Act concerning the admission and qualification of solicitors and attornies," *Laws of Maryland* (Annapolis, MD: Frederick Green, 1787), chap. XVII.

10 *Spragins v. Houghton*, 3 Ill. 377, 2 Scam. 380 (1840).

11 J. Hector St. John de Crevecoeur, *Letters From an American Farmer* (Belfast: James Magee, 1783), 34.

12 *A Century of Lawmaking for a New Nation: U.S. Congressional Documents and Debates*, 1774–1875 Annals of Congress, House of Representatives, 3rd Congress, 2nd Session, 1004.

13 Douglas Bradburn, *The Citizenship Revolution* (Charlottesville, VA: University of Virginia Press, 2009), 152, 160–61.

14 Annals of Congress, House of Representatives, 3rd Congress, 2nd Session, 1004.

15 James Madison, *Notes of Debates in the Federal Convention of 1787* (New York: W. W. Norton & Company, 1987), 402.

16 Madison, "Foreign Influence," January 23, 1799, in *Madison: Writings*, ed. Jack Rakove (New York: The Library of America, 1999), 593.

17 Simon Snyder, *Journal of the Senate of the Commonwealth of Pennsylvania*, vol. XX (Lancaster: William Greer, 1809), 12.

18 Daniel Raymond, *The Elements of Political Economy*, 2 vols. (Baltimore, MD: F. Lucas, Jun, and E.J. Coale, 1823), 2:208, 215, 205.

19 Jefferson, *Notes on the State of Virginia*, in *Jefferson: Writings*, ed. Merrill D. Peterson (New York: The Library of America, 1984), 291.

20 Samuel Dana, *A Specimen of Republican Institutions* (Philadelphia, PA: Maxwell and Humphreys, 1802), 76, 73.

21 Zephaniah Swift, *A System of the Laws of the State of Connecticut*, 2 vols. (Windham, CT: John Byrne, 1795), 1:152.

22 John Witherspoon, "Queries, and Answers Thereto, Respecting Marriage," in *The American Museum, or Repository*, vol. 4 (Philadelphia: Mathew Carey, 1788), 315.

23 Wilson, *Collected Works*, 2:1068–83; John Daniel Gros, *Natural Principles of Rectitude* (New York: T and J Swords, 1795), 313, 303.

24 Witherspoon, "Queries," 315; Gros, *Natural Principles*, 323–24.

25 Gros, *Natural Principles*, 303; Francis Wayland, *The Elements of Moral Science* (Boston, MA: Gould, Kendall, and Lincoln, 1835), 295.

26 Swift, *A System of the Laws of the State of Connecticut*, 183.

27 Theophilus Parsons, *Milford v. Worcester*, in *Commentaries on American Law*, (New York, 1836), 367.

28 John Witherspoon, "Lecture XI," *Lectures on Moral Philosophy*, in *The Works of John Witherspoon* (Edinburgh, 1805), 7:88.

29 *Trustees of Dartmouth Coll. v. Woodward*, 17 U.S. 696–97 (1819).

30 Wilson, *Collected Works*, 2:1071.

31 James Kent, *Commentaries on American Law*, 2 vols. (New York: O. Halsted, 1827), 2:70.

32 "Philosophy, Moral," §31, *The American Edition of the British Encyclopedia or Dictionary of Arts and Sciences, Comprising an Accurate and Popular View of the Present Improved State of Human Knowledge* (Philadelphia, PA: Mitchell, Ames, and White, 1821), 9:NIC...PHO.

33 Jacob Rush, *Charges, and Extracts of Charges on Moral and Religious Subjects; Delivered at Sundry Times* (Philadelphia, PA: George Forman, 1804), 46–48.

34 "An Act for the Orderly Solemnization of Marriage," *The Perpetual Laws of the Commonwealth of Massachusetts* (Boston, MA: Adams and Nourse, 1789), pt. I.14; "An Act to Prevent Clandestine Marriages," *The Public Laws of the State of Rhode-Island and Providence Plantations* (Providence, RI: Carter and Wilkinson, 1798), 481.

35 Witherspoon, "Queries," 315–16.

36 *The Conductor Generalis: Or, the Office, Duty and Authority of Justices of the Peace...and Overseers of the Poor* (Philadelphia, PA: Printed for

Robert Campbell, 1792), 64; *The Perpetual Laws of the Commonwealth of Massachusetts*, pt. IV.187.

37 See *The Perpetual Laws of the Commonwealth of* Massachusetts, pt. IV.211–13.

38 *Fenton v. Reed,* 4 Johns. (NY) 52 (1809), a decision attributed to Kent, cited by the Pennsylvania Supreme Court in *Hantz v. Seeley* (1814) and the Vermont Supreme Court in *Newbury v. Brunswick* (1829). The Supreme Court ruled in *Hallet v. Collins,* 51 U.S. 174, 182 (1850) that consent and the will to marry constituted a marriage.

39 *Vaigneur v. Kirk,* 2 SC Eq. 646, 2 Des. Eq. 640 (1808).

40 Joseph Story, *Commentaries on the Conflict of Laws* (Boston, MA: Charles C. Little and James Brown, 1841), 100n3 (§108).

41 Caleb Bingham, *The American preceptor; being a new selection of lessons for reading and speaking. Designed for the use of schools.* (Boston: Manning and Loring, 1794), 48.

42 Lydia Maria Child, *The Mother's Book* (Boston, MA: Carter, Hender and Babcock, 1831).

43 Child, *The American Frugal Housewife: Dedicated to Those Who are Not Ashamed of Economy* (Boston, MA: Carter, Hendee, and Co., 1833), 99–100, 5.

44 Wayland, *The Elements of Moral Science,* 310.

45 *Martin v. Commonwealth of Massachusetts* (1 Mass. Reports 348).

46 Married women and their families turned to state legislatures rather than the courts for freedom from coverture and the right to control their own property. In 1821 in Maine and Massachusetts, if a wife were deserted, she could sue, make contracts, and convey real estate as if unmarried. Similar laws were passed in New Hampshire, Vermont, Tennessee, Kentucky, and Michigan before 1850. Massachusetts and Rhode Island allowed a wife separate use in life insurance contracts. In 1845, Massachusetts passed public recognition of marriage settlements and trusts for a wife's separate benefit. Illinois, Pennsylvania, Michigan, and Connecticut recognized the right of a married woman to dispose of her property. Connecticut, Ohio, Indiana, and Missouri exempted a wife's property from her husband's debts. Mississippi recognized a woman's "separate estate" in 1839, followed by Alabama and North Carolina.

47 Andrews Norton, *A Collection of the Miscellaneous Writings of Professor Frisbie* (Boston, MA: Cummings, Hilliard, & Co., 1823), 134.

48 Jefferson to Adams, October 28, 1813, *Jefferson: Writings,* 1308.

49 Benjamin Franklin to Benjamin Vaughan, July 26, 1784, *The Papers of Benjamin Franklin,* 42:444.

50 *The Constitutions of the United States* (Philadelphia, PA: John Conrad & Co., 1804), 59 (Massachusetts), 27 (New Hampshire).

51 Henry St. George Tucker, *Blackstone's Commentaries: With Notes of Reference, to The Constitution and Laws, of the Federal Government of the United States; and of the Commonwealth of Virginia,* 5 vols. (Philadelphia, PA: William Young Birch and Abraham Small, 1803), 1:xvi–xvii.

52 Thomas G. West, *The Political Theory of the American Founding* (Cambridge University Press, 2017), 201–12.

53 *The Constitution of the Presbyterian Church in the United States of America* (Philadelphia, PA: Jane Aitken, 1806), 115–16.

54 George Washington, "General Orders," November 5, 1775, in *The Writings of George Washington*, ed. John Fitzpatrick, 37 vols. (Washington, D.C.: Government Printing Office, 1931–44), 4:65.

55 John Carroll, "To the Editor of the gazette of the united states," *American Museum: Or Repository*...vol. 6 (Philadelphia: Mathew Carey, 1789), 42–43.

56 John Gilmary Shea, *Life and Times of the Most Reverend John Carroll* (New York: John G. Shea, 1888), 505.

57 See *Private Laws of the State of New York, Passed at the Thirty-Third Session of the Legislature* (Albany: Solomon Southwick, 1810), 3, 47, 143, 173.

58 "The Governor's Address to the Legislature," *Public Papers of Daniel D. Thomkins, Governor of New York, 1807–1817*, 3 vols. (Albany, NY: J. B. Lyon Company, State Printers, 1902), 2:234.

59 *The Perpetual Laws of the Commonwealth of Massachusetts* (Worcester, MA: Isaiah Thomas, 1788), 345; *Gibbons v. Ogden*, 22 U.S. 203 (1824); on infected bales, *Gilman v. Philadelphia*, 70 U.S. 713 (1865); on flammable oil, *Patterson v. Kentucky*, 97 U.S. 501 (1878).

60 *Rex v. Vantandillo*, 4 Maule & S. 73 (1815); on a tort for negligently spreading whooping cough, *Smith v. Baker*, (Circuit court S.D New York, July 5 1884, 22 rep. 240).

61 *Laws of the Commonwealth of Massachusetts, from February 28, 1807, to February 29, 1812* (Boston, MA: Greenough and Stebbins, 1812), 167.

62 *The Cow Pox Act with the Order of the Legislature: And a Communication, Relative to the Subject, from the Selectmen of the Town of Milton* (Boston, MA: Joshua Belcher, 1810), 9.

63 *Small pox destroys, vaccination saves, the life of thousands* (Philadelphia, PA: Philadelphia Society for Promoting Vaccination, 1803); *Address of the New York Vaccine Institution; with the Act of Incorporation and By-Laws* (New York: Burns & Bauer, 1847), 2.

64 Samuel Bayard Woodward, "The Story of Smallpox in Massachusetts," *The New England Journal of Medicine* 206, no. 23 (June 9, 1932): 1190.

65 *Annual Report of the City Inspector of the City of New York, for...1860* (New York: Edmund Jones & Co., 1861), 42–43.

66 Ronald Hamowy, "The Early Development of Medical Licensing in the United States, 1875–1900," *The Journal of Libertarian Studies* 3, no. 1 (1979): 104n2.

67 John B. Beck, *Introductory Lecture, Delivered at the College of Physicians and Surgeons of the City of New York, November 6, 1829* (New York: Charles S. Francis, 1829), 24.

68 *Laws of the State of New-York...; Passed, From 1828, to 1841, Inclusive* (Rochester, NY: Thomas H. Hyatt, 1841), 444.

69 *The Cherokee Nation v. The State of Georgia* 30 U.S. 1. 5 Pet. 1. 8 L. Ed. 25 (1831); *Elk v. Wilkins*, 112 U.S. 99 (1884).

70 In 1802 the US government extinguished all Indian titles to land in the state of Georgia; see *Register of Debates in Congress…of the Second Session of the Twentieth Congress* (Washington: Gales and Seaton, 1830), 5: 229–230.

71 Madison, *Notes of Debates in the Federal Convention*, 295, 502.

72 Jefferson, *Notes on the State of Virginia* in *Writings*, 264; Madison, *Memorandum on Colonizing Freed Slaves*, in *Writings*, 472–73.

73 Tucker, *Commentaries*, 1-2:75–76.

74 Tucker, *Commentaries*, 1-1:257; Ramsay, *A Dissertation*, 3–4: "Negroes are inhabitants, not citizens," with "security for his person and property, agreeably to fixed laws, but without any participation in its government"; see *Annals of Congress*, House of Representatives, 16th Congress, 2nd Session, 545–56; *Rankin v. Lydia*, 9 Ky. (2 A.K. Marsh.) 476 (1820): "Free people of color in all the States are, it is believed, *quasi* citizens, or, at least, denizens. Although none of the States may allow them the privilege of office and suffrage, yet all other civil and conventional rights are secured to them."

75 Free blacks could vote in North Carolina, New York, New Jersey, Pennsylvania, Massachusetts, Rhode Island, New Hampshire, Delaware, Maryland, and Vermont. Suffrage was revoked in Delaware (1792), Kentucky (1799), New Jersey (1807), Maryland (1809), Connecticut (1818), North Carolina (1835), Pennsylvania (1835; by constitution in 1838), and New York (1821). New Hampshire barred blacks from serving in the militia in 1815.

76 Chief Justice David Daggett, in *Connecticut v. Prudence Crandall* (1834); *Hobbs et al. v. Fogg*, 6 Watts 553 (1837); *State v. Claiborne*, 19 Tenn. 331, 1 Meigs 331 (1838): "Free blacks are not citizens within the meaning of the provisions of the Constitution of the United States, Art. 4, §2."

77 Kent, *Commentaries on American Law* (New York: E. B. Clayton, James Van Norden, 1836), 2:258nd.

78 *The Public statute Laws of the State of Connecticut, Passed at the Session of the General Assembly, in 1833* (Hartford, CT: John Russell, 1833), 425–26.

79 *Barkshire v. State*, 7 Ind. 389-90, Ind. Supreme Court (1856).

80 *Naval Documents Related to the Quasi-War Between the United States and France: Naval Operations from February 1797 to December 1801*, ed. Dudley W. Knox, 7 vols. (Washington: Government Printing Office, 1935–38), 1:41, see 281, 326, 490, 517.

81 William Wirt, "Rights of Free Negroes in Virginia," November 7, 1821, in *The Founders' Constitution*, ed. Kurland and Lerner, 4:495–96.

82 In subsequent acts, Congress granted voting rights for immigrants in the new territories of Washington, Kansas, Nebraska, Nevada, the Dakotas, Wyoming, and Oklahoma.

83 The new states prohibiting suffrage were Louisiana (1812), Indiana (1816), Mississippi (1817), Alabama (1819), Maine (1920), and Missouri (1821); the states revoking suffrage were New Hampshire (1814), Connecticut (1819), New Jersey (1820), Massachusetts (1822), Vermont (1828), and Virginia (1818).

84 Alexander Keyssar, *The Right to Vote: The Contested History of Democracy in the United States* (New York: Basic Books, 2000), 63, 32–33.

85 "A supplement to the act entitled 'An act to regulate the election of members of the legislative council'..." in *Laws of the State of New Jersey*, Joseph Bloomfield (Trenton, NJ: James J. Wilson, 1811), 33–34.

86 Delaware (1831), Tennessee (1834), Pennsylvania (1838), Rhode Island (1842), Ohio (1851), North Carolina (1856).

87 *The Perpetual Laws of the Commonwealth of Massachusetts*, 2 vols. (Worcester, MA: Isaiah Thomas, 1799), 2:232.

88 Lincoln, "Fourth Lincoln-Douglas Debate, Charleston, Illinois," *Speeches and Writings*, 2 vols. (New York: Library of America, 1989), 1:675, 636.

89 Lincoln, "Speech on the Dred Scott Decision at Springfield, Illinois," *Speeches and Writings*, 1:397–98.

90 Lincoln, "Address on Colonization to a Deputation of Negroes," *Collected Works of Abraham Lincoln*, vol. 5, ed. Roy P. Basler (New Brunswick, N.J.: Rutgers Univ. Press, 1953), 371, 372.

91 Lincoln, "Speech on Reconstruction, April 11–12, 1865," *Speeches and Writings*, 2:699.

92 Grover Cleveland supported Indian reform via education, private ownership, and federal oversight. Francis Walker, *The Indian Question* (Boston, MA: James R. Osgood and Company, 1874), argued for slow change on reservations, while the intention of the 1887 Dawes Act was rapid Indian assimilation through private property.

93 *Civil Rights Cases*, 109 U.S. 3 (1883); on contracts, *Yick Wo v. Hopkins*, 118 U.S. 356 (1886).

94 *Fourth Report of the United States Civil Service Commission* (Washington, D.C.: U.S. Government Printing Office, 1888), 134–35.

95 *The Congressional Globe*, First Session, 33rd Congress, vol. 28, pt. 3 (Washington, D.C.: John C. Rives, 1854), 1708–9.

96 *Munn v. Illinois*, 94 U.S. 113 (1876).

97 *Wabash, St. Louis & Pacific Railway Company v. Illinois*, 118 U.S. 557 (1886).

98 *In re Pacific Railway Commission*, 32 F. 249 (1887); *Kilbourn v. Thompson*, 103 U.S. 168.

99 *In re Pacific Railway Commission*, 32 F. 256 (1887), quoting John Marshall.

100 H. G. Wood, *A Treatise on the Law of Master and Servant* (Albany, NY: John D. Parsons, Ja., Publisher, 1877), sections 134, 272.

101 *Adair v. United States*, 208 U.S. 161, 174–75 (1908).

102 State of New York, *First Annual Report of the State Board of Arbitration. For the Year 1886* (Albany, NY: The Argus Company, Printers, 1887), 13.

103 Winfield Davis, *History of Political Conventions in California, 1849-1892* (Sacramento, CA: Publications of the California State Library, no. 1, 1893), 368–69.

104 Theodore Roosevelt, "National Life and Character," *The Sewanee Review* 2, no. 3 (May 1894): 366.

105 *Constitution of the State of California and Summary of Amendments* (California State Printing Office, 1915), 23 (Art 1, Sec. 17).

106 *Chae Chan Ping v. United States* 130 U.S. 595, 603–604 (1889).

107 *Reynolds v. United States*, 98 U.S. 145 (1878).

108 *Annual Report of the City Inspector of the City of New York, for the Year Ending December 31, 1860* (New York: Edmund Jones & Co., 1861), 11, 14, ix, vii.

109 *Report of the Council of Hygiene and Public Health of the Citizens' Association of New York upon the Sanitary Condition of the City* (New York: D. Appleton and Company, 1865), vii–viii.

110 *Patterson v. Kentucky*, 97 U.S. 503 (1878).

111 *Holden v. Hardy*, 169 U.S. 366 (1898).

112 Ray A. Brown, "Due Process of Law, Police Power, and the Supreme Court," *Harvard Law Review* 40, no. 7 (May 1927): 953.

113 *State Ex Rel. Adams v. Burdge*, 95 Wis. 393 (Wis. 1897).

114 *Abel v. Clark*, 84 Cal. 226 (1890), challenging California's 1889 school vaccination law; *Duffield v. School Dist.*, 162 Pa. 476, 483–84, 29 A. 742, 742–43 (1894).

115 *Smyth v. Ames* (1898) 169 U.S. 546.

2 / PROGRESSIVISM

1 Noah Porter, "The Collapse of Faith," *The Princeton Review, Fifty-Eighth Year* (May 1882): 166, 165.

2 Porter, "The Collapse of Faith," 179.

3 Fiske, *Excursions of an Evolutionist* (Boston, MA: Houghton, Mifflin and Company, 1896), 369.

4 G. W. F. Hegel, *Phenomenology of Spirit*, tr. A. V. Miller (Oxford University Press, 1977), 263; *Elements of the Philosophy of Right*, ed. Allen Wood, tr. H. B. Nisbet (Cambridge University Press, 1991), 35.

5 Hegel, *Philosophy of Right*, 35, 195; *The Philosophy of History*, tr. J. Sibree (New York: Dover Publications, Inc., 1956), 40, 322–23 ("the completion of his nature"), 417; on Africa, *Philosophy of History*, 99.

6 Hegel, *Philosophy of Mind*, tr. William Wallace (Oxford: Clarendon Press, 1971), 314–15.

7 William James, "On Some Hegelisms," *Mind*, no. 26 (April 1882): 193, 186.

8 John Dewey, "Kant and Philosophic Method," *The Early Works of John Dewey, 1882–1898*, 5 vols. (Carbondale and Edwardsville: Southern Illinois University Press, 1972), 1:43–44.

9 Dewey, "From Absolutism to Experimentalism," *The Later Works of John Dewey, 1925–1953*, 17 vols. (Carbondale and Edwardsville: Southern Illinois University Press, 1985), 5:153.

10 Dewey, *Hegel's Philosophy of Spirit: Lectures by John Dewey* (Chicago: 1897), 9.

11 Woodrow Wilson, "The Study of Administration," *Political Science Quarterly* 2, no. 2 (June 1887): 202.

12 Walter Rauschenbusch, *Christianizing the Social Order* (Boston, MA: The Pilgrim Press, 1912), 121, 119.

13 Richard T. Ely, *Social Aspects of Christianity* (New York: Thomas Y. Crowell and Company, 1889), 53, 119.

14 Ely, "Introduction," *Science: Economic Discussion* (New York: The Science Company, 1886), xi.

15 Edward House, *Philip Dru, Administrator: A Story of Tomorrow, 1920–1935* (New York: B. W. Huebsch, 1912), 66.

16 Josiah Strong, *Our Country*, ed. Jurgen Herbst (Cambridge, MA: The Belknap Press of Harvard University Press, 1963), ix, 26, 201.

17 Roosevelt, in Mrs. John Van Vorst and Marie Van Vorst, *The Woman Who Toils* (Toronto: George N. Morang, Co. Limited, 1903), viii.

18 Grenville Stanley Hall, *Adolescence*, 2 vols. (New York: D. Appleton and Company, 1905), 2:97–98.

19 *The Quarterly Calendar* 3, no. 4 (February 1895): 15.

20 Roosevelt, in Edward A. Ross, *Sin and Society: An Analysis of Latter-Day Iniquity* (New York: Houghton, Mifflin and Company, 1907), xi.

21 Washington Gladden, *Tools and the Man: Property and Industry Under the Christian Law* (Boston, MA: Houghton, Mifflin and Company, 1893), 1.

22 John Burgess, *Political Science and Comparative Constitutional Law*, 2 vols. (Boston, MA: Ginn & Company, 1891), 1:49–58.

23 Herbert Croly, *The Promise of American Life* (Boston, MA: Northeastern University press, 1989), 400.

24 Ely, "Ethics and Economics," in *Science: Economic Discussion*, 50.

25 James, "Great Men, Great Thoughts and the Environment," *Atlantic Monthly* 46 (1880): 441–59; Cooley, "Genius, Fame, and the Comparison of Races," *Annals of the American Academy of Political and Social Science* 9 (May 1897): 1–42; Fiske, *Excursions*, 175–210.

26 Ely, "Ethics and Economics," 51.

27 Wilson, *The State* (Boston, MA: D.C. Heath & Co., 1889), 2–7, 22–29, 625–26.

28 Charles Merriam, *A History of American Political Theories* (New York: Russell & Russell, 1903), 329–30; Ross, *Sin and Society*, ix.

29 Lester Ward, *Dynamic Sociology, or, Applied Social Science*, 2 vols. (New York: D. Appleton and Company, 1926), 1:60, 137; *The Psychic Factors of Civilization* (Boston, MA: Ginn & Company, Publishers, 1893), 324; *Glimpses of the Cosmos*, 6 vols. (New York: G.P. Putnam's Sons, 1913), 2:353.

30 Strong, *Our Country*, 216–17.

31 Roosevelt, "National Life and Character," 369; Wilson, *The State*, 2.

32 Roosevelt, in *The Woman Who Toils*, vii–iii.

33 Ross, "The Causes of Race Superiority," *The Annals of the American Academy of Political and Social Science* 18 (July 1901): 85.

34 Hall, *Adolescence*, 2:93 [emphasis added].

35 Charlotte Perkins Gilman, "A Suggestion on the Negro Problem," *American Journal of Sociology* 14, no. 1 (July 1908): 78.

36 Ross, *Sin and Society*, viii.

37 Edward Bellamy, *Looking Backward: 1887–2000* (New York: Magnum Books, 1968), 287, 286.

38 Bellamy, *Looking Backward*, 288–89.

39 Gilman, *Women and Economics*, (Mineola, NY: Dover Publications, Inc., 1998), 49.

40 Gilman, *Women and Economics*, 136.

41 Ely, "Ethics and Economics," 54.

42 Gilman, *Concerning Children* (London: G. P. Putnam's Sons, 1903), 132.

43 Hall, *Adolescence*, 2:94, 494.

44 H. C. Markham, "State Regulation and the Practice of Medicine—Its Value and Importance," *Journal of the American Medical Association* 10, no. 1 (January 1888): 5.

45 Samuel G. Dixon, "Law, the Foundation of State Medicine," *Journal of the American Medical Association* 48, no. 23 (June 1907): 1926.

46 Ephraim Cutter, "More Physicians and Less Lawyers in Congress and Legislature," *The Journal of the American Medical Association* 29, iss. 17 (October 1897): 838.

47 Dixon, "Law, the Foundation of State Medicine," 1926.

48 "Physicians as Politicians," *Journal of the American Medical Association* (January 16, 1892): 84.

49 Dixon, "Law, the Foundation of State Medicine," 1926, 1929, 1930–31, 1927.

50 Cutter, "More Physicians and Less Lawyers in Congress and Legislature," 839.

51 Dixon, "Law, the Foundation of State Medicine," 1926–27.

52 "Treason Against the Government," *Journal of the American Medical Association* 45, no. 18 (October 1905): 1331.

53 Cutter, "More Physicians and Less Lawyers in Congress and Legislature," 839.

54 Dixon, "Law, the Foundation of State Medicine," 1928.

55 Charles Warren, "The Progressiveness of the United States Supreme Court, *Columbia Law Review* 13, no. 4 (April 1913): 294–313.

56 *Jacobson v. Massachusetts*, 197 U.S. 11–12 (1905) ruled that vaccination could be required if "necessary for the public health or the public safety" (27).

57 *Zucht v. King*, 260 U.S. 176 (1922). By the 1930s, four states prohibited compulsory smallpox vaccination, twenty-eight had no vaccination laws, six provided for local option, and ten had compulsory vaccination laws.

58 "Entire Country Near Closed; Few Hopeful Reports Received," *Variety* 52, no. 8 (October 18, 1918): 1.

59 George M. Price, MD, "Influenza—Destroyer and Teacher: A General Confession by the Public Health Authorities of a Continent," *The Survey*, December 21, 1918: 368.

60 Price, "After-War Public Health Problems," *The Survey*, December 21, 1918: 369.

61 Gilman, *Concerning Children*, 26; Gilman, "Parasitism and Civilised Vice," in *Women Coming of Age*. ed. Calverton and Schmalhausen (New York: Horace Liveright, Inc., 1931), 124; Roosevelt, "National Life and Character," 372; Annie Riley Hale, *The Eden Sphinx* (New York, 1916), 166, 206–7.

62 Ellen Key, *The Renaisance of Motherhood* (New York: G. P. Putnam's Sons, 1914), 91, 105; Hale, *Eden Sphinx*, 209, 74, 80, 78: "Motherhood is the greatest of all the many services that women can render to the State."

63 Roosevelt, in Mrs. John Van Vorst and Marie Van Vorst, *The Woman Who Toils*, vii–viii.

64 Hiram Stanley, "Artificial Selection and the Marriage Problem," *The Monist* 2, no. 1 (October 1891): 51n*, 52.

65 Ely, *Studies in the Evolution of Industrial Society* (New York: The Chautauqua Press, 1903), 167.

66 Dixon, "Law, the Foundation of State Medicine," 1928.

67 Margaret Sanger, *Woman and the New Race* (New York: Truth Publishing Company, 1920), 8, 40–41.

68 "Purity Congress Meets," *New York Times*, October 15, 1895, 16.

69 Gilman, *Women and Economics*, 15.

70 Jane Addams, *A New Conscience and an Ancient Evil* (New York: The Macmillan Company, 1913), 27–28, 209–10.

71 Hale, *Eden Sphinx*, 253, 206.

72 George Elliott Howard, *A History of Matrimonial Institutions*, 3 vols. (Chicago: The University of Chicago Press, 1904), 3:225–28.

73 Roscoe Pound, in Edward F. Waite, "Courts of Domestic Relations," *Minnesota Law Review* 5, no. 3 (February 1921): 167; "The End of Law as Developed in Juristic Thought," *Harvard Law Review* 27, no. 7 (May 1914): 621–22; on Pound's critique of founding thought, 622–25; "The End of Law as Developed in Legal Rules and Doctrines," *Harvard Law Review* 27, no. 3 (January 1914): 204–11.

74 Pound, "The Administration of Justice in the Modern City," *Harvard Law Review* 26, no. 4 (February 1913): 325.

75 Pound, "The End of Law as Developed in Juristic Thought, II," *Harvard Law Review* 30, no. 3 (January 1917): 202, 222; "The End of Law as Developed in Legal Rules and Doctrines," 196, 198.

76 *Maynard v. Hill*, 125 U.S. 213–14 (1888).

77 Pound, in Waite, "Courts of Domestic Relations," 167.

78 Pound, "The Administration of Justice in the Modern City," 312, 323.

79 Pound, "Foreword," in Pauline V. Young, *Social Treatment in Probation and Delinquency* (New York: McGraw-Hill Book Company, Inc., 1937), xxvii.

80 Ida Tarbell, "A Court of Hope and Goodwill," *The American Magazine* 77 (January–June 1914): 43, 44.

81 Waite, "Courts of Domestic Relations," 164–65.

82 Pound, "The Administration of Justice in the Modern City," 318.

83 David Rothman, *Conscience and Convenience: the Asylum and its Alternatives in Progressive America* (Boston, MA: Little, Brown, 1980), 44.

84 Charles L. Chute, "Developing Standards in the Work of Domestic Relations Courts," *Journal of the American Institute of Criminal Law and Criminology* 8, no. 2 (July 1917): 273.

85 Charles Hoffman, "Domestic Relations Courts," in *The Social Work of the Courts: Annual Report and Proceedings of the Tenth Annual Conference of the National Probation Association, held in Kansas City, MO., May 14-20, 1918* (Albany, NY: National Probation Association, 1919), 135–38.

86 Waite, "Courts of Domestic Relations," 169.

87 Merriam, *American Political Theories*, 306, 307, 308-9, 313, 311.

88 Dewey and James Tufts, *Ethics* (New York: Henry Holt and Company, 1908), 444, 446–47.

89 Merriam, *American Political Theories*, 324.

90 Theodore Woolsey, *Political Science*, 2 vols. (New York: Charles Scribner's Sons, 1877), 1:211, 223.

91 Burgess, *Reconstruction and the Constitution, 1866-1876* (New York: Charles Scribner's Sons, 1902), viii.

92 Wilson, "The Modern Democratic State," in *The Papers of Woodrow Wilson*, ed. Arthur S. Link, 69 vols. (Princeton, N.J.: Princeton University Press, 1966–1983), 5:76, 90.

93 Wilson, *The New Freedom* (New York: Doubleday, Page &Company, 1913), 49, 47.

94 Frank Goodnow, *Politics and Administration* (New York: The Macmillan Company, 1900), 14.

95 Wilson, "The Study of Administration," 210–11; Croly, *Progressive Democracy* (New York: The Macmillan Company, 1914), 364, advocated a "Fourth department of government" with the powers of all three branches.

96 Goodnow, *Politics and Administration*, 91.

97 Wilson, "The Study of Administration," 203, 212–13.

98 Wilson, "The Modern Democratic State," 5:79.

99 Wilson, "The Study of Administration," 201, 214 [emphasis added], 215, 216, 217.

100 Ely, "The Inheritance of Property," *North American Review* 153, no. 146 (July 1891): 54–66; Ely, Thomas Adams, Max Lorenz, and Allyn Young, *Outlines of Economics* (New York: Macmillan, 1922), 461–63.

101 *United States v. E. C. Knight Co.*, 156 U.S. 1 (1895).

102 Louis Brandeis, "The Solution of the Trust Problem: A Program," *Harper's Weekly* 58, no. 2968 (November 8, 1913): 18; *Other People's Money: And How the Bankers Use It* (New York: Frederick A. Stokes Company, 1914), chap. 8.

103 Brandeis, in John B. Cheadle, "Government Control of Business," *Columbia Law Review* 20, no. 5 (May 1920): 580; Taft, *The Anti-Trust Act and the Supreme Court* (New York: Harper & Brothers Publishers, 1914), 124.

104 Brandeis, *Business—A Profession* (Boston, MA: Small, Maynard & Company, 1914), 253.

105 Charles Van Hise, *Concentration and Control: A Solution of the Trust Problem in the United States* (New York: The Macmillan Company, 1912), 227.

106 Pound, "Mechanical Jurisprudence," *Columbia Law Review* 8, no. 8 (December 1908): 615.

107 Pound, "The Need of a Sociological Jurisprudence," 392.

108 Pingree, *Annual Address of Hazen S. Pingree, Mayor of the City of Detroit, Delivered January 9, 1894* (Lansing, MI: Robert Smith Printing Co., 1897), 16–18.

109 Pingree, *Ex-augural Message of Governor Hazen S. Pingree to the Forty-first Legislature of Michigan January, 1901* (Lansing, MI: Wynkoop Hallenbeck Crawford, 1900), 22.

110 William Allen White, "On Mr. Steffens's Book, 'The Shame of the Cities,'" *McClure's Magazine* 23, no. 2 (June 1904): 221.

111 White, "On Mr. Steffens's Book," 221; "A Municipal Business Manager in Staunton, Va," *The City Hall: Bulletin of the League of American Municipalities* (April 1909): 348.

112 "A Municipal Business Manager in Staunton, Va," 349.

113 Roosevelt, "First Annual Message, December 3, 1901" [emphasis added].

114 Roosevelt, "Eighth Annual Message, December 8, 1908."

115 "Theodore Roosevelt to William Jennings Bryan, October 22, 1912."

116 Roosevelt, *Progressive Principles* (New York: Progressive National Service, 1913), 190.

117 "Annual Report of the Commissioner of Corporations to the Secretary of Commerce," Bureau of Corporations (Washington, D.C.: U.S. Government Printing Office, 1904), 41 [emphasis added].

118 Taft, "The Boundaries Between the Executive, the Legislative and the Judicial Branches of Government," *Yale Law Journal* 25, no. 8 (June 1916): 616.

119 Taft, "Introduction," in William Draper Lewis, *The Life of Theodore Roosevelt* (Philadelphia, PA: The John C. Winston Company, 1919), viii.

120 Taft, "Special Message, January 7, 1910."

121 Taft, *The Anti-trust Act and the Supreme Court*, 114.

122 "Politics and Banking," *New Republic*, November 14, 1914: 11.

123 Croly, *Progressive Democracy*, 15–25.

124 *Harriman v. ICC*, 211 U.S. 407, 419–20 (1908); *Smith v. ICC*, 245 U.S. 33 (1917).

125 *FTC v. American Tobacco Co.*, 264 US 298, 305–6 (1924).

126 Roosevelt, *The New Nationalism* (New York: The Outlook Company, 1910) 3.

127 General James Rusling, "Interview with President William McKinley," *The Christian Advocate* 22 (January 1903): 17.

128 Taft, "Remarks at the Banquet of the Washington Corral of the Military Order of the Carabaos, January 22, 1910," justified the occupation as furthering "the progress of civilization in the world."

129 Merriam, *American Political Ideas* (New York: The Macmillan Company, 1920), 251–52.

130 Taft, "Remarks at the Banquet of the Washington Corral"; McKinley called it "benevolent assimilation."

131 Burton J. Hendrick, *The Life and Letters of Walter H. Page*, 2 vols. (Garden City, NJ: Doubleday, Page & Company, 1922), 1:204.

132 Wilson, "Address to Congress Advising that Germany's Course Be Declared War Against the United States."

133 Robert La Follette, *Robert M. La Follette, June 14, 1855–June 18, 1925*, ed. Belle Case La Follette, 2 vols. (New York: The Macmillan Company, 1953), 2:767.

134 "La Follette as a Foe of Democracy," *The Literary Digest*, October 6, 1917: 15.

135 Smedley Butler, *War is a Racket* (New York: Skyhorse Publishing, 2013), 16–17.

136 "National Affairs: Protestants," *Time* 4, no. 12 (September 22, 1924).

137 Wilson, "The Modern Democratic State," 5:79.

138 Gilman, *Women and Economics*, 117.

139 Burgess, *The Reconciliation of Government with Liberty* (New York: Charles Scribner's Sons, 1915), 382.

140 *Wilson v. New* 243 U.S. 378 (1917).

141 "Where Are the Pre-War Radicals?" *The Survey* 55, no. 9 (February 1926): 563.

142 Otis L. Graham, Jr., *An Encore for Reform: The Old Progressives and the New Deal* (New York: Oxford University Press, 1967), 195, 78–84.

3 / LIBERALISM

1 Walter Lippmann, "Liberalism in America," *New Republic*, December 31, 1919: 150.

2 Dewey's, "Liberalism and Social Action," *The Later* Works, 11:40: "The ends [of liberalism] can now be achieved *only* by reversal of the means to which early liberalism was committed."

3 Dewey, "The Influence of Darwin on Philosophy," *The Middle Works of John Dewey, 1899–1924*. 15 vols. (Carbondale and Edwardsville: Southern Illinois University Press, 1978), 4:3–10.

4 Dewey, "The Influence of Darwin on Philosophy," *The Middle Works*, 4:7–8.

5 Dewey, "Reconstruction in Philosophy," *The Middle Works*, 12:179; "Logic: The Theory of Inquiry," *The Later Works*, 12:11–15.

6 Dewey, "The Relation of Theory to Practice in Education," *The Middle Works*, 3:263; "Context and Thought," *The Later Works*, 6:3–21.

7 Dewey, "Individualism, Old and New," *The Later Works*, 5:120.

8 Lippmann, "The Footnote," *New Republic*, July 17, 1915: 284.

9 Randolph Bourne, "John Dewey's Philosophy," *New Republic*, March 13, 1915: 154, 155.

10 Dewey, "Authority and Social Change," *The Later Works*, 11:142–43.

11 Dewey, "Authority and Social Change," *The Later Works*, 11:141.

12 Sigmund Freud, *Totem and Taboo*, tr. James Strachey (New York: W. W. Norton & Company, 1950), 30–35.

13 Freud, *The Question of Lay Analysis*, tr. James Strachey (New York: W. W. Norton & Company, 1989), 85–86.

14 John B. Watson, *Psychology from the Standpoint of a Behaviorist*, 2nd. ed. (Philadelphia, PA: J. B. Lippincott Company, 1924), viii, 354–55, 12, xi–xii, xii–xiii, 5, 7.

15 Watson, *Psychology from the Standpoint of a Behaviorist*, 4, 8, 8–9.

16 Clifford Beers, *The Mental Hygiene Movement: Origin and Growth* (Norwood, MA: The Plimpton Press, 1917), 337; Watson, *Psychology from the Standpoint of a Behaviorist*, 8.

17 Watson, *Behaviorism* (London: Kegan Paul, Trench, Trubner & Co., Ltd., 1925), 82.

18 Freud, *Civilization and Its Discontents*, tr. James Strachey (New York: W. W. Norton & Company, 1989), 69.

19 Freud, "My contact with Josef Popp-Lynkeus," in *Collected Papers*, 5 vols, tr. Joan Riviere (New York: Basic Books, 1959), 5:297.

20 Dewey, "Individuality in Our Day," *The Later Works*, 5.118–19; on rejecting altruism, Freud, *Civilization and Its Discontents*, 108–9.

21 Dewey, "Liberalism and Social Action," *The Later Works*, 12:190–92.

22 Dewey, "Education and the Social Order," *The Later Works*, 9:178.

23 Dewey, "Individualism, Old and New," *The Later Works*, 5:122–21.

24 Dewey, "Human Nature and Conduct," *The Middle Works*, 14:197, 223–26.

25 William B. Munro, *The Invisible Government* (New York: The Macmillan Company, 1928), 2, 56.

26 Lippmann, *Public Opinion* (New York: Harcourt, Brace and Company, 1922), 248–49.

27 Abraham Myerson, "Freud's Theory of Sex: A Criticism," in *Sex in Civilization*, 510. Schmalhausen, "The Sexual Revolution," in *Sex in Civilization*, 405.

28 Dorothy Dunbar Bromley, "Feminist—New Style," *Harper's Monthly Magazine* 155 (October 1927): 552–60.

29 H. L. Mencken, *In Defense of Women* (New York: Alfred A. Knopf, 1922), 184–185, 186–87.

30 Wilhelm Reich, *The Sexual Revolution*, tr. Therese Pol (New York: Pocket Books, 1975), 23–28, 176–77.

31 D. H. Lawrence, *Psychoanalysis and the Unconscious* (New York: Thomas Seltzer, 1921), 19–21, 86–87, 94, 101.

32 Robert Latou Dickinson and Lura Beam, *A Thousand Marriages* (Baltimore: The Williams & Wilkins Company, 1931), 369.

33 Edward Bernays, *Propaganda* (New York: Liveright Publishing Corporation, 1928), 92, 117–18.

34 Israel Zangwill, *The Melting-Pot: Drama in Four Acts* (New York: the Macmillan Company, 1915), 184.

35 Franz Boas, "Changes in the Bodily Form of Descendants of Immigrants," *American Anthropologist*, New Series, 14, no. 3 (July–September 1912): 557.

36 Robert E. Park, "Human Migration and the Marginal Man," *American Journal of Sociology* 33, no. 6 (May 1928): 881.

37 Park, "The University and the Community of Races," *Pacific Affairs* 5, no. 8 (August 1932): 695–703.

38 Maurice Samuel, *You Gentiles* (New York: Harcourt, Brace and Co., 1924), 122, 76-77, 31–32, 218–19.

39 Adolf Hitler, *Mein Kampf* (New York: Reynal & Hitchcock, 1941), 20, 8, 15, 55–59, 39–40.

40 Paul Hollander, *Political Pilgrims: Travels of Western Intellectuals to the Soviet Union, China, and Cuba* (New York: Oxford University Press, 1981), xi; Eugene Lyons, *The Red Decade* (New York: Arlington House, 1970), 70–81, 170–94.

41 Franklin Delano Roosevelt, "State of the Union Message to Congress, January 11, 1944."

42 Raymond Moley, *After Seven Years* (New York: Harper & Brothers Publishers, 1939), 184.

43 Adolf Berle, author of FDR's "Commonwealth Club Address"; Rexford Tugwell, "The Principle of Planning and the Institution of Laissez Faire," *The American Economic Review* 22, no. 1 (March 1932): 76–84.

44 Federal Housing Administration, *Underwriting and Valuation Procedure...to April 1, 1936*, in Charles Abrams, *Forbidden Neighbors* (New York: Harper & Brothers, 1955), 162.

45 James Landis, *The Administrative Process* (New Haven, CT: Yale University Press, 1938), 1.

46 McCraw, *Prophets*, 213–14, 186–88; *Humphrey's Executor v. United States*, 295 U.S. 602-603 (1935); *FTC v. Ruberoid Co.*, 343 U.S. 487-8 (1952).

47 *KFKB Broadcasting Association v. FRC* (1931) 47 F. 2d 670.

48 *FCC v. Pottsville Broadcasting Co.*, 309 U.S. 138 (1940); *KFKB Broadcasting Association, Inc. v. FRC*, 47 F. 2d 670, 672 (DC Cir. 1931)(using the station to sell medicines); *Norman Baker*, FRC Docket No. 967 (June 5, 1931) (attacks on doctors and soliciting cures for cancer).

49 *Trinity Methodist Church, South v. FRC*, 62 F.2d 850 (DC Cir. 1932); *Adelaide L. Carrell*, 7 FCC 219, 222 (1939); *Scroggin & Co. Bank*, 1 FCC. 194 (1935).

50 *Mayflower Broadcasting Corp.*, 8 F.C.C. 333, 340 (1941).

51 "The Mayflower Doctrine Scuttled," *Yale Law Journal* 59 (1950): 763n23; FCC, "Editorializing by Broadcast Licensees," *Reports, July 1, 1948-June 30, 1949*, vol. 13, no. 2 (1949): 1257.

52 "Comments," *The University of Chicago Law Review* 18, no. 1 (Autumn 1950): 87n53.

53 Jerome Frank, *Law and the Modern Mind* (New York: Anchor Books, 1963), 261.

54 *Buchanan v. Warley*, 245 U.S. 60 (1917) overturned a city ordinance prohibiting the sale of property to blacks; in *Corrigan v. Buckley*, 271 U.S. 323 (1926), the Court did not overturn a racial restrictive covenant; *United States v. Carolene Products Co.*, 304 U.S. 155n4 (1938).

55 Robert M. Cover, "The Supreme Court. 1982 Term. Foreword: Nomos and Narrative," *Harvard Law Review* 97, no. 4 (1983–84): 4-68; Suzanne Last Stone, "In Pursuit of the Counter-Text: The Turn to the Jewish Legal Model in Contemporary American Legal Theory," *Harvard Law Review* 106, no. 4 (February 1993): 813–94.

56 Alan M. Dershowitz, *Chutzpah* (New York: Simon and Schuster, 1992), 58–9; Will Maslow, "The Uses of Law in the Struggle For Equality," *Social Research* 22, no. 3 (Autumn 1955): 310–14.

57 Carol Glassman, "Women in the Welfare System," in *Sisterhood is Powerful: An Anthology of Writings From the Women's Liberation Movement*, ed. Robin Morgan (New York: Vintage Books, 1970), 103.

58 Moreno, *From Direct Action to Affirmative Action, 1933–1972* (Baton Rouge, LA: LSU Press, 1999), 43–44.

59 Moreno, *From Direct Action to Affirmative Action*, 60.

60 *Steele v. Louisville & Nashville Railway Co.*, 323 U.S. 202-3 (1944).

61 *James v. Marinship Corp.* 25 Cal.2d 721 (1944).

62 *Hughes v. Superior Court*, 339 U.S. 463-64 (1950).

63 Thurman Arnold, "Antitrust Law Enforcement, Past and Future," *Law and Contemporary Problems* 7 (Winter 1940): 8, 7.

64 Cal Lewis, "The Pauper Vote," *The North American Review* 246, no. 1 (Autumn 1938): 87–95.

65 Lloyd C. Gardner, *Economic Aspects of New Deal Diplomacy* (University of Wisconsin Press, 1964); William L. Neumann, "How American Policy Toward Japan Contributed to War in the Pacific," in *Perpetual War for Perpetual Peace*, ed. Harry Elmer Barnes (Caldwell, ID: Caxton Printers, 1953), 245–46.

66 Charles Beard, *President Roosevelt and the Coming of the War, 1941: A Study of Appearances and Realities* (New Haven, CT: Yale University Press, 1948).

67 Thomas Fleming, *The New Dealers' War: FDR and the War Within World War II* (New York: Basic Books, 2002), 281–304.

68 "Vice President Henry Wallace," *Life*, April 21, 1941: 32.

69 "Looking Ahead with Albert Einstein," *The Rotarian* (June 1948): 8.

70 Walter A. McDougall, *Promised Land, Crusader State: The American Encounter with the World Since 1776* (New York: Houghton Mifflin Company, 1997), 173–74.

71 Henry Morgenthau, *Germany is Our Problem* (New York: Harper & Brothers Publishers, 1945), 16–29; on German tariffs, 58; on the State Department's own agricultural plan, Cordell Hull, *The Memoirs of Cordell Hull*, 2 vols. (New York: The Macmillan company, 1948), 2:1609.

72 William H. Draper, Economics Division, Office of Military Government for Germany, *A Year of Potsdam: German Economy Since Surrender*, 190; on German cartels, Morgenthau, *Germany is Our Problem*, 30–47.

73 Freda Utley, *The High Cost of Vengeance* (Chicago: Henry Regnery Company, 1949), 183–84, 163–64.

74 Hull, *The Memoirs of Cordell Hull*, 2:1602–3.

75 James Bacque, *Other Losses* (Toronto: General Paperbacks, 1991), 29.

76 William E. Griffith, "Denazification in the United States Zone of Germany," *The Annals of the American Academy of Political and Social Science 267, Military Government* (January 1950): 68–76; McDougall, *Promised Land*, 177–79.

77 Bacque, *Crimes and Mercies: the Fate of German Civilians Under Allied Occupation, 1944–1950* (Vancouver, British Columbia: 2007), xxiv, 107–25, estimates a larger and more controversial number.

78 *Trials of War Criminals Before the Nuremberg Military Tribunals under Control Council Law No. 10 Nuremberg, October 1946–April 1949* (Washington, D.C.: U.S. Government Printing Office, 1949), 964, 966.

79 Utley, *The High Cost of Vengeance*, 179; Morgenthau, *Germany is Our Problem*, 154.

80 Utley, *The High Cost of Vengeance*, 167–72.

81 Alpheus Thomas Mason, *Harlan Fiske Stone: Pillar of the Law* (New York: Viking Press, 1956), 716.

82 Thomas A. Breslin, "Mystifying the Past: Establishment historians and the origins of the Pacific War," *Bulletin of Concerned Asian Scholars* 8, no. 4 (1976): 18–36.

83 "The Sedition Trial: A Study in Delay and Obstruction," *The University of Chicago Law Review* 15, iss. 3 (1947): 691–702.

84 Edward L. Van Roden, "American Atrocities in Germany," *The Progressive* (February 1949): 21ff., "American investigators . . . used the following methods to obtain confessions: Beatings and brutal kickings. Knocking out teeth and breaking jaws. Mock trials. Solitary confinement. Posturing as priests. Very limited rations. Spiritual deprivation. Promises of acquittal." The Senate, *Malmedy Massacre: Investigation Hearings Before a Subcommittee of The Committee on Armed Services, United States Senate, Eighty-First Congress, First Session* (Washington D.C.: U.S. Government Printing Office, 1949), 606–7. The hearings confirmed German POWs' broken jaws, teeth, and crushed testicles (212, 233–34, 244, 250–51).

85 James Burnham, *The Struggle For the World* (London: Jonathan Cape, 1947), 52, 27, 227, 27.

86 Walter Lippmann, *The Cold War: A Study in U.S. Foreign Policy* (New York: Harper Brothers Publishers, 1947), 23.

87 Seymour M. Hersh, "Ex-Analyst Says C.I.A. Rejected Warning on Shah," *New York Times*, January 7, 1979, quoting Jesse J. Leaf, chief CIA analyst in Iran from 1968–73, alleged that the CIA's "torture seminars" to train the Shah's SAVAK secret police were "based on German torture techniques from World War II."

88 George F. Kennan, *Realities of American Foreign Policy* (Princeton, NJ: Princeton University Press, 1954), 49.

89 *Brown Shoe Co., Inc. v. United States*, 370 U.S. 294 (1962); *United States v. Von's Grocery Co.*, 384 U.S. 270 (1966).

90 Arthur Schlesinger, Jr., *The Vital Center* (Boston, MA: Houghton Mifflin Company, 1962), xiii.

91 Daniel Bell, *The End of Ideology: On the Exhaustion of Political Ideas in the Fifties* (New York: The Free Press, 1962).

92 Eric Hoffer, *The True Believer* (New York: Harper & Row, 1951), 135.

93 Schlesinger, *A Thousand Days: John F. Kennedy in the White House* (Boston: Houghton Mifflin Co., 1965), 679.

94 Karl Mannheim, *Ideology and Utopia* (London: Routledge & Kegan Paul LTD, 1960), 203.

95 E. Michael Jones, *The Slaughter of Cities: Urban Renewal as Ethnic Cleansing* (South Bend, IN: Fidelity Press, 2017).

96 "Manners & Morals: The Coffee Hour," *Time*, March 5, 1951.

97 Floyd Mansfield Martinson, *Family in Society* (New York: Dodd, Mead & Company, 1970), 341.

98 Thomas P. Monahan, "Family Fugitives," *Marriage and Family Living* 20, no. 2 (May 1958): 146.

99 Monahan, "Family Fugitives," 148.

100 Max Rheinstein, "Our Dual Law of Divorce: The Law in Action Versus The Law of the Books," *Conference on Divorce 9, The University of Chicago Conference Series* (1952), 39, 41; *Marriage, Stability, Divorce, and the Law* (Chicago: The University of Chicago Press, 1972), 261.

101 John Wayne interview, *Playboy* (May 1971).

102 Scott Eyman, *John Wayne: The Life and Legend* (New York: Simon & Schuster, 2014), 293.

103 Will Herberg, *Protestant, Catholic, Jew* (Garden City, NY: Anchor Books, 1960), 49, 46–47. Membership was 63 percent in 1958; as self-perceived, 73 percent.

104 Seward Hiltner, *Ferment in the Ministry* (Nashville, TN: Abingdon Press, 1969), 100–1.

105 Herberg, *Protestant, Catholic, Jew*, 16–17, 38, 23, 31; Negroes and Asians still held inferior status (38).

106 Jones, *Slaughter of Cities*, 120–71.

107 Where Catholics leaned Democratic and Jews voted overwhelmingly liberal, both groups agreed on economic liberalism and civil rights. The two disagreed on entry into the war and communism. Saul Brenner, "Patterns of

Jewish-Catholic Democratic Voting and the 1960 Presidential Vote," *Jewish Social Studies* 26, no. 3 (July 1964): 169–78.

108 Charles S. Liebman, *The Ambivalent American Jew* (Philadelphia, PA: Jewish Publication Society, 1973), 24–25.

109 Herberg, *Protestant, Catholic, Jew*, 190: "Friendliness to the State of Israel"; David Verbeeten, *The Politics of Nonassimilation* (DeKalb, IL: NIU Press, 2017), 119.

110 *Whom We Shall Welcome: Report of the President's Commission on Immigration and Naturalization* (Washington, D.C.: U.S. Government Printing Office, 1953), 12, 23; John F. Kennedy, *A Nation of Immigrants* (New York: Harper & Row Publishers, 1964).

111 Oscar Handlin, *The Uprooted* (Boston, MA: Little, Brown and Company, 1952), 3.

112 *Whom We Shall Welcome*, 4–5.

113 Harvey Breit, "A Second Novel," *Partisan Review* 27 (Summer 1960): 561.

114 Raymond S. Franklin and Solomon Resnik, *The Political Economy of Racism* (New York, Holt, Rinehart and Winston, 1973), 29. In 1963, the labor movement helped mobilize forty thousand union members for the March on Washington for Jobs and Freedom.

115 "Business: The Negro Market," *Time*, Monday, July 5, 1954.

116 Joseph H. Jackson, *Unholy Shadows and Freedom's Holy Light* (Nashville, TN: Townsend Press, 1967), 136–57.

117 UNESCO, *The Race Concept: Results of an Inquiry* (Paris: UNESCO, 1952), 5–35.

118 P.G.A. and M.C.G, "Racial Discrimination in Housing," *University of Pennsylvania Law Review* 107, no. 4 (February 1959): 515–50; Oscar Cohen, "The Case for Benign Quotas in Housing," *Phylon* 21, no. 1 (1st Quarter 1960): 20–29; "Racial Quotas Urged For Chicago Schools," *The Christian Science Monitor*, December 2, 1961, 6.

119 Michael Harrington, *The Other America: Poverty in the United States* (Baltimore, MD: Penguin Books, 1962), 64, 69, 70, 72, 79, 73, 131.

120 Gunnar Myrdal, *An American Dilemma, the Negro Problem and Modern Democracy*, 2 vols. (Brunswick, New Jersey: Transaction Publishers, 1996), 2:929.

121 Those who made statements against quotas or reverse discrimination included Roy Wilkins, Whitney Young, Secretary of Labor Willard Wirtz, Eisenhower, and JFK: "Wirtz says JFK nixes job quotas, *The Baltimore Afro-American*, November 23, 1963, 13; "Eisenhower States Quotas Hurt Negro," *New York Times*, October 13, 1963, 44; Cabell Phillips, "Kennedy Opposes Quotas For Jobs On Basis Of Race," *Special to The New York Times*, August 21, 1963, 1.

122 Will Maslow, "The Uses of Law in The Struggle For Equality," 306 [emphasis added].

123 Johnson, "Remarks at the Signing of the Immigration Bill, Liberty Island, New York, October 3, 1965."

124 "A New Mix for America's Melting Pot in 1965," *U.S. News & World Report,* October 11, 1965.

125 Hugh Davis Graham, *Collision Course: The Strange Convergence of Affirmative Action and Immigration Policy in America* (New York: Oxford University Press, 2002), 94, 57; Kevin MacDonald, "Jewish Involvement in Shaping American Immigration Policy, 1881–1965," 295–356.

126 Marc Dollinger, *Quest for Inclusion* (Princeton, NJ: Princeton University, 2000), 133.

127 Verbeeten, *The Politics of Nonassimilation,* 117.

4 / RADICALISM

1 Fleming, *The New Dealers' War,* 164.

2 Morton White, *Social Thought in America: The Revolt Against Formalism* (Boston, MA: Beacon Press, 1957), 4.

3 Vernon Parrington, *Main Currents in American Thought,* 3 vols. (New York: Harcourt, Brace, and Company, 1927-30), 3:401.

4 Martin Heidegger, *Being and Time,* tr. John Macquarrie and Edward Robinson (New York: HarperCollins, 1962), 163–68, 225–26, 312–13, 370–82.

5 Heidegger, *The Question Concerning Technology,* tr. William Lovitt (New York: Harper Colophon Books, 1977), 17.

6 Barrett, *Irrational Man* (Garden City, NY: Doubleday Anchor Books, 1962), 20, 6.

7 Marjorie Grene, *Introduction to Existentialism* (Chicago: The University of Chicago Press, 1959), 9.

8 Max Horkheimer, *Eclipse of Reason* (New York: Oxford University Press, 1947), 84.

9 Horkheimer and Theodor Adorno, *Dialectic of Enlightenment,* tr. John Cumming (New York: The Continuum Publishing Company, 1994), 9.

10 Herbert Marcuse, "Review of John Dewey's Logic: The Theory of Inquiry," tr. Phillip Deen, *Transactions of the Charles S. Peirce Society* 46, iss. 2 (Spring 2010): 261–62.

11 Marcuse, *One-Dimensional Man* (New York: Routledge, 2002), 135–46; *Reason and Revolution* (Boston, MA: Beacon Press, 1960), vii–xiv; Adorno, *Negative Dialectics,* tr. E. B. Ashton (New York: Routledge, 1973), 146–48; Horkheimer and Adorno, *Dialectic of Enlightenment,* 24–25.

12 Marcuse, *Eros and Civilization,* 111, 118–19, 124–25; 111–12.

13 Horkheimer and Adorno, *Dialectic of Enlightenment,* 168–208; Adorno et al., *The Authoritarian Personality,* Vol. I of *Studies in Prejudice,* ed. Horkheimer and Samuel H. Flowerman (New York: Harper & Brothers, 1950), 1–11; Marcuse, *Studies in Critical Philosophy,* tr. Joris De Bres (Boston, MA: Beacon Press, 1972), 141.

14 Paul Goodman, *Growing Up Absurd* (New York: Vintage Books, 1960), 3–8; Abraham Maslow, *Toward a Psychology of Being* (Princeton, NJ: D. Van

Nostrand Co., Inc.), 5; Erich Fromm, *The Sane Society* (Greenwich, CT: Fawcett Publications, Inc., 1955), 139–47.

15 Maslow, *Toward a Psychology of Being*, 3; on looking to existentialism, 9–17.

16 Reich, *The Sexual Revolution*, 5.

17 Carl Rogers, "Reinhold Niebuhr's The Self and the Dramas of History: A Criticism," *Pastoral Psychology* 9 (June 1958): 16; Marcuse, *Eros and Civilization*, 143, 178, 182.

18 Maslow, *Toward a Psychology of Being*, 194.

19 Rogers, *On Becoming a Person* (Boston, MA: Houghton Mifflin Company, 1961), 119, 203.

20 Marcuse, *Eros and Civilization* 124, 166.

21 Maslow, *The Journals of A. H. Maslow*, 2 vols. (Monterey, CA: Brooks/Cole, 1979), 1:650–51, soured on the movement.

22 Rogers, *Counseling and Psychotherapy* (Boston, MA: Houghton Mifflin Company, 1942), 126–27.

23 "Paul Tillich," in *Carl Rogers: Dialogues*, ed. Howard Kirschenbaum and Valerie Land Henderson (Boston, MA: Houghton Mifflin Company, 1989), 68, 69, 71.

24 Tillich, *The Courage to Be* (New Haven, CT: Yale University Press, 1952), 185; Rogers, *Counseling and Psychotherapy*, 109: "Therapy and authority cannot be coexistent in the same relationship."

25 *The Documents of Vatican II*, tr. Rev. Msgr. Joseph Gallagher (New York: Guild Press, 1966), 146–63, 341–70; for criticism, see Alfredo Cardinal Ottaviani, "A Brief Critical Study of The New Order of Mass," June 5, 1969.

26 Discrimination and Christian Conscience: A Statement Issued by the Catholic Bishops of the United States, November 14, 1958, 203; On Racial Harmony: A Statement Approved by the Administrative Board, National Catholic Welfare Conference, August 23, 1963.

27 Robert Schuller, *Self-Esteem: The New Reformation* (Waco, TX: Word Books, 1982): 68–69.

28 *Lesbian Nuns: Breaking Silence*, ed. Rosemary Curb and Nancy Manahan (Tallahassee, FL: Naiad Press, 1985), 3–4.

29 Jones, *Slaughter of Cities*, 41.

30 William H. Whyte, Jr., *The Organization Man* (Garden City, NY: Doubleday Anchor Books, 1956), 295.

31 David Riesman, *The Lonely Crowd: A Study of the Changing American Character*, abr. ed. (New Haven, CT: Yale University Press, 1961), 256, 239, 259.

32 Mills, *Sociology and Pragmatism*, ed. Irving Louis Horowitz (New York: Oxford University Press, 1966), 379, 382.

33 Mills, *The Causes of World War Three* (New York: Simon and Schuster, 1958), 81–89.

34 "Pressures on Federal Regulatory Commissions," *Congressional Quarterly*, April 2, 1958.

35 "Iron triangle: Clout, background, and outlook," *Congressional Quarterly Weekly Report* 30 (1956): 1627–34.

36 Marcuse, *Eros and Civilization*, xvi.

37 Marcuse, *One-Dimensional Man*, 260.

38 Marcuse, *Eros and Civilization*, 87–88; 194.

39 Mills, *The Sociological Imagination* (New York: Oxford university Press, 2000), 195–226; 181, 187.

40 Mills, "The Politics of Responsibility," *The New Left Reader*, ed. Carl Oglesby (New York: Grove Press, Inc., 1969), 30.

41 Mills, *The Causes of World War Three*, 101–4.

42 Stokely Carmichael, "Black Power," in *To Free a Generation: The Dialectics of Liberation*, ed. David Cooper (London: Collier Books, 1968), 165.

43 Fromm, "The Basis of Humanist Socialism," *The Socialist Call* 28, no. 1 (Spring 1960): 10.

44 Maslow, *Toward a Psychology of Being*, 12–13; Marcuse, *Eros and Civilization*, 193n48; Rogers, *On Becoming a Person*, 192–93.

45 Norman Mailer, "The White Negro," *Dissent* (Fall 1957); Jack Kerouac, *On the Road* (New York: Penguin, 1976), 179–80: "At lilac evening I walked…wishing I were a Negro, feeling that the best the white world had offered was not enough ecstasy for me"; Allen Ginsberg, *Howl and Other Poems* (San Francisco: City Lights, 2001), 9: "I saw the best minds of my generation destroyed by madness, starving hysterical naked, dragging themselves through the negro streets at dawn looking for an angry fix."

46 *Roth v. United States*, 354 U.S. 476 (1957); *Memoirs v. Massachusetts*, 383 U.S. 413–14 (1966).

47 Jackson, *Unholy Shadows*, 48, 49.

48 Martin Luther King., Jr., *Where do We Go From Here?: Chaos or Community* (Boston, MA: Beacon Press, 1968), 39; Theodore H. White, "Backlash," *Life* 67, no. 16 (October 16, 1964): 100–10.

49 Whitney Young, *To Be Equal* (New York: McGraw-Hill Book Company, 1964), 27–33, 19.

50 "The Negro and the American Promise," *Perspectives, National Education Television*, WGBH Archives; Malcolm X changed his view of King, *The Autobiography of Malcolm X* (New York: Random House, 1965), 377–78.

51 Huey Newton, *Huey Newton Talks to the Movement* (Chicago: Students for a Democratic Society, 1968), 4.

52 Chicago Office of SNCC, "We Must Fill Ourselves With Hate for All White Things," in *Black Protest Thought in the Twentieth Century*, ed. August Meier, Elliot Rudwick, and Francis L. Boderick (Indianapolis, IN: The Bobbs-Merrill Company, Inc., 1971), 486.

53 E. Franklin Frazier, *Black Bourgeois: The Rise of a New Middle Class* (New York: The Free Press, 1957), 130–49.

54 Carmichael, "Black Power," 150.

55 William Melvin Kelley, "If You're Woke You Dig It," *New York Times*, May 20, 1962; Carmichael, "Black Power" (October 29, 1966), 44.

56 Carmichael, "Black Power" (October 29, 1966), 13–14.

57 Sy Landy and Charles Capper, "In Defense of Black Power," *New Left Notes* 1, no. 34 (September 9, 1966): 4; Robert Bone, "Negro Literature in the Secondary School: Problems and Perspectives," *The English Journal* 58, no. 4 (April 1969): 514; *If They Come in the Morning: Voices of Resistance*, ed. Angela Y. Davis and Bettina Aptheker (New York: Third Press, Joseph Okpaku Publishing Company, 1971), 30–31.

58 King, "The Other America," Grosse Point High School, March 14, 1968.

59 On King's teaching of "unconscious racism," David Halberstam, "When 'Civil Rights' and 'Peace' Join Forces," in *Martin Luther King, Jr.: A Profile*, ed. C. Eric Lincoln (New York: Hill & Wang, 1970), 201–2; King, *The Trumpet of Conscience* (New York: Harper & Row, 1989), 6; *Where do We Go From Here?*, 94.

60 King, *The Trumpet of Conscience* (London: Hodder and Stoughton, 1968), 6.

61 King, *Where Do We Go From Here?*, 94.

62 James H. Cone, *A Black Theology of Liberation* (Maryknoll, NY: Orbis Books, 2003), 107.

63 Cone, *A Black Theology of Liberation*, 45, 29–30, 104–109, 108, 108.

64 Cone, *A Black Theology of Liberation*, 107, 134, 20, 33; Frazier, "The Failure of the Negro Intellectual," *Negro Digest* 11, no. 4 (February 1962): 35; Malcolm X, *The Autobiography*, 236–237; Frazier, *The Negro Church in America*, in C. Eric Lincoln, *The Black Church Since Frazier* (New York: Shocken Books, 1974), 80–85; 135–52.

65 Robert Gilman, "Review: White Standards and Negro Writing," *Negro American Literature Forum* 3, no. 4 (Winter 1969): 111–13.

66 FBI, File #: 62-HQ-116395, Serial Scope: 1153-Bulky, https://www.archives.gov/files/research/jfk/releases/docid-32989551.pdf, 17–18.

67 Taylor Branch, *Pillar of Fire: America in the King Years, 1963–65* (New York: Simon & Schuster, 1999), 207.

68 FBI, File #: 62-HQ-116395, Serial Scope: 1153-Bulky, https://www.archives.gov/files/research/jfk/releases/docid-32989551.pdf, 13.

69 Marshall Frady, *Martin Luther King, Jr.: A Life* (New York: Penguin Books, 2006), 63.

70 *Black Manifesto: Religion, Racism & Reparations*, ed. Robert Lecky and H. Elliott Wright (New York: Search Books, 1969), 119, see 114–26.

71 Berman, *America in the Sixties*, 31, 26, 7.

72 Greg Calvert, "In White America: Liberal Conscience vs. Radical Consciousness," in *Revolutionary Youth and the New Working Class: Lost Writings of SDS*, ed. Carl Davidson; (Pittsburgh PA: Changemaker Publications, 2011), 12, 13, 19.

73 Marcuse, "Repressive tolerance," in *A Critique of Pure Tolerance* (Boston, MA: Beacon Press, 1965), 109.

74 Johan Galtung, "Violence, Peace and Peace Research," *Journal of Peace Research* 6 (1969): 168; on speech as a form of violence, Marcuse, "Repressive Tolerance," 106–15.

75 Cleaver, *Soul on Ice* (New York: Delta, 1968), 81.

76 Charles Levy, *Voluntary Servitude: Whites in the Negro Movement* (New York: Meredith Corporation, 1968).

77 Armando Rendón, *Chicano Manifesto* (New York: Collier Books, 1971), 262, 263, 248–49, 280, 281, 278.

78 *In re Rodriguez*, 81 F. 337 (May 3, 1897, United States District Court for the Western District of Texas).

79 *Westminster School Dist. of Orange County v. Mendez*, 161 F.2d 780 (9th Cir. 1947).

80 *Cisneros v. Corpus Christi Independent School District*, 330 F. Supp. 1377 (S.D. Tex. 1971).

81 Richard Avila and James Romo, "The Undocumented Worker," *Chicana/o Latina/o Law Review*, 3 (1976): 170n35, 174–75. *Graham v. Richardson*, 403 U.S. 365 (1971) classified "resident aliens" as a strict scrutiny category.

82 Casey Hayden and Mary King, "Sex and Caste: A Kind of Memo" (November 18, 1965), in Evans, *Personal Politics*, 235–38; "Liberation of Women," *New Left Notes* (July 10, 1967), in Evans, *Personal Politics*, 240–42; Gloria Steinem, "Women Freeing the Men, Too," *Washington Post*, June 17, 1970.

83 Carol Hanisch, "The Personal Is Political," in *Notes from the Second Year: Women's Liberation*, ed. Shulamith Firestone and Anne Koedt (New York: Radical Feminism, 1970), 76–78.

84 Radicalesbians, *The Woman-Identified Woman* (Pittsburgh, PA: Know, Inc., 1970); Shulamith Firestone, *The Dialectic of Sex* (New York: Bantam Books, 1972), 2, 15.

85 "Regional Conference," *Berkeley Tribe* 3, no. 20, iss. 72 (November 20–27, 1970): 13.

86 Firestone, *Dialectic of Sex*, 11.

87 Firestone, *Dialectic of Sex*, 2, 8–11; Herma Hill Kay, "Making Marriage and Divorce Safe for Women," *California Law Review* 60, no. 6 (November 1972): 1696.

88 "Regional Conference," *Berkeley Tribe* 3, no. 20, iss. 72 (November 20–27, 1970): 15.

89 Steinem, "Women Freeing the Men, Too."

90 Katherine Turk, "Out of the Revolution, into the Mainstream: Employment Activism in the NOW Sears Campaign and the Growing Pains of Liberal Feminism," *The Journal of American History* 97, no. 2 (September 2010): 403.

91 Susan Jacoby, "The Flatbush Feminists," *The Possible She* (New York: Ballantine Books, 1973), 3.

92 "The Combahee River Collective Statement," *Home Girls: A Black Feminist Anthology*, ed. Barbara Smith (New York: Kitchen Table, 1983), 272, 275, 278, 277.

93 *Gay Liberation* (New York: The Red Butterfly, 1970), 4–5; John Money and Anke A. Ehrhardt, *Man & Woman, Boy & Girl* (Baltimore, MD: The Johns Hopkins University Press, 1972), 1, 176.

94 Lars Ullerstam, *A Sexual Bill of Rights for The Erotic Minorities*, tr. Anselm Hollo (New York: Grove Press, 1966), 161.

95 Paul Goodman, "The Politics of Being Queer," in *Nature Heals: The Psychological Essays of Paul Goodman*, ed. Timothy Stoehr (New York: Free Life Editions, 1977), 216.

96 Dennis Altman, *Homosexual: Oppression and Liberation* (St. Lucia: University of Queensland Press, 2012), 2.

97 Altman, *Homosexual*, 19.

98 Carl Wittman, *The Gay Manifesto* (New York: A Red Butterfly Publication, 1970), 3.

99 Altman, *Homosexual*, 80, 19, 26, 28–29, xii, 17.

100 George Weinberg, *Society and the Healthy Homosexual* (New York: Macmillan, 1972), 1-21.

101 "Press Release from The Johns Hopkins Medical Institutions, November 21, 1966, Announcing the Establishment of the Gender Identity Clinic for Transsexuals," in John Money, *Gendermaps: Social Constructionism, Feminism and Sexosophical History* (London: Bloomsbury Academic, 2016), 139.

102 Laura Wexler, "Identity Crisis," *Baltimore Style Magazine* (January/February 2007).

103 Dr. Lindsay R. Curtis, "Obsessive desire to cross sex lines," *Boston Globe*, June 12, 1972, 19; "Hundreds Wait to Change their Sex," *Jet* 43, no. 5 (October 26, 1972): 47.

104 Janice Raymond, *The Transsexual Empire: The Making of the She-Male* (New York: Teachers College Press, 1994), 183, 104.

105 Julius Lester, *Look Out, Whitey!: Black Power's Gon' Get Your Mama!* (New York: Grove Press, Inc., 1968), x; Carmichael, "Black Power" (1966), 11.

106 Gitlin, "Foreword," in *The War Within*, xvii.

107 Hayden, *Trial* (New York: Holt, Rinehart and Winston, 1970), 33–43; 33; Marcuse, *Eros and Civilization*, xvi.

108 Carmichael, "Black Power" (1966), 38.

109 Berman, *America in the Sixties* 30, 29.

110 Morgan, *Sisterhood is Powerful*, xxxv.

111 "Regional Conference," *Berkeley Tribe* 3, no. 20, iss. 72 (November 20–27, 1970): 14.

112 Fred Dutton, *Changing Sources of Power: American Politics in the 1970s* (New York: McGraw-Hill Book Company, 1971), 224.

113 Dutton, *Changing Sources of Power*, 230; *Mandate for Reform, the Report of the Commission on Party Structure and Delegate Selection to the Democratic National Committee* (Washington, D.C.: U.S. Government Printing Office, 1970), 34.

114 Victor S. Navasky, "A Funny Thing Happened on the Way to the Coronation," *New York Times*, July 23, 1972.

115 Jeane Kirkpatrick, "Representation in the American National Conventions: The Case of 1972," *British Journal of Political Science* 5, no. 3 (July 1975): 279.

116 "New Directions: 1972–76," 1972 Democratic Party Platform, July 10, 1972.

117 "U.S. Funds Helping to Pay Rent Of 4 at 'Hate Whitey' School," *Philadelphia Daily News*, August 8, 1967, 2; Myles H. Whitney and Paul J. Champagne, "New Left Organizers and the Poor," *The Journal of Sociology & Social Welfare* 5, iss. 5 (September 1978): 678–92.

118 Leroi Jones, in "The Task of the Negro Writer as Artist: A Symposium," *Negro Digest* 14, no. 6 (April 1965): 65.

119 Jane Martin, "What Should We Do With a Hidden Curriculum When We Find One?" *Curriculum Inquiry* 6, no. 2 (1976): 140.

120 James A. Banks, "Imperatives in Ethnic Minority Education," *The Phi Delta Kappan* 53, no. 5 (January, 1972): 267; "Curriculum Strategies for Black Liberation," *The School Review* 81, no. 3, The Future of Education for Black Americans (May 1973): 405–14.

121 Paulo Freire, *Education for the Oppressed*, tr. Myra Bergman Ramos (New York: Continuum, 1993), 30.

122 John Schuyler Gibson and William Clement Kvaraceus, *The Development of Instructional Materials Pertaining to Race and Culture in American Life* (Medford, MA: Trustees of Tufts College, 1966), 1; *Schooling for a Global Age*, ed. James M. Becker (New York: McGraw Hill, 1979), xiii, xiv.

123 Lee F. Anderson, "Education and Social Science in the Context of an Emerging Global Society," in *International Dimensions in the Social Studies*, ed. James M. Becker and Howard D. Mehlinger (National Council for the Social studies, 1968), 78.

124 Pat A. Bidol, *Developing New Perspectives on Race: an innovative multimedia social studies curriculum in race relations for secondary level* (Detroit: New Detroit Speakers Bureau, 1970).

125 National Education Association, *Education & Racism: An Action Manual* (Washington, D.C.: National Education Association, 1973).

126 Judy Katz and Allen Ivy, "White Awareness: The Frontier of Racism Awareness Training, *Personnel and Guidance Journal* 55, no. 8 (April 1977): 487.

127 *Education & Racism*, 27–35.

128 *Hearings Before the General Subcommittee on Education of the Committee on Education and Labor, House of Representatives, 92nd Congress, 1st Session, on H.R. 3101 and H.R. 10641* (Washington D.C.: U.S. Government Printing Office, 1972), 43–46.

129 Katz, "White Awareness," 485–89.

130 "Racism films trigger orientation discussions," *The Heights* 50, September 9, 1969, 5.

131 R. Shep Melnick, "The Odd Evolution of the Civil Rights State," *Harvard Journal of Law & Public Policy* 37, no. 1 (2014): 124, 116.

132 Samuel C. Jackson, "Using the Law to Attack Discrimination in Unemployment," *Washburn Law Journal* 8 (1968–9): 189, 190.

133 Timothy L. Jenkins, "Study of Federal effort to end job bias: a history, a status report, and a prognosis," *Howard Law Journal* 14, no. 259 (Summer 1968): 259–329.

134 *Swann v. Charlotte-Mecklenburg Bd. of Educ.*, 402 U.S. 2 (1971) [emphasis added].

135 Judge J. Braxton Craven had approved the school board plan in *Swann v. Charlotte-Mecklenburg Board of Education*, 243 F. Supp. 667 (W.D.N.C. 1965). After *Green v. County School Board*, 391 U.S. 430, the Swann case was filed again and this time taken by Judge James B. McMillan.

136 *Keyes v. School District No. 1, Denver*, 413 U.S. 189 (1973).

137 *Morgan v. Hennigan*, 379 F. Supp. 410 (D. Mass. 1974).

138 Nathan Glazer, "A Breakdown in Civil Rights Enforcement? Review Essay," *The Public Interest* 23 (Spring 1971): 109, 112.

139 US Commission on Civil Rights, *Racism in America: and How to Combat It*, Clearinghouse Publication, Urban Series, no. 1 (January 1970), 3, 5, 7, 5, 17, 6, 19, 30, 35, 36, 37.

140 Margaret Dunkle and Bernice Sandler, *Sex Discrimination Against Students: Implications of Title IX of the Education Amendments of 1972* (N.W. Washington, D.C.: Association of American Colleges, 1975), 5.

141 Mark Green and Ralph Nader, "Economic Regulation vs. Competition: Uncle Sam the Monopoly Man," *Yale Law Journal* 82 (1973): 871, 876.

142 Richard B. Stewart, "The Reformation of American Administrative Law," *Harvard Law Review* 88, no. 8 (June 1975): 1712.

143 Theodore J. Lowi, *The End of Liberalism: Ideology, Policy, and the Crisis of Public Authority* (New York: W. W. Norton, 1969), 125.

144 Stewart, "The Reformation of American Administrative Law," 1670.

145 *Colonnade Catering Corp. v. United States*, 397 U.S. 74 (1970) (involving liquor, based on a history of supervision of the industry), expanded in *United States v. Biswell*, 406 U.S. 311 (1972) (involving firearms); *Marshall v. Barlow's, Inc.*, 436 U.S. 307 (1978) (affirming a warrantless administrative inspection of business premises).

146 *Red Lion Broadcasting Co., Inc. v. FCC* 395 US 367 (1969); the Fairness Doctrine made Smoot's radio program impossible for stations—his last broadcast was in 1971.

147 Alvin Toffler, *Future Shock* (New York: Bantam Books, 1970), 270, 224.

148 Richard Blackhurst, Nicolas Marian, and Jan Tumlir, "Trade Liberalization, Protectionism and Interdependence," *GATT Studies in International Trade* 5 (November 1977): 18–19.

5 / NEOLIBERALISM

1 *Citizens to Preserve Overton Park v. Volpe*, 401 U.S. 402, 415–16 (1971).

2 *Vermont Yankee Nuclear Power Corp. v. NRDC*, 435 U.S. 519 (1978).

3 *Industrial Union Department, AFL-CIO v. American Petroleum Institute* 448 U.S. 672 (1980).

4 *Industrial Union Department, AFL-CIO v. American Petroleum Institute* 448 U.S. 609 (1980): OSHA had incorrectly applied the no-risk policy it applied to carcinogens.

5 *Industrial Union Department, AFL-CIO v. American Petroleum Institute* 448 U.S. 607 (1980); *Industrial Union Department, AFL-CIO v. Hodgson* 499 F.2d 467, 4 ELR 20415 (D.C. Cir. 1974); *American Textile Mfrs. Inst., Inc. v. Donovan*, 452 U.S. 490 (1981).

6 Edward P. Denison, *Accounting for Slower Economic Growth: The United States in the 1970s* (Washington: The Brookings Institution, 1979); Wayne B. Gray, "The Cost of Regulation: OSHA, EPA and the Productivity Slowdown," *The American Economic Review* 77, no. 5 (December 1987): 998.

7 Matusow, *The Unraveling of Liberalism*, 232–37.

8 Gurr, "Historical Trends in Violent Crime," 321–23.

9 Graham, *The Civil Rights Era*, 454–55.

10 In 1976 Pennsylvania became the first state to pass legislation for protective orders for battered women, and Oregon became the first state to legislate mandated arrest in domestic violence cases.

11 Kay, "Making Marriage and Divorce Safe for Women," 1696.

12 Emma Rothschild, "Reagan and the Real America," *New York Review of Books*, February 5, 1981.

13 Daniel Yergin and Joseph Stanislaw, *The Commanding Heights: The Battle Between Government and the Marketplace That Is Remaking the Modern World* (New York: Simon & Schuster, 1998), 63.

14 Gene Healy, "Remembering Nixon's Wage and Price Controls," *Cato Institute*, August 16, 2011.

15 Michael Hudson, *Super Imperialism: The Economic Strategy of American Empire* (New York: Holt, Rinehart and Winston, 1972).

16 Alan Greenspan, "Antitrust," in Ayn Rand, *Capitalism: The Unknown Ideal* (New York: Signet Books, 1966), 70.

17 Robert Bork, "The Goals of Antitrust Policy," *The American Economic Review* 57, no. 2 (May 1967): 242.

18 "Milton Friedman on Antitrust," *YouTube*, https://www.youtube.com/watch?v=vMvVmlDNonY.

19 Quinn Slobodian, *Globalists: The End of Empire and the Birth of Neoliberalism* (Cambridge, MA: Harvard University Press, 2018), 148.

20 Rawls, *A Theory of Justice* (Cambridge, MA: Harvard University Press, 1971), 85, 17–22; Rawls, *Political Liberalism* (New York: Columbia University Press, 1993), 338–39, argued that philosophy, which he likened to religion or an individual good, could no longer serve the purpose of discovering truth.

21 Rawls, *A Theory of Justice*, 505; *Justice as Fairness: A Restatement*, ed. Erin Kelly (Cambridge, MA: Harvard University Press, 2001), 20, was grounded on what he later called "public reason" (15, 45).

22 Rawls, *A Theory of Justice*, 136–39.

23 Rawls, *Justice as Fairness*, 112–13.

24 Rawls, *A Theory of Justice*, 61, 302–3, 542, 301–2, 339.

25 Friedman, *Capitalism and Freedom* (Chicago: The University of Chicago Press, 2002), 190–91; Rawls, *Justice as Fairness*, 106–10.

26 Rawls, *A Theory of Justice*, 536.

27 Friedman, *Capitalism and Freedom*, 107; Rawls, *A Theory of Justice*, 536.

28 Rawls, *A Theory of Justice*, 331.

29 Rawls, *Political Liberalism*, 243.

30 Michelman, "Economic Power," 46; on welfare rights, Michelman, "The Supreme Court, 1968 Term—Forward: On Protecting the Poor through the Fourteenth Amendment," *Harvard Law Review* 83, no. 1 (November 1969): 7–59; "Welfare Rights in a Constitutional Democracy," *Washington University Law Quarterly* 1979, iss. 3 (Summer 1979): 659–93.

31 Charles Reich, "The New Property," *The Yale Law Journal* 73, no. 5 (April 1964): 733–87.

32 Mark Glick, "Antitrust and Economic History: The Historic Failure of the Chicago School of Antitrust," *Institute for New Economic Thinking*, Working Paper No. 95 (May 2019): 56–57; *Continental T.V. Inc. v. GTE Sylvania Inc*, 433 U.S. 36 (1977); *Monsanto Co. v. Spray-Rite Service Corp.*, 465 U.S. 752 (1984); *United States v. General Dynamics Corp.*, 415 U.S. 486 (1974).

33 David Harvey, *A Brief History of Neoliberalism* (New York: Oxford University Press, 2005), 120–51.

34 McCraw, *Prophets*, 63–64, 212.

35 Marc Allen Eisner, *Regulatory Politics in Transition* (Baltimore, MD: The Johns Hopkins University Press, 2000), 177.

36 Stewart, "Reformation of American Administrative Law," 1690.

37 *Economic Report of the President: Transmitted to the Congress, February 1975* (Washington, D.C.: U.S. Government Printing Office, 1975), 159.

38 Eisner, *Regulatory Politics in Transition*, 191.

39 Gerald Berk, "The Financialization of the U.S. Economy Has Produced Mechanisms That Lead Toward Concentration," *ProMarket*, June 2, 2017.

40 McDougall, *Promised Land*, 196.

41 Steven Gillon, *The Democrats' Dilemma: Walter F. Mondale and the Liberal Legacy* (New York; Columbia University Press, 1992), 220.

42 *Economic Report of the President, Transmitted to the Congress, February 1982* (Washington, D.C.: U.S. Government Printing Office, 1982), 22, 7, 22.

43 William F. Buckley, "Standing Athwart History," in *Athwart History: Half a Century of Polemics, Animadversions, and Illuminations*, ed. Linda Bridges and Roger Kimball (New York: Encounter Books, 2010), 7.

44 Emma Rothschild, "Reagan and the Real America," *New York Review of Books* (February 5, 1981).

45 Reagan, "Remarks at a Fundraising Dinner for Senator Strom Thurmond in

Columbia, South Carolina September 20, 1983."

46 David Stockman, "How to Avoid an Economic Dunkirk," *Challenge* 24, no. 1 (March/April 1981): 17–21.

47 Eisner, *Regulatory Politics in Transition*, 183.

48 *Chevron U.S.A., Inc. v. Natural Resources Defense Council*, 467 U.S. 837, 842–43 (1984).

49 Eisner, *Regulatory Politics in Transition*, 188.

50 Jonathan Tepper and Denise Hearn, *The Myth of Capitalism: Monopolies and the Death of Competition* (Hoboken, NJ: Wiley, 2019), 158.

51 Eisner, *Regulatory Politics in Transition*, 188.

52 Tepper and Hearn, *The Myth of Capitalism*, 159.

53 John Komlos, "Reaganomics: A Watershed Moment on the Road to Trumpism," *The Economists' Voice* 16, no. 1 (January 2019): 4.

54 Richard Morin, "America's Middle-Class Meltdown," *Washington Post*, December 1, 1991.

55 Reagan, "Apples," November 29, 1977, *In His Own Hand: The Writings of Ronald Reagan That Reveal His Revolutionary Vision for America*, ed. Kiron K. Skinner, Annelise Anderson, and Martin Anderson (New York: Touchstone, 2001), 302.

56 "In Praise of Huddled Mases," *Wall Street Journal*, July 3, 1984.

57 Eric Weinstein, "How and Why Government, Universities and Industry Create 'Labor Shortages' of Skill," https://www.ineteconomics.org/uploads/papers/Weinstein-GUI_NSF_SG_Complete_INET.pdf; "Editorial," *Wall Street Journal*, February 1, 1990.

58 Komlos, "Reaganomics," 2, 6: "The average hourly wage of men without a high-school diploma was $17.47 per hour in 1980 (in 2017 prices). The precipitous decline began in 1981; by 1984 it was down by $1.35 to reach $16.12; by 1988 it was $15.73."

59 Timothy J. Minchin, *Empty Mills: The Fight Against Imports and the Decline of the U.S. Textile Industry* (Lanham, MD: Rowman & Littlefield, 2013), 167–68.

60 Kevin Phillips, *The Politics of Rich and Poor: Wealth and the American Electorate in the Reagan Aftermath* (New York: Harper Perennial, 1991), 87.

61 Dan Rottenberg, "About That Urban Renaissance...there'll be a slight delay," *Chicago Magazine*, May 1, 1980.

62 Randall Rothenberg, "The Neoliberal Club," *Esquire* (February 1982): 37–46, included Gary Hart, Paul Tsongas, Max Baucus, Dick Gephardt, Tim Worth, Chris Dodd, Michael Dukakis, opinion makers in journalism and academia, economist Lester Thurow, Morton Kondracke of the *New Republic*, Michael Kinsley (*Harper's*), and James Fallows (*Atlantic Monthly*). Their "guru" was Charles Peters, editor of the *Washington Monthly*.

63 Rothenberg, "The Neoliberal Club," 37, 38, 44.

64 Gillon, *The Democrats' Dilemma*, 290, 327, 309.

65 Gillon, *The Democrats' Dilemma*, 307–17. Liberal views changed on the

middle class and poor, tax cuts, high interest rates, economic growth, and deregulation as well as embracing race and environmental policies.

66 John B. Judis and Ruy Teixeira, *The Emerging Democratic Majority* (New York: Scribner, 2002), 42.

67 Saskia Sassen, *The Global City* (Princeton, NJ: Princeton University Press, 1991), 335, 337, describes the "new urbane regime."

68 David Brooks, *Bobos in Paradise* (New York: Simon & Schuster, 2000), 53.

69 *EPA 1997 Strategic Plan*, United States Environmental Protection Agency (September 1997), 13.

70 Eisner, *Regulatory Politics in Transition*, 198.

71 Manfred Steger and Ravi K. Roy, *Neoliberalism: A Very Short Introduction* (New York: Oxford University Press, 2010), 51.

72 Clinton, "Remarks on Signing the North American Free Trade Agreement Implementation Act," December 8, 1993.

73 Steger and Roy, *Neoliberalism*, 89.

74 Thomas Friedman, *The Lexus and the Olive Tree: Understanding Globalization* (New York: Anchor Books, 2000), 109, 105, 107 (109, "produced by large historical forces"), 112, 438, 117–27.

75 William Greider, *One World, Ready or Not: The Manic Logic of Global Capitalism* (New York: Simon & Schuster Paperbacks, 1997), 334.

76 Myron Magnet, "What Is Compassionate Conservatism?" *Wall Street Journal*, February 5, 1999.

77 David Boaz, "Bush's Third Way Betrays True Conservatism," *Cato Institute*, January 31, 2003.

78 George W. Bush, "Statement on Affirmative Action," *New York Times*, January 15, 2003.

79 Warren Vieth and Edwin Chen, "Bush Supports Shift of Jobs Overseas," *Los Angeles Times*, February 10, 2004.

80 Gwynn Guilford, "The epic mistake about manufacturing that's cost Americans millions of jobs," *Quartz*, May 3, 2018.

81 Naomi Schaefer Riley, "Mr. Compassionate Conservative," *Wall Street Journal*, October 21, 2006.

82 Office of the Press Secretary, "President and Prime Minister Blair Discussed Iraq, Middle East," *The White House: George W. Bush*, November 12, 2004.

83 Peter Van Buren, *We Meant Well* (New York: Metropolitan Books, 2011), 157.

84 Matt Stoller and Lucas Kunce, "America's Monopoly Crisis Hits the Military," *The American Conservative*, June 27, 2019.

85 Chrystia Freeland, "The Rise of the New Global Elite," *The Atlantic* (January/February 2011).

86 Roger Kimball, *The Long March: How the Cultural Revolution of the 1960s Changed America* (San Francisco, CA: Encounter Books, 2000), 247.

87 Christopher Buckley, "Sorry, Dad, I'm Voting for Obama," *Daily Beast*, October 10, 2008; Maureen Dowd, "Those Hard-Boiled Eggheads," *New York Times*, October 14, 2008.

6 / IDENTITY POLITICS

1 Robert D. Putnam, "Bowling Alone: America's Declining Social Capital," *Journal of Democracy* 6, no. 1 (January 1995): 65–78; "Tuning In, Tuning Out: The Strange Disappearance of Social Capital in America," *PS: Political Science and Politics* 28, no. 4 (December 1995): 664–83.

2 Putnam, "Civic Disengagement in Contemporary America," *Government and Opposition* 36, no. 2 (Spring 2001): 135–36.

3 Victoria A. Brownworth, "Return to the scene of the crime," *Bay Area Reporter* 34, no. 49, December 2, 2004: 36.

4 Frank Rich, "Journal; Summer of Matthew Shepard," *New York Times*, July 3, 1999.

5 Elizabeth Siegel Watkins, "How the Pill Became a Lifestyle Drug: The Pharmaceutical Industry and Birth Control in the United States Since 1960," *American Journal of Public Health* 102, no. 8 (August 2012): 1463–64.

6 Shanna Swan: "Most couples may have to use assisted reproduction by 2045," *Guardian*, March 28, 2021.

7 Tyrone B. Hayes et al, "Atrazine induces complete feminization and chemical castration in male African clawed frogs (Xenopus laevis)," *Proceedings of the National Academy of Sciences of the United States of America* 107, no. 10 (March 2010): 4612–17.

8 Charles Duhigg, "Debating How Much Weed Killer Is Safe in Your Water Glass," *New York Times*, August 22, 2009; "The Farm-Bill: An Antidote for Atrazine?" *National Resources Defense Council*: "EPA conducted a special monitoring program of selected drinking water supplies in ten states from 2003 to 2005. The study found that 94 of the 136 public water systems tested had atrazine concentrations above the 3 ppb drinking water standard in their raw (untreated) water for at least one 90-day period."

9 Jatinder Bhatia, Frank Greer, and the Committee on Nutrition, "Use of Soy Protein-Based Formulas in Infant Feeding," *Pediatrics* 121. no. 5 (May 2008): 1062–68.

10 K. D. Setchell et al., "Exposure of infants to phyto-oestrogens from soy-based infant formula," *Lancet* 350, no. 69 (July 5, 1997): 203–7; C. H. Irvine et al., "Phytoestrogens in soy-based infant foods: concentrations, daily intake, and possible biological effects," *Proceedings of the Society for Experimental Biology and Medicine* 217, no. 3 (March 1998): 247–53; "Soy Infant Formula," *National Institute of Environmental Health Sciences*, https://www.niehs.nih.gov/health/topics/agents/sya-soy-formula/index.cfm.

11 Anne Harding, "Men's testosterone levels declined in last 20 years," *Reuters*, January 19, 2007.

12 Teresa A. Rummans, MD; M. Caroline Burton, MD; and Nancy L. Dawson, MD, "How Good Intentions Contributed to Bad Outcomes: The Opioid Crisis," *Mayo Clinic* (December 2017).

13 Art Van Zee, MD, "The Promotion and Marketing of OxyContin: Commercial Triumph, Public Health Tragedy," *American Journal of Public Health* 99, no. 2 (February 2009): 221–27.

14 "Understanding the Epidemic," CDC, https://www.cdc.gov/opioids/basics/epidemic.html.

15 Ames Grawert et al., "Crime Trends: 1990–2016," *Brennan Center*, April 18, 2017: "The national crime rate peaked in 1991 at 5,856 crimes per 100,000 people"; "The violent crime rate also peaked in 1991 at 716 violent crimes per 100,000."

16 Toni Morrison, "Comment," *The New Yorker* (October 5, 1998).

17 William Henry III, "Beyond the Melting Pot," *Time*, April 9, 1990.

18 Victor Davis Hanson, *Mexifornia* (San Francisco, CA, Encounter Books, 2003), 7.

19 Clinton, "Commencement Address at Portland State University in Portland, Oregon, June 13, 1998."

20 Paul Starr, "An Emerging Democratic Majority," in *The New Majority: Toward a Popular Progressive Politics*, ed. Stanley B. Greenberg and Theda Skocpol (New Haven, CT: Yale University Press, 1997), 221–37; Judis and Teixeira, *The Emerging Democratic Majority*, 49–62.

21 Sam Francis, "Anarcho-tyranny, USA," *Chronicles* (July 1994).

22 Martha Nussbaum, *For Love of Country: Debating the Limits of Patriotism*, ed. Joshua Cohen (Boston, MA: Beacon Press, 1996), 11.

23 The exception here is Gertrude Himmelfarb, a neocon, who argued that democracy and liberty are "predominantly, perhaps even uniquely, Western values."

24 Giddens, *Third Way: The Renewal of Social Democracy* (Cambridge, UK: Polity Press, 1998), 136; Bhikhu Parekh, "Cosmopolitanism and Global Citizenship," *Review of International Studies* 29, no. 1 (January 2003): 3–17.

25 Natasha Lehrer, "Review: War of the Words," *frieze*, iss. 20 (January-February 1995).

26 Iris Marion Young, *Justice and the Politics of Difference* (Princeton, NJ: Princeton University Press, 1990), 10.

27 Cornel West, "The New Cultural Politics of Difference," *October* 53, *The Humanities as Social Technology* (Summer 1990): 103, 105; *Race Matters* (Boston, MA: Beacon Press, 1993).

28 Amory Starr, "Is The North American Anti-Globalization Movement Racist? Critical Reflections," *Social Register* (2003): 269–74.

29 Young, *Justice and the Politics of Difference*, 98.

30 Patricia Hill Collins, "Toward a New Vision: Race, Class and Gender as Categories of Analysis and Connection," *Race, Sex & Class* 1, no. 1 (Fall 1993): 27–34.

31 Collins, "Toward a New Vision," 29; Jana Sawicki, "Foucault and Feminism: Toward a Politics of Difference," *Hypatia* 1, no. 2, Motherhood and Sexuality (Autumn 1986): 32–33; Harvey, *Justice, Nature & the Geography of Difference* (Malden, MA: Blackwell Publishers, 1996), 349–50, 362–63.

32 Martin Seligman and Mihaly Csikszentmihalyi, "Positive Psychology: An Introduction," *American Psychologist* 55, no. 1 (January 2000): 5; Seligman, *Authentic Happiness* (New York: Free Press, 2002), 129–30.

33 Michael S. Kimmel and Abby L. Ferber, *Privilege: A Reader* (Cambridge, MA: Westview Press, 2003), xii.

34 Kimberlé W. Crenshaw, "Demarginalizing the Intersection of Race and Sex: A Black Feminist Critique of Antidiscrimination Doctrine, Feminist Theory and Anti-racist Politics," *University of Chicago Legal Forum* iss. 1, art. 8 (1989): 151, 167.

35 Collins, "Toward a New Vision," 29–35.

36 Stuart Hall, "New Ethnicities," in *Race, Culture & Difference*, eds. James Donald and Ali Rattansi (London: Sage Publications, 1992), 252, 254.

37 Taylor, *Multiculturalism*, 38; West, "The New Cultural Politics of Difference," 103; Parekh, *A New Politics of Identity* (New York: Palgrave Macmillan, 2008), 51–53.

38 SDA: Survey Documentation and Analysis, "General Social Survey Cumulative Datafile 1972–2014"; Pew Research Center, "America's Changing Religious Landscape," May 12, 2015.

39 Frank S. Pittman III, *Man Enough: Fathers, Sons, and the Search for Masculinity* (New York: Perigee, 1993), xvi, 107.

40 Marilyn Frye, "Oppression," in *Privilege*, 19.

41 Kimmel, *Privilege*, 9.

42 Richard Dyer, *White: Essays on Race and Culture* (London: Routledge, 1997), 4, 10.

43 Raymond J. Wlodkowski and Margery B. Ginsberg, *Diversity & Motivation: Culturally Responsive Teaching* (San Francisco, CA: Jossey-Bass, 1995), xii, 284.

44 Charles Mills, *The Racial Contract* (Ithaca, NY: Cornell University Press, 1997), 1.

45 Mills, "Global White Ignorance," in *Routledge International Handbook of Ignorance Studies*, ed. Matthias Gross and Linsey McGoey (New York: Routledge, 2015), 217.

46 Mills, *The Racial Contract*, 18.

47 George Yancy, *On Race: 34 Conversations in a Time of Crisis* (New York: Oxford University Press, 2017), 188.

48 Young, *Justice and the Politics of Difference*, 157, on "democratizing workplaces" and attacking "the division between task-defining and task-executing work," 10–13, 37–38, 81; *The Wealth of Races: the Present Value of Benefits from Past Injustices*, ed. Richard F. America (New York: Greenwood Press, 1990).

49 Young, *Justice and the Politics of Difference*, 9–10.

50 Rawls, *Justice as Fairness*, 11; see 10n8, 12, 72, 93, 100, 163; "Justice as fairness does not seek to cultivate the distinctive virtues and values of the liberalisms of autonomy and individuality, or indeed any other comprehensive doctrine. For in that case it ceases to be a form of political liberalism" (157); Susan Moller Okin, *Justice, Gender, and the Family* (New York: Basic Books, Inc., Publishers, 1989), 89–109.

51 Christine Littleton, "Reconstructing Sexual Equality," *California Law Review* 75 (July 1987): 1297.

52 Roberto Unger, *The Critical Legal Studies Movement* (Cambridge, MA: Harvard University Press, 1983), 119, 99, 43–90.

53 Stephanie Ross, "How Words Hurt: Attitudes, Metaphor and Oppression," in *Sexist Language: A Modern Philosophical Analysis*, ed. Mary Vetterling-Braggin (Totowa, NJ: Littlefield, Adams, & Co., 1981), 194–216; Madhavi Sunder, "Authorship and Autonomy as Rites of Exclusion: The Intellectual Propertization of Free Speech in Hurley v. Irish-American Gay, Lesbian and Bisexual Group of Boston," *Stanford Law Review* 49, no. 1 (November 1996): 143–72; Catharine MacKinnon, *Only Words* (Cambridge, MA: Harvard University Press, 1993), 71–110.

54 Parekh, *Rethinking Multiculturalism: Cultural Diversity and Political Theory* (London: Macmillan Press, 2000), 312–21.

55 Elazar Barkan, *The Guilt of Nations*, 320, 336–42; Young, *Justice and the Politics of Difference*, 47, 11.

56 Christopher Lebron, *The Color of Our Shame* (New York: Oxford University Press, 2015), 14.

57 Frank Garcia, "Between Cosmopolis and Community: Globalization and the Emerging Basis for Global Justice," *NYU Journal of International Law & Politics* 46, no. 1 (2013): 10–11.

58 Young, *Justice and the Politics of Difference*, 13.

59 Young, *Justice and the Politics of Difference*, 108, 234; Lebron, *The Making of Black Lives Matter: A Brief History of an Idea* (New York: Oxford University Press, 2017), 45.

60 Young, *Justice and the Politics of Difference*, 13.

61 Peter Singer, *One World Now: The Ethics of Globalization* (New Haven, CT: Yale University Press, 2016), 14; *The Life You Can Save* (New York: Random House, 2010), 153.

62 Singer, *One World*, (New Haven, CT: Yale University Press, 2004), ix.

63 Singer, *One World Now*, 8.

64 Singer, *One World Now*, 8.

65 Michelman, "Economic Power," 48.

66 Singer, *One World*, xiii–xiv; Held, "Cosmopolitan Democracy and the Global Order: Reflections on the 200th Anniversary of Kant's Perpetual Peace," *Alternatives: Global, Local, Political* 20, no. 4 (October–December 1995): 426.

67 Singer, *One World Now*, 4–5.

68 Giddens, *Third Way*, 131.

69 Naomi Klein, "Obama's Chicago Boys," *The Nation*, June 12, 2008; Joseph G. Peschek, "The Obama Presidency and the Great Recession: Political Economy, Ideology, and Public Policy," *New Political Science* 33, no. 4 (December 2011): 429–44.

70 Tepper and Hearn, *The Myth of Capitalism*, xvii.

71 Steve LeVine, "Farm bankruptcies shed new light on perils of Big Agriculture," *Axios*, March 31, 2019; James M. MacDonald, "Competition in Seed and Agricultural Chemical Markets," *USDA Economic Research Service*, April 3, 2017.

72 Charles Murray, "The New American Divide," *Wall Street Journal*, January 21, 2012.

73 NYU business professor Scott Galloway, "The Rant: The College Implosion | NO MERCY, NO MALICE," *YouTube*, May 15, 2020.

74 "Some Universities Are About to Be 'Walking Dead' | Amanpour and Company," *YouTube*, May 25, 2020.

75 Jeffrey Avina, "The Evolution of Corporate Social Responsibility (CSR) in the Arab Spring," *The Middle East Journal* 67, no. 1 (Winter 2013): 84.

76 William A. Galston, *Anti-Pluralism: The Populist Threat to Liberal Democracy* (New Haven, CT: Yale University Press, 2020), 14.

77 Chrystia Freeland, "The Rise of the New Global Elite," *Atlantic* (January/ February 2011).

78 Jonathan Turley, "James Clapper's perjury, and why DC made men don't get charged for lying to Congress," *USA Today*, January 19, 2018.

79 Radley Balko, *Rise of the Warrior Cop: The Militarization of America's Police Forces* (New York: PublicAffairs, 2013).

80 Cass Sunstein, "Chevron Step Zero," *Virginia Law Review* 92, no. 2 (April 2006): 187–249.

81 Michael S. Greve and Ashley C. Parrish, "Administrative Law Without Congress," *George Mason Law & Economics Research Paper*, no. 14–56 at http://ssrn.com/abstract=2514484: 1-49; Philip Hamburger, *Is Administrative Law Unlawful?* (Chicago: The University of Chicago Press, 2014), 120–27.

82 Government Accountability Office, *Federal Rulemaking: Agencies Could Take Additional Steps to Respond to Public Comments* (December 2012), https://www.gao.gov/assets/gao-13-21.pdf.

83 Jeffery H Anderson, "Bailing Out Health Insurers and Helping Obamacare," *Washington Examiner*, January 13, 2014.

84 Dan Berrett, "Intellectual Roots of Wall St. Protest Lie in Academe," *Chronicles of Higher Education*, October 16, 2011.

85 L. Randall Wray, *Understanding Modern Money: The Key to Full Employment and Price Stability* (Northampton, MA: Edward Elgar, 1998), ix.

86 Wray, William Mitchell, and Martin Watts, *Macroeconomics* (London: Red Globe Press, 2019), 320–21.

87 Wray, *Understanding Modern Money*, viii, 1, 2.

88 Wray, Mitchell, and Watts, *Macroeconomics*, 303–4.

89 Wray, *Understanding Modern Money*, 9.

90 Wray, *Understanding Modern Money*, viii.

91 According to the Federal Reserve, in October 2020, there were $1.99 trillion of physical currency (M1) in circulation (excluding financial assets, savings

accounts, and bonds), with about two-thirds of that overseas. M2, or "near money," refers to savings deposits, money market securities, mutual funds, and other time deposits, which totaled about $18 trillion.

92 Warren Mosler, in "MMT vs. Austrian School Debate," *YouTube*, June 19, 2013.

93 Atossa Araxia Abrahamian, "The Rock-Star Appeal of Modern Monetary Theory," *The Nation*, May 8, 2017.

94 Alain Badiou, *Metapolitics*, tr. Jason Barker (New York: Verso, 2005), xxxiv.

95 Slavoj Žižek, *In Defense of Lost Causes* (New York: Verso, 2008), 162.

96 Žižek, *In Defense of Lost Causes*, 310–11.

97 Badiou, *Metapolitics*, 24.

98 Friedman, "Our One-Party Democracy," *New York Times*, September 9, 2009.

99 A. Barton Hinkle, "OWS protesters have strange ideas about fairness," *Richmond Times-Dispatch*, November 4, 2011.

100 *Without Borders or Limits*, ed. Jorell A. Melendez Badillo and Nathan J. Jun (Cambridge Scholars Publishing, 2013), xiii.

101 Ray Sanchez, "Occupy Wall Street: 5 years later," *CNN*, September 16, 2016.

102 Peter Baker, "Court Choice Brings Issue of 'Identity' Back Out," *New York Times*, May 30, 2009.

103 *Baldwin v. Department of Transportation*, EEOC Appeal No. 0120133080 (July 15, 2015).

104 "I am Part of the Resistance Inside the Trump Administration," *New York Times*, September 5, 2018.

105 Katie Bo Williams, "Outgoing Syria Envoy Admits Hiding US Troop Numbers; Praises Trump's Mideast Record," *Defense One*, November 12, 2020; "A Letter From G.O.P. National Security Officials Opposing Donald Trump," *New York Times*, August 8, 2016.

106 Max Eden, "Harvard vs. the Family," *City Journal*, April 24, 2020.

107 Eric Levitz, "David Shor's Unified Theory of the 2020 Election," *New York Intelligencer*, July 17, 2020.

108 "Spies who lie: 51 'intelligence' experts refuse to apologize for discrediting true Hunter Biden story," *New York Post*, March 18, 2022; "Hunter Biden's Laptop Is Finally News Fit to Print," *Wall Street Journal*, March 18, 2022.

7 / DESPOTISM

1 Thomas Dye, *Who's Running America? The Obama Reign* (New York: Routledge, 2014), 10.

2 Michelle Malkin, *Open Borders, Inc.: Who's Funding America's Destruction?* (New York: Regnery, 2019), 39–81; Peter Schweizer, *Throw Them All Out* (Boston, MA: Houghton Mifflin Harcourt, 2011), 105–33.

3 Darrell M. West, *Billionaires: Reflections on the Upper Crust* (Washington, D.C.: Brookings Institution Press, 2014), 15–16.

4   Schweizer, *Secret Empires*, on the Bidens (21–73), the McConnells (75–89), Obama (111–83); See Schweizer, *Extortion* (Boston, MA: Houghton Mifflin Harcourt, 2013), 151–70, on the Reid and Blunt families in Nevada and Missouri; Schweizer, *Clinton Cash* (New York: HarperCollins Publishers, 2015), 6: John Kerry is worth at least $100 million, George W. Bush, $40 million; the Clintons rose from "dead broke" to make $136.5 million from 2001–12 (Bill's reported net worth was $55 million).

5   West, *Billionaires*, 43.

6   John Mauldin, "America has a Monopoly Problem," *Forbes*, April 11, 2019.

7   Ethan McAfee, "3 Reasons Why Amazon Will Likely Continue To Gain E-Commerce Market Share," *Forbes*, March 31, 2021; Josh Sandbulte, "Why the Post Office Gives Amazon Special Delivery," *Wall Street Journal*, July 13, 2017; Kasia Tarczynska, "Taxpayer Subsidies to Amazon Now Exceed $3.7 Billion," *GoodJobsFirst*, December 16, 2020.

8   Yasha Levine, "Google's Earth: how the tech giant is helping the state spy on us," *The Guardian*, December 20, 2018: "including civilian federal agencies, cities, states, local police departments, emergency responders, hospitals, public schools and all sorts of companies and nonprofits."

9   Greg Ip, "The Antitrust Case Against Facebook, Google and Amazon," *Wall Street Journal*, January 16, 2018.

10 William Isaac, "Don't Like an Industry? Send a Message to Its Bankers," *Wall Street Journal*, November 21, 2014; Schweizer, *Secret Empires*, 156–57.

11 Arnoud Boot et al., "What Is Really New in Fintech," *IMFBlog*, December 17, 2020.

12 Schweizer, *Extortion*, 21–99.

13 Schweizer, *Secret Empires*, 141–83, provides the examples in coal, for-profit colleges, and payday lending.

14 Matthew Stewart, "The Birth of the New American Aristocracy," *The Atlantic*, June 15, 2018.

15 Aarian Marshall, "Google's New Union Is Already Addressing Political Issues," *Wired*, January 12, 2021.

16 Schweizer, *Secret Empires*, 163–83.

17 Michael Donnelly, "Consuming the 'Planet of the Humans:' The Most Important Documentary of the Century," *Counterpunch*, August 9, 2019; L. Michael Buchsbaum, "The secret burning of trees: the often overlooked role of biomass," *Energy Transition*, July 8, 2020.

18 *County of Butler v. Wolf* 486 F. Supp. 3d 899–900 (W.D. Pa. 2020).

19 *County of Butler v. Wolf* 486 F. Supp. 3d 900 (W.D. Pa. 2020).

20 Janet Green et al. "The implications of face masks for babies and families during the COVID-19 pandemic: A discussion paper, *The Journal of Neonatal Nursing* 27, no. 1 (February 2021): 21–25.

21 Krystal Hur, "Toddlers Can't Shake Pandemic Habits. Parents Are Rattled," *Wall Street Journal*, August 25, 2021.

22 Javier C. Hernández, "How China Brought Nearly 200 Million Students Back to School," *New York Times*, September 12, 2020.

23 Peter Navarro, *The Immaculate Deception: Six Key Dimensions of Election Irregularities*, *The Thinking Conservative*, December 15, 2020.

24 William Doyle, "The Wisconsin Purchase," *American Conservative*, December 24, 2021; Office of the Special Counsel, Second Interim Investigative Report, On the Apparatus & Procedures of the Wisconsin Elections System, Delivered to the Wisconsin State Assembly on March 1, 2022.

25 Hagai Levine et. al, "Temporal trends in sperm count: a systematic review and meta-regression analysis," *Human Reproduction Update* 23, iss. 6 (November-December 2017): 646–59; Neil Howe, "You're Not the Man Your Father Was," *Forbes*, October 2, 2017: "A 60-year-old man in 2004 had testosterone levels 17% lower than those of a 60-year-old in 1987"; Thomas G. Travison et al., "A Population-Level Decline in Serum Testosterone Levels in American Men," *The Journal of Clinical Endocrinology & Metabolism* 92, iss. 1 (January 2007): 196–202.

26 Collier Meyerson, "How our racist child support laws hurt poor, black fathers the most," *Splinternews*, August, 10, 2016; Frances Robles and Shaila Dewan, "Skip Child Support. Go to Jail. Lose Job. Repeat," *New York Times*, April 19, 2015; Elaine Sorensen et al., "Assessing Child Support Arrears in Nine Large States and the Nation," *Urban Institute*, January 14, 2009.

27 Paul Vitz, *Faith of the Fatherless: The Psychology of Atheism* (Dallas, TX: Spence Publishing Company, 1999).

28 Stacy Trasancos, "How Aborted Children Are Used in Medical Research in 2020," *National Catholic Register*, December 15, 2020.

29 Tom Parfitt, "Beauty salons fuel trade in aborted babies," *Guardian*, April 16, 2005.

30 Patrick Hauf, "Government-Funded Researchers Sought Aborted Minorities for Organ Harvesting," *Washington Free Beacon*, August 5, 2021; see the FOIA request documents at https://www.centerformedicalprogress.org/wp-content/uploads/2021/07/NIH-FOIA-54074-06.07.2021-Production.pdf.

31 "FDA purchased baby heads and other body parts, documents show," *WND*, September 14, 2021.

32 Meredith Wadman, "Abortion opponents protest COVID-19 vaccines' use of fetal cells," *Science*, June 5, 2020.

33 "5 Times 'Transgender' Men Abused Women and Children in Bathrooms," *Daily Wire*, April 26, 2016; Matt Masterson, "Lawsuit: Female Prisoner Says She Was Raped by Transgender Inmate," *WTTW*, February 19, 2020.

34 Katie Herzog, "Med Schools are Now Denying Biological Sex," *RealClearEducation*, July 28, 2021.

35 Jonathan Kay, "An Interview With Lisa Littman, Who Coined the Term 'Rapid Onset Gender Dysphoria,'" *Quillette*, March 19, 2019; Dan Avery,

"Nearly 1 in 10 Teens Identify as Gender-diverse in Pittsburgh Study," *NBC News*, May 21, 2021.

36 Joyce C. Abma et al., "Sexual Activity and Contraceptive Use Among Teenagers in the United States, 2011–2015," *National Health Statistics Report*, CDC, no. 104 (November 22, 2017); Christopher Ingraham, "The share of Americans not having sex has reached a record high," *Washington Post*, March 29, 2019.

37 Sinéad Bakerfeb, "The US accused China of forcing American diplomats to take anal swab tests for COVID-19," *Business Insider*, February 25, 2021; April Glaser, "A U.S.-built biometric system sparks concerns for Afghans," *NBC News*, August 31, 2021.

38 Melanie Evans, "Hospitals Retreat from Early COVID Treatment and Return to Basics," *Wall Street Journal*, December 20, 2020.

39 Eddie Scarry, "Black police officers are putting up with a lot in the George Floyd protests," *Washington Examiner*, June 3, 2020; Bill Miston, "Milwaukee police: 60-year-old man killed in shooting near Bremen and Wright," *Fox6*, July 23, 2020.

40 Jon Brown, "Lawmakers Who Attended John Lewis Funeral Do Not Have to Undergo D.C. Quarantine," *The Daily Wire*, August 1, 2020; Hundreds of migrants broke coronavirus rules to attend the funeral of Sudanese migrant Badreddin Abadlla Adam, who carried out a mass stabbing attack in Glasgow.

41 Adele-Momoko Fraser, "Google bans two websites from its ad platform due to Protest Coverage," *WRJN*, June 16, 2020.

42 John L. Allen, Jr., "Italian judge latest example of Church's new test for 'martyrdom,'" *Crux*, December 23, 2020.

43 Ibram X. Kendi, *How to Be an Antiracist* (New York: Random House Publishing Group, 2019), 20.

44 "Charles W. Mills," in *The Philosophical I: Personal Reflections on Life in Philosophy*, ed. George Yancy (Lanham, MD: Roman & Littlefield, 2002), 156–157; Mills, *Racial Contract*, xi.

45 Lawrence Otis Graham, *Our Kind of People: Inside America's Black Upper Class* (New York: HarperCollins, 1999), ix.

46 Razib Khan, "Genetic variation among African Americans," *Discover* magazine, May 5, 2010.

47 Max Ehrenfreund and Jeff Guo, "How a controversial study found that police are more likely to shoot whites, not blacks," *Washington Post*, July 13, 2016.

48 Michigan State University, "White police officers are not more likely to shoot minorities," *PhysOrg*, July 22, 2019.

49 Charles A. Gallagher, Cameron D. Lippard, *Race and Racism in the United States: An Encyclopedia of the American Mosaic, Vol 1: A-E* (Santa Barbara, CA: Greenwood, 2014), 313.

50 Heather Mac Donald, "The Myth of Systemic Police Racism," *Wall Street Journal*, June 2, 2020.

51 Mac Donald, "Race, crime, and police: A closer look," *Manhattan Institute*, October 12, 2015.

52 "Wisconsin Town Mourns Those Who Died in Holiday Parade," *New York Times*, November 22, 2021.

53 Phillip Magness, "The Statistical Errors of the Reparations Agenda," *American Institute for Economic Research*, June 23, 2019; Bradley Hansen, "The Back of Ed Baptist's Envelope," *Bradley A. Hansen's Blog*, October 30, 2014; "A Description of the Problems with Edward Baptist's 'The Half Has Never Been Told' for Non-Economists," *Bradley A. Hansen's Blog*, September 2, 2019.

54 Hansen, "Was Slavery Central to American Economic Development?" *Bradley A. Hansen's Blog*, June 11, 2018.

55 Robert L. Woodson, Sr., "Fighting Poverty: Welfare vs. A Way Out," *Ripon Forum* 50, no. 2 (April 2016).

56 Armstrong Williams, "Many of America's Black youths cannot read or do math—and that imperils us all," *The Hill*, November 4, 2021.

57 Jason L. Reilly, "The Other Ferguson Tragedy," *Wall Street Journal*, November 25, 2014.

58 Dye, *Who's Running America?*, 180.

59 Ron Unz, "The Myth of American Meritocracy," *American Conservative*, November 28, 2012; Jay M., "Racial preferences at elite American universities," *Reason Without Restraint*, November 20, 2021.

60 "Courthouse confusion continues: Court clerk claims it's 'racist' to ask 'why?,'" *WGN TV*, July 29, 2020.

61 Stoller, "Boeing's travails show what's wrong with modern capitalism," *Guardian*, September 11, 2019.

62 Peter Robison, "Boeing's 737 Max Software Outsourced to $9-an-Hour Engineers," *IndustryWeek*, June 28, 2019; David Gelles et al., "How 'Boeing's Fatal Flaw' Grounded the 737 Max and Exposed Failed Oversight," *New York Times*, September 13, 2021.

63 Stoller, "Counterfeit Capitalism: Why a Monopolized Economy Leads to Inflation and Shortages," *Substack*, September 9, 2021.

64 J. D. Tuccille, "After 20 Years of Failure, Kill the TSA," *Reason*, November 19, 2021.

65 *Vice Media*, "Is This What Winning Looks Like?" May 27, 2013.

66 Nick Timiraos, "Automakers, Technology Firms Are Largest Components of Fed's Corporate-Bond Purchases," *Wall Street Journal*, June 28, 2020.

67 Schweizer, *Secret Empires*, 125–40.

68 Summer Said and Stephen Kalin, "Saudi Arabia Considers Accepting Yuan Instead of Dollars for Chinese Oil Sales," *Wall Street Journal*, March 15, 2022.

69 Klaus Schwab and Thierry Malleret, *COVID-19: The Great Reset* (Geneva: Forum Publishing, 2020), 56.

70 Nicholas Wade, "The origin of COVID: Did people or nature open Pandora's box at Wuhan?" *Bulletin of the Atomic Scientists*, May 5, 2021.

71 Tunku Varadarajan, "How Science Lost the Public's Trust," *Wall Street Journal*, June 23, 2021.

CONCLUSION

1 "Firing Line with Margaret Hoover," *PBS*, September 27, 2019; Ben Schott, "China Is More Democratic Than America, Say the People," *Bloomberg*, June 26, 2020.

2 Jack Goldsmith and Andrew Keane Woods, "Internet Speech Will Never Go Back to Normal," *The Atlantic*, April 25, 2020.

3 Alex Padilla, California Secretary of State, "Elections and Voter Information," January 1, 2019.

4 Williams, "Outgoing Syria Envoy Admits Hiding US Troop Numbers; Juliet Eilperin, Lisa Rein, and Marc Fisher, "Resistance from within: Federal workers push back against Trump," *Washington Post*, January 31, 2017.

5 Jesse Merriam, "Is Legal Conservatism as Accomplished as It Thinks It Is?" *Law and Liberty*, July 1, 2019.

6 Laura Bassett, "Why Violent Protests Work," *GQ*, June 2, 2020.

7 David Azerrad, "On the Peculiar Character of American 'Racism,'" *RealClearPolitics*, October 7, 2020.

8 A. Richard et al., "Racial variation in sex steroid hormone concentration in black and white men: a meta-analysis," *Andrology* 2, no. 3 (May 2014): 428–35; Laura Gerace, "Skeletal differences between black and white men and their relevance to body composition estimates," *American Journal of Human Biology* 6, iss. 2 (1994): 255–62; Maria E. Bleil et al., "Race disparities in pubertal timing: Implications for cardiovascular disease risk among African American women," *Population Research and Policy Review* 36, no. 5 (October 2017): 717–38.

9 Jon Entine, "The DNA Olympics–Jamaicans Win Sprinting 'Genetic Lottery'—and Why We Should All Care," *Forbes*, August 12, 2012.

10 Jason Reid and Jane McManus, "The NFL's Racial Divide," *The Undefeated*, April 26, 2017. Note a division of labor: black players dominate most positions, including that requiring the greatest athleticism, cornerback, while whites excel at the positions of quarterback and center.

11 Zupei Luo et al., "Fine motor skills and mathematics achievement in East Asian American and European American kindergartners and first graders," *British Journal of Developmental Psychology* (2007): 25, 595–614.

12 Elinor McKone et al., "Asia has the global advantage: Race and visual attention," *Vision Research* 50, iss. 16 (July 2010): 1540–49; "Physics Degrees by Race/Ethnicity," *American Physical Society*.

13 "Bill Gates Interview," (November 30–December 1, 1993), National Museum of American History, Smithsonian Institution.

14 Noah Smith, "It Isn't Just Asian Immigrants Who Thrive in the U.S.," *Bloomberg*, October 13, 2015; Chanda Chisala, "The IQ Gap Is No Longer a Black and White Issue," *The Unz Review*, June 25, 2015.

15 Steven Pinker, "Groups and Genes," *New Republic*, June 26, 2006.

16 Ron Unz, "The Myth of American Meritocracy," *The American Conservative*, November 28, 2012.

17 John Blake, "White supremacy, with a tan," *CNN*, September 4, 2021.

18 Simeon Howard, "A Sermon Preached to the Ancient and Honorable Artillery Company in Boston (1773), in *American Political Writing during the Founding Era, 1760–1805*, ed. Charles Hyneman and Donald Lutz, 2 vols. (Indianapolis, IN: Liberty Fund, 1983), 1:202.

19 Abigail Adams to John Quincy Adams, January 19, 1780, in *Letters of Mrs. Adams, the Wife of John Adams* (Boston, MA: Wilkins, Carter, and Company, 1848), 111–12 [emphasis added].

INDEX